A Social Cognition Perspective of the Psychology of Religion

Scientific Studies of Religion: Inquiry and Explanation

Series editors: Luther H. Martin, Donald Wiebe,
Radek Kundt and Dimitris Xygalatas

Scientific Studies of Religion: Inquiry and Explanation publishes cutting- edge research in the new and growing field of scientific studies in religion. Its aim is to publish empirical, experimental, historical, and ethnographic research on religious thought, behavior, and institutional structures. The series works with a broad notion of scientific that includes innovative work on understanding religion(s), both past and present. With an emphasis on the cognitive science of religion, the series includes complementary approaches to the study of religion, such as psychology and computer modeling of religious data. Titles seek to provide explanatory accounts for the religious behaviors under review, both past and present.

The Attraction of Religion, Edited by D. Jason Slone and James A. Van Slyke
The Cognitive Science of Religion, Edited by D. Jason Slone and William W. McCorkle Jr.
Connecting the Isiac Cults, Tomáš Glomb
The Construction of the Supernatural in Euro-American Cultures, Benson Saler
Contemporary Evolutionary Theories of Culture and the Study of Religion, Radek Kundt
Death Anxiety and Religious Belief, Jonathan Jong and Jamin Halberstadt
Gnosticism and the History of Religions, David G. Robertson
Imagining the Cognitive Science of Religion, E. Thomas Lawson
The Impact of Ritual on Child Cognition, Veronika Rybanska
Language, Cognition, and Biblical Exegesis, Edited by Ronit Nikolsky, Istvan Czachesz, Frederick S. Tappenden & Tamas Biro
The Learned Practice of Religion in the Modern University, Donald Wiebe
The Mind of Mithraists, Luther H. Martin
The Minds of Gods, Edited by Benjamin Grant Purzycki and Theiss Bendixen
Naturalism and Protectionism in the Study of Religion, Juraj Franek

New Patterns for Comparative Religion, William E. Paden
Philosophical Foundations of the Cognitive Science of Religion,
Robert N. McCauley with E. Thomas Lawson
Religion, Disease, and Immunology, Thomas B. Ellis
Religion Explained?, edited by Luther H. Martin and Donald Wiebe
Religion in Science Fiction, Steven Hrotic
Religious Evolution and the Axial Age, Stephen K. Sanderson
The Roman Mithras Cult, Olympia Panagiotidou with Roger Beck
Solving the Evolutionary Puzzle of Human Cooperation, Glenn Barenthin
The Study of Greek and Roman Religions, Nickolas P. Roubekas
Understanding Religion Through Artificial Intelligance, Justin E. Lane

A Social Cognition Perspective of the Psychology of Religion

"Why God Thinks Like You"

Luke Galen

BLOOMSBURY ACADEMIC
LONDON · NEW YORK · OXFORD · NEW DELHI · SYDNEY

BLOOMSBURY ACADEMIC
Bloomsbury Publishing Plc
50 Bedford Square, London, WC1B 3DP, UK
1385 Broadway, New York, NY 10018, USA
29 Earlsfort Terrace, Dublin 2, Ireland

BLOOMSBURY, BLOOMSBURY ACADEMIC and the Diana logo
are trademarks of Bloomsbury Publishing Plc

First published in Great Britain 2023
This paperback edition published 2025

Copyright © Luke Galen, 2023

Luke Galen has asserted his right under the Copyright,
Designs and Patents Act, 1988, to be identified as Author of this work.

For legal purposes the Acknowledgments on p. ix constitute an
extension of this copyright page.

All rights reserved. No part of this publication may be reproduced or transmitted
in any form or by any means, electronic or mechanical, including photocopying,
recording, or any information storage or retrieval system, without prior
permission in writing from the publishers.

Bloomsbury Publishing Plc does not have any control over, or responsibility for,
any third-party websites referred to or in this book. All internet addresses given
in this book were correct at the time of going to press. The author and publisher
regret any inconvenience caused if addresses have changed or sites have
ceased to exist, but can accept no responsibility for any such changes.

A catalogue record for this book is available from the British Library.

Library of Congress Control Number: 2023931559

ISBN: HB: 978-1-3502-9390-8
PB: 978-1-3502-9394-6
ePDF: 978-1-3502-9391-5
eBook: 978-1-3502-9392-2

Series: Scientific Studies of Religion: Inquiry and Explanation

Typeset by Integra Software Services Pvt. Ltd.

To find out more about our authors and books visit www.bloomsbury.com
and sign up for our newsletters.

Contents

List of Illustrations	viii
Acknowledgments	ix
Introduction: The Psychology of Religious Belief from a Social Cognition Perspective	1

Part 1 Mechanisms of Social Cognition and Religious Manifestations

1	Cognition, Dual Process Models, and Introspective Opacity	19
2	Social Cognition and Attribution Theory	39
3	Functional and Compensatory Mechanisms of Religion	73
4	Influence of the Social and Group Context	103

Part 2 Misattribution of the Effects of Religion

5	Exceptional Religious and Spiritual Experiences	127
6	Mental Health	159
7	Morality and Prosociality	185

Conclusion	227
References	239
Index	287

List of Illustrations

Figures

3.1	Compensatory Functions of Religion	74
4.1	Social Paths of Religious Internalization and Externalization	116
6.1	Transitive Fallacy of Composition	160
6.2	Religious Continuum	177

Table

1	Academic Discipline and Common Conceptual Areas of Study	4

Acknowledgments

Many thanks to: Elise Fles, Christine Smith, Walter Sa, Lucretia Dunlap, Samantha Selik, Amy Jarchow, and Toby Galen.

The figures were designed by Olivia Brenner.

Introduction: The Psychology of Religious Belief from a Social Cognition Perspective

"Man created God in his own image." *Ludwig Feuerbach, The Essence of Christianity.*

(1841)

The Origins of Belief

Why are some people religious, whereas others are not? Although the question seems simple enough, answers are likely to be very different, depending on who is responding. One straightforward perspective is that individuals are exposed to religious content that either seems plausible to them, or it does not; beliefs result from an interaction between exposure to religious ideas (e.g., from social learning) together with the plausibility of the content. However, even people exposed to the same content, raised in the same environment, or the same family, often disagree regarding their religious beliefs. How do we account for individual differences in these cases? As we will see later in this chapter, people also give different answers to such questions depending upon whether they are explaining their own religious beliefs (e.g., "Why I believe in God") as opposed to others (e.g., "Why do people in general believe in God"—or "Why do people whose beliefs differ from mine believe?"). One way to introduce this topic with greater complexity is to use a specific person as an example.

Consider this as a case vignette: Once, a disaffected young law student was walking back to his university during a thunderstorm. This student had been having conflicts with his father, who was pressuring him to continue with his legal studies, but studying the law was not appealing. The student was also having an internal religious struggle. He believed that reason itself was useful for dealing with worldly affairs, but it was insufficient for knowing about God.

Rather, he thought the study of scripture and perhaps personal revelation could provide religious certainties. On the night that he was walking during the storm, a lightning bolt struck close to him causing him to cry out in terror for help. The thought of being killed and facing divine judgment led him to vow that, if he survived the storm, he would quit law school and devote his life to becoming a monk. Later, despite his father's disapproval, he did enter a monastery. Even there, however, he was unhappy with his life, often engaging in grueling rituals of fasting, long hours of prayer, and even self-flagellation. No matter how much he attempted to be worthy of God's love, he merely became more aware of his own sinfulness. He was also repelled by what he saw as hypocrisy and a lack of faith among some church leaders. His studies eventually led him to form a new understanding of his religious beliefs. He concluded that his own spiritual efforts were beside the point. God was not merely a stern taskmaster, but was benevolent and forgiving; in many ways, an ideal type of father figure. It was through God's grace that he was saved, not through any merit of his own. He boldly challenged conventional religious thought and the Church's teachings at the time, putting his life in jeopardy.

We could ask a question similar to those at the beginning of the chapter: Why did this man have these particular beliefs, or more specifically, why did his beliefs change? Among the numerous ways to explain religious phenomena, some are considered "insider" perspectives, compatible with assumptions made within a given belief system such as taking individuals' religious responses at face value (McCutcheon, 1999). By contrast, "outside" perspectives are those provided from scientists and scholars who may not share the same worldviews as their subjects of study. In the case described above an example of an insider account could be that perhaps this man formed his beliefs because that is the correct interpretation of scripture and he was responding to God's influence. Consistent with his subjective experience, his beliefs were simply a valid result of his studies, and God was trying to guide him to the truth through divine intervention. Outside perspectives can produce some controversy because they may involve explanations that deviate from this man's subjective perspective, even including ones that he may not even have been aware of. A psychological version of an outsider perspective may pose questions such as: What role did his emotional needs play in the development of his religious thinking? Was there a connection between his strained relationship with his father and his earlier view that God was also stern and unforgiving? Did his religious revelation experience function as a convenient "solution" to some of his existential conflicts? The lightning-induced promise to abandon his (already less than happy) legal studies seems particularly well-timed. Could his attribution of what God wanted and his novel interpretation of scripture really have been just his way of telling himself the things that he wished to hear?

Many other psychologically informed interpretations could be applied, but these are sufficient to demonstrate the complexity involved in answering the original question: "Why did he have those religious beliefs?" In case you have not already recognized the individual in this story, his name was Martin Luther. His life serves as a particularly good example of examining the origin of beliefs and has already attracted much attention from historians and psychologists (e.g., Erikson, 1958). However, just one more type of question pertains to issues covered throughout the rest of this book—one regarding ultimate interpretive accuracy. If we are limited to choosing between accepting Luther's own subjective description—that his beliefs were merely a response to the actual events as they happened to him, including God's intervention—as opposed to adopting an outsider perspective—implying that his beliefs were created by his own psychological needs rather than actual spiritual agency—would we ever be able to determine which is correct?

Psychological Perspectives: The Cognitive Science of Religion and Social Cognition

There are many scientific approaches that can be applied to understanding religious belief and behavior. One of the most broad and productive of these is the field of Cognitive Science of Religion (CSR). It draws upon a range of academic disciplines including Cognitive Psychology, Social Psychology, Evolutionary Psychology, Cultural Anthropology, and the Neurosciences. The current series published by Bloomsbury includes several CSR accounts such as *Philosophical Foundations of the Cognitive Science of Religion: A Head Start* (McCauley, 2017) and *The Cognitive Science of Religion: A Methodological Introduction to Key Empirical Studies* (Slone & McCorkle, 2019). One theme of this book is that our understanding of religion can be enhanced by synthesizing knowledge from the CSR together with perspectives from other subdisciplines subsumed within Social and Personality Psychology, particularly that of Social Cognition.

Social Cognition (SC) examines the processes governing how individuals think about themselves and each other, how they interpret and encode this information, how they form interpersonal attitudes and impressions, function in groups, and interact with the social world. One example of a familiar SC concept is attribution theory, the process by which individuals perceive the causes of experiences such as assigning causal responsibility, including how these processes can be biased (i.e., misattribution). The field of CSR has operated largely independently from that of SC and has not fully taken advantage of combining these complementary approaches. The CSR emphasizes religion as being a product of the evolved human brain, exhibiting similar, even universal features across cultures and time periods. By contrast, Social Cognition focuses to a greater extent on how beliefs and behaviors are influenced by situational factors and how individually varying characteristics interact with particular contexts. For instance, most social psychologists view religious belief as primarily a product of the surrounding cultural milieu, social group norms, learning history, personality traits, and personal background.

The CSR and SC approaches also tend to differ in their preferred level of analyses. The concepts studied in the CSR more often refer to ultimate explanations pertaining to the core evolved origins of religion. However, while some fundamental aspects of religion (e.g., belief in the agency of spiritual powers) do appear to be near ubiquitous throughout history and across cultures, other aspects of religious phenomena show more variation across time, place, person, and the individual human life span. Events or stimuli from the social environment can induce shifts in religious beliefs just as overall cultural religiosity can wax and wane. Over the past century (a blink of the eye in evolutionary time) some societies have moved from being highly religious to secular or vice versa. The field of SC focuses more on these proximal influences, including how beliefs and

Table 1 Academic Discipline and Common Conceptual Areas of Study.

Discipline	Examples of Terms and Concepts
Cognitive Science of Religion	Cognitive byproducts, functional adaptations, agency detection, promiscuous teleology, costly signaling and rituals, credibility-enhancing displays.
Cognitive Psychology	Types of cognitive abilities, memory, heuristics and biases, dual processing theories.
Interpersonal Social Psychology	Cultural and ecological psychology, social influence, group dynamics, conformity, social identity theory, obedience.
Social Cognition	Attribution theory, compensatory functioning, cognitive dissonance theory, social-cognitive biases, motivated reasoning, stereotype theory, system justification, belief in a just world.

behaviors are shaped by the cultural and group context. Although many aspects of religious beliefs can be conceptualized as general human tendencies, many also vary as a function of individual differences and can be altered via social influence. The field of Social Psychology also involves adopting an individual differences or personality psychology approach to religion, wherein beliefs are the product of the interplay between traits and social contexts.

Thus, the SC approach can complement the types of distal questions typically addressed from the CSR approach (e.g., "Why are religious beliefs ubiquitous?") by adding more specificity and proximal influence ("Why do some people endorse particular beliefs more than others in particular contexts?"). In this sense, the differing emphases of the CSR and SC approaches reflect Tinbergen's (1963) distinction between explanatory "why" questions of ultimate functional purpose, as opposed to those relating to specific proximal casual mechanisms. Another analogy could be the use of audio equipment where a signal is processed or altered using a graphic equalizer with different frequency settings. Whereas CSR is more likely to focus on studying the general properties of the audio signal and its origin, the field of Social Cognition would be more concerned with the effect of specific settings such as how boosting certain frequencies and attenuating others changes the character of the music in specific spaces.

To use one concept as an example of such a complementary approach, the "hyperactive agency detection" (HAAD) function of the human mind has received a great deal of attention in the CSR. This refers to an evolved predisposition to over-attribute intentionality and purpose, even in the case of randomly occurring stimuli, making beliefs in spiritual agents more plausible. A SC approach can contribute to the study of the HAAD concept by focusing more on proximal factors such as individual differences in misattributions that interact with specific situations (i.e., what cognitive and personality traits are associated with the over-detection of causality operating within contexts that elicit agency attributions). The use of concepts such as attribution theory also enables a more refined analysis of R/S content, such as allowing us to ascertain why particular spiritual agents are believed to have specific desires or goals and how these relate to individuals' personal motivations, social identity, or moral values (e.g., "Why do spiritual agents tend to make moral judgments of human actions in some situations?").

An additional benefit of a combined SCR and SC approach pertains to research methodology. As previously mentioned, CSR has often attempted to identify general or universal human propensities, such as by using a cultural anthropology perspective. As Conway and Schaller (2002) point out, whereas proximate mechanisms can usually be tested directly, distal evolutionary mechanisms are more elusive. Many studies in the field of SC assess changes in religious beliefs as a function of the interaction between cognitive styles or personality dimensions as they are manifested in particular contexts. As will be seen from the material in this book, this experimental approach (e.g., manipulating variables in laboratory settings) adds additional levels of control that complement other methods such as cross-cultural or anthropological comparisons. Clearly, any alteration or change in R/S beliefs resulting from experimental manipulation of variables yields advantages in establishing causal pathways.

An additional benefit of integrating the CSR and SC approaches pertains to the ability to address potential criticisms that could be leveled at either field individually. As mentioned above, it is often difficult to verify or design falsifiable tests on universally evolved predispositions. In another example, some have suggested that the implications of finding innate precursors of religious thought such as intuitive tendencies (e.g., Hyperactive Agency Detection) are limited in their ramifications for the ultimate reliability and origin of these faculties. This argument suggests that the mere identification of any "natural" cognitive function has no bearing on the existence or nonexistence of the actual ontological referent detected by its operation. However, methodological traditions and techniques from SC strengthen the validity of the conclusions to be drawn from results by allowing testable comparisons with objective referents, a topic that will be revisited in the concluding chapter.

Themes

One of the main themes of this book pertains to how religious and nonreligious cognitions alike are shaped by the same basic underlying processes. Religious concepts are not products of some unique or *sui generis* function of the mind, but rather they exhibit the same psychological contours, patterns, and biases as other secular beliefs. Consequently, there are nonreligious analogues of religious cognition that differ in content and are attributed to distinct sources, but that nonetheless serve similar psychological features and functions. Just as our day-to-day secular cognition is affected by mental biases and heuristics, religious concepts are similarly affected. Examples of these will be covered in detail in Chapter 1. As mentioned above, humans have the tendency to over-detect intentionality and agency. One manifestation of this is the tendency to attribute personal culpability for misfortune, as opposed to believing that outcomes are random (i.e., "there must be a responsible agent, things do not just happen"). Social Cognition research has identified general cognitive biases related to this tendency, such as the Fundamental Attribution Error (under-weighting situational explanations), the Belief in a Just World (viewing outcomes as being deserved), and System Justification (the tendency to defend, bolster, and justify aspects of the societal status quo). Attributions produced by these mental heuristics can lead to blaming victims of misfortune. The content of these attributions can be secular (e.g., "Careless people put themselves in harm's way") as well as religious ("God is punishing them for their sins"). The tendency to rely on rules of thumb, or to be biased differs as a function of inter-individual traits (e.g., cognitive and personality traits) and contextual conditions (e.g., threats or ambiguity).

Some aspects of religious belief content have been created by these cognitive processes. Religious traditions, textual interpretations, and doctrines have been subject to humans' biases and heuristics, resulting in change and adaptation over the course of history. Some religious concepts are memorable and selectively emphasized while others are overlooked or downplayed. Some are shaped to be more intuitively appealing. This psychological harmonization process has been the subject of CSR study, such as in Pascal Boyer's book *Religion Explained* (2001). Boyer suggests that concepts like supernatural punishment, ghosts, witches, and the evil eye originate as byproducts of our evolved intuitive mental processes such as Theory of Mind and the tendency to affix social explanations for misfortune. Cognitively compatible or "sticky" intuitive concepts are expanded into more elaborate attributional accounts by more explicit processes. Interestingly, intuitions about religious and spiritual matters do not always consistently line up with explicit theological beliefs and doctrines. Such states of affairs can lead to psychological tension and the resulting motivation to resolve any inconsistency between opposing intuitive and explicit beliefs. In *Mind and Gods* (2006), Todd Tremlin outlined the process in which conflict between "basic" religious intuitions on the one hand, and "theological" concepts on the other can create new religious doctrines.

The field of SC contributes to the study of phenomena such as explanations of misfortune and victim blaming via the concept of cognitive dissonance, demonstrating how tension produced by psychological conflicts can generate novel attributions. For example, questions of theodicy or "Why would a just God allow innocent people to suffer?" can result in an intuitive conflict between the concept of a benevolent deity juxtaposed with observations that evil is nonetheless occurring. The most psychologically satisfying solutions to such questions are internalized, disseminated with greater ease, and become culturally popular. Concepts that resolve dissonance become harmonized with other "theologically correct" doctrines over time (Barrett & Keil, 1996). In the above mentioned case of attributing blame for misfortune, the apparent suffering of innocent individuals creates cognitive dissonance on an intuitive level that can be reduced by invoking explicit religious concepts such as supernatural punishment ("maybe they were not innocent, so God is punishing them"), heaven, hell, and purgatory. Interpersonal social-psychological processes also help further explain how beliefs are shared and consensually validated by fellow group members such as the process of internalizing social norms. Individual differences in beliefs can be harmonized to match the group belief. This process of conformity to group norms reduces cognitive dissonance by shaping beliefs to be more consonant with those of others. In sum, explicit religious concepts often represent the harmonization with, and outcome of, the same implicit cognitive dynamics that are used in processing social information. This process will be explored in more detail in Chapters 2 and 3.

Dual Process and Intuitive Origins

These different levels of cognition represent another theme of the book, the utility of Dual Process theories (Evans, 2008; Kahneman, 2011). Mental content is the combined product of separate psychological modes of functioning. One such distinction is that between System one or Type one (T1) thinking, which operates automatically and effortlessly at an unconscious, intuitive level, and Type two (T2) cognition, which functions in a manner that is slow, effortful, conscious, and analytical. Although many, if not most of daily thought processes, our intuitions and motivations, are produced using T1 processes, we do not have conscious access to these operations. Likewise, the impact of social learning and exposure to contextual stimuli interacting with our temperament and personality characteristics also influence our thoughts and behaviors in ways that are not necessarily consciously perceived. Many experiments demonstrate that participants can be influenced by cues such as priming techniques (e.g., subtle or subliminal exposure to certain concepts), without being consciously aware of connections between the cue and their behavior. Such results indicate that we are often unaware of the actual reasons why we believe certain things or behave certain ways; religious thought is no exception to this.

One implication of Dual Processing modes of cognition is that we are unable to accurately access our intuitive or implicit processes. Type two is afflicted by "introspective opacity"—the inability to direct the spotlight of our conscious mind and discern the operations of Type one—again, which often are the ultimate origins of why we think or feel as we do (Wilson, 2002). As such, humans are prone to the Blind Spot Bias (Pronin, 2008). We tend to assume that we see the world as it is (i.e., naïve realism), and therefore we assume that others will view the world as we do. When others arrive at different conclusions from ours (while also believing they see the world as it is), we generate reasons to explain why *they* are biased, rather than looking for sources of our own biases. Although we can use our analytic mind (primarily T2 processes) to have an intellectual understanding of how things may contribute to bias in general (e.g., "Humans believe as they do in order to maintain self-esteem"), this is used primarily for attributions about others, not typically about our own judgment in any given situation. Rather, our own intuition (T1) is accepted as a valid source of information, in accordance with naïve realism. This is a consequence of the independent function of our existing mental structures, which paradoxically encourages a reliance on our own personal introspection but a rejection of the reliability of others' introspection.

As a result, biases such as these are very difficult to consciously overcome. A related religious manifestation of this type of introspection bias is the tendency to refer to seemingly rational, internally generated reasons for our own belief or lack of belief ("I believe in a god because the world seems well-designed," "I have given religion much thought") but to make attributions to emotional and contextual reasons to explain why others believe ("They need religion to cope with life"; Kenworthy, 2003). This is related to the motivated skepticism bias in which we (again, unconsciously) hold different standards for evidence that supports our preexisting beliefs versus potentially contradictory information. The consequences of our inability to correctly access the implicit origins of our cognition will be a recurrent theme in the book, discussed as contributing to religious beliefs in several ways.

Rationalization, Confabulation, and Projection

One might think that this lack of introspective access into nonconscious processes would produce a hesitancy or uncertainty in T2 processing when providing explanations for thoughts and behaviors. If we are consciously unaware of these intuitive influences, it would stand to reason that we would admit: "I don't know why I feel a spiritual presence" or "I have no idea of the origin of my beliefs." However, as will be discussed in subsequent chapters, there is ample evidence that, when confronted with gaps in introspective awareness, we generate explicit justifications for beliefs originating from implicit mechanisms (Wilson, 2002). Consequently, many of our attributions about our beliefs and motivations are inaccurate or only partially true. Intuitively generated content is altered and smoothed-over, making it more consistent and comprehensible. We often refer to deliberative processes ("I thought about the evidence for my beliefs and carefully decided") even in instances that can be demonstrated to originate without deliberation (e.g., subliminal priming with contextual cues). These plausible but mistaken rationales for why we think or act the way we do can be characterized as confabulations or *post hoc* rationalizations (i.e., not the actual reasons).

A manifestation of rationalized intuitions in the case of religious and spiritual belief is that we may misattribute their source as coming from outside ourselves in a form of externalization or projection onto supernatural entities. In other words, phenomena that are experienced not as coming from "in here" but rather from "out there." In the case of blaming victims who suffer misfortune (i.e., because of the belief in a just world), the attributed origin for our thoughts regarding culpability for misfortune can be externalized as "God meting out justice," rather than internalized (e.g., "I am scapegoating because of my need to avoid randomness"). Indeed, individuals project onto "God" their own attitudes and opinions on a range of issues in what is known as egocentric bias. It is common for religious believers to state that their beliefs about the characteristics and desires of God are derived from religious sources such as theological or philosophical teachings, scripture and tradition, or personal revelation. However, consider a series of experiments conducted by Epley et al. (2008) wherein the relationship was shown to run in the other direction—from person onto "God." Participants' attitudes about various issues (e.g., the death penalty, gay marriage) were subtly changed by the experimenters (e.g., under conditions providing the participants with strong versus weak arguments), with the result that participants came to believe that "God" also shared the same (shifted) attitudes, consistent with egocentric projection. Throughout this book we will see other examples of causality running in a similar direction—people attributing religious beliefs externally onto "God." We will see that motivational factors, personal traits, changes in mental states, or the influence of social groups and cultural norms, can lead individuals to misattribute their thoughts and feelings to "God." Such findings are the most profound and useful contribution of Social Psychology and Social Cognition toward the understanding religious and spiritual belief.

Religious Concepts Are Internalized or Introjected

When people believe something in a religious sense, this could refer to more than one type of concept. One could have a religious belief that refers to statements of ostensible facts, or semantic information ("Jesus died for our sins," "My religion stresses obedience to the Ten Commandments"), or alternatively a belief could refer to personal, phenomenological ways of knowing ("Jesus changed my heart," "God wants us to reconcile"). The term "belief" does not adequately distinguish between the former type of conceptual religious content and the latter, more personal phenomenological sense. A linguistic analogy for this distinction pertains to the two Spanish verbs that both translate as "to know" in English. Whereas *saber* refers to knowledge in the sense of facts or information ("I know the tenets of a religion"), *conocer* refers to knowing in the sense of being familiar with people or things ("I know God's will"). Rather than focusing primarily on the acquisition of religious concepts (e.g., doctrine, denominational identity, belief tenets), this book will primarily discuss the influence on the phenomenological types of religious beliefs and attributions (e.g., "God is sending me a sign," "I believe this event is evidence of God's influence"). Accordingly, the focus will be on how beliefs move from being perceived as external in origin ("I was taught by my parents that God wants X," "In the Bible, Jesus asked children to come to him"), to being internalized ("It seems to me that God wants X," "The birth of my child is a sign"). In the terminology used in psychodynamic theories of human consciousness, I will focus on how beliefs become introjected and ego-syntonic—seen as compatible with our own Self.

Implications: What Is at Stake?

With any scientific discussion pertaining to the origins of religious belief, questions arise regarding ontological and metaphysical implications such as: "Does the identification of naturalistic mechanisms have any bearing on the ultimate reality or bases of R/S beliefs and experiences?" and "Are the R/S thoughts and intuitions reliable in tracking external reality?" A complete and comprehensive discussion of such philosophical questions is beyond the scope of the present coverage. However, because the implications of findings from the field of CSR are topics of ongoing deliberation (Barrett, 2007; Jong et al., 2015; Shults, 2016), it is appropriate to discuss any additional contribution of fields of Social Psychology and Social Cognition to that debate.

Possible positions in these debates generally fall into one of several categories (or in a dimensional sense, on a continuum). At the metaphysical supernaturalist or spiritually believing end, the psychological mechanisms revealed by CSR are viewed as reliable indicators of authentic R/S phenomena (Barrett & Church, 2013). Some have suggested that the very existence of belief-promoting functions (e.g., agency detection) constitutes a type of *sensus divinitatus* through which spiritual powers or Gods interact with human brains or give rise to religious experiences when influenced by external agency (Barrett, 2007; Clark & Barrett, 2010). In the terminology of this debate, this camp considers the psychological mechanisms to be generally "truth-tracking."

Another position, somewhere in the middle of the continuum, states that scientific findings pertaining to R/S phenomena are metaphysically neutral, capable of neither supporting nor refuting the ontological reality of R/S phenomena. This view maintains that merely because CSR research has identified evolved, brain-based mechanisms that promote R/S beliefs, this has no bearing on the ultimate genuineness of the beliefs, nor on whether any predispositions are reflective of intentional design. For example, Van Eyghen (2020) argues that the epistemic bases for religious belief cannot be undermined by findings from CSR.

One version of this position, relevant to the output of cognitive mechanisms such as agency detection, intentionality, and promiscuous teleology, involves taking a neutral stance regarding the veracity of their output. According to this line of reasoning, if religious believers and nonbelievers differ in their capacity to detect spiritual agency, we cannot necessarily say that one group over-detects (i.e., false positives) and the other under-detects (false negatives) without making assumptions about the existence of what is being detected. Without objective criteria, the reliability of these functions is an open question. Barrett (2007) argues that there are many times where human experience testifies that agency detection and the theory of mind are in fact reliable and that "to call genuinely religious beliefs 'illusions' we need to be able to demonstrate that they too … are in error" which "requires a metaphysical commitment" (p. 63). Perhaps it could be that atheists have some sort of epistemic impairment that causes them to be oblivious to spiritual realities (Barrett & Church, 2013).

The evidence needed to address issues of accuracy of beliefs (again, often said to be lacking in correlational CSR studies) would have to include some sort of objective benchmark by which to judge individual differences in R/S detection abilities. For example, to make statements of accuracy there would have to be a verifiable criterion or target with a comparison of the relative accuracy of believers and nonbelievers. A related question pertaining to the reliability of belief-forming functions is whether their initial intuitive output can be corrected by other non-intuitive processes. Some advocates for the ultimate reliability of belief-forming mechanisms suggest that, although the initial output from T1 may indeed be unreliable or "coarse grained," subsequent processing by rational mechanisms operating at the level of T2 (logic, reason, theological teachings), can assist or scaffold the fuzzy output, ultimately resulting in reliable R/S beliefs (Barrett, 2007). In other words, this position would concede the potential for biases or inaccuracies but hold that these can be overcome by referring to other types of evidence.

Finally, at the other end of the continuum, the metaphysical naturalist or debunking type positions hold that evidence of the function of naturalistic mechanisms implies that supernatural explanations are demonstrably unreliable or at least not the most parsimonious accounts (Galen, 2017). Such arguments refer to findings indicating that mental functions associated with R/S belief deliver objectively biased output (i.e., not just fuzzy or coarse-grained). Notably, debates involving these implications have focused almost exclusively on concepts associated with the field of CSR (e.g., hyperactive inferences of agency, teleology, minimally counterintuitive concepts, etc.). However, the additional contribution from the fields of Social Psychology and Social Cognition, particularly the use of experimental designs featuring clear objective criteria, makes a unique contribution to this debate, a topic that will be emphasized in the concluding chapter.

Misattribution of Study Effects

Another theme of the book is that misattributions of R/S influences do not occur solely as part of the phenomenology of believers, but also in the form of the results of scientific studies. Such third-party misattributions occur when a given study result is interpreted to indicate that R/S has had some unique causal influence, when the methodology did not allow for that idea to be tested, or the results did not necessarily support that interpretation because competing explanations were not eliminated. For example, many studies lack controls for basic expectancy or placebo-type effects. As I will argue throughout the book, R/S research often has not incorporated basic scientific controls at multiple levels such as in the choice of participant samples, measures, and comparison conditions in experiments.

One point of contention among scholars of religion regards whether the effects of R/S are unique or *sui generis* in terms of being irreducible to more basic naturalistic or secular mechanisms. This book will examine three domains of the literature arguably discussed most often in terms of R/S uniqueness: Exceptional experiences, morality, and mental health/ well-being. Just as with the range of views on the ontological implications of CSR, there is a similar range of positions on the issue of *sui generis* effects in these domains. On one end of the continuum is the stance that research evidence supports R/S having a singular influence on cognition and behavior, one without secular equivalent (Slife et al., 2012). An example of this is the concept of sanctity or sacredness, which is argued to have a unique impact on relationships and well-being (Pargament et al., 2005). In another example, some theories suggest that R/S-related contexts are particularly able to elicit positive emotional states such as awe, collective uplift, and flow via the unique footing found in features of religious worship (Van Cappellen et al., 2016). It should be mentioned, however, that not all researchers suggest that the *sui generis* qualities of R/S influences necessarily constitute evidence of actual external agency. Many sanctification researchers, for instance, suggest that the concept represents unique variance in terms of people's phenomenological experiences, but is not necessarily indicative of actual ontological reality (Wong et al., 2018).

As I will argue in subsequent chapters, one major contribution to the misinterpretation of R/S having *sui generis* effects is a lack of experimental control for secular confounding influences, including the inability to institute comparisons that are fully equivalent, save for the R/S belief components. For example, religious attendance has been found to be associated with many positive aspects of moral and mental health functioning, often leading researchers to suggest that it is uniquely R/S content (e.g., belief in God, scriptural study, a group "sacred canopy") that is necessary for producing other positive aspects such as social support or community embeddedness. However, more recent studies have found modest effects, if any, of R/S belief components when controlling for the secular aspects or when religious congregations are compared to equivalent secular congregations (Charles et al., 2021; Shor & Roelfs, 2013). Thus, this represents a misattribution of one effect (i.e., salubrious outcome) erroneously to another (R/S belief).

Implications of Misattribution for Self-Reports

Another theme of the book will examine how findings from areas of basic psychological research such as dual process and attribution theories have implications for the proper interpretation of R/S phenomena such as the self-reports of believers. Specifically, I will focus on how phenomenological, subjective reports (e.g., "God spoke to me in prayer," "The Holy Spirit is moving through me," or "My religion is the cause of my behavior") can be shown to constitute misattributions of inner processes. This is particularly relevant to domains such as exceptional experiences, morality, and well-being in which theories of unique R/S influences are based on such introspections. Just as with the interpretations of sanctification and positive spiritual influences, one position on self-reports of R/S effects is that of ontological neutrality, in which the phenomenology of the believer is accepted without taking a stance either way on the ultimate source or referent. For example, this position would entail that if a given group of participants in a study attribute improvement in their mental well-being to the effects of R/S, a neutral researcher cannot rule out that actual spiritual agency was involved as opposed to purely naturalistic processes.

Such neutrality is standard practice in fields such as cultural anthropology where the beliefs and experiences are described from the *emic* perspective of the subject without taking a position on ultimate accuracy, rather than an *etic* perspective based on the observer's point of view. In the accounts of Charismatic Christian "Renewalist" believers, Luhrmann (2012) describes their interactive prayer experiences of speaking with God or of demonic presences using terms reflecting the *emic* perspective such as "… the demons *become real to those* who pray …" Often, when psychological accounts of R/S belief have not adopted this neutral approach or when researchers have not demonstrated sufficient acceptance of R/S self-reports, this has elicited charges of outsider bias or reductionism (Wong et al., 2018). In reference to sanctification research, Mahoney (2021) warns of the risk of reductionism in failing to acknowledge conceptual uniqueness in the substantive content of participants' R/S thoughts or feelings, such as "feeling a sense of comfort from a loving deity or perceptions of the sanctity of an aspect of life" (p. 29).

Certainly, researchers must tread lightly when describing the worldviews or the phenomenological accounts of participants or patients, particularly those from different cultures. However, one question that will be discussed throughout the book is whether a completely neutral stance is warranted when referring to evidence that includes objective standards of perceptual accuracy or is based on known experimental manipulations under controlled conditions. In virtually every other area of social sciences, it is unusual to adopt such a neutral stance. Using an example from a non-R/S scientific domain, the case of a double-blind, placebo-controlled drug study, characterizing a participant's experience in the manner of: "A patient in the placebo condition believed that her depression was alleviated by an antidepressant drug, but we cannot say for certain if this was a misattribution," would be viewed as unnecessarily neutral, if not inaccurate. Many scientists maintain that since religion and spirituality involve references to unfalsifiable concepts and experiences, no stance can be taken on their accuracy. However, in studies such as the abovementioned Epley et al. (in which the dependent variable—participants' views of what "God thinks"—were manipulated by the independent variable of essay type), it is not reductionist or biased for the researchers to suggest that attributions to "God" represented evidence of egocentric bias, rather, it is a neutral description of the effect of a known manipulation, the results, and the implications.

Warnings of the perils of reductionism are almost *de rigueur* when defending the acceptance of R/S self-reports at face value. However, the identification of basic underlying processes is properly an element of the scientific method. Slingerland (2008) distinguishes between productive, explanatory reductionism versus crudely eliminative reductionism, concluding that the general label of reductionism is ultimately an empty term of abuse. In the case of R/S processes that putatively add unique elements to moral or well-being outcomes, making a distinction between components that are causal versus those that are superfluous is a practice of "good reductionism" following the principle of Occam's Razor.

Organization

The chapters that follow are organized into two broad sections. The first part of the book is devoted to areas of cognitive psychology, social cognition, and interpersonal social psychology in relation to basic concepts that are applied to religious belief. The second part of the book will use this combined set of concepts to address the phenomena of exceptional religious experiences, morality, and mental well-being. Finally, the concluding chapter will revisit the overarching themes mentioned in this introductory chapter such as general implications of the findings described.

Part One

Mechanisms of Social Cognition and Religious Manifestations

1

Cognition, Dual Process Models, and Introspective Opacity

Among the most productive fields of study subsumed within the cross-disciplinary Cognitive Sciences of Religion (CSR) is Cognitive Psychology (and the associated Cognitive sciences). These disciplines have not only identified plausible mechanisms and modes of thought that constitute the underpinnings of religious and spiritual beliefs, but they have also gone further in uncovering how mental systems enable the conceptualization and believability of some ideas. Previous work from the CSR perspective has described how evolved modules, functions, or modes of thought (e.g., Hyperactive Agency Detection, Promiscuous Teleology, Theory of Mind) produce different types of religious or spiritual (R/S) beliefs (Boyer, 2001; Tremlin, 2006). Compared to other avenues of study that exert influence at "higher" interpersonal or social levels, Cognitive Psychology is better able to capture fundamental or "basic" mental operations such as those involving attention, perception, memory, and the ability to think analytically and abstractly. This chapter will illustrate how R/S belief is associated with impaired performance on tasks of reasoning, analytic cognition, and perception. The first portion of the chapter will simply describe the empirical findings pertaining to cognitive traits and R/S belief. The latter portion of the chapter will place these findings into a theoretical framework, specifically how these cognitive patterns can contribute to misattributions of supernatural agency.

Cognitive Traits and Religiosity/Spirituality

There are some occasions when we must use our cognitive reasoning abilities to avoid the biasing influence of common stereotypic information. Consider the following pieces of information:

> "In a study 1000 people were tested. Among the participants there were 995 nurses and 5 doctors. Paul is a randomly chosen participant of this study. Paul

is 34 years old. He lives in a beautiful home in a posh suburb. He is well spoken and very interested in politics. He invests a lot of time in his career. What is the probability that Paul is a nurse?"

This type of problem is structured so that the base rate data (i.e., more nurses than doctors) conflicts with stereotypic information (e.g., Nurses tend to be predominantly female, Paul is affluent). To correctly ascertain the probability requires the subordination of the latter stereotypic information in favor of the former base rate. Studies have shown that greater religiosity is associated with lower reasoning ability on tasks requiring the attenuation of intuitive stereotypic information (Pennycook et al., 2014). Likewise, Daws and Hampshire (2017) found that religiosity was negatively related to performance on problems involving response inhibition conflict (e.g., a version of the Stroop color naming task). Other studies have also found negative correlations between religious belief and successful performance on a range of reasoning tasks involving numeracy and deduction (e.g., syllogisms; Pennycook et al., 2013; Pennycook et al., 2016; Ross et al., 2016). Relative to the nonreligious, religious individuals tend to make decisions quickly, seek less additional information (Vonk et al., 2021), and engage in types of strategic processing marked by lower degrees of cognitive flexibility and planning (Zmigrod et al., 2019; Zmigrod et al., 2021). In sum, performance across a range of cognitive tasks is inversely related to individuals' degree of religious belief.

Similar to this pattern on basic reasoning tasks, religious believers also tend to have lower performance on "higher level" or "top-down" tasks involving cognitive styles ("thinking dispositions") such as a lesser inclination to engage in effortful cognitive activities (i.e., Need for Cognition; Lobato et al., 2014). These stylistic thinking traits include susceptibility to confirmation bias, faith in intuition, and anti-intellectualism (Baimel et al., 2021; Jasinskaja-Lahti & Jetten, 2019; Nilsson et al., 2019). The belief that one's own beliefs should change in accordance with empirical evidence, or "actively open-minded thinking" is less common among the religious (Pennycook et al., 2023; Pennycook et al., 2020). Religiosity is positively related to "bullshit receptivity"—the tendency to ascribe profundity to randomly generated content (e.g., "Imagination is inside exponential space time events"; Erlandsson et al., 2018; Pennycook et al., 2023). Conversely, religiosity is related to lower "bullshit-sensitivity"—the ability to distinguish the pseudo-profound from the genuinely profound (Nilsson et al., 2019). Again, these patterns are notable because the tasks all feature objective performance criteria unrelated to any religious content.

Beyond cognitive tasks and skills, religious and nonreligious individuals differ in their perceptual sets and views of reality or ontology. Some of these tendencies resemble features of interest within the Cognitive Sciences of Religion such as agency detection, mentalizing, anthropomorphism, and teleological (purpose-driven) mindsets. The degree of personal religiosity has been found to predict the attribution of agency to non-human entities (Wlodarski & Pearce, 2016). Religious, spiritual, and supernatural believers have a greater tendency to over-attribute meaningfulness and intentionality to a variety of stimuli. These include believing in coincidences (Coleman & Beitman, 2009), assigning purpose to randomly moving geometric figures (Riekki et al., 2014), and over-perceiving faces (i.e., when viewing non-face stimuli; Riekki et al., 2013). Greater religiosity is also predictive of confusing ontological properties such as viewing lifeless entities as possessing attributes of living entities (e.g., "Stars live in the sky"), or attributing mental states to material objects (e.g., "A plan lives in nature"; Lindeman et al., 2015; Lindeman & Svedholm-Häkkinen, 2016). Those with more devout religious orientations report greater belief in fantastical cognitions and behaviors (Thibodeau et al., 2018). Viewed in the aggregate, such findings indicate that the perceptual tendencies of believers, relative to nonbelievers, are more prone to apophenia—the tendency to detect patterns or causality when none exists—and making perceptual misattribution in the form of "false-positives" to neutral stimuli.

Religious believers also differ from the nonreligious in possessing higher levels of traits that themselves are associated with the types of cognitive, perceptual, and ontological errors mentioned above. For instance, the personality trait of absorption (i.e., the tendency to become immersed in one's own thoughts and feelings) is associated with greater susceptibility to fantasy and hypnotic states and fluctuations in phenomenal experience (Tellegen & Atkinson, 1974). Those who are high on absorption are more likely to report a range of pseudo-hallucinatory experiences, including hearing voices and experiencing paranormal phenomena (Glickson & Barrett, 2003; Granqvist et al., 2005; Spanos & Morettti, 1988) and to interpret ambiguous sensations in accordance with prior expectation, perceiving signal where there is only noise (Lifshitz et al., 2019). Apropos to the current topic, absorption is positively associated with religiosity (Levin et al., 1998; Luhrmann et al., 2010). This trait will be discussed in greater detail in the chapter on religious experiences because of its association with spiritual and quasi-mystical experiences as well as engagement in person-like prayer interactions (Levin et al., 1998; Luhrmann et al., 2010; Luhrmann et al., 2021).

Just as absorption is related to the blurring of boundaries between inner and outer experiences, a similar trait associated with perceptual anomalies is schizotypy, which involves having odd ideas, magical thinking, unusual experiences, and ideas of reference (belief that innocuous events refer to oneself). Those high in schizotypy display an increased tendency to perceive complex meaning in random visual noise and the employment of a looser criterion (i.e., response bias) when determining what constitutes a meaningful image (Partos et al., 2016). Higher levels of schizotypy are not only associated with religious and spiritual belief, but also increased attributions of mental states to God and to non-agentic objects like trees and the dead (Gray et al., 2011; Lindeman & Lipsanen, 2016; Schuurmans-Stekhoven, 2013a; Willard & Norenzayan, 2017). In sum, religious and spiritual belief is associated with the perceptual styles of absorption and schizotypy, traits themselves linked with apophenic over-detection and a more porous internal-external boundary (Wlodarski & Pearce, 2016).

Dual Process Models of Thinking

What ultimately accounts for this pattern of association between cognitive-perceptual tendencies and individual differences in R/S? One general framework that may help explain this connection is Dual Process Theory. Dual Process (DP) models are based on results from cognitive sciences suggesting that, despite our subjective experience of a seamless and unitary self, mental functioning involves more than one type of cognition (Evans, 2008; Kahneman, 2011). As mentioned briefly in the introductory chapter, classic DP theory suggests that System or Type One (T1) is automatic, fast, intuitive, and implicit, whereas System or Type Two (T2) is slow, analytical, and explicit. Intuitions from T1 function without conscious awareness, whereas cognitions from T2 involve deliberative processing and mental effort. This distinction between types of thinking allows for the separate measurement of functions performed by T2 on tasks of analytic cognition from T1 operations, the latter of which resemble heuristics or automatic "rules of thumb" (Stanovich et al., 2008).

Debate regarding the precise nature or boundary limitations of Dual Process models is ongoing. For instance, some theoretical frameworks suggest that there may be more than two systems or state-like modes of functioning, or even a continuum of thought with greater or lesser degrees of analytic deliberation (De Neys, 2021; Morgan, 2016). Further, any given content area (i.e., including religion as well as other domains such as music or language) can involve both T1 and T2 operations, depending on the stage or level at which information is being processed. For example, when an interactive and emotional prayer experience with a perceived spiritual agent may be best characterized as occurring in the T1 mode of cognition, whereas the study of scripture or learning to pray in a new language utilizes T2 cognitive processing. CSR researchers have pointed to differences in the types of religious content produced by the separate types (Oviedo, 2015). Tremlin (2006) suggests that while T1 religious content is implicit or imagistic, content processed by T2 is more doctrinal or theological. The imagistic concepts (e.g., anthropomorphized agents) can be at odds with doctrinal or "theologically correct" concepts disseminated via religious instruction (Barrett & Keil, 1996). In this sense, different types of religious beliefs can be suited to analytic as well as intuitive processing.

The nuances and qualifications of DP models certainly should be incorporated into any comprehensive discussion of religion and cognitive processing. However, for the present purposes of generally characterizing cognitive performance in relation to R/S, these caveats do not fundamentally change the overall pattern of results. Religious and spiritual beliefs, such as the general tendency to endorse supernatural concepts, are inversely related to performance on measures associated with Type Two cognitive processes.

Analytic Cognition

As outlined above, religious believers show a differing pattern of results from nonbelievers on a range of cognitive tasks. Dual Process models distinguishing Type 1 (intuitive) from Type 2 (analytic) cognition may provide an explanation for this difference. Analytic cognition tends to be relatively slow, careful, and deliberative relative to intuitive cognition. To illustrate, consider the following problem: "*A bat and a ball cost $1.10 in total. The bat costs $1.00 more than the ball. How much does the ball cost?*" The intuitive answer given by most individuals is ten cents. But this is incorrect because a 10¢ ball plus a $1.10 bat (required for a difference of $1.00) would add up to $1.20. More careful consideration of the phrasing of the question, however, reveals that the correct answer is five cents ($0.05 plus $1.05 bat equaling $1.10). Successful performance on this type of item, taken from the Cognitive Reflection Test (CRT; Frederick, 2005), requires the ability and motivation to suppress a prepotent (but incorrect) response, and to instead use analytical skills associated with Type Two thinking to deliberately calculate an answer. When aggregated together with other similar items, individual performance forms a continuum from greater to lesser analytical skill.

How does the construct of analytic cognition and performance on related tasks connect with individual differences in R/S belief? As mentioned in the introductory chapter, many CSR researchers have focused on general human intuitive processes that produce R/S beliefs (as well as secular equivalents) via functions like hyperactive agency detection, teleological and meaning-making tendencies, and theory of mind. If intuitive tendencies produce the near-universal attribution of spiritual agency, an individual difference perspective suggests that those with greater intuitive activation (or less analytic thought or inhibition of intuition) will display higher levels of R/S belief. This intuitive belief hypothesis posits that non-analytic thinking will be most pronounced among R/S believers, whereas greater analytical thought should be associated with skepticism and lower levels of belief (Yilmaz, 2021).

Numerous studies, including a meta-analysis by Pennycook, Ross, Koehler, and Fugelsang (2016), have found a negative relationship between trait analytic cognition and religiosity. Some early studies have been criticized on the grounds of poor operationalization of constructs. For example, the Cognitive Reflection Test (Frederick, 2005), which features the aforementioned ball and bat problem, has a limited item range and emphasizes mathematical ability. However, other studies using non-numeric items to assess the ability to analytically override intuitive responses have found similar inverse relationships with religiosity, spirituality, and supernatural belief (Gervais et al., 2021; Roberts et al., 2021; Weiss et al., 2021; Yilmaz & Isler, 2019). In sum, the same pattern of negative relationships with religiosity also holds using numerous measures of analytic cognition (Ross et al., 2016).

The analytic cognition—religiosity relationship has several caveats and qualifications. Recent work has suggested that the religiosity-analytic cognition association may vary as a function of, or be moderated by, conditions such as individual differences in valuing epistemic rationality (Ståhl & van Prooijen, 2021). There is also a debate regarding whether the relationship holds in other cultures featuring differing levels of religious predominance (Gervais et al., 2018; Stagnaro et al., 2019). Attempts have been made to substantiate causality by experimentally enhancing the level of analytic cognition (e.g., via semantic priming) to attenuate levels of religious belief. Although several earlier studies suggested that this was indeed the case (e.g., Gervais & Norenzayan, 2012) more recent pre-registered replication attempts using similar methodology with large samples have failed (Sanchez et al., 2017; Saribay et al., 2020). Therefore, it does not appear that the temporary activation or enhancement of analytic thought reliably decreases religiosity.

Further, some research has supported a "reflective religious belief" hypothesis, suggesting that some religious content is processed using higher levels of analytic cognition (Yilmaz, 2021). One instance of this may occur with R/S belief in contexts emphasizing intellectual reflection, and therefore utilizing more Type Two processes. Among samples drawn from Christian colleges, Yonker et al. (2016) found that priming of analytic thought led to greater, not lesser, levels of intrinsic religiosity (although this study obtained the association with intrinsic religiosity while also controlling for general religiosity). Another implication of the reflective belief hypothesis is that increased analytic cognition may lead not only to re-evaluation of religious belief, but to a similar critical processing and attenuation of nonreligious belief. Yilmaz and Isler (2019) found that inducing reflection increased, rather than decreased, belief in God among non-believers. The authors reasoned that activation of analytic cognition increases doubts about any previous stance regarding God's existence or nonexistence, leading to a kind of regression to the uncertain middle in believers and nonbelievers alike. In general, studies that have used priming have had problems with replication, indicating that the phenomenon is, at best, tenuous and inconsistent (Watanabe & Laurent, 2021). However, despite the results from studies using experimental activation of analytic versus intuitive mindsets, it should be re-iterated that the general association between individual differences in R/S and trait analytic cognition measured as an ability or level of performance has been widely confirmed.

Intelligence and General Cognitive Ability

One of the more contentious topics pertaining to the connection between cognition and religiosity is that involving general cognitive ability or overall intelligence ("IQ"). Perhaps one reason for the controversy is the sensitive nature of research questions such as "is belief in God related to lower intelligence?" A separate scientific debate concerns the construct of general cognitive ability itself, how best to define it, and the proper interpretation of results. As with analytic cognition however, the basic relationship between general cognitive ability and religiosity has been reasonably consistent across studies. In a meta-analysis of sixty-three studies, Zuckerman, Li, Lin, and Hall (2020) found an overall correlation between intelligence and religiosity in the −0.20 to −0.23 range. This was similar to the obtained range in Zuckerman's earlier (2013) findings (−0.20 to −0.25). Ross et al. (2016) also arrived at a similar figure (−0.19) using a variety of cognitive ability measures. Whether using individual-level or country-level data, religiosity is related to lower fluid intelligence or "g" (Dutton & Kirkegaard, 2022; Stankov & Lee, 2018). Other meta-analyses also confirm a small but robust negative association between intelligence and religiosity ($r = -.14$), particularly when the latter is measured as religious belief (Dürlinger & Pietschnig, 2022).

As with other research involving cognitive ability, the usual caveats must be kept in mind such as the implications of different studies using different ability measures and samples featuring different characteristics (e.g., nationality, level of education, and variable range). For example, Ganzach, Ellis, and Gotlibovski, (2013) found that the negative association between intelligence and religiosity was stronger in situations where religious background itself was strong rather than weak. This stands to reason, given that in some social contexts, nearly all individuals are religious, such that any resulting restriction of range would render the relationship with other variables negligible. Still, such methodological factors and moderating effects do not appear to negate the overall inverse relationship between the two constructs (Dürlinger & Pietschnig, 2022).

Aside from the association between general cognitive ability and R/S, an issue that is perhaps more theoretically important is the relative primacy of intelligence versus analytic cognition, which are correlated constructs. Some studies indicate that the analytic cognition—religiosity relationship is independent of cognitive ability, while others suggest that rational thinking exerts a lesser influence on religiosity than cognitive ability (Pennycook et al., 2016; Razmyar & Reeve, 2013). Also, religiosity has been found to be specifically related to the type of analytic performance involving conflicts between intuition and logic rather than with general intelligence (Daws & Hampshire, 2017). The Zuckerman et al. (2020) meta-analyses also indicated that analytic cognition partially mediates the relationship between general intelligence and religiosity.

Clearly, further research is necessary to substantiate the boundary conditions and nuances of the relationship between R/S beliefs and cognitive processes. This body of work has also been criticized regarding the use of specific individual measures. As mentioned above, the original CRT has a limited item range and only includes numeracy problems. Nonetheless, more recent studies using measures with expanded item ranges and non-numeric problems have yielded similar results (Weiss et al., 2021). There is also debate regarding whether intuition and rationality constitute two opposite endpoints on a single continuum as opposed to being independent constructs (Epstein et al., 1996). Despite these specific methodological issues, however, when the totality of results featuring the broad array of cognitive measures is viewed in the aggregate, there remains a clear general trend of an inverse association between analytic cognitive ability and R/S belief. This is not merely an issue of R/S believers being more intuitively perspicacious such as displaying greater skill at detecting actual patterns in stimuli. Rather, it is an issue of poorer performance and lower accuracy on tasks featuring objective criteria (i.e., misattribution). By contrast, those who are less religious display higher analytic performance and increased perceptual accuracy.

The link between greater religiosity and lower analytic cognition, as interpreted through the lens of DP models, increases our understanding of how religious beliefs are formed and the interpretation of the phenomenological experience of those beliefs. Initial, broad intuitions, whether of agency, teleology, or purposefulness, are generated largely by Type One processing. The processes creating these operate in a manner akin to other cognitive heuristics in that, while they function effortlessly and automatically, are also prone to biases. Whereas T1 operations produce intuitions similarly across individuals, people differ in the ability and motivation to use T2 processing to overrule or attenuate these intuitions. Dual processing models may not completely capture the nature of operations used to solve the specific tasks. Type Two thinking likely subsumes different analytic components (e.g., as measured by tasks such as the CRT) that tap not only the "reflective mind" that detects and overrides incorrect intuitive responses, but also the "algorithmic mind," which sustains the override and identifies a correct solution (Stanovich et al., 2011; Zuckerman et al., 2020).

The component most relevant to religious cognition across studies involves the concept of cognitive style. The intuitive religious belief hypothesis posits that the divergent beliefs of religious and nonreligious individuals primarily occur with T2 processes specifically as a difference in using an "override" thinking style. Religious individuals do not generate more intuitions than the nonreligious, but rather T1 output is more likely to emerge unchecked by T2 processing. The resulting (unchecked) intuitions are then integrated with other existing religious schemas. Religious and nonreligious individuals differ (by definition) in the attributional labeling by T2 processes of intuitions generated via T1 processes. An unexplained coincidence may trigger an intuition that something exceptional occurred, however this may be labeled by T2 as merely an uncanny statistical fluke. Likewise, whereas religious individuals attribute these intuitions as seeming as if they originate from external (e.g., spiritual) sources or agency, nonreligious people may attribute them as being natural errors akin to optical illusions or superstitions (Risen, 2016).

However, on some occasions or in some contexts, despite having adequate ability to override intuitions generated using T1 processes, T2 operations are not utilized to do so. There may be several explanations for the failure of T2 to override T1. Rather than a dichotomy of initial intuitions being corrected by rational cognition, other type of "partial beliefs" may be formed where content is recognized as being technically in error or irrational (e.g., magical thinking), but individuals nonetheless acquiesce or act upon the belief. As a result, people "believe things they know they shouldn't" such as avoiding anything that could "jinx" an outcome even when denying a belief in superstition "just in case" (Risen, 2016). This occurs in contexts where the costs of ignoring rationality are low relative to the costs of ignoring intuition. In some cases, aspects of neural functioning may be attenuated, such as when fatigued, leading to a cognitive pattern marked by attenuation of hesitancy and doubt. For example, evidence for the False Tagging Theory suggests that lower levels of frontal cortex functioning are associated with excessive certainty and conviction, including religious fundamentalism (Zhong et al., 2017). Also, specific types of content areas may be processed in such a way as to restrain T2 processes from correcting T1 processes. Apropos to the current topic, R/S intuitions are particularly likely to be viewed as being incompatible with objective analysis such that believers more readily "go with what feels true." For instance, subliminal priming (i.e., without conscious awareness) with religious concepts can increase the misattribution of agentic, intentional features onto natural phenomena (Nieuwboer et al., 2014), indicating that contextualizing specific content within a religious frame of reference can attenuate analytic correction.

Perhaps the most robust factor attenuating the analytic override of intuitive R/S cognition may be exposure to a social environment featuring normative religious practices. One such concept identified in the Cognitive Science of Religion, is the Credibility Enhancing Display (CRED); a display of behavior, often costly or extravagant, that increases the transmission of socially shared beliefs. Indeed, interpersonal modeling and social transmission may have an even greater impact on R/S beliefs than the intra-individual functions of mentalizing and analytic thought (Maij et al., 2017). Gervais, Najle, and Caluori (2021) found that analytic, reflective cognition was only predictive of nonbelief in contexts with a low prevalence of CREDs. In that study, belief was present in contexts with high CREDs even among those with high levels of analytic cognition. Thus, rather than a model in which analytic cognition always overrides intuitive cognition resulting in an attenuation of R/S beliefs, environmental and social contextualization can influence this relationship, such as discouraging effortful processing (i.e., lower Need for Cognition; Lobato et al., 2014). In one example of such contextual effects, when facts are presented in a nonscientific context, religious people require less evidence to endorse the claim than when presented in a scientific context (McPhetres & Zuckerman, 2017). This suggests that framing information as R/S-related for individuals who endorse a spiritual epistemology can result in a greater openness to intuitively based attributions (e.g., the efficacy of prayer and good wishes) rather than analytically based ones.

Even broader contexts can interact with individuals' cognitive styles, including how they relate to religiosity. According to the Social Foundations hypothesis (Morgan et al., 2018), cognitive style shows cross-cultural variation; societies such as those in Western Europe exhibit greater preferences for analytical cognition compared to non-European societies. Accordingly, the relationship between higher analytic cognition and lower religiosity may be related to the lower levels of religiosity in certain societies. Conversely, broader societal values (e.g., social density, respect for hierarchy) interact with the relationship between cognition and religiosity, and a person's choice of community is itself influenced by their cognitive style. For example, those with more intuitive cognitive styles may gravitate toward dense social networks in which religious beliefs function as signals of group affiliation. These findings indicate that socially shared and instantiated belief systems can influence how or even whether R/S-related beliefs are analytically or rationally processed.

Even with secular, non-R/S related content, it is not uncommon for people to perseverate in holding beliefs, even when the factual bases of the beliefs are demonstrably incorrect (Lewandowsky et al., 2012; Shtulman & Valcarcel, 2012). This is especially likely when the new information would contradict emotionally based worldviews. Instead, worldview-threatening information is processed in a filtered or selective way, greatly diminishing the likelihood that individuals will engage in Bayesian updating by recognizing and admitting that their views have been contradicted by evidence. Such findings indicate that any general model suggesting that analytic or reflective processes uniformly correct intuitive errors is overly simplistic. Merely having the capacity for analytic cognition is necessary but not sufficient for such updating. Analytic, Type Two processes are selectively utilized and can also be biased. Individuals may learn, via inculcation or sociocultural exposure, ways of thinking that attenuate or restrain T2 correction and reinforce intuitive content, a topic that will be explored in subsequent chapters.

Nonreligious Equivalents: Paranormal Superstitious Beliefs

Mental content attributed to R/S is not the only type of output associated with greater intuitive and lower analytic cognition. Superstitious thinking, belief in the paranormal, and the endorsement of conspiracy theories are also associated with relatively poorer performance on the same standard cognitive tasks as those mentioned above (Kokis et al., 2002; Toplak et al., 2011). Paranormal believers have less reflective and more intuitive thinking dispositions (Lindeman & Aarnio, 2006, 2007). Low analytical thinking distinguishes both religious and paranormal believers from skeptics (Aarnio & Lindeman, 2007). Greater belief in the paranormal is associated with lower scholastic performance (Musch & Ehrenberg, 2002), logical conjunction errors (Rogers et al., 2018), and endorsement of pseudo-profound "bullshit" statements (Pennycook et al., 2015). Perceptual over-detection (e.g., seeing patterns in random coin tosses or abstract paintings) is also correlated with superstitious and conspiracy-related beliefs (van Prooijen et al., 2018). As with R/S beliefs, the tendency to commit ontological confusions is a predictor of paranormal and superstitious beliefs (Lobato et al., 2014).

Just as with R/S beliefs, there are debates regarding the relative primacy of different cognitive traits in their association with belief in the paranormal or superstitions, such as whether general cognitive ability versus specific analytic thinking style has the greater attenuating influence (Ståhl & Van Prooijen, 2018). Lindeman and Aarnio (2007) found that measures of ontological confusion were superior to analytic cognition in discriminating superstitious believers from skeptics. Similarly, Rizeq, Flora & Toplak (2021) found that although both general cognitive ability and analytic cognition were negatively related to paranormal beliefs and anti-science attitudes, ontological confusions and actively open-minded thinking were the more influential predictors. It is likely that R/S and paranormal beliefs are particularly closely related to ontological confusions because of shared measurement content. For example, measures of ontological confusion contain item statements such as "force lives in the universe" and "a plan lives in nature," which may be interpreted as compatible with, or even specifically referring to, spiritual concepts. Thus, the greater relevance of ontological confusion in the prediction of paranormal and supernatural beliefs may be attributable to the greater criterion overlap between measures.

Just as the same cognitive precursors (e.g., high intuitive, low analytic style) give rise to a range of general apophenic over-detection of patterns (R/S, paranormal, or superstitious beliefs), intuitive thinking and errors on cognitive tasks may also lead to greater beliefs in conspiracy theories (Brotherton & French, 2014; Swami et al., 2014; Toplak et al., 2011). As with R/S belief, analytic thinking appears to be necessary but not fully sufficient to override intuitive beliefs that form the basis of conspiracy theories. Rather, individuals must also be motivated to value epistemic rationality and to base conclusions on evidence to attenuate conspiracy beliefs (Ståhl & Van Prooijen, 2018). In sum, we see that a similar constellation of cognitive abilities and the motivation to use (or not use) them is associated with not only R/S beliefs, but also with attributions to paranormal, superstitious, and conspiracy-related content. The aspects of rational cognition discussed above (i.e., general ability, analytic cognition, rejection of pseudo-profound bullshit) may even serve a protective function in attenuating a broad range of apophenic manifestations.

Introspective Opacity and Estrangement from Ourselves

As we have seen, Dual Process models suggest that in some situations, intuitive content can form the basis for beliefs that may not be modified or updated by the analytic T2 operations. Beyond merely a failure of correction, another implication of DP type models is that functional separation of operations can contribute to misattributions due to "introspective opacity"—the lack of awareness of T2 into T1 processing. Our conscious awareness consists solely of T2 operations, which is compartmentalized from access into T1 processes that generate intuitive content. Consequently, we are largely unaware of the functions producing and influencing our emotions and behaviors. In his book *Strangers to Ourselves* (2002), Timothy Wilson compiles a body of evidence from fields as diverse as split-brain research, cortical stimulation experiments, observations of amnestic patients, subliminal priming, and hypnotic induction to illustrate the existence of the Adaptive Unconscious (AU). The AU consists of cognitive, memory, personality, and other psychological processes that are vital to our everyday functioning but of which we are unaware. The AU differs from psychoanalytically based notions of the unconscious in that, whereas Freud suggested that some mental content was inaccessible due to a motivated lack of awareness (i.e., repression, trauma, anxiety-driven defenses), the inaccessibility of the AU is attributable to the divided structure of the mind, which involves different processing modules used for different tasks. The lack of conscious access into the AU is due to functional separation, reasons of efficiency (e.g., cognitive heuristics and biases), automatization of operations, or simple inattention.

Largely overlapping with T1 processes, the Adaptive Unconscious can only be observed indirectly via its eventual distal output in the form of explicit thoughts and behavior but without direct access to the underlying mechanisms. Consequently, when providing an attribution or justification for this output, "we" (i.e., the explicit, conscious T2 operations) omit from explanatory accounts influences of which we are unaware. This includes the intra-individual intuitive processes as well as extra-individual stimuli such as contextual primes and frames, social cues, and other subliminal phenomena. Wilson points to the consequences of this compartmentalization including, but not limited to, discrepancies between self- and peer-reports of our own personality traits, biased recall for our past behavior, enhanced views of our own morality, and misattributed causes of our emotions. This is most evident in the context of experiments where participants are blinded to manipulations, yet they nonetheless provide introspectively based alternative explanations for their behavior. For example, Latane and Darley's (1970) classic experiments testing diffusion of responsibility garnered attention primarily because of the counterintuitive finding that greater numbers of bystanders decreased the likelihood that any given participant would assist in a crisis. However, this study also found that when participants were debriefed, they repeatedly denied that their behavior was influenced by the number of others present despite the observable effect of the manipulation. This type of failure to correctly attribute the causes of beliefs and behavior to their actual sources is commonplace in psychological experiments.

Research has consistently shown that, although we may be able to gain partial self-knowledge by observing our own behavior or receiving feedback from others, introspection is not reliable. Type Two operations interpret the cognitive and behavioral output of which it is unaware by offering explanations that are based on idiosyncratic personal theories and shared cultural stereotypes ("I am a male, and males tend to do X"). It is for this reason that analytic ability and associated T2 functions are necessary, but not sufficient to correct T1 intuitions: T2 functions can be biased in a way that contributes to misattribution. Much of the subsequent material from this book will illustrate how, in the case of religious belief, introspective inaccessibility across different domains can lead to "spiritual misattributions"—seemingly plausible accounts of mental interaction with, or influence from external agents. In reality, the origins of these influences are generated by non-R/S factors.

Manifestations of Misattributions

As outlined in the introductory chapter, the inaccessibility of mental processes contributes to misattribution in several ways. The lack of awareness into influences originating in the Adaptive Unconscious does not simply result in attributional ignorance or dumbfounding (e.g., "I do not know why I believe that"). Instead, T2 operations can generate justifications, rationalizations, confabulations, or externalized, projected accounts of mental content. These attempts at producing plausible, coherent accounts of why we have such intuitions can take the form of R/S-associated explanations (Baimel et al., 2021; Baumard & Boyer, 2013b). One source of T2 rationalizations, suggested by Wilson (2002), draws upon a priori "folk" theories such as shared cultural stereotypes. If a religious person behaves morally, they may assume that their motivation is derived from their personal beliefs or is a result of religious teachings in accordance with the stereotype that religion promotes morality. Again, this can be observed even when the actual moral influences are known to have originated elsewhere, such as in the experimental manipulation of conditions or in unrelated dispositional and situational sources.

Similarly, we may retroactively misremember our behaviors as conforming to certain narratives by substituting what we believe we intended to do, based on presumptive stereotypes (e.g., "I wanted to help, therefore I must have been helpful"). Shaver et al. (2021) found the accuracy of individuals' self-reported religious service attendance was inferior to the accuracy reported by third-party peer observers. Instead, those people who fit the stereotypic profile of churchgoing exemplars (i.e., women with young children) were particularly likely to inflate estimates of their own attendance, possibly because they based their self-report on what they stereotypically believed they should be doing or intended to do. This illustrates how a lack of introspective access combined with the malleability of memory recall can lead to a misattributed account for motivation and behaviors. A similar process occurs when we harmonize our own past with the present, such as retroactively re-working memories to create an inferior past, enabling the perception that our personal history represents a narrative arc of improvement over time ("I had to hit bottom before God changed my heart"; Wilson & Ross, 2001). As will be discussed in subsequent chapters, this may have relevance for some R/S conversion experiences.

A lack of introspective access on the part of T2 operations into the Automatic Unconscious and T1 processes can also contribute to other varieties of misattribution in the form of justifications, confabulations, and rationalizations.

These incorrect causal accounts may involve the alteration of certain facts or memories but are nonetheless believed with confidence. Nisbett and Wilson (1977) documented numerous instances in which participants confabulated verbal explanations for behaviors that were influenced or manipulated by stimuli or conditions of which they were unaware. For example, participants were asked to select the best item from an array of identical products. But many participants were unaware that the products were identical, instead offering various confabulated justifications for their preferences. The factors that did determine preference (e.g., products placed on the right side of the display) were not mentioned in their explanations. Such confabulations can also be motivated by a need to maintain a coherent self-concept that plausibly matches our sense of identity. The choice blindness phenomenon demonstrates that justificatory accounts can be generated even in cases where experimenters completely revise participants' attitudes. Hall, Johansson, and Strandberg, (2012) recorded participants' views on social and moral issues using a response sheet that allowed surreptitious reversal of answers (e.g., changing a participant's answers from pro- to anti-immigration). When the participants were shown their (reversed) responses and asked to elaborate, most of them failed to notice at least one of the changed responses. Incredibly, fully half argued for positions that were the opposite of their original attitude in at least one of the manipulated trials, and subsequently provided justificatory confabulated reasons. This accords with other similar phenomena in which individuals provide justifications for whichever conclusion they have been influenced to believe (Evans & Wason, 1976).

Even in studies where participants are informed that their thoughts and behaviors were experimentally influenced, they often deny that they were personally affected, yet most believe that others are susceptible to such influences (Pronin, 2008). In general, we believe that our own introspection has an enlightening influence, while rejecting the notion that others' introspection could be a valid source of knowledge. When providing explanatory accounts, individuals tend to substitute their own idiosyncratic theories that accord with what they ought to think or feel. These "useful fictions" of rationalizations can be adaptive in creating a coherent self-narrative and sense of meaning (Cushman, 2020). Wilson (2002) offers the political analogy that our conscious mind, rather than being a chief executive with decision-making powers, is more akin to a press secretary who issues explanations for decisions that were made elsewhere.

In terms of relevance to Dual Process models of cognition, the intuitions that give rise to R/S beliefs are usually products of T1 (e.g., conformity to CREDs, hyperactive agency detection). Previous work in the field of CSR has pointed out that "theologically correct" beliefs generated by Type Two processes are overlaid upon the more basic "theologically incorrect" Type One intuitions (Slone, 2007). As we have seen above however, the T2 output is not merely "second-hand wares" existing in contradiction to, or being undermined by beliefs from T1 (Tremlin, 2006). Rather, T2 functions can also rationalize and justify the intuitions. Despite the greater influence on belief of non-rational, non-deliberative processes (e.g., childhood inculcation, hyperactive agency detection), if an individual is asked to introspect in response to questions such as "Why do you believe in God?," T2 processes substitute a rational response such as "Because the universe seems well-designed" or "The Bible says so." Rather than being an impediment to intuitive beliefs, in religious believers the refined "theologically correct" concepts from T2 such as "God is omniscient" are used to defend and justify "theologically incorrect" concepts from T1 such as "God is anthropomorphic" (Barrett & Keil, 1996).

Misattribution to R/S sources is not the only outcome of intuitive output that is not updated or corrected by analytic T2 processes. As with the association between lower analytic cognition and R/S content, T2 justifications may also take the form of paranormal beliefs (Van Prooijen et al., 2020). Bouvet and Bonnefon (2015) found that intuitive, non-reflective thinkers were particularly likely to make paranormal, supernatural attributions after being presented with (bogus) uncanny experiences such as a rigged ESP demonstration or an astrology horoscope with seemingly apt descriptions (i.e., high base rate, vague "Barnum effect" statements). By contrast, even though reflective thinkers also rated such experiences as being uncanny, they endorsed more naturalistic explanations such as a statistical fluke.

Another consequence of the opaque nature of T1 processes is misattribution of an internally generated intuition as originating from an external source. This is similar to the psychodynamic theory of the defense mechanism of projection (again, not in the Freudian sense of being motivated by anxiety avoidance). The field of social cognition recognizes other (non-religious) psychological processes that resemble projection, such as the false consensus effect in which one assumes that one's beliefs are shared by others. Likewise, the egocentric bias in early childhood development involves the inability to think from others' perspectives ("Theory of Mind"). Because children cannot conceptualize others as having different or false beliefs, they assume that others share their perspective. In the context of R/S beliefs, again, T2 processes do not involve explicit awareness of the actual formative sources so other explanations are subsequently generated explaining why a particular belief seems plausible or an attitude is endorsed; in this case, an externalized one such as "this is what God wants." In actuality, the causal origin of the belief runs in the opposite direction—personal intuitions drive the attribution that "God" holds those beliefs. This sense of "God" as representing a projection of man's inner nature can be traced back to early anthropological work such as Ludwig Feuerbach's 1841 book *The Essence of Christianity*.

Summary and Implications

Findings from Cognitive Psychology, particularly those related to Dual Processing theory have implications for the proper interpretation and conceptualization of R/S beliefs. We have seen that stimuli processed by intuitive mechanisms such as random patterns or ambiguous images can lead to false positives in the sense of being misattributed as meaningful or purposeful. However, the tendency to over-attribute is more likely to occur to the extent that the intuitive processing remains unchecked by Type Two analytical thinking. Performance on measures of cognitive ability, particularly analytic cognition is inversely related to the degree of religious and spiritual belief endorsement. The ability and motivation to use T2 thinking are related to lower religiosity, but content processed by the intuitive systems may emerge unchecked because analytic cognition is attenuated in some contexts. Although experiences that are ambiguous or unexplained may, for most people, be difficult to make sense of or to classify, those with intuitive cognitive styles are particularly likely to misattribute them as being supernaturally caused. Therefore, to the extent that we are not conscious of the origin of intuitions in T1 processes, the resulting material will remain unchecked by analytic T2 processes and there will be a greater likelihood of misattributing the origin and meaning of thoughts and beliefs.

We have also seen that, although analytic T2 thinking is necessary to override intuitive beliefs, this is itself not always sufficient to provide correction. Type Two thinking can also produce rationalizations, confabulations, and other misattributions. Those in religiously predominant social contexts (e.g., high prevalence of CREDs) may actually be socialized to use analytic cognition to promote and justify, rather than attenuate, religious intuitions. The topic of how social cognitive biases—often in the form of concepts that are socially acquired or absorbed from cultural influences—can affect this process will be the subject of the subsequent chapters.

This has implications for the interpretation of phenomenological accounts of R/S experiences in the form of causal attributions. Some authors have suggested that identified differences between believers and nonbelievers on agency detection and attributions of purposefulness or meaning are ontologically neutral. In that case, findings illustrating overdetection (or false positives) on the part of R/S believers rather than underdetection (or false negatives) on the part of nonbelievers constitute a form of question-begging, since no objective standards exist to calibrate the reliability of the detection faculties or for validating the accuracy of what is being perceived (Barrett & Church, 2013). In the findings reported in this chapter that use objective criteria, we have seen that this is not the case.

Another implication of these findings pertains to the validity of verbal self-reports such as providing rational reasons and justifications for beliefs (e.g., apologetics). Individuals are not accurate in their introspective ability to identify the origins of their thoughts, beliefs, and behaviors. Merely because an individual or participant has generated a rational justification for their belief does not indicate this is the actual origin of the belief, as opposed to a rationalization or confabulation. In the language of philosophical debates about the meaning of findings from the CSR, T2 thinking does not necessarily refine ("scaffold") intuitions produced by T1 thinking.

2

Social Cognition and Attribution Theory

"I distrust those people who know so well what God wants them to do because I notice it always coincides with their own desires."
—Susan B. Anthony National-American Woman Suffrage Association Convention (1896)

Attribution Theory

Social Cognition (SC), the study of mental processes and content involving other people, draws upon the disciplines of Social Psychology and Cognitive Psychology. Particularly pertinent to the topic of religious and spiritual (R/S) beliefs are SC concepts related to attribution theory and the biased nature of social-cognitive processes. This chapter will discuss how people form attributions—explanation of events in their environment such as why things happen or why others act or believe as they do. Causal attributions can be secular (referring to naturalistic forces), but for the present chapter the main focus will be on R/S attributions, such as explanations for events involving a divine purpose or the will of God. As seen in the previous chapter, cognitive processes are commonly susceptible to biases, which can result in misattributions such as mistakenly inferring a causal connection where none exists. The chapter will demonstrate how cognitive biases can produce misattributions of R/S agency.

Attributions are a "gateway" into Social Cognition because of their centrality in shaping how we make sense of the world (Reeder, 2013). They are inferences about the causes of events and the motivation for others' behavior, as well as that of our own. Causal attributions are attempts to answer questions such as: Why did something happen? What caused another person to act the way they did? Why do I believe something? Why did I just behave in a particular way? Rather than objective statements about reality, they are, by definition, subjective perceptions, most of which can be classified using several basic dimensions of explanation and causation. One such dimension refers to the extent to which something is perceived as being stable as opposed to unstable (Wimer & Kelley, 1982). Another causal dimension pertains to explanations of others that are internal (i.e., dispositional traits) as opposed to external or situational (e.g., the context in which one operates). As we will see, attributions to R/S causal influences can be conceptualized using the same dimensions that describe secular causal attributions.

Religious beliefs themselves can be construed as attributions because they involve presumptions of causality. For example, beliefs such as: "This is evidence of God's actions" or "God wants me to take action" or "I had a spiritual experience" all include attributions about the role of R/S. These attributions may be implicit – existing on unconscious levels rather than being explicitly articulated. An individual may make the attribution for a natural disaster that "It was a result of divine retribution for sinfulness." This belief is in turn predicated upon other, more basic implicit attributions such as "God is responsible for all events, even negative ones" and "God has a justifiable reason for allowing all events" or "God can be wrathful as well as benevolent."

The vast body of information regarding attribution theory derived from SC research complements a parallel body of work produced by the Cognitive Sciences of Religion. Indeed, Hill and Gibson (2008) suggested that attribution theory is an "ideal bridge" for the integration of CSR with the psychology of religion. Often, the two disciplines study identical phenomena using different terminology or address different levels of assumed causation. Attributions, as conceptualized in SC theory are similar to "intuitive inferences" or "implicit causal explanations" in the CSR except in the latter, there is an emphasis on the presumed evolved mechanisms generating the beliefs. The CSR has traditionally focused on how supernatural properties of gods and spirits are cognitively represented and transmitted to others. Attribution theory can provide additional insight into how believers construe their relationship with R/S agents believed to possess specific qualities or characteristics, as well as the situational determinants and individual differences in attribution formation.

Work from the CSR perspective has conceptualized the "Hyperactive Agency Detection" (HAAD) tendency as producing intuitions that agents are present and active, which is hypothesized to have been adaptive in an earlier environment. These intuitions could involve non-R/S content (e.g., "The twig snapped so there may be a tiger") but the content can also contain R/S elements such as "That sound indicated the spirits are watching and telling me something." Other similar tendencies to infer agentic qualities such as intentionality can also be conceptualized as systematic misattributions (e.g., anthropomorphism, personification, and promiscuous teleology). In *Religion Explained* (2001), Pascal Boyer suggested that causal inferences represent the combined output or byproduct of separate mental modules or systems evolved for other purposes (e.g., social exchange, theory of mind, morality). Boyer points to folk explanations for misfortune that are the aggregate product of systems processing social exchange, causal relationships, or moral culpability. These explanations involve attributions of intentional harm rather than random happenstance such as "It is a witch's curse," or "Ostentatious displays of wealth invited the Evil Eye." Boyer suggests that inferences that are particularly memorable tend to be those with socially relevant or "strategic" information (e.g., norm violations) rather than general facts (precise mechanisms of how agents act).

Attribution theory expands upon such CSR accounts at more proximal levels of explanation, adding not only detail and complexity but also evidence of boundary conditions and situational malleability. As mentioned in the introduction, the CSR perspective has tended to conceptualize intuitions as the product of more universal, distal, ultimate mechanisms rather than emphasizing contextual moderators or individual differences. By contrast, a social-cognitive approach emphasizes proximal influences and the identification of traits that predict the likelihood of attribution formation. The following sections will outline the parameters of R/S attributions—different categories or dimensions, the process by which they are formulated, and several common types of misattributions produced by biases in social cognition.

Dimensions of Religious and Spiritual Attributions

When an event occurs, there is a spontaneous tendency to assign causation: "Why did this happen?" A given event or phenomenon can be attributed to naturalistic causes, such as the laws of the physical universe, random chance, or luck. Some attributions may assign ultimate causal responsibility onto supernatural agents such as God, Jesus, Satan, or the Holy Spirit, or impersonal forces such as fate or karma. Agentic attributions also include references to teleological elements such as the agent's motivations or goals. For example, in the case of extremely unfortunate events such as the death of a child, parents often conclude that God had a specific reason for "allowing this to happen" (e.g., Calling the child home; testing the parents' faith, or using them as exemplars for how to properly cope; Cook & Wimberly, 1983; McIntosh et al., 1993).

One role that R/S attributions play is to provide explanations when no other obvious materialistic cause is evident. Typically, naturalistic explanations are used for events with obvious causality. Supernatural or spiritual explanations can be used in instances of ambiguous causation. This is known as the "God of the gaps" heuristic (Lupfer et al., 1996). In practice, however, natural and supernatural causes are not always mutually exclusive antipodes of a single dimension (Lupfer & Layman, 1996). Rather, individuals often blend explanations in which naturalistic and R/S attributions play different roles such as representing proximal versus ultimate causes. Legare and Gelman (2008) found that even people who are aware of the proximal role of biological factors in disease or death may still refer to supernatural influences as ultimate causes. One may make a naturalistic attribution for how cancer develops (e.g., smoking) while simultaneously stating that God determines the timing and underlying reason (e.g., "why did one person have a remission but not another?").

Legare and Gelman (2008) also describe those enculturated with beliefs in folk-healing and witchcraft as combining supernatural and naturalistic explanations for diseases such as AIDS (e.g., "yes the person contracted a virus but why at this particular time?"). These believers are not ignorant of biological explanations, but they create a causal chain in which the ultimate origin for misfortune is attributed to bewitchment (e.g., "Witchcraft can make you have sex with someone who has AIDS"). This type of blending suggests that the God-of-the-gaps account in which supernatural attributions are only made in instances where biological explanations are lacking may be simplistic. Attributional blending also shows how intuitive beliefs such as teleological biases (e.g., "important life-threatening conditions must be intentionally caused by something") are elaborated and harmonized with more explicit, culturally learned concepts (Legare et al., 2012).

Factors That Predict Making R/S Attributions

Dispositional

According to Spilka and colleagues (1985) the two major categories of attributional influence are characteristics of the attributor (e.g., traits) and those of the situation (e.g., event or context). The former includes influences from the perceiver's background and social-learning history, personality traits, familial beliefs, childhood instruction, and cultural exposure. Because of social-acquired cognitive schema, those with a stronger religious background are more likely to make R/S causal attributions compared to those from a weakly religious or secular background, although even religious people use secular attributions for most situations (Lupfer et al., 1994; Weeks & Lupfer, 2000).

Among those who have a general belief in God, those whose religious orientation is highly intrinsic (i.e., deeply held) and fundamentalist (exclusivist, particularist) use R/S attributions in a wider range of situations and with more specificity than those who are less intrinsically religious and they view God as possessing more anthropomorphic and agentic qualities (Mallery et al., 2000; Vonk & Pitzen, 2016). A similar trend is seen in demographic, sectarian, and denominational backgrounds, some of which particularly emphasize imbuing R/S with more personified and interventionist concepts. Specifically, in the United States, people who identify as evangelical or charismatic (as opposed to moderate or mainline) Christians are more likely to make R/S attributions for a wider range of phenomena. Evangelical Protestants are especially likely to view negative agents like Satan as responsible for misfortune (Pew Research Center, 2021). Similarly, R/S attributions vary as a function of demographic differences in ethnicity, race, education, and geographic area of residence, to name only a few (Stephens et al., 2013). For example, beliefs in malevolent supernatural agents such as Satan and in the existence of hell are more common among the less educated compared to those with higher levels of education.

As mentioned in the previous chapter, other dispositional characteristics associated with making R/S attributions include cognitive ability, thinking style, and personality traits. Attributions to God and Satan are less commonly made by those with higher levels of analytic cognition, skepticism, and open-mindedness and are more commonly made by those with experiential/ intuitive thinking, and schizotypic, absorptive, and dissociative tendencies (Wilt et al., 2022a; Wilt et al., 2022b). Although the broad intuitions constituting the focus of study in the CSR (e.g., agency, anthropomorphism) are often conceptualized as being universally evolved tendencies, they also produce a range of output that differs as a function of individual traits. The over-attribution of meaning, purpose, and teleology is more common in people with cognitive styles marked by lower analytic cognition, greater schizotypy, and more ontological confusions (Partos et al., 2016; Svedholm et al., 2010; Zemla et al., 2016). Epley, Waytz, and Cacioppo (2007) found that anthropomorphism was more common among those with lower need for cognition (disinclination to think effortfully), greater need for closure (desire for quick resolution and unambiguous answers), and a greater need for control.

Situational and Contextual Influences on R/S Attributions

R/S attributions are influenced by factors associated with the phenomenon, event, or action that is being explained or evaluated. The "availability hypothesis" posits that religious attributions are used when religious cues are situationally salient (Spilka et al., 1985). This is a religious version of the cognitive availability heuristic in which judgments of the probability of events are based on the ease with which relevant instances come to mind, such as their importance or recency (Tversky & Kahneman, 1973). Although intuitions made using this heuristic may be accurate, as with other processes that feature Type One cognitive processing, it is subject to co-occurrence biases such as illusory correlation. However, Lupfer and Layman (1996) argue that a more accurate characterization of religious attribution is based on the representativeness heuristic—explanations are made that best match salient features of the event, not those that are most quickly or easily retrieved. For many events with ambiguous etiology, the actions of God or a higher power may be perceived as the most plausible among competing accounts (Dijksterhuis et al., 2008). For example, some medical conditions such as cancer are particularly likely to elicit R/S attributions because they have origins that are ambiguous and they feature stochastic progression (Lupfer et al., 1996; Spilka & Schmidt, 1983).

Another contextual factor affecting R/S attribution is the importance of the event. Generally, highly consequential and/ or disruptive events are more likely to elicit R/S attributions relative to mundane occurrences (e.g., God causes tidal waves or earthquakes, but is unconcerned with lost keys; Cragun & Sumerau, 2015; Stephens et al., 2013). Likewise, over-attributions of intentionality, purposefulness, and teleology are more likely to occur with events that are important, uncontrollable, and unpredictable (Scott, 2022). However, what is subjectively important to one person is not always important to another (Gorsuch & Smith, 1983). Consequently, general attributional rules about occurrences deemed to be R/S in nature are flexible and not consistently applied to others and to ourselves. The likelihood that an individual will attribute a disaster—even one that is objectively large—to God as opposed to naturalistic factors is lower when the event did not have a personal impact. This can be seen in the case of the 2005 Indian Ocean earthquake and tsunami, which caused massive damage and loss of life (e.g., approximately 250,000 dead). In one international poll, half of Malaysian respondents felt that it was "an act of God," but only 27 percent of Russians, 26 percent of Americans, and 15 percent of Koreans felt similarly (Global Market Insite, Inc., 2005). By contrast, despite the greater objective impact of the tsunami relative to the terrorist attacks on September 11, 2001 (e.g., approximately 3,000 dead), many in the United States believed that 9/11 had theological implications. In a lighter vein, given the importance of sports team loyalty for many people, perhaps it should not be surprising that a quarter of those in the United States agree that "God plays a role in determining which team wins sporting events" (PRRI, 2015).

A related attributional distinction pertains to the observed causal chain preceding events. Attributions to God are more likely when events or behaviors are seen to passively occur or merely "happen" as opposed to being voluntarily initiated (Lupfer et al., 1992, 1996). As alluded to in the previous section, some situations lack predictability or control, and therefore are especially likely to elicit R/S attributions on the part of those who have a greater need to control and predict the environment (i.e., the process of making attributions brings a sense of control). Thus, the formation of R/S attributions results from a combination of contextual factors, including an increased need for understanding. This will be discussed in greater detail in the chapter on compensatory mechanisms.

Perhaps the most influential set of factors affecting the likelihood of R/S attributions are those relating to the predominant worldview of an individual's surrounding culture, nation, ethnicity, family, or other relevant social groups. Just as the proverbial goldfish does not notice the water in the bowl, the sheer ubiquity of shared social assumptions often leads to their attributional influence as being taken for granted. Those who live in social contexts marked by certain R/S attributions are likely to acquire propensities to explain the world accordingly, often without conscious notice. As mentioned in the previous chapter, exposure to the Credibility Enhancing Displays such as ritual behaviors performed by others can strongly influence R/S attributions (Exline & Pait, 2021; Gervais et al., 2021).

Person by Situation Interaction and the Role of Expectancy

Among the range of factors that influence the formation of R/S attributions, no one single category plays an exclusive role. Attributions result from an accumulation of interactions between individual traits, social learning history, and event-related factors. Some of these factors are early or distal in the causal chain such as cognitive abilities or early inculcation, whereas others are causally proximal to the attribution formation. Exline and Pait (2021) identified several proximal influences such as mental states that promote unusual perceptions (e.g., substance use), or a stress-induced need for comfort. Likewise, Spilka, Shaver, and Kirkpatrick (1985) suggest that, because they provide a sense of meaning, control, and mastery, R/S attributions are particularly common when epistemic needs are challenged or depleted. Such deficit states are interactive products of both the individual's personal needs and the situation or context. Those with a high need for control or who have chronic uncertainty may be particularly likely to form R/S attributions in situations when those are lacking.

Previously learned concepts can potentiate other related beliefs by creating expectations (e.g., "When I pray, I will feel God's presence" or "God's role is to intervene to protect his followers"). Exline and Pait (2021) found that spiritual attributions are more easily adopted when they confirm prior beliefs such as those pertaining to the supernatural agent's abilities, intentions, or functions. One must first believe that a spiritual agent is willing and able to communicate with people and is of benevolent character, prior to making attributions such as "The spirit is helping me by sending a sign." These anticipatory cognitions increase the likelihood that certain R/S attributions will be made for experiences, which further reinforce the schematic network of beliefs in a re-iterative process (Exline & Pait, 2021). In this manner, foundational *a priori* assumptions about R/S agents give rise to other attributions as *post hoc* elaborations or concepts that conceptually follow.

Several of the broad intuitive tendencies of interest in CSR research such as agency detection respond to expectational mindsets. Although there is equivocal evidence that trait differences in agency detection are closely associated with (or even required for) supernatural beliefs (Maij et al., 2019; Willard, 2019), several studies have indicated that establishing an expectational set can increase the likelihood of agency detection. Often, merely providing a suggestive context that certain phenomena are likely to occur can be sufficient to produce attributions of R/S or paranormal experiences in most participants. For instance, experiences of agency and sensed presences have been induced by informing participants that devices could plausibly mediate their perceptions such as virtual reality goggles or brain stimulating "God helmets" (Andersen et al., 2014; Andersen et al., 2019; Granqvist et al., 2005; Maij & van Elk, 2018; Tratner et al., 2020). Just as a particular context and mindset (the "set and setting") or the placebo effect can influence the subjective experience of using a drug, expectational sets function to channel or alter the probability of specific R/S attributions.

In accordance with interactive person by situation models, the effects of expectational sets or contextual reminders are often contingent upon individual difference characteristics. For example, Dijksterhuis et al. (2008) found that the sense of personal (versus external) volition was altered by priming with

God-related concepts—but only for religious believers. Van Elk et al. (2016) similarly found that priming with supernatural concepts increased the perception of agency in visual stimuli, but again, this also was only true for believers. As discussed in the previous chapter, those with cognitive styles such as high trait absorption are particularly susceptible to suggestions regarding potential agents or presences (Erickson-Davis et al., 2021; Maij et al., 2019).

Unfortunately, the ability to experimentally influence specific belief content (as opposed to superficial temporary increases in a sense of general agency or presence) in a meaningful way is often limited. Interventions such as semantic priming or conceptual reminders are difficult to implement without inducing demand effects. Further, such methodologies can have inconsistent and fragile influences unlikely to impact robust religious belief systems. As such, these limitations have resulted in several failures to replicate earlier findings (Watanabe & Laurent, 2021). Despite this, there is evidence that activating concepts associated with R/S agency can elicit or change the likelihood of R/S-related attributions due to the stereotypic associations between R/S agents and expected agentic actions. There appears to be a bidirectional relationship between metaphysical agent concepts (e.g., God, spirit) and actions or events such that experimentally activating or priming one category increases attribution in the other. In one study, priming with supernatural concepts enhanced the attribution of intentionality to natural phenomena (Nieuwboer et al., 2014). Another study found that altering the perceived unpredictability of an agent's actions or increasing individuals' incentive for control and mastery increased anthropomorphizing (Waytz et al., 2010). Clearly, these results should be considered provisional in the absence of appropriate replication and validation. However, they broadly support a model that R/S attributions are malleable as a function of dispositional traits within certain conditions, particularly those involving expectational sets. These are indicative of a re-iterative process such that religious teachings produce expectations in believers, which increase the likelihood of perceptual detection (of agency, anthropomorphism, or teleology), which in turn further confirm existing cultural narratives and worldviews.

Attributional Biases and Misattribution

We have seen that common mental processes produce R/S as well as secular content. Accordingly, R/S beliefs are susceptible to the same attributional biases as with secular (e.g., social and political) worldviews. Some of these biases pertain to the selective processing of information, evidence gathering, and argumentation, such as myside bias and confirmation bias (e.g., tendencies to evaluate or consider evidence in a manner that supports pre-existing beliefs). Attribution formation can be affected by motivated reasoning and emotional factors that defend existing beliefs (Kunda, 1990). For example, religious self-identification or being a member of a denomination leads to more criticism of belief-incongruent information and the use of lower standards of evidence for religious-relevant claims (Klaczynski & Gordon, 1996; Lobato et al., 2020). Likewise, greater religious belief attenuates the ability to distinguish weak from strong religious arguments (Cardwell & Halberstadt, 2019).

The number of attributional biases is so great as to preclude an enumeration of equivalent R/S examples for each. Several such biases produce particularly inferentially rich output relevant to R/S beliefs. Much of the extant work from the CSR has focused on such general mechanisms that produce attributions that agents exist, that they have anthropomorphic qualities, or have certain desires such as moral enforcement. However, the following examples illustrate biases that produce more specific attributions (e.g., "What God thinks" or "What God is like"). These demonstrate that beliefs about God's beliefs and qualities are malleable and susceptible to systematic misattribution.

Misattribution of Divine Responsibility and Blame: God-Serving Biases

We tend to take personal credit for positive outcomes but blame negative ones on external causes or the actions of others ("I aced the first test because I am smart but failed the second test because it was unfair"). This self-serving bias (Miller & Ross, 1975) helps to preserve and enhance our self-esteem. An R/S version of the self-serving bias exists such that religious people assign "good" outcomes to the actions of God, but "bad" event outcomes are often attributed to poor luck or human error (Krull, 2022; Lupfer et al., 1992). In one study (Riggio et al., 2018), participants read vignettes of a disaster that differed in outcome valence. In accordance with a God-serving bias, Christians made more causal attributions to God when no one died compared to the version in which deaths were involved. Similarly, Riggio et al. (2014) found that God was given greater credit for outcomes in which victims engaged in faith-supporting behaviors (e.g., prayer) and who survived disaster. The God-serving bias shapes attributions that protect God from responsibility for negative events (Mallery et al., 2000). In such cases, one option is to frame God's causal role as ultimately serving a more positive purpose (Bulman & Wortman, 1977; Ray et al., 2015). The believer may contextualize a negative event as ephemeral such as "God is testing me" or "God gives me the strength to cope with problems." By making this temporal distinction, a believer can acknowledge short-term negativity, while retaining God-serving beliefs in the long term.

Beyond specific good or bad event outcomes, reconciling the general existence of misfortune (or "evil") in a universe ostensibly controlled by a benevolent God has been a perennial task in human history. This dilemma, known as the problem of theodicy, plays a role in the formation and interpretation of religious ideas. Accordingly, the invocation of a causal role for an array of other R/S agents allows more God-serving attributional possibilities. For instance, malevolent agents (e.g., Satan, witches, or demons) are often seen as bearing responsibility for negative outcomes (Legare & Gelman, 2008; Ray et al., 2015), attributions more common among conservative Christians (Lupfer et al., 1992). Further, negative events may be seen as part of an ongoing struggle between good and evil (Spilka & Schmidt, 1983)—God can be seen as allowing Satan to smite a target, though with ultimate control in God's hands.

Some scholars of religion have asserted that scriptures and doctrines themselves have evolved over time to elaborate and personify malevolent agents such as Satan or the Anti-Christ, thereby creating an attributional scapegoat and preventing God from being blamed for negative occurrences. In *The Origin of Satan* (2005), Elaine Pagels points out that the earliest depiction of Satan in Hebrew scripture was as a relatively minor character—not even a specific person but a generic adversary or opponent. In this first appearance, in the book of Numbers 22: 22-23, Yahweh sends "a satan" to perform an obstructive function by blocking a pathway. The term also refers to angels who act as a sort of subordinate prosecutor, testing the loyalty of Yahweh's followers such as in the book of Job. In Greek scripture, the term "satan" was used along with "diabolos," to refer to a slanderer or as an antagonist who tempts or thwarts. Over time however, Satan evolved to become a virtual antipode or counterweight to God. Likewise, the figure of the Anti-Christ was used by early Christians as a powerful, independent, and malevolent figure that explained the death of the Messiah and persecution of followers. Viewed from a psycho-historical perspective, the depiction of malevolent agents can be seen performing a God-serving bias role by assuming responsibility for misfortune.

The invocation of malevolent R/S agents as perpetrators can be used to explain indiscriminate misfortune (e.g., "Satan causes suffering"). But this becomes more cognitively complicated when we attempt to explain why certain people are victims of misfortune including why their plight is a justified result of our own aggression. Although some events such as death and destruction may seem objectively negative, whether they are seen as good or bad often depends upon the relationship between attributor and victim. Specifically, if the victim is an antagonist, their misfortune could be seen as beneficial to us. Attributions about God's intending the occurrence of misfortune (e.g., smiting the enemy) are often made when negative events happen to outgroup members, value-violators, or moral scapegoats. Dispositional attributions can be used to explain our opponent's culpability ("They were evil"). Thus, attributing malevolence or demonizing opponents also performs a God-serving function. Misfortune inflicted on those who deserve it does not violate a view that God is benevolent.

Early psychological theories attempting to explain the assignation of malevolence to others have often focused on intrapsychic processes such as the psychoanalytic defense mechanism of projection—disowning aspects originating in one's own psyche and assigning them to others. For instance, the Jungian analytic tradition features the archetype of the Shadow (i.e., the underdeveloped or negative aspects of our personality that are denied and projected onto persons or groups). According to Jungian depth psychology, the apparent independence of archetypal forces from our conscious ego (i.e., not "us") leads us to assume that they originate externally rather than from our own psyche. Although not grounded in empirical science, this approach to religion suggests that malevolent agents such as Satan, the Anti-Christ, or other adversaries represent external personifications of Shadow elements (Wulff, 1991). Nonetheless, empirical work suggests that the tendency to focus on broad supernatural concepts such as "evil" can lead to polarized judgments of others, to form dispositional attributions, and increase punitive tendencies toward them (Burris & Rempel, 2011).

The assignation of causal responsibility for negative outcomes to God (versus humans) is malleable, depending on a variety of factors. In one study, Riggio et al. (2014) had participants read vignettes in which a target either performed religious behaviors (e.g., prayer, church attendance) or health-related behaviors (e.g., diet, sleep) and then either lived or died. The target was seen as less personally responsible when he engaged in religious behaviors and survived compared to when he engaged in health behaviors and survived. Conversely, participants assigned greater blame when he performed religious behaviors and died compared to when he used health behaviors and died. This indicates that even if a person voluntarily engages in certain behaviors, the resulting outcomes are not consistently attributed as being under the control of the person. Similarly, De Bono, Poepsel, and Corley (2020) found that religious participants attributed a greater role for God when they played and won versus lost a game. Therefore, the responsibility attributed to God varies as a function of the implications of a given outcome for maintaining a positive view of God.

The God-serving bias also can involve a merging of believers' own identity with that of God. In contrast to other secular interpersonal attributions where there is a clear distinction between an actor and an observer, the ontological intangibility of spiritual agents can create an inchoate boundary. The nebulosity of this distinction allows for the possibility that personal identity can blend with external agentic identity (i.e., "God" merged with "self"; Hodges et al., 2013). Self-God merging does not refer to exceptional experiences involving the dramatic alternation of one's identity such as possession or spirit channeling (the subject of a later chapter). Rather, in the present context this merely refers to individuals attributing some of their thoughts, desires, and motivations as linked to those of "God" (e.g., "God wants me to take the new job," "God says we should marry"). As a result, the outcomes of external events (controlled by God) have relevance for enhancing and preserving personal self-esteem. De Bono et al. (2020) found that when participants experienced a success, it was the personal feeling of God's presence that explained attributions to God for success. In this sense of attributional merging, for a believer, the self-serving bias and the God-serving bias are essentially the same process.

Viewing oneself as merged with God can have positive effects on believers' self-esteem, such as viewing one's own actions and motivations as part of God's purposes. If God is viewed as acting to promote justice or morality, and God is part of one's own identity, this enhances a religious individual's self-perceived morality. Religiosity is positively associated with various forms of self-enhancement such as communal narcissism (e.g., "I am the best friend someone could have," "I am the most helpful person I know"), over-claiming of certain forms of knowledge, and a "better-than-average" self-image (Eriksson & Funcke, 2014; Gebauer et al., 2017). Even traits such as humility can be self-enhanced, which can lead to benign religious "humble bragging" such as when an athlete "gives all glory to God" after winning. However, there are more problematic consequences when a God-serving attributional bias exists in conjunction with a belief that God is part of the self and is imminent or present. Rosenblatt et al. (1991) found that those employed as spiritual directors drew an unclear boundary between their own identity and that of God, which promoted the attribution of having internal dialogues. The more porous the boundary between self and

God, the easier it is to attribute to God our own desires or to view ourselves as a divine mouthpiece or an instrument in God's hands.

To summarize: the self-esteem and self-enhancement functions resulting from the construal of outcomes make certain beliefs more plausible and likely. Because religious individuals are motivated to form R/S explanations that are relatively pleasant (Exline & Pait, 2021), those events that feature people being rewarded with good outcomes after engaging in religious behaviors are viewed as consonant with religious worldviews (a "Hallelujah effect"; Riggio et at., 2014). In general, those high in religiosity are particularly likely to make supernatural attributions when the character of a target individual or protagonist (good or bad) matches the valence of event that occur (positive or negative, respectively), consistent with the expectation of "appropriate" or "fair" interventions from God (Vonk & Pitzen, 2016). This attributional heuristic is tantamount to: "If it was good, it was God." However, God-serving biases also operate in the other causal direction—if an outcome is attributed as being caused by God, then there must be a good reason or purpose for it ("If its God, it's good"). This implies that when negative outcomes do occur, responsibility is likely to be seen as residing within the person suffering misfortune.

Misattribution of Deservingness for Misfortune: The Belief in a Just World and Karma

Humans are generally biased in that responsibility and deservingness are attributed as being consequences of prior behavior or character. In other words, on average, most people tend to believe that the world operates out of a principle of justice (Lerner & Simmons, 1966). However, the degree to which consequences are viewed as "just desserts" and blame is assigned varies across individuals and is malleable as a function of different motivational and situational factors. The just world belief (JWB) can take several forms. Belief in immanent justice is a view that one's present status is a direct consequence of one's actions such that valence of the outcome reflects the morality of prior behaviors. In one set of experiments (Callan et al., 2006), participants viewed scenarios of persons who either committed a misdeed (e.g., had an affair) or did not, who then subsequently experienced an unrelated outcome that was either good or bad (e.g., died in an accident). Participants endorsed cause-and-effect thinking in that when the prior action matched the outcome (i.e., virtue with positive, vice with negative), the outcome was believed to be a consequence of the action (again, even with no evident causal mechanism). Thus, matched outcomes are casually linked outcomes. Immanent justice beliefs motivate attributions of deservingness, which bring into alignment views of another person's moral character and actions with their outcomes. Alternatively, ultimate justice refers to an eventual, rather than immediate alignment between actions and outcome, such as compensation for misfortune "in the long run" (Maes, 1998).

There is evidence that the JWB is motivated by self-defense mechanisms that protect one's ego. Because we perceive ourselves to be virtuous (in accordance with the self-serving attributional bias), we can distance ourselves from those who experience misfortune by attributing their outcome to missteps or sinful living, believing that a similar fate will not befall us (i.e., "It couldn't happen to me"). A sense of control and predictability is derived from believing that working hard and playing by the rules will eventually lead to reward. As with other cognitive biases, the JWB exists as both a population level attributional bias while also reflecting individual differences in degrees of endorsement (Hafer & Begue, 2005). Despite much evidence that "the rain falls on the just and unjust alike," some people are more motivated to believe the world is just. Whereas high JW believers firmly assert that outcomes result from character, low just world believers are more likely to attribute a person's outcome to random circumstance, fate, or luck. Some work suggests that, although strong JW believers feel that the world is more predictable, they also are more complacent, feeling less need to change society or to alleviate the plight of victims. Lerner (1965) believed that for these people it was easier to assume that forces beyond their control distributed justice. Consequently, those with a strong JWB experience less psychological distress and greater life satisfaction (Depalma et al., 1999; Ritter et al., 1990). Strong JW believers are more likely to have conservative socio-political attitudes marked by support for the status quo (Furnham, 2003).

Religion and Just World Beliefs

Although most studies have found a positive relationship between endorsement of general JWB and religiosity, this has not always been consistent (Begue, 2002; Dalbert, 2001; Harvey & Callan, 2014; Jost et al., 2014; Rubin & Peplau, 1975; Schuurmans-Stekhoven, 2021). Religious content such as beliefs, doctrines, and teachings emphasize connections between actions and consequences. Correspondingly, ultimate justice beliefs are often blended with beliefs in specific R/S mechanisms acting to align behavior with outcome. That is, gods or spirits are attributed the role of accountants for merit and misbehavior, which will eventually result in rewards or punishments not only in this life but in heaven, hell, or some other eschatological consequence (Jugel & Lecigne, 2015).

Moreover, those who attribute events as being caused by God are more likely to see present negative events as eventually (i.e., in accordance with ultimate justice) yielding positive downstream consequences (Bannerjee & Boom, 2014). Some types of justice beliefs show a stronger relationship to religiosity than others (Crozier & Joseph, 1997). Conversely, different manifestations of religiosity display greater or lesser endorsement of JWB than others (Zweigenhaft et al., 1985). Specifically, forms of religion emphasizing political conservatism and authoritarianism, such as fundamentalism or orthodoxy are more closely associated with JWB (Osborne & Sibley, 2014; Pichon & Saroglou, 2009). Some evidence indicates that the need to believe in a just world can itself affect belief in God, especially the attribution of God's qualities related to morality. In experiments, conditions in which people contemplate injustice (compared to justice) have the effect of increasing belief in divine moral authority (Stanley & Kay, 2022). This suggests that for believers, particularly those who need a structured and orderly world, threats to a default JWB lead to a compensatory assertion that God is indeed a supreme moral authority so that psychological equanimity can be restored.

The pattern involving a motivation to believe in a just world is part of an even broader need to defend and justify existing systems, whether religious, social, economic, or political. This "system justification" bias leads individuals to conclude that the status quo is desirable; that "If it is, therefore it ought to be." The above mentioned ultimate justice belief is one form of system justification associated with greater religiosity (e.g., "people will eventually be compensated for injustices"; Jost et al., 2014). One way that such a view can be maintained is via a biased tendency to presume that outcomes must be relatively fair. The motivation to see life as being just reinforces the legitimacy of the status quo while simultaneously leading to acceptance of otherwise illegitimate situations (Hafer & Choma, 2009). Indeed, a greater level of religiosity in a society is associated with a weaker relationship between perceived injustice and life satisfaction (Joshanloo et al., 2021). That is, whereas life satisfaction is lower in societies with greater levels of injustice, religiosity buffers or attenuates this relationship, discouraging the motivation to alter an unjust status quo (e.g., "It's God's will"). Further, because of the motivational role they play in maintaining a predictable worldview, justice beliefs are also malleable. Under conditions of threats to their worldview, those with a particularly strong JWB are even more likely to form attributions of victim responsibility in a compensatory and defensive manner (Hafer & Choma, 2009), a topic which will be discussed in the following chapter.

Consistent with dual processing theories, immanent justice attributions and the role of perceived deservingness have been found to be enhanced when analytical thinking is inhibited by a cognitive load manipulation (Callan et al., 2010). Such a relationship suggests that attributions of intentionality are automatic and may lack conscious awareness (i.e., products of Type one cognition) as with other cognitive defaults (Rossett, 2008). Significantly, although individuals often deny explicit endorsement of justice principles (e.g., declaring that outcomes are randomly determined), they are nonetheless influenced by implicit intuitions and their accompanying biases (Baumard & Chevallier, 2012), indicating that JWB-like cognition may be akin to a cognitive default.

Supernatural Punishment and Attributions of Deservingness

Beliefs that the world is just and therefore that good behaviors are justly rewarded are predicated upon even more basic underlying assumptions. One must first have the belief that behaviors or character traits have moral relevance, that there is a mechanism of accounting, and that some agency has the power to reward or punish. In other words, we must have the foundational beliefs that something in the universe cares about our actions, that behaviors are consequential, and something keeps track of such matters. These fundamental beliefs have also been implicated as foundational in the development of religion itself. Perspectives from the Cognitive Sciences of Religion (CSR) have emphasized the significance of intuitive morality and the belief in supernatural monitoring and punishment (Johnson, 2016). Banerjee and Bloom (2014) suggest that supernatural explanations for outcomes are products of the evolved teleological tendency to ascribe purpose to events and actions. Likewise, Baumard and Chevallier (2012) posit that when a misdeed is followed by a misfortune, our innate sense of fairness construes the latter as compensation for the former (i.e., immanent justice). Evolutionarily based accounts suggest that there is a particular bias toward inferring causal relationships with moral content, as opposed to situations in which behaviors have no moral implications.

Supernatural Punishment (SP) theories stipulate that evolved mechanisms promote intuitions that our moral behaviors are monitored by agents, and that cooperative behavior will be rewarded, whereas antisocial behavior will be punished (Johnson, 2016). Accordingly, this may have provided a selective advantage by allowing identification of strategically adaptive behaviors, such as deterring cheating or promoting cooperation and group cohesion. Social cognition research has provided additional information by identifying situational influences and boundary conditions when attributions of deservingness are used to explain misfortune. For example, although humans have a general bias toward intentionality (Kelemen, 1999; Rossett, 2008), attributions of purposefulness are also malleable as a function of the perceived moral consequences of actions. Notably, a side effect of an action is more likely to be attributed as intentional when it leads to a bad, rather than good outcome (Knobe, 2003). Such a propensity is consistent with a broader pattern in which we are biased to over-weight negative information compared to positive information (Baumeister et al., 2001).

Whereas the CSR perspective has emphasized the role of SP beliefs in promoting the believer's own morality (Johnson, 2016) the same mechanisms also generate attributions about others. The common basic tendencies of agency detection, teleology, mentalizing, fair exchange, and immanent justice (Fitouchi, & Singh, 2022) not only produce beliefs that one's own behavior is monitored and that personal misfortune constitutes punishment for misbehavior, but leads us to assume that others' misfortune must have been caused by their misbehavior.

Karma and Immanent Justice

The belief that good behavior produces good outcomes and bad behavior produces bad outcomes—karma—is a quasi-religious concept implicated in the general psychological motivation to connect actions with appropriate consequences (White & Norenzayan, 2019). On the one hand, karmic beliefs do not necessarily require belief in personified, agentic, supernatural monitoring. Some karmic believers restrict their worldview to a naturalistic belief that actions inherently produce consequences. Alternatively, conceptions of karma may include unspecified supernatural principles ("the universe operates in accordance with balanced justice") but that differ from belief in God in being non-agentic and impersonal. Other karmic beliefs incorporate concepts of reincarnation such as that behavior from past lives can affect one's present status, and that current behavior can affect future incarnations. However, on an implicit level the way in which people actually implement general karmic beliefs is more complex and fluid. Karmic beliefs contain a mixture of non-agentic and personified attributions, such as belief in God (White & Norenzayan, 2022).

This may be another example of dual processing in which "theologically correct" explicit beliefs diverge from implicit intuitions.

Karmic beliefs play a role similar to JWB in aligning attributions of responsibility with immanent justice reasoning so that a person's behavior is seen as causing a deserved outcome (Taylor et al., 2022). As with intuitions of supernatural punishment, endorsement of karma can lead to believing that a victim of misfortune had built up a moral debt necessitating a payback; they "had it coming." This can be the case even in instances where there is no observable culpability, as with some Buddhist and Hindu beliefs that current misfortune is caused by transgressions in a past life (White & Norenzayan, 2019). Karmic concepts are also associated with motivations to justify current systems. Cotterill, Sidanius, Bhardwaj, and Kumar (2014) found that belief in karma was stronger among Indians high in authoritarianism and social dominance orientation who would be expected to endorse the appropriateness of caste-related hierarchy.

Victim Blaming and Derogation

In the previous sections, we have seen that people have the tendency to form causal connections between actions and outcome that are morally balanced such as misfortune being linked with prior culpability. This connection links psychological biases such as the Just World Belief with R/S concepts such as karma and supernatural punishment. This bias also affects how we view other people, such as how much empathy we extend to victims of misfortune. In one early study, after allowing participants to view confederates who were ostensibly receiving shocks in a "learning experiment," Lerner and Simmons (1966) measured subsequent perceptions of the victim. Remarkably, they found that participants derogated the character of those who voluntarily elected to remain in the experiment relative to those who were not shocked or who had no choice in the matter. Lerner and Simmons concluded that the sight of an innocent person suffering without compensation motivated people to devalue the victim to align her character with her outcome. Conversely, when others are observed to incur fortunate outcomes, impressions are aligned by "upgrading" their deservingness. Lerner (1965) reported that someone described as having won a lottery was rated as more hardworking than another who did not win.

Attribution of responsibility and deservingness in service of maintaining a JWB can lead to victim blaming and derogation even in the absence of any evident causal connection (Callan et al., 2010; Furnham, 2003). Although this occurs in situations having nothing to do with religion, it is exacerbated by, and justified with beliefs such as in supernatural punishment and karma. Similarly, victim blaming and dispositional attributions for misfortune are more common among the religious, with some explanations specifically invoking religious content. Divine attributions for poverty as "God's will" or arising because of a "lack of faith" are more common among Protestant Christians (Brimeyer, 2008). Likewise, it is not uncommon for HIV+/ AIDS status to be viewed as a "punishment from God" (Zou et al., 2009). Even individuals directly impacted by the disease or who themselves are HIV positive endorse such religiously related stigmatizing views (Muturi & An, 2010; Parsons, 2022). Further, belief in Karma has also been linked to greater attributions of deservingness of misfortune (Taylor et al., 2022).

The motivation to preserve a benevolent view of God can promote victim blaming as part of attempts to reconcile how bad things can happen to good people (i.e., theodicy or the "problem of evil"). If God is just and misfortune is a form of punishment, this is reconciled by attributing greater victim deservingness (Furnham & Brown, 1992). Surprisingly, dispositional attributions of blame of a religious nature can be self-directed as well. In one study (Pargament & Hahn, 1986) students were asked to imagine scenarios of misfortune including those featuring blameless actions (e.g., "What if you slipped and hurt yourself on the ice?"). When participants imagined experiencing a negative outcome, some assumed that they had behaved irresponsibly or had sinned elsewhere. One wrote: "God never punishes when there is no reason. Did I act wrong?" Similarly, in a study of paraplegic accident victims (Bulman & Wortman, 1977) youths higher in religiosity made attributions consistent with a stronger JWB, blaming themselves for the accidents but attributing positive ultimate purposes to God. Thus, a reluctance to view God as unjust leads to misattributing personal blame for a negative outcome.

The tendency to blame victims by making dispositional attributions for their plight varies as a function of individual difference traits including socio-political conservatism, social dominance orientation, and authoritarianism (Altemeyer, 1988; Skitka, 1999; Williams, 1984). On the one hand, this presents a classic third variable problem and should caution against drawing any simplistic direct connection between general religiosity and just world-induced victim blaming. It is difficult to determine the relative primacy of religious versus specifically nonreligious traits.

On the other hand, the association between these traits does involve common belief content that potentiates victim blaming (Jost et al., 2014; Osborne &

Sibley, 2014). Individuals with traits of religious fundamentalism, conservatism, and authoritarianism tend to share similar cognitive and personality characteristics (Ludeke et al., 2013). Moreover, the correlation between religious conservatism and internal attributions for poverty holds even controlling for political conservatism (Bergmann & Todd, 2019). Both authoritarian and religious fundamentalist belief content promote dispositional attributions and just world beliefs. For example, the belief in a just world partially mediates the tendency for orthodox/literalistic believers to perceive victims as more responsible for their plight (Pichon & Saroglou, 2009). The use of dispositional attributions ("some people are evil") also explains why those with conservative religious beliefs are more punitive towards criminal offenders (Grasmick & McGill, 1994). Likewise, Levy & Reuven (2017) found that juvenile care workers who were religiously observant as well as high in JWB showed more punitive disciplinary behaviors. Such findings may explain why religious fundamentalists rate even victims who are not responsible for misfortune as being somehow more deserving (Galen & Miller, 2011). Indeed, the belief that people get what they deserve may explain why religiosity has been found to correlate with some sadistic traits involving the lack of empathy (Schofield et al., 2022).

Beyond overt victim derogation, there are more indirect, subtle ways by which religion is involved with the principles of a just world and the alignment with outcomes. As mentioned earlier, one of these is to minimize negative effects by altering one's overall construal of fairness. Galen, Kurby, and Fles (2022) found that, compared to those low in religiosity, those high in religiosity rated an objectively unequal third-party economic exchange as being relatively fair. Similarly, VanDeursen, Pope, Warner, (2012) found that those with high intrinsic religious orientations engaged in "silver lining" attributions for victims by looking for possible benefits in misfortune ("being assaulted eventually made them a stronger person").

Further, a motivation to see the world as just and associated attributions of deservingness also affects how memory is reconstructed. In one study (Callan et al., 2009), those who experienced a misfortune selectively remembered committing more bad deeds compared to those who did not experience a misfortune. These researchers also found that recall of the amount another individual won in a lottery was systematically lower when they were portrayed as a "bad" person, illustrating how memory is malleable when aligning character with outcomes.

Attributions of deservingness produced by the interaction between religiosity and JWB are also malleable as a function of situational and contextual factors.

Lea and Hunsberger (1990) found that those high in Christian orthodoxy showed greater levels of victim derogation only when reminded of their religion. Indeed, religiosity interacts with the relative degree of threat to a JWB. VanDeursen, Pope, & Warner (2012) found that high intrinsically religious participants were particularly likely to look for potential benefits for a victim of a crime upon learning that the perpetrator was not apprehended (which is more threatening to a JWB). Such findings point to defensive or compensatory mechanisms (i.e., greater victim blaming when worldviews are threatened), which will be discussed in greater detail in the following chapter. These are just some examples illustrating how religiosity is reflected in worldview beliefs pertaining to justice, and how this can result in the motivated re-working of information so that outcomes align with character.

Religious Concepts of Vicarious Punishment and Victim Blaming

Misattributions of victim deservingness can have an impact on the plausibility of specific religious beliefs. That is, we react differently to people we perceive as deserving of supernatural punishment as opposed to those we view as innocent victims of chance. Any violations of JWB, such as the existence of perpetrators who deserve punishment but who are not held to account, can contribute to distress. Consequently, in the absence of present justice, punishment and blame can be psychologically shifted into the future by imagining justice in the afterlife. In this case, rather than aligning the elements of: 1) actions, 2) deservingness, and 3) outcomes by altering the middle component (i.e., attributing someone as being more deserving via blaming), the two components of immoral actions leading to deservingness are "held constant" and it is the imagined outcome that is psychologically altered. In a modification of the supernatural punishment hypothesis, hell and heaven do not exist solely to enforce morality by generating intuitions of consequences, they also maintain a sense of fairness and justice. Indeed, as Johnson (2016) alludes, if supernatural punishment is more effective than human retribution, the seeming excess of eternal damnation may be even more appealing, a divine "supernormal stimuli."

The psychologically motivated nature of religious forms of ultimate justice beliefs are most clearly seen in concepts that go beyond vague attributions of victim deservingness by filling in specific detail regarding punishments awaiting wrongdoers. For example, common conceptions of hell contain different levels such as in Dante's *Inferno*, in which the severity of torment is proportional to the transgression of the wrongdoer. Alternatively, rather than waiting until an unspecified future time, beliefs in apocalyptic or end-times events such as the Rapture (the removal of the elect to heaven, leaving behind the nonbelievers) represent ways to imagine ultimate justice occurring in a more immanent or tangible way. Millenarist beliefs often refer to a period of worldly tribulations after which evil is defeated and justice is restored. A substantial number of Americans have eschatological beliefs such as in the immanent second coming of Christ and in the events outlined in the book of Revelations (Benson & Herrmann, 1999). This suggests that concepts such as the Rapture clearly serve a psychological function similar to heaven or hell beliefs, and that JW beliefs motivate the imagined selective punishment of wrongdoers.

An additional benefit of religious forms of punishment beyond secular victim blaming is that it allows the "outsourcing" or projection of our justice intuitions; "I believe they should be punished" is converted to "God will punish them." One example of this impulse is so-called "imprecatory prayer"—invocations of judgment or curses against one's enemies and, by extension, the enemies of God. Scriptural exemplars include verses from Psalms such as "Let death seize upon them, [and] let them go down quick into hell" (Ps. 55) and "Let his children be fatherless, and his wife a widow" (Ps 109:9 9). In the Evangelical Christian subculture, the enlistment of divinely sanctioned punishment is sought by "Prayer Warriors" who envision themselves as battling malevolent forces. A related psychological motivation is a religious version of schadenfreude in which fantasies of elaborate forms of damnation for wrongdoers can be imagined, but absent any guilt that would ordinarily accompany the enjoyment of others' suffering. Feelings of schadenfreude can be justified by projecting the deservingness and righteousness of the punishment as stemming from God's will rather than our own wish-fulfillment (Portmann, 2000).

Underlying psychological motivations can also work in the opposite direction when it is psychologically necessary to mitigate victim blaming. Baumard and Boyer (2013) describe the evolution of moralizing religions that emphasize proportionality between deeds and supernatural rewards and punishments (e.g., leniency). Concepts such as purgatory and limbo are plausible because intuitions of fairness produce the belief that punishment should be lessened in the case of innocence or extenuating circumstances. In the case of the Christian belief in limbo, a rigid assertion that all who die without baptism will suffer eternal damnation violates a sense of justice and proportionality. It strikes many believers as unfair that some people may lack knowledge of Jesus

Christ through no fault of their own (e.g., virtuous pagans such as Aristotle, who lived in an earlier era) or who die prior to baptism. Tellingly, limbo is not based upon scripture nor is it an official doctrine of the Catholic church, yet it has gained widespread folk acceptance. For example, a Catholic advisory body, the International Theological Commission, published "The Hope of Salvation for Infants Who Die Without Being Baptized" (2007). In this study, submitted to the Vatican, the commission members state that, although these infants are punished in hell, they will suffer only the lightest punishment of all, "for there are diverse punishments in proportion to the guilt of the sinner." This is clearly an attempt to harmonize theological doctrine with intuitions of proportional guilt. Likewise, the concept of purgatory refers to a temporary post-mortem state of expiation for souls (i.e., not eternal damnation) prior to entering heaven, representing an acquiescence to the intuitive need for proportional punishment. Al-Issa et al. (2021) points out that in the Islamic world, the doctrine of purgatory is also prevalent despite its contradiction with other theological doctrines, representing another example of theologically incorrect intuitions overriding "correct" official versions.

There are several qualifications to the linkage between JWB and victim blaming. Individuals who have the opportunity to remedy injustice often prefer that option to derogating the victim of injustice (Furnham, 2003; Hafer & Bègue, 2005; Maes, 1998). Lerner found that participants will help rather than derogate victims, although this tends to be applied only to victims deemed not responsible for their plight (Depalma et al., 1999). In situations where options for justice remediation exist, victims are viewed as being relatively virtuous, but in contexts with disincentives for justice-restorative action in which nothing can be done to enact justice, more blame is attributed to victims (Jordan & Kouchaki, 2021). Since studies typically only provide restorative options in cases of secular misfortune, it remains to be seen whether specifically referring to something akin to divinely sanctioned punishment would deter efforts to perform restorative actions.

Summary of Just World Beliefs and Malleability of Attributions

Taken in the aggregate, research regarding JWB and attributional tendencies illustrate that humans are inclined toward presuming the existence of a just, fair, and proportional universe in which actions lead to appropriate consequences. Religious beliefs such as in supernatural punishment can exacerbate misattributions of deservingness. The various components by which actions, deservingness, and outcomes are aligned can be psychologically re-worked and altered so that, particularly for those with a strong JWB, a stable and predictable worldview is maintained. Examples (and associated religious concepts) include:

- Actions seen as causally leading to, rather than randomly associated with outcome, consistent with immanent justice so that outcomes are deserved. (Supernatural punishment, karma).
- In cases of negative outcome, attributions of deservingness increased in the form of victim blaming or derogation. (Victims seen as violating morality or religious rules).
- The valence—relatively badness or goodness—of an outcome changed by God-serving or fairness attributions. ("God always opens doors," "You are never given anything you cannot handle").
- Shifting justice to the future (ultimate) when not achieved in present. (Heaven, hell, Rapture, Limbo, Purgatory).
- When contemplating injustice, increased compensatory belief in a morally controlling God (Stanley & Kay, 2022).

Misattribution of God's Character: God Representations and Moral Typecasting

In addition to the assignment of general causal agency such as God's responsibility for events, many R/S beliefs are based on attributions of specific personal traits or characteristics such as images, representations, concepts, and other qualities of God. A God image refers to how a believer affectively experiences the deity (e.g., as benevolent, available vs. wrathful, rejecting), whereas a God concept or representation involves more cognitive (e.g., doctrinal and theological) elements. The most influential factors shaping these attributions stem from socio-cultural learning, familial inculcation, and exposure to credibility-enhancing behaviors (Gunnoe & Moore, 2002; Lanman & Buhrmeister, 2017). However, there is still individual variation in God concepts that cannot be accounted for by social learning factors, as evidenced by diversity even among members of the same religious group or culture (Froese & Bader, 2010). Personal characteristics such as demographics (gender, education, geographical region), political orientation, developmental history, and temperament all influence conceptualizations of God (Froese & Bader, 2007).

It is self-evident that images of God and R/S agents often correspond to, or parallel, similar qualities in believers themselves. Given that aspects of the self can become merged with views of God it is not surprising that people tend to view God as sharing their own traits, worldviews, and interests. Those who describe themselves as nurturing (e.g., generous) tend to describe God similarly, whereas those who perceive themselves as critical describe God as more disciplinarian (Roberts, 1989). Self-perceived positive personality traits such as self-liking are associated with people perceiving God as caring, whereas self-perceived negative traits are associated with viewing God as not caring and punitive (Greenway et al., 2003). Those with more agreeable personalities attribute more supportive characteristics onto God; those with higher neuroticism have more feelings of anxiety towards God (Braam et al., 2008). Such forms of Self-God parallelism exist even for divergent and contradictory socio-political views; Ross, Lelkes, and Russell, (2012) found that groups of political liberals and conservatives both believe that Jesus would share their opinions and attitudes.

The interpretation of the etiology of parallelism, however, is ambiguous. As with any other correlational relationship, the possible explanations could include either casual direction or common third variable influences. Unfortunately, many studies use language that conflates different causal hypotheses. For example, Mencken, Bader, and Embry (2009) describe associations between individuals' levels of interpersonal trust and their images of God in ways that state one causal direction ("how one views God affects how one views others") then shift to the opposite, more anthropomorphic hypothesis that attributions to God reflect our preferred human traits. Alternatively, traits of believers as well as views of God may stem from even more basic common influences, such as early parental relationships. Certainly, the relationships between personal traits and those attributed to God are bidirectional and multi-causal. However, there is evidence that at least some characteristics attributed to God originate from characteristics of the believer. This can be seen with traits that are causally prior in the sense of being basic and early developing. For example, a meta-analysis of the association between religion and personality (Saroglou, 2010) concluded that the latter has chronological priority (i.e., agreeable personality at younger ages predicted religiosity at older ages).

The domain that arguably provides the clearest evidence of early characteristics predicting later formation of conceptualizations of God is the child development perspective. Numerous studies have found that children's representations of God (and of other people) are modeled on parental relationships and child-rearing practices. Hertel and Donahue (1995) found parallels between parents' images of God and childrens' impressions of parenting styles, and in turn, childrens' images of God. In another study, mothers' authoritarian rearing practices were associated with punishing God concepts in children (De Roos et al., 2001). On an anthropological scale, cultures in which nurturing parenting is the norm tend to believe in deities that are more benevolent compared to cultures with authoritarian practices, who tend to have more malevolent deities (Lambert et al., 1959). Thus, childrens' early relationships with and views of their parents can shape their later attributions of God's characteristics.

Perhaps the most fully articulated developmental explanation for God image attributions comes from the field of attachment theory. This posits that children internalize a representation or "working model" of the relationship with their caregiver that serves as a template for subsequent relationships with significant others, including God (Birgegard & Granqvist, 2004). Most children are characterized as securely attached, for whom the parental model is perceived as a stable and secure base, providing a sense of safety that can buffer and attenuate anxiety. In other cases, however, parents are perceived as unavailable or rejecting, resulting in attachment that is insecure, avoidant, or ambivalent. Children with a secure attachment style tend to have images of God as loving, whereas those with an avoidant style tend to imbue view God with negative qualities such as being controlling (Eurelings-Bontekoe et al., 2005).

As with other associations between personal characteristics and attributions to God, correlation does not necessarily indicate causation. However, longitudinal studies have found that attachment patterns at an earlier point in time predict later images of God. For example, Thauvoye et al. (2018) found that individuals' earlier depressive feelings predicted avoidant attachment to God over time. Likewise, Van Tongeren et al. (2019) found that earlier R/S struggles and doubts predicted later images of God as being more punishing and less good. Further, these changes in God images altered future God concepts (e.g., involving cognitive, doctrinal content). The authors interpreted these findings as consistent with the hypothesis that "people create a doctrine and theology to fit their experiences, rather than alter their perception of their experiences to align with their theological beliefs" (p. 231). Longitudinal studies also point to a bidirectional relationship between individuals' own traits such as aggression or benevolence, and attributions of God's characteristics. Shepperd et al. (2019) found that not only did views of God as punitive at an earlier time point correspond with greater aggressive and lower benevolent behavior later, but also individuals' earlier aggression predicted lowered future belief in a loving

God, and benevolence predicted later belief in a loving, nonpunitive God. These findings indicate that behavior can be a cause, as well as a consequence of God attributions.

Perhaps the best evidence of the malleability and projection of attributions of God's characteristics is derived from manipulations of the salience of believers' motivational states. Some studies have utilized priming methods to activate the attachment-related internal working models, such as exposing participants to threatening stimuli. For example, Birgegard and Granqvist (2004) found that participants' history of parental attachment interacted with subliminal priming of attachment threats in changing their perceptions of God as a close, available figure. Likewise, those with avoidant attachment history reacted more to threat-related primes by subsequently displaying weaker associations with God as a safe haven (Granqvist et al., 2012). The link between attachment styles and changes in religiosity, particularly that of a sudden increase in faith or conversion experience, will be explored in more detail in the chapters on compensatory mechanisms and mental health.

A separate field of social cognition research that also has particular relevance to the process by which attitudes are projected onto "God," involves biased cognition such that others are seen as sharing our own views and judgments (e.g., the "false consensus effect"). Interestingly, people believe that "God's beliefs" on important social and ethical issues are particularly aligned with their own beliefs, even more than are the views of other people. For instance, Epley et al. (2009) found an egocentric bias (i.e., our view of what God thinks is based on what we think) via experimentally altering participants' views on social and moral issues. These researchers shifted participants' views by presenting strong (versus weak) supporting arguments, finding that changing believers' attitudes on issues led to changing what they believed God thought about these issues. Such evidence indicates that R/S agents constitute externalized representations of believers' mental states. This also explains why malevolent agents such as Satan are often seen as influencing negative thoughts, poor choices, or providing temptation (Ray et al., 2015).

Furthermore, another attributional heuristic or bias that creates the attribution of God's responsibility for events involves the combination of two separate intuitive tendencies: 1) making inferences about the mental states of others (i.e., theory of mind), and 2) forming moral judgments. According to Moral Typecasting Theory, humans have the tendency to construe situations that involve moral consequences (e.g., harm or misfortune) as being caused by active agents who inflict consequences on passive recipients or "patients." Therefore, perceived harm or misfortune is construed as involving two "typecast" roles: Moral agents do good or bad, and moral patients experience good or bad. The mechanism of effect involves "dyadic completion"—a motivation to balance the existence of a perceived experiencer with the need for a responsible "inflictor" and vice versa.

Moral Typecasting Theory (MTT) has also been integrated into concepts frequently used in the field of CSR such as inferences of agency detection, promiscuous teleology, and the theory of mind. Specifically, people tend to have intuitions that those who suffer misfortune must be acted upon by an agent dispensing supernatural punishment—attributions that satisfy the dyadic completion of moral patient and agentic God. For example, Gray and Wegner (2009) presented participants with a disaster scenario (a flood) that, in some conditions resulted in harm (death) versus other conditions with no harm, and that was either caused by a known agent (a worker) or in other conditions by an unknown cause. Only the combination of harm with an unknown cause elicited attributions of an agentic God as a cause. These authors also point to a typecasting pattern occurring at a much higher social level of analysis—geographical regions with high levels of misery and suffering also tend to feature the highest levels of religiosity. Thus, suffering of patients evokes attributions of external agency.

The motivation to complete the dyad of moral agent versus patient is yet another instance in which attributions to God are malleable. Experimentally shaping situations that involve perceived harm with no other obvious human agent can produce attributions to God as the responsible agent. MTT also explains why attributions to God often consist solely of God's actions while being devoid of descriptions of God's agentic experience (God is not seen as having patient-like feelings or reactions). In the terms of MTT, high agency with no capacity for experience is due to God's typecast role as moral author. Moral agents can only "do" good or bad, whereas moral patients can only experience good or bad. For the dyad to be completed, a moral action needs an agent acting upon a patient.

In addition, MTT offers qualifications to other work on religious causal attributions and JWB. The generality that God's agentic role is only attributed in cases of positive events is simplistic. Specifically, Gray and Wegner argue that negative events that involve a moral patient evoke the greatest anthropomorphism because the completion of the dyad requires an inflicting agent, which would explain the coexistence of wrathful, punishing God images alongside benevolent ones. Just World theories also explain why any action with moral consequences elicits the attribution that the victim must have deserved it, which in turn elicits an intuition of supernatural punishment. However, Gray and Wegner (2009) articulate different areas of relevance between JWB and MTT theories—the former pertain more to perceptions of the victim or patient, whereas the latter are more relevant to the agent, in this case, God. Indeed, these authors suggest that, beyond merely evoking characteristics of the agent, MTT also explains the evocation of belief in God in general and that the ubiquity of R/S intuitions is due to the completion of the dyad: Observed suffering invokes a need for an agent.

In sum, believers often form attributions regarding the characteristics of R/S agents as a function of their own motivations, wishes, and current affective states. In the cases of Supernatural Punishment, Just World Belief, and Moral Typecasting theories, observing distress or misfortune (even in oneself) triggers attributions of God as a punishing agent. Although believers perceive their own attitudes to be internalizations of external agentic influences (e.g., "I'm following God's commands"), the process is actually an externalization or projection of internal influences (e.g., "I think that is wrong, therefore God does as well").

Blind Spot Bias: Misattributions about Our Own Thoughts and Beliefs

In addition to explanations for external events (e.g., natural disasters, health-related outcomes), attributions are also used to explain subjective psychological phenomena such as the origin and accuracy of our own thoughts and beliefs. Whereas one person may attribute their own religiosity to a formative emotional experience, another may view their faith as the product of careful intellectual evaluation of the evidence. Using the dimensions of dispositional and situational influences, it would seem logical for a believer to reflect upon the circumstances of their upbringing, exposure to religion, and instruction from parents, and conclude that their beliefs were the inevitable result of these factors ("I'm religious because I was raised to be"). However, when asked why they believe, individuals more often make an internal attribution that they carefully weighed and considered the evidence and independently arrived at certain religious conclusions. Believers are more likely to attribute their own R/S beliefs to internal, intellectual processes, whereas they tend to use emotional or situational explanations for others' beliefs. In one survey, 22 percent of respondents said others believe what they do "because they were raised to" while only 7 percent of people said this was true of their own belief (Shermer, 2000). Conversely, 29 percent said that their own beliefs were attributable to intellectual reasons such as perceiving that the universe was well designed; only 6 percent thought that others believe for that reason. Religious individuals appear to think that even fellow believers (along with disbelievers) are more influenced by external, emotional factors compared to the internal, rational reasons used for their own beliefs (Kenworthy, 2003).

What can explain the Self-Other disconnect between the attributed sources for beliefs? This "Blind Spot Bias" is the combined effect of several heuristics. First, people tend to believe that their view of the world is fundamentally accurate—Naïve Realism. This affects our ability to objectively evaluate the validity of others' differing worldviews. Our views are taken to be objectively accurate whereas the beliefs of others are seen as reflecting the influence of biases, such as their group allegiances, upbringing, and pre-existing commitments. Other factors that contribute to making different attributions for ourselves versus others lead us back to the formative cognitive processes involved in misattributions.

Dual Processing and Misattributions

The earlier chapters referred to the opacity of Type one processes into which Type two cognition lacks access. This gives rise to the Introspection Illusion, featuring overconfidence in the accuracy of our perceptions because we mistakenly assume that we have full access to the origins of our mental states (Pronin, 2008; Wilson, 2002). By contrast, we are skeptical and dismissive of the reliability of others' introspection (e.g., "My introspection has an enlightening effect, yours has a biasing effect"). We only have access to others' verbal reports and behaviors, not their internal thought processes. We mistakenly assume that our access to our thoughts lends an advantage in reliability (i.e., direct introspective access). Although we can be informed and warned about potential cognitive biases, this knowledge tends to be applied to others, not ourselves. We may entertain the hypothetical possibility of our being biased, but we believe that our introspection acts as a corrective mechanism (e.g., "I may sometimes be guilty of bias in general, but not after introspecting about this particular instance"). As a result, we are more likely to attribute others' beliefs to non-rational and external influences ("she was raised to believe," "he receives emotional comfort"), while considering those to be less influential for our beliefs relative to internal, rational explanations (e.g., "I read about and compared various religions"). However, in the majority of cases, rational and intellectual reasons are the result of prior implicit beliefs and attitudes.

Dual processing theory also helps explain the divergence between "theologically incorrect versus correct" beliefs in which R/S attributions formed at an implicit level diverge from explicit (e.g., doctrinal) ones. Work from the CSR perspective has indicated that nonbelievers such as atheists may have latent tendencies to implicitly endorse intuitions characteristic of supernatural belief. As mentioned in the previous chapter, nonbelievers may override such intuitions with Type two analytic processing, but under conditions that interfere with Type two processes, such as responding under time pressure, they make more teleological attributions (Roberts et al., 2020). Järnefelt, Canfield, & Kelemen (2015) also found that nonbelievers endorse teleological attributions that nature was purposefully created when under conditions of speeded responding, thus attenuating T2 correction.

Questions remain regarding the degree to which attributions can be cleanly categorized as being either products of T1 type processes (e.g., general agency, teleology) versus T2 processes (e.g., theological, doctrinal). Others may stem from a mixture of the two depending on the stage of formation such as a transfer over time from effortfully learned "correct," culturally shared beliefs into familiar, stereotypic concepts that are internalized, where they function as automatic, nonreflective attributions (e.g., "God is always in control," "God will ultimately reward good people"). The presence of attributive biases even in nonbelievers can be explained not only by evoking evolved universal mechanisms but also via exposure to ubiquitous cultural beliefs. For example, nonbelievers raised in an overwhelmingly religious culture may attribute moral advantages to being religious because of internalized stereotypes (Gervais, 2014).

The methods by which attributions are elicited and measured can assist in differentiating their processing origins. When participants are responding to questions regarding God attributes, their answers can differ depending on how a scenario or item is framed (Riggio et al., 2018). Implicit tasks, such as reaction time-based methods, or items that do not directly cue religious concepts can help minimize defensive or socially desirable sets and therefore increase the likelihood of tapping automatic attitudes and beliefs (Heiphetz et al., 2013). For example, the use of color naming latency (i.e., Stroop) tasks has revealed the predicted effect of victim derogation attributions in response to threats to a just world (Hafer, 2000). The susceptibility of T1 type cognition to implicit, nonconscious influences can also be seen in studies using subliminal stimuli.

Religious priming can increase the attribution of agency to natural phenomena (Nieuwboer et al., 2014). Likewise, among believers, subliminal God priming can decrease attributions of one's own contributions to an event (Dijksterhuis et al., 2008). The malleability for attributions produced by Type one could be enhanced due to the lack of conscious awareness.

Implications of Social Cognition for the Cognitive Science of Religion

Attribution theory represents an important bridge between the fields of CSR and Social Cognition. Theories regarding the deep origins of general religious cognition benefit from increasing explanatory specificity. For example, Boyer (2001) describes the chain of intuitions leading to beliefs about the effectiveness of religious rituals such as sacrifice, atonement, penance, and requests made to the deity. These are said to derive from social exchange-based systems that construe situations in terms of bargaining and compensation such as "If I want something, I have to give something first" and "penance could counterbalance sins" (Baumard & Boyer, 2013a). However, for this output to occur, attributional factors must be interwoven in numerous places within the cascade of intuitions. To construe something as a moral violation or supernatural punishment, there first need to be distinctions of intentional versus accidental harm, judgments of appropriate consequences based on degrees of dispositional responsibility, assessments of deservingness based on moral culpability, and so on. Attribution theory provides a much finer-grained analysis than CSR regarding how these judgments are made.

An additional contribution from Social Cognition is an appreciation of the role of individual differences in the propensity for R/S belief and temporal variation in motivational states. We have seen that people differ in traits such as the tendency to view the world as just, and that the need to restore justice and fairness can be enhanced or attenuated as a function of defensive responsiveness. In addition to trait differences in JWB, people also differ in terms of their sensitivity to injustice, leading to varying degrees of empathy for victims (Schmitt et al., 2005). Rather than being universal, invariant mechanisms as is often implied in CSR research, inference-generating systems are quite variable.

The implications of SC findings for debates regarding theology, philosophy, and the ontological existence of supernatural agents constitute a much broader topic and will be covered in greater detail in the concluding chapter. However, it bears mentioning when summarizing these findings that many of the attribution types mentioned above serve as the evidentiary basis for foundational R/S beliefs such as: "Since the world seems well-designed then only God could explain this," or "God is just because the wrongdoer was punished." As we have seen, these attributions are subject to systematically biased mental processes, indicating that resulting R/S beliefs can be objectively classified as misattributions. This is seen most clearly in the cases of experimental malleability in which R/S attributions can be altered by known manipulations.

3

Functional and Compensatory Mechanisms of Religion

Epistemic Functions of Religion

A functional approach to understanding religion holds that beliefs are motivated by basic psychological needs. In general, humans need to believe that they live in a coherent and predictable world. This includes: 1) *epistemic* motives to attain consistency, certainty, predictability, and control; 2) *existential* motives to manage anxiety, fear, and threat; and 3) *relational* motives to affiliate with others and share a consensually validated reality. For some, religious and spiritual (R/S) worldviews help to maintain equanimity and satisfy these needs by providing a set of coherent tenets and doctrines, moral codes, and social groups that engage in shared demonstrations of faith. A functional approach to religion suggests that this worldview constitutes a fungible resource that evinces a "fluid compensation" response when epistemic and existential needs are threatened. The perceived availability of these needs, on the one hand, and the perceived certainty of R/S worldviews on the other interact in a hydraulic-type relationship (Figure 3.1). That is, threats to beliefs, worldviews, and convictions produce an increased need for a sense of consistency, control, certainty, meaning, and companionship. Conversely, being in a state of deficit or incurring recent threats to epistemic, existential, and social equanimity results in compensatory bolstering of worldview beliefs. This process of belief bolstering reduces anxiety and re-establishes equanimity. The compensatory response enlisted to meet these needs includes not only a general increase in religious conviction, but also involves specific types of attributions such as that God is in control, and that religion provides a consistent, coherent, meaningful explanation. The following sections will illustrate the many ways in which changes in R/S belief occur in response to fluctuating psychological states in domains functioning to meet various needs.

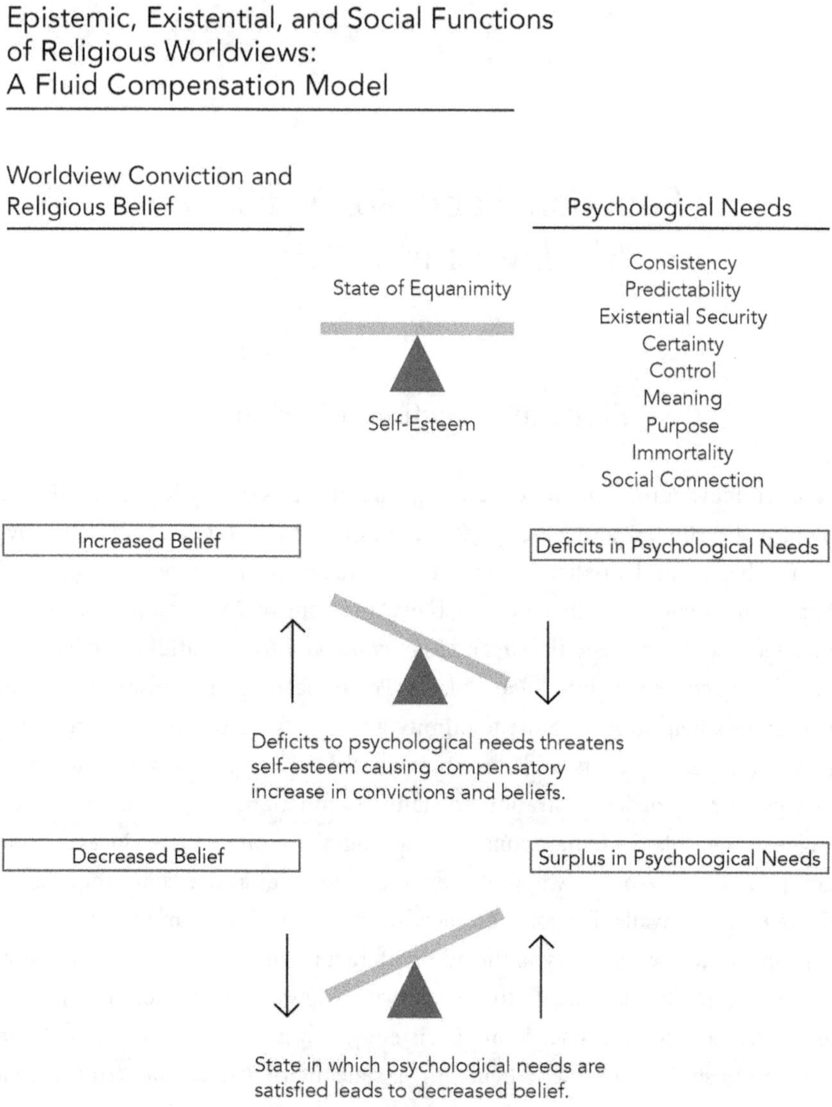

Epistemic, Existential, and Social Functions of Religious Worldviews: A Fluid Compensation Model

Figure 3.1 Compensatory Functions of Religion. Source: Olivia Brenner.

Need for Consistency

Individuals prefer to maintain consistency among beliefs, attitudes, and behaviors (Gawronski & Brannon, 2019). These include representations of the world that are regarded as factually true or false ("The meteorologist predicted a heat wave" paired with "The thermometer indicates a record high"), the logical relationship between cognitions ("I am on a diet" linked to "I probably shouldn't eat dessert"), as well as consistency in stereotypes or cultural mores ("People in the Midwest are nice," "Joe is from Nebraska," "Joe helped me shovel snow"). The ability to recognize inconsistencies serves an epistemic function of detecting potential errors that may require updating. When inconsistencies or doubts do occur, such as discrepancies between one's worldviews and contrary information, an aversive state is triggered that motivates a realignment of the conflicting attitudes. This general motivation for consistency forms the basis for theories of cognitive dissonance, self-perception, and effort justification.

The specific manner of aligning contradictory beliefs can differ as a function of multiple factors. First, the domains in question must be deemed sufficiently important and self-relevant to generate unease or dissonance. Hence, the motivation to update beliefs may be absent if the beliefs in question are deemed trivial or irrelevant (Festinger, 1957). Similarly, perceptions of inconsistency and the accompanying dissonance can be prevented by avoiding exposure to threatening information, thus stripping the information of its potential to contradict existing beliefs.

Although reconciling inconsistent cognitions may appear to be a process that would ultimately lead to greater accuracy in the manner of Bayesian updating, aligning beliefs can also introduce bias. That is, although some changes in beliefs, attitudes, or worldviews may resolve contradictions and inconsistencies in the direction of greater accuracy, this is not always the case. These, and other processes of inconsistency reduction can be particularly useful when explored in the context of R/S beliefs and behaviors. The following overview will focus on how religious beliefs change through the process of resolving conflicts between the beliefs themselves, from religious concepts that are threatened or unsupported (e.g., disconfirming events, failed prophesy), and inconsistencies between beliefs as well as between beliefs and one's behavior.

Avoidance of Inconsistency

As mentioned earlier, the motivation to change beliefs or resolve contradictions can be reduced by avoiding inconsistency altogether (Festinger, 1957). One can easily and unknowingly engage in selective exposure only to information conducive to existing worldviews while ignoring potentially threatening information (Shepherd & Kay, 2012). In an example of this pertaining to religion, Brock and Baloun (1967) asked participants to listen to audio recordings that contained information attacking Christianity. However, the audio recordings were designed to have episodes of static that could be corrected only if participants performed periodic adjustments to the player. Whereas non-believing subjects made such adjustments to clarify the audio, religious subjects refrained from adjusting the player, allowing the (threatening) message to remain incomprehensible. Another process that can prevent the perception of inconsistency is the derogation of the source of any information that may be threatening or may contradict previous views (Prasad et al., 2009). The tendency to dispute new information makes updating beliefs difficult, as predicted by the "belief perseverance" effect in which even information explicitly shown to be false can nonetheless persist. In fact, attempts to use factual correction may even produce a "backfire" effect in which new information is distrusted and existing beliefs are further entrenched (Garret & Weeks, 2013).

Yet another option to avoid inconsistencies and contradictions is to recategorize the underlying issue as one of opinion or faith rather than evidence and reason, such as by disputing the notion of objective truth (e.g., "postmodernism;" Prasad et al., 2009). In one study, students taking a course featuring a historical—critical study of the Bible (i.e., objectively determining authorship and chronological development of scripture) responded in several ways when this perspective conflicted with their beliefs (Burns, 2006). Some students misremembered their earlier position of scriptural inerrancy to be consistent with the new evidence. If the students' attention was drawn to contradictions between the four Gospels, they often denied their prior belief (e.g., "I never said the Gospels were all exactly the same"). Others took a relativist or postmodern approach to challenging facts such as "I have faith, so it doesn't matter." In this way, the realization that one's beliefs are inconsistent with reality is avoided by re-assigning their epistemological status to be immune from contradiction or falsification.

The contents of religious beliefs are often described as belonging to a separate epistemological domain from that of empirical or scientifically based information—or what Steven J. Gould identified as "non-overlapping magisteria." This suggests that factual discrepancies or logical contradictions involving religion do not, or should not, lead to a perception of inconsistency. Indeed, there is evidence that some religious claims are held to different standards of evidence from scientific claims. This is particularly true for religious believers, suggesting a motivational component to protect their beliefs from falsification (Liquin et al., 2020; McPhetres & Zuckerman, 2017). Therefore, the epistemological status of R/S beliefs is not a fixed property of R/S beliefs themselves, but rather one that can change in the mind of the believer as needed to defend against inconsistency, such as psychologically "shifting" in the direction of being construed as impervious to disconfirmation. In a similar process, pseudoscientific beliefs (e.g., ESP, alternative medicines) undergo preparatory "*ad hoc* immunization" prior to scrutiny. This involves forms of special pleading or "bet-hedging" that renders them difficult to falsify (e.g., "My psychic predictions are not always accurate when reading nonbelievers;" Carroll, 2003). The process of belief immunization is often encouraged via the dissemination of religious truisms such as "reason can only take you so far" or "you have to read through the eyes of faith." Believers may be referred to Biblical passages emphasizing religious concepts as being distinct from secular knowledge such as Corinthians 1:18–25 "Has not God made foolish the wisdom of this world?" or Proverbs 3:5: "Trust in the Lord with all your heart and lean not on your own understanding." Consequently, if religious inconsistencies or contradictions appear, they can be framed in such a way that normal standards of logic or reason do not apply.

In addition to the epistemological status of belief content itself, the motivation of the believer to engage in belief immunization versus critical analysis varies as a function of individual differences. As mentioned in the earlier chapter on cognition, the process of belief updating and correction requires the effortful engagement of Type Two processing (Risen, 2016). If such motivation is absent, believers can selectively disengage from identifying informational inconsistencies. For example, in accordance with the process of motivated reasoning, individuals who are religious are less likely to distinguish between good and bad reasons for believing in God, which contrasts with the distinctions they are capable of making when reasoning about nonreligious issues (Cardwell & Halberstadt, 2019).

Religious *ad hoc* protection against inconsistency can also be observed when requests are framed as "petitionary prayer." Prayer requests for specific outcomes are often modest, yet ambiguous, such as asking for strength to endure illness rather than for a miraculous cure. This phenomenon has often been framed from the Cognitive Science of Religion perspective as a contrast between doctrinal, "theologically correct" beliefs versus "theologically incorrect" ones. The limited nature of the requests has been seen as a natural inclination of human cognition (Barrett & Keil, 1996; Boyer, 2001). That is, petitionary prayer often includes requests for God to intervene in a manner that is more human-like rather than reflective of God's ostensible omnipotence, because the former is shaped by anthropomorphic tendencies (i.e., "what is a human-like agent most likely to do"). From a motivated cognition perspective, such prayer requests may be influenced by the need to immunize beliefs from possible inconsistency and disconfirmation (Boudry & De Smedt, 2011). For example, Dein and Pargament (2012) describe petitionary prayer requests for outcomes that are more "attainable" for God (e.g., not requesting the return of an amputated limb) as being motivated to "conserve the sacred." As a result, believers can pre-emptively avoid dissonance by marshaling rationalization for possible failure such as "Perhaps my prayer will be answered in a different way, according to God's plan."

As with most other human cognitive abilities, the tendency to engage in informational avoidance, recategorization, and selective exposure varies as a function of individually varying traits. Whereas those who are cognitively open-minded are more likely to approach new information, those who are closed-minded (i.e., high dogmatism) are less likely to expose themselves to material that is discrepant with prior beliefs (Innes, 1978; Sorrentino & Roney, 2013). Greater dogmatism is associated with lower recall of opinion-inconsistent information as well as selective support-seeking for belief-confirming information out of a need for cognitive consistency (Clarke & James, 1967; Kleck & Wheaton, 1967). A related trait, authoritarianism, is also associated with selective information exposure, particularly under conditions of perceived threat (Lavine et al., 2005). Also reminiscent of the traits mentioned in the earlier chapter on cognition, those whose thinking style is lower in Need for Cognition are less motivated to process conflicting information (Cacioppo & Petty, 1982). It is notable that religious belief itself is positively correlated with the traits of authoritarianism and dogmatism and negatively correlated with Need for Cognition and a related trait, open-minded thinking (Friedman & Jack, 2018; Yilmaz, 2021).

The motivated nature of immunizing beliefs against inconsistency can be seen more clearly in responses to contextual threats. Beliefs can be cognitively immunized in an effort to avoid inconsistency by recategorizing their epistemic status, making them less susceptible to disconfirmation. In one experiment, Friesen, Campbell, and Kay (2015) allowed participants to rate the degree to which support for their religious beliefs was based on evidence (e.g., "archeological findings support the Bible") as opposed to subjective and unfalsifiable views (e.g., "because I feel God's presence"). After reading an article stating that scientific findings threaten the existence of God, religious participants engaged in anticipatory defense by increasing their ratings of the importance of unfalsifiable reasons for their beliefs. Further, the process of framing religious beliefs as unfalsifiable made them more appealing to those who were religious. In contrast to those who read an article that stated God's existence would eventually be disproven, those who read an article concluding that God's existence would never be proven or disproven, if they were high in religiosity, showed increased religious conviction relative to those low in religiosity. Taken together, these findings indicate that the epistemic status of religious beliefs as subjective and unfalsifiable, as opposed to objective and falsifiable, is a malleable property, susceptible to alteration as a function of the motivation to avoid disconfirmation.

In summary, religious content is often framed as being unmoored from empirical refutation or logical contradiction, diminishing the possibility of inconsistency. However, the degree to which beliefs are immune to disconfirmation is subject to change. Belief immunization is particularly likely to occur under conditions of threat or with the anticipation of future dissonance. The personal traits that enable the reprocessing of information as being unfalsifiable are positively associated with religious belief.

Inconsistency and Cognitive Dissonance

Despite efforts to avoid inconsistency, individuals inevitably encounter instances where their beliefs and worldviews are threatened by external reality in the form of contradictory information. Inconsistencies and mutual incoherence can also be detected between one's beliefs and one's behavior. For instance, one may consider oneself an environmentalist while also enjoying driving large inefficient vehicles. Cognitive Dissonance theory posits that the tension aroused by inconsistency motivates the believer to change beliefs (Festinger, 1957). For example, a student may believe that she is a moral person, and that cheating is immoral, but she cheated on an exam to pass a class. This untenable state of inconsistency could be resolved by changing attributions in several ways such as believing that: 1) She is not a moral person; 2) The professor was wrong to give such an unreasonably difficult exam; 3) Other students are cheating and it would disadvantage her to be the only one not to cheat, among numerous other rationalizations that serve to align attitudes with behaviors.

The belief change process driven by cognitive dissonance reduction often begins at a relatively deep, intuitive level, but beliefs can also be re-worked in a more deliberative manner, connecting them together into more coherent, rational explanations. This is consistent with the Dual Processing theories discussed in Chapter 1, suggesting that individuals are not necessarily aware of the influences that change their beliefs. Further, they may misattribute their views as being conscious decisions or they may be unaware of the rationalization process. One study found that the "induced compliance" procedure (a standard method for changing attitudes by requiring participant to write positions contrary to their previous views) changed explicit, but not implicit (i.e., unconscious) attitudes (Gawronski & Strack, 2004). Similarly, behavior-induced attitude change can occur in the absence of explicit, conscious memory (i.e., solely at a Type One processing level) but the change is nonetheless experienced as genuine, consistent with a misattribution process (Lieberman et al., 2001).

Dissonance Reduction via Alteration of R/S Attributions

Dissonance raised by conflicting beliefs can be resolved by attributional reframing. Perhaps the most frequently cited religious examples of this are cases of failed prophesy. Indeed, the seminal work in the field, *When Prophecy Fails* by Festinger, Reicken, and Schachter (1956), used dissonance theory to explain how beliefs could be maintained even in cases of unambiguously failed prophecy. The study focused on a quasi-religious UFO group formed around a charismatic leader, Mrs. Keech, who delivered channeled messages via automatic writing with a specific time and date for a world-ending flood. Essentially, the group was assured that they would be transported up to a waiting UFO craft at the specified hour. When the hour came and went without any of the prophesized events taking place, the (increasingly agitated) believers were given a new revelation by Mrs. Keech that the cataclysm was called off due to their faith and group solidarity. This unequivocal failure of occurrence did not lead to abandonment of the belief system. Based on these events, Festinger et al. specified that certain elements were necessary for beliefs to be maintained. Specifically, members must 1) have taken some public or irrevocable action to demonstrate their sincere commitment, and 2) there must have been a clear refutation of the prophesy (for maximal dissonance pressure) followed by high levels of group-based social support.

The phenomenon of end-times prediction is not limited to small groups or sects. A substantial proportion of Christians in the United States believe that the Second Coming of Christ and/or Judgment Day will occur in the twenty-first century, within their own lifetime (Benson & Herrmann, 1999). Extra-Biblical literature dealing with themes such as the end times or apocalypse has enjoyed a wide public interest. Examples include *The Late Great Planet Earth* and *The 1980's: Countdown to Armageddon* by Hal Lindsey as well as the *Left Behind* series by Tim LaHaye. However, subsequent studies of failed prophesy and apocalyptic doomsday groups have called portions of Festinger et al.'s original theory into question (Stone, 2000). Rather than construing events as clear failures of prophesy, it may be more common for groups to reattribute events in a way that denies failure (Melton, 1985). A common rationalization is that the original prediction was misinterpreted, an attribution that prevents a broader collapse of the belief system.

History abounds with instances of believers who, far from having their faith weakened by a failure of events to conform to predictions, continued to believe. In the cases of American Christian followers of William Miller in the late 1800s or Jehovah's Witnesses in the twentieth century, groups attributed prophetical failure to errors in the calculations based on scripture (which may have contributed to a more common practice of not specifying the predicted date of the cataclysm). Some groups re-attribute prophetic messages as referring to spiritual, rather than literal fulfillment such as "The world did not physically end, but a new realm began" (Melton, 1985). These partial or symbolic fulfillments are often sufficient to reduce dissonance. Predictions are adjusted in the manner of attributional "goal post-moving," helping to preserve the belief systems. These *post hoc* rationalizations are similar to *ad hoc* immunizations formed prior to the event in their function of reducing dissonance. Thus, Festinger's original requirement of wholehearted commitment to a literal and clearly unfulfilled prophesy is not only atypical due to the slippery nature of prophecy but may be unnecessary for belief maintenance. More to the present point, these types of dissonance reduction that rely on shifting standards are likely to be accompanied by causal attributions of God's intentions reflecting believers' rationalizations (e.g., "God was testing our faith," "God is merciful," "God gave us time to gather more followers").

Although failed prophesy is the most well-known example of religious cognitive dissonance (not only because of the historical role played by Festinger et al.'s seminal study, but also the dramatic nature of prophetic groups), it is not the most commonplace example. Dissonance theory is also relevant to several religious concepts discussed in the previous chapter in the context of attribution theory; we return to them now for further elaboration. Specifically, religious-based dissonance plays a role in the resolution of "the problem of evil" or theodicy: How can an omnipotent, benevolent God allow suffering and evil in the world? Restated in a way to accentuate the contradictory nature of the attributions, when there is an observed misfortune that has befallen an apparently innocent victim ("Person X"), a state of logical inconsistency exists between propositions: (a) "God is benevolent and just"; (b) "Misfortune has befallen Person X," and (c) "Person X was undeserving of misfortune."

Resolving the dissonance by believing that God is, in fact, not all good is an unviable option for most people. Rather, common re-attributions of theodicy often focus on alternative interpretations of what constitutes "just," including "Injustice is a consequence of God's gift of free will to man," or "Though things may appear unjust to man, we are not able to discern God's ultimate purposes" or "God uses injustice to test our faith." In a study exploring the attributions for unanswered prayer, Sharp (2013) found that individuals create "face saving" attributions for God that include similar themes (human free will, ultimate benefit, shifting blame) in an effort to reduce the dissonance brought on by theodicy. A similar religious method of reconciling inconsistent cognitions according to Abelson (1959) is transcendence—the harmonizing of apparently contradictory cognitions under a superordinate principle. In one study, (Burris et al., 1997), Christians read a passage designed to induce dissonance by highlighting a contrast between a benevolent God concept and a tragic occurrence (an infant boy killed in a shooting despite his grandfather praying for protection). Those participants who were provided with transcendent concepts like "God would cause a person to die—but only in order to protect them," "God doesn't cause things but allows them to happen," and "God works in mysterious ways or for greater purposes" had lower negative affect after reading the scenario—evidence of reduced dissonance.

As discussed in the previous chapter, attributions tend to be God-serving, such that causal responsibility for negative events is rarely attributed to God; rather they are changed into positively framed attributions. Viewed in the light of dissonance theory, we can see a similar phenomenon in the attributional responses to contexts or events that threaten beliefs. For example, dissonance caused by negative events can be reduced by attributing responsibility to Satan (Beck & Taylor, 2008). Dissonance resolution also helps explain the previously discussed phenomenon of victim blaming in the form of deservingness attributions. Given that religious believers, particularly those with a fundamentalist or orthodox orientation, also tend to have strong beliefs in a just world, they are more "locked" into attributions that misfortune must have been deserved. To the extent that one believes that God controls all events (i.e., nothing is random), there is little choice but to conclude that an outcome occurred for a reason and that victims of misfortune are deserving of their plight.

Violations of beliefs about justice and proportionality can produce dissonance in relation to afterlife related concepts such as heaven, hell, purgatory, and limbo. Recall that in instances where punishment by eternal damnation is deemed excessive, such as for those who have not been exposed to the correct religious teachings or in the case of ignorant young children, a sort of "lighter sentence" or "do-over" is envisioned in the form of purgatory or limbo. This resolves the dissonance generated between the theologically correct doctrine of eternal punishment versus intuitions of excessive, disproportionate punishment. In an example from the Islamic world, Al-Issa et al. (2021) found that folk intuitions of purgatory are prevalent despite their contradiction with Islamic theology and suggested that proportionality and immanent justice intuitions play a causal role. Thus, one way that the dissonance generated by bad things happening to innocent people can be resolved is to change the latter attribution (e.g., to "they deserved damnation") resulting in victim blaming, whereas another solution is produced by changing the former (e.g., to "their fate will be temporary and not so bad"), realigning afterlife consequences to be more proportional.

The process of creating religious attributions via cognitive dissonance resolution has been alluded to in accounts from the Cognitive Science of Religion perspective, albeit absent the concepts and terminology used in the domain of social cognition. We have already mentioned instances where a "theologically correct," doctrine has conflicted with "theologically incorrect" intuitions. In one account, Boyer (2001: 222–4) discussed inferences related to death, corpses, and grief as originating from different cognitive systems. Boyer posits that the output of modules functioning to detect animacy and distinguish it from in-animacy yields information indicating a permanently dead, inanimate corpse while at the same time modules that identify familiar people and those that infer their thoughts (i.e., Theory of Mind) continue to generate intuitions about the deceased loved one's thoughts and wishes. Boyer uses phrases such as that the "conflicting" output from different systems is "dissociated" and that they "undercut" each other or are "not in harmony" (p. 219). However, another way to describe these conflicts is to use the concept of dissonance. In this example, dissonant output is resolved by creating beliefs of dualism and the afterlife such as "the soul of a dead person is still around." The resolution of cognitive dissonance produces more internally consistent attributions of "God's" thoughts and intentions.

Dissonance Resolution via Effort Justification

Individuals prefer outcomes that were obtained through effort over those that are obtained effortlessly. Effort Justification theory (EJ) is one facet of consistency theory predicting that engaging in arduous or costly behavior will result in intensified beliefs that justify the expenditure. Stated conversely, the behavior of exerting unpleasant effort is inconsistent with the cognition that one would have preferred not to have engaged in that effort (Harmon-Jones & Mills, 1999). Consequently, the person concludes "it must have been worth it." Effort Justification explains a variety of group-level phenomena including group cohesion, initiations, and strict membership criteria. Groups such as fraternities, the military, and gangs often require initiation rituals or costly investments of effort, time, and money prior to full membership (Gerard & Mathewson, 1966). Although common sense would dictate that being asked for increasingly costly commitment or adhering to strict requirements would have a negative impact on attitudes toward groups, EJ predicts that such sacrifices lead to an increase in allegiance. With greater effort expended comes greater pressure to justify: "why did I go through this?," leading to greater valuation; "it was worth it."

This has implications for costly and time-consuming religious practices. Phenomena involving arduous rites and rituals have been studied extensively in the Cognitive Sciences of Religion and from anthropological perspectives. This coverage has primarily focused on the social meaning of behaviors such as information communicated to others by individual participation. Theories such as Credibility Enhancing Displays (CREDs) and Costly Signaling posit that extreme rituals send a message to observers that the participant is sincerely committed to the belief in question, leading to greater status and perceptions of group loyalty (Henrich, 2009). Some CSR researchers have discussed the effect of ritual participation as also impacting believers' own attitudes toward their group membership (Whitehouse & Lanman, 2014). Likewise, Xygalatas et al. (2019) specifically points to the role that EJ plays on participants' beliefs about themselves vis-à-vis their group. Said differently, aside from any external audience, the recipient of the costly signal is also oneself. Ritual participation can be a bridge-burning act that results in increased belief conviction to better align with costly behavior ("If I did such a thing, I must fervently believe"). Notable in CSR accounts of religion, Tremlin (2006) refers to dissonance theory in stating that "people's thinking is affected by their behaviors as much as their behaviors are determined by their thinking" because "acting as if we believe something promotes belief itself" (p. 131).

Despite the undeniably fascinating phenomena of extreme rituals, Effort Justification plays an equally relevant role in less dramatic forms of religious commitment. Strict religious denominations (e.g., fundamentalist groups) often have inconvenient rules and require large commitments of time and money but they retain members at a higher rate than those with more relaxed membership criteria (Iannaccone, 1994). Requiring that members engage in such committed behaviors leads to EJ-induced belief solidification ("My beliefs must really be valid because I have devoted myself to the cause").

A social cognition concept related to consistency theory and effort justification is the sunk cost fallacy. Individuals are more likely to continue pursuing behavioral goals to the extent that effort has already been invested in this pursuit. This helps explain the tenacity or lingering effects of having expended efforts (i.e., justification via "post-decisional dissonance reduction") because a believer can only enjoy the effects of lower dissonance if they stick with their earlier course of action (Cunha & Caldieraro, 2009). The biased or fallacious nature of the sunk cost effect is often apparent in believers who do not consider abandoning their group or relinquishing their beliefs to be viable options despite having endured setbacks such as failed prophesy or depletion of resources. Rather, participants in apocalyptic movements or strict groups perceive that they have few alternatives; sacrifices would be wasted if they drop out (Ferrero, 2014). Consequently, they stick with their movement to an extent proportional to the degree of initial sacrifice.

Effort Justification also casts a different light onto activities that are ostensibly for the purposes of gaining converts. The Church of Jesus Christ of Latter-Day Saints (LDS; or "Mormons") emphasizes, from a very young age, the importance of missionary work. Similarly, Jehovah's Witnesses devote time to evangelizing, going door to door handing out literature and discussing their beliefs. There are certainly stories of converts who have been won by relationships established through missionary work, but the increase in church membership obtained by such efforts is quite modest. However, an outcome that is even more valuable than gaining new members via conversion is the increase in devotion and loyalty of the missionaries themselves. After investing a substantial amount of effort and having given up other activities (in economics parlance—"opportunity costs"), missionaries return with greater zeal for their beliefs and their church. One LDS member reflecting on his mission experience admitted that when he had first embarked, he was somewhat tentative in his beliefs. However, after being asked to publicly defend his faith he said: "[t]he conviction I had been searching for came ... That was the moment when really my hope and my tender belief turned into something really solid which has been the foundation for the rest of my life. So, when people say 'how was your mission', I say, 'It was everything'" (Whitney & Barnes, 2007). In this manner, the alignment between effort and belief conviction generates attributions about the self (e.g., "This must be important to me"), which can also take the form of an externalized attribution (e.g., "God has called me to do something important").

Dissonance Reduction via Proselytization and Increased Conviction

A seemingly paradoxical effect predicted by classical CD theory is that those whose beliefs are threatened or disconfirmed will not merely maintain, but increase in conviction, as well as engage in proselytization. In Festinger et al.'s seminal study of the failed UFO prophesy, rather than becoming discouraged and dissolving their group, the members increased their efforts to win new converts. The researchers suggested that the inconsistency between their beliefs and the unequivocal failure of the expected cataclysm created dissonance, which motivated compensatory proselytization. As with other forms of missionary work, recruiting others to one's own belief system can reaffirm conviction through consensual validation (i.e., "My beliefs must be correct because others are also convinced").

Although Festinger et al.'s field study lacked internal validity and was not a true experiment, other studies of religious dissonance have been conducted under more controlled conditions, finding consistent results. Batson (1975) used a belief-challenge paradigm, first asking women in a youth program to state, in a social context, belief or disbelief in Christ's divinity. Next, they were presented with a (bogus) article suggesting that the major writings of scripture were fraudulent. After this challenge, the participants' beliefs were again measured, as well as their view of the article's authenticity. It was found that those who both: (1) believed in Jesus's divinity; and (2) believed that the threatening information was authentic, intensified their level of conviction. By contrast, those who either: (1) did not believe in Jesus's divinity; or (2) rejected the article as false did not intensify their stance. This latter portion of the findings is reminiscent of the previously mentioned phenomenon of dissonance avoidance via dismissal or derogation of contradictory evidence. The belief-intensifying effect in those who perceived a threat to their faith (i.e., who deemed the article valid) reflects Festinger et al.'s belief-bolstering effect. Batson also found that the students who experienced the threat-induced increase in conviction responded by wanting to talk about their belief, in effect saying, "Let me tell you why I really believe this." This suggests a motivation akin to proselytization (albeit in a more artificial setting than in Festinger et al.'s group). Other studies of religious dissonance have also indicated that the function of belief intensification is to reduce the anxiety raised by threatened beliefs. In the abovementioned Burris et al. (1997) study (participants who were exposed to a scenario of an innocent victim who died despite prayer), providing participants an opportunity to reaffirm their faith by filling out a belief questionnaire had the effect of reducing the negative emotions raised after reading the threatening scenario, illustrating a distress reduction role for simply being given an opportunity to reaffirm beliefs.

Based on such findings, the cognitive dissonance perspective relating to the need to resolve inconsistency can be conceptualized as being subsumed within a broader epistemic need for certainty and conviction. Efforts to compensate for dissonance by increasing the certainty of belief in God have even been observed in studies using dissonance-producing tasks that contain no religious content (Randles et al., 2015). In one such study, those who were made to feel uncertain by reading an incomprehensible text showed increased religious idealism in the form of statements like "I would give my life for my religious beliefs" (McGregor et al., 2010). In other words, beyond any specific need for consistency in religious beliefs themselves, individuals need to have a broad sense of epistemic certainty. More pertinent to the present point however, the responses to any uncertainty led to increases in specifically religious beliefs, suggesting a model of fluid compensation.

Need for Epistemic Certainty

Feelings of ambiguity, doubt, and randomness pose threats to a sense of epistemic clarity, and are avoided, if possible. Therefore, deficits in certainty involve responses not altogether different from those triggered by contradictory knowledge or belief inconsistency; all are experienced as threats to epistemic equanimity. In the narrower instance of cognitive dissonance, consistency is directly restored by adjusting attitudes to make them consistent with each other (or consistent with behavior), whereas in the case of general epistemic certainty, the compensatory mechanism can be indirect, such as assuagement by bolstering conviction in other domains (McGregor et al., 2001). Viewed from this perspective, the increase in belief conviction and proselytization following threats (as seen in the classic cognitive dissonance model) represents a compensatory response to weakened conviction or doubting. This has been demonstrated experimentally by inducing doubts in participants (e.g., having them write about feeling uncertain) and then offering them a chance to engage in advocacy (e.g., Gal & Rucker, 2010). Paradoxically, the most fervent efforts to convince others, which are often assumed to indicate high degrees of confident conviction, are frequently motivated instead by high levels of doubt. Efforts which appear aimed at convincing others are better understood as attempts to reassure the proselytizer themselves. The increases in conviction and proselytization function to reduce anxiety and preserve self-esteem.

In an illustration of the mechanisms of religious compensatory conviction, Van Tongeren et al. (2021) exposed participants to existentially threatening material (disaster footage) and recorded their beliefs about God's attributes in two ways: doctrinal (i.e., what God's characteristics "ought" to be), as opposed to rating God's traits based on the participant's own subjective experience of God. The authors conceptualized a wider discrepancy between the two ratings as indicative of greater dissonance (i.e., between how God "ought to be" versus how he is based on experience). Results indicated that, whereas those low in intrinsic religiosity showed the predicted increase in dissonance following the disaster footage, those high in intrinsic religiosity showed lower dissonance (reduced gap between the two ratings). Although the authors suggested that the reduced dissonance among the highly religious was attributable to factors such as having more integrated religious schema, the results are also consistent with a greater compensatory defensive reaction on the part of those whose belief systems are most entrenched. Specifically, for the highly religious participants, the gap between their ratings of God's doctrinal versus personally experienced characteristics was narrower for those in the threat condition than their "normal default" gap in the non-threat/control condition. That is, from a compensatory conviction perspective, those whose beliefs are central to their identity are most likely to "double down" in the face of threat. Other studies suggest that a double-down response to religious threats can even lead to extremist religious beliefs (Hogg, 2014). The induction of uncertainty that initially produces greater religious faith can be reversed by allowing individuals to engage in self-affirmation (Wichman, 2010). This suggests that religious worldviews function to maintain self-esteem, which produces compensatory conviction in the face of threat. It also explains why those who are most anxious regarding uncertainty and who feel disempowered in life respond with not only increased zeal but also negative emotions such as anger when their religious convictions are threatened (McGregor et al., 2010; Van den Bos et al., 2006).

The compensatory nature of epistemic certainty can also have social manifestations. Recall that in the Festinger et al. study of disconfirmation and inconsistency, individuals were motivated to seek out support from like-minded others who helped reduce dissonance by providing consensual validation. Likewise, feeling uncertain increases the motivation to identify with others who share strong, even extreme beliefs. For example, studies have found that not only does induced uncertainty increase identification with radical protest actions of extremist groups, but it increases support for suicide bombing (Hogg & Adelman, 2013; Hogg et al., 2010). Threats to personal certainty can accentuate religious "zeal," which can include intolerance and antipathy toward nonbelievers (Kossowska et al., 2017; McGregor et al., 2008). Thus, in both dissonance and compensatory conviction models, a believer in a state of doubt often engages in a reaction formation-like double down by becoming more extreme in conviction and in seeking out others who are most suited to shore up wavering belief systems.

Compensatory Conviction and Individual Difference Traits

The increase in R/S beliefs following uncertainty is potentiated for those with certain cognitive traits. Being uncertain is especially aversive for those with high needs for cognitive closure who desire clear, firm answers to epistemic questions. Cognitive styles marked by high levels of dogmatism, need for closure, and lower tolerance for ambiguity are associated with a greater compensatory reaction to threats. In the case of religious beliefs, a challenge to the literal accuracy of scripture may not threaten those who have relatively lower needs for certain epistemic knowledge in that domain, but it may be quite threatening to those with less tolerance for ambiguity (e.g., fundamentalist type of beliefs). In one study, when exposed to texts that pointed out inconsistencies and contradictions in the Biblical accounts of Christ's resurrection, students higher in dogmatism were more likely to maintain that the Bible is literally God's word and without contradiction compared to those low in dogmatism (Altemeyer, 2002). Similarly, Shaffer and Hastings (2007) asked Catholic participants to read an article that was either, in one group, threatening to their faith ("scandals in the church") or a neutral article (spiritual development). Those in the former group subsequently scored higher on a measure of religious fundamentalist ideals and identified more fervently with their affiliation compared to those reading the non-threatening article. Notably, those participants high in authoritarianism were particularly reactive to the threat and responded with increased fundamentalist belief and fewer doubts. These experiments suggest that compensatory conviction effects are a product of the interaction between external threats to beliefs and one's personal traits such as cognitive style and strongly held worldviews. Firm, even rigid belief, can develop in those who are engaged in defense against doubting.

Epistemic Needs for Meaning and Control

The need to feel that one's life has purpose and meaning can be a powerful epistemic motivation. Whether or not one subjectively feels the presence of meaning is an interaction between factors in the environment that may objectively provide meaning and an individual's subjective motivational state (i.e., in a satisfactory state versus one of deficits in meaning). For many, religion serves as a source of meaning by providing a transcendent purpose and a sense that their lives are consequential. Indeed, religious people tend to report having a greater overall presence of meaning in life than atheists (Schnell & Keenan, 2011; Steger & Frazier, 2005). Therefore, R/S worldviews, when stable, are associated with low motivation to search for meaning (Abeyta & Routledge, 2018; Nelson et al., 2020). However, as predicted by the fluid compensation phenomenon, threats to a sense of meaning result in increased R/S beliefs (Koenig & Schneider, 2019; Routledge et al., 2017). In accordance with dual processing theory, there is evidence that this effect occurs even on an implicit cognitive level such that subliminal exposure to meaning threat can lead to increased religiosity (Van Tongeren & Green, 2010). However, a generalized compensatory response to threatened meaning has not always replicated. For example, Routledge, Abeyta, and Roylance (2016) found threats to meaning increased belief in magical evil only among those reporting high levels of religiosity. In accordance with an individual differences approach to fluid compensation models, it is specifically those high in epistemic needs who may be most susceptible to chronic and situational threats to meaning.

In addition to certainty and meaning, humans need to feel that their lives are in control and that they have a sense of agency. Religion can meet these needs by providing a coherent worldview, moral codes, and ritual practices, all of which give a sense of self-efficacy. Believing in God as a controlling agent provides a sense of reassurance that something or someone is in charge, especially when that feeling of agency is threatened (e.g., "it's in God's hands now"). As we saw in the previous chapter, R/S believers make attributions for a wide range of events as being God-controlled. That negative events are sometimes attributed to God is notable, suggesting that even a capricious or wrathful deity is preferable to a random universe.

As predicted by compensatory theories, those who have a lower sense of personal control tend to have a stronger belief in God (specifically, in a controlling God; Hoogeveen et al., 2018). Even belief in quasi-spiritual phenomena such as conspiracy theories and paranormal beliefs is greater among those who lack a sense of control over their lives (van Elk & Lodder, 2018). Earlier experiments found that inducing a sense of randomness or a lack of control (by asking participants to recall positive autobiographical events perceived as beyond their control) promoted increased belief in a controlling God (Kay et al., 2010a). Other studies found that similar inducements also boosted endorsement in a range of pattern-seeking superstition such as belief in the efficacy of rituals (Whitson & Galinsky, 2008). Some studies have illustrated the hydraulic nature of the control-religiosity relationship by priming with God concepts, which decreases religious believers' sense of personal authorship and autonomy (Dijksterhuis et al., 2008). However, the recent failures of large-scale preregistered replication attempts have called into question the degree to which religious compensatory control induction is a robust phenomenon (Hoogeveen et al., 2018; Van Elk & Lodder, 2018). It may be difficult to meaningfully alter participants' sense of control in a relatively superficial experimental context.

As with the epistemic domains of certainty and meaning, however, the inverse relationship between personal control and religious belief is more robust when analyzed as a function of individual difference traits rather than by activating states of lower control. Those who have a lower trait sense of personal control report greater religiosity, and (as with other epistemic motivations) this is particularly so for those with a greater cognitive need for structure and clarity. Living in a state in which control is doubtful is more impactful and distressing for those who have a greater need for structure (Noordewier & Rutjens, 2021). This contrasts with those who perceive their environment to be reasonably predictable and for whom any momentary destabilization of their sense of equanimity is not as threatening. Hoogeveen et al. (2018) found that, although lower personal control was related to greater religiosity in the United States, this was not the case for those in the Netherlands, indicating that culture differences in religiosity, possibly driven by existential security, moderate the effects. Having a sense of perceived personal control thus involves not only intra-individual epistemic needs, but also varies as a function of interpersonal and social conditions (e.g., groups, cultures). For example, reminders of low personal control lead to increased identification with agentic ingroups (Fritsche, 2022). This points to a compensatory motivation for aspects of religious group affiliation. Said differently, believers can regain control and compensate for epistemic deficits by viewing their group or organization as being an agentic extension of themselves. This will be discussed in more detail in the next chapter on interpersonal social phenomena.

Living Conditions and Existential Security Theory

The role of religion in compensating for deficits in epistemic needs can also be observed in the covariation between these constructs across disparate regions and societies. There is wide variation in individuals' sense of personal control, certainty, meaning, health, perception of social cohesion, and safety as a function of different living conditions. Social, political, and environmental circumstances contribute to a sense of existential security via factors such as a stable economy, public health, functional institutions, states of conflict versus peace, among others. Higher religiosity is more common in societies with difficult and insecure existential conditions and is less prevalent in places with stable living conditions where existential security is sufficient (Barber, 2011; Diener et al., 2011). This relationship is found using numerous measures of security (Immerzeel & van Tubergen, 2013), and via the use of country-level comparisons, state-level comparisons, or even across a variety of time periods (Barber, 2015). According to Existential Security Theory (EST; Norris & Inglehart, 2011) living in less secure societies increases the salience of religious values due to the increased need for reassurance; a relationship that exists both at a societal (or sociotropic), as well as intra-personal (ego-tropic) level. Religious faith and personal well-being are most closely related in nations with high levels of uncertainty avoidance (Kogan et al., 2013), indicating that religion functions to compensate or buffer the effects of social insecurity.

The plethora of potential variables involved in comparing societies obviates any simple explanation for regional differences in religiosity. To complicate matters further, these factors are also difficult to study under controlled conditions. However, some predictions of EST have been tested by examining the impact of "natural experiments" such as acute shifts in living conditions caused by traumatic social events. Such research has shown that religiosity is greater in countries and districts that suffer from more wars and/conflicts (Du & Chi, 2016), and the degree or intensity of exposure to warfare is associated with increased participation in religious groups and rituals, even following the cessation of conflict (Henrich et al., 2019). The increase in religious behaviors following war constitutes a way of coping with negative psychological effects (Shai, 2022). Similarly, religiosity is also associated with adverse environmental conditions such as ecological duress (Botero et al., 2014). Religiosity tends to increase in areas struck by earthquakes (Bentzen, 2019; Sibley & Bulbulia, 2012). Relatedly, an analysis of Google data indicated that searches for life-threatening illnesses in a prior week were followed by searches for religious content the following week (Pelham et al., 2018). In line with projective hypotheses, social and existential stressors produce compensatory beliefs about the character and intentions of God/s. Skoggard et al. (2020) found that resource stress brought on by famine led to increased belief in "God's" involvement and concern with the weather. Although studies of environmental and social changes do not constitute experimental manipulations in the strictest sense, they are arguably more ecologically valid in explaining real-world fluctuations in religiosity. Taken together, these findings suggest that R/S beliefs increase in response to chronic deficits and to acute threats to existential and epistemic security.

Social Connection and Attachment Compensation

As discussed in the cognition chapter, religious individuals are likely to have perceptual tendencies producing greater anthropomorphism and the personification of agents. Supernatural believers tend to over-attribute intentionality to randomly moving geometric figures (Riekki et al., 2014), and over-perceive faces in random stimuli (Riekki et al., 2013). Beyond general agentic qualities, many believers also make attributions of having a close social connection and interactive relationship with a personally available God. This tendency is accentuated in those who lack meaningful human relationships or who are chronically lonely. Demographic patterns reveal that the unmarried and widowed have more devout religious belief and report greater closeness to God than those who are partnered (Brown et al., 2004; Granqvist & Hagekull, 2000). In accordance with a model of compensatory social connection, the sense of closeness inherent in personified religious beliefs functions to reduce anxiety and provides a sense of meaning and purpose for those who feel socially disconnected (Chan et al., 2019).

The need to feel close to God can be manipulated by experimentally increasing the salience of interpersonal loneliness. Epley et al. (2008) found that exposing participants to stimuli increasing their sense of social disconnection (e.g., bogus personality feedback predicting future loneliness, clips of the film Cast Away), increased supernatural beliefs, including in God. Likewise, other studies have found that self-reported intrinsic religiosity increases following reminders of social isolation (Aydin et al., 2010; Burris et al., 1994). The compensatory nature of this relationship is also evident in that the anthropomorphism induced by loneliness can be reversed by reminding people of a close, supportive relationship (Bartz et al., 2016).

Beyond general increases in religiosity, experimentally enhancing the salience of social disconnection increases those specific aspects of supernatural or theistic beliefs most relevant to companionship and belonging. For example, Niemyjska and Drat-Ruszczak (2013) found that participants induced to feel socially disconnected (i.e., by remembering when someone left them) were more likely to make anthropomorphic attributions that included communal qualities. Similarly, Gebauer and Maio (2012) found that the experimental induction of God beliefs occurred only among those whose image of God was accepting and loving (not distant or wrathful). This indicates that the motivation to believe is affiliative because only an accepting God fulfills belongingness needs. Such findings suggest that attributions of God's personal availability are partially motivated by a compensatory need for social contact.

Recall that the previous chapter discussed how images of God are based on early parental attachment relationships. Specifically, individuals' attachment style tends to correspond with their views of God's attributes and character. The many examples of parental qualities attributed to religious figures (e.g., God the Father, Mother Mary) have been the frequent subject of psychological theorizing. In the present context, this process can also be seen through the lens of compensatory social motivation in which perceived deficits in attachment needs can be compensated for by viewing God as a personally available and close figure. Although this is superficially reminiscent of psychoanalytic theories suggesting that God is a projection of infantile needs for a parental figure, contemporary attachment theories of religion have a firmer empirical grounding. This can be seen in the correlation between children's self-reported attachment relationship with parents and their perceptions of God. In one meta-analysis, Granqvist and Kirkpatrick (2004) found that those who experienced sudden conversions and whose religiosity was more emotionally based (i.e., emphasizing qualities most related to attachment such as need for proximity, and distress at the prospect of separation) were also likely to report having an insecurely attached relationship with parents. Apropos to the abovementioned effect of social isolation, subjective anxiety involving emotionally based attachment themes is an even stronger predictor of anthropomorphic tendencies than is loneliness (Bartz et al., 2016).

The correlation between, on the one hand, believers' insecure style of attachment (e.g., fear of abandonment, feeling ignored), and on the other, their views of God as being available, close, and loving, may have more than one causal interpretation. It is possible that believers acquire theological beliefs that then serve as a template for their social and familial relationships. However, there are reasons to posit that the most likely causal pathway runs in the other direction—from an initial attachment deficit or personal need for a close relationship to subsequent increases in religiosity, including views of God as an idealized attachment figure (Thauvoye et al., 2018). One method to establish causal priority is to compare attachment patterns or relationships at an earlier point in time to later changes in religious beliefs such as increased devotion or conversion. Longitudinal studies have found that those with an insecure attachment style at an earlier point in time are more likely to subsequently turn to God as a close attachment figure (Kirkpatrick, 1997; 1998). These effects are not limited to parental attachment. Those with insecure romantic attachment styles are more likely to establish a "new relationship with God" and report exceptional religious experiences compared to the securely attached (Kirkpatrick, 1998). Further, these changes are a product of an interaction between individuals' attachment history together with changes in their relational status. Granqvist and Hagekull (2003) found that individuals' insecure attachment history was associated with increased religiousness only for those who had experienced a breakup or separation, in contrast to the decreased religiousness in those who had gained a new romantic relationship. In other words, believers' perceived relationship with God tracked changes in their interpersonal relationships in a compensatory manner.

Although it is obviously difficult to experimentally manipulate perceptions of interpersonal or parental relationships in a meaningful way, researchers have used indirect methods to establish causal priority in attachment patterns. One method similar to the induction of feelings of social isolation is by priming with threatening stimuli conceptually related to insecure attachment themes. Laurin, Schumann, and Holmes (2014) used priming to test compensatory theory in the context of romantic relationships. Participants who were asked to imagine things that could cause problems in their relationships with significant others subsequently reported feeling closer to God. Likewise, those participants whose relationship with God was threatened responded by drawing closer to their romantic partner. This indicates that sources of connectedness (whether social or religious) may be interchangeable; deprivation from one can be compensated for by drawing closer to an alternative. In sum, attributions of God as being a close and available companion are generated as a function of individual differences in attachment needs or deficits (i.e., based on parental, social, and romantic relationship history) interacting with contextual events such as social isolation or losing/gaining close relationships.

Existential Needs

Perhaps our most fundamental existential need is to maintain a sense of meaning and self-esteem in the face of inevitable death. As befitting the great psychological importance of mortality, there is a substantial literature pertaining to religion and concepts of death anxiety. Readers seeking more comprehensive coverage of the topic are encouraged to consult another volume in the present series: *Death anxiety and religious belief: An existential psychology of religion* (Jong & Halberstadt, 2018), the definitive work in this area. Somewhat surprisingly however, Jong (2021) has found little evidence of a consistent relationship between individuals' level of death anxiety and their religiosity. Relatedly, there is a lack of coherence in theoretical predictions themselves, given that, on the one hand, the fear of death itself is believed to motivate religious belief, yet on the other hand religious belief should assuage that same fear.

One of the most informative and widely studied experimental social psychology perspectives on death is Terror Management Theory (TMT: Greenberg et al., 1997). Based on the theories of Ernest Becker emphasizing the centrality of death denial and its relationship with human culture, TMT has inspired a substantial body of work. Specifically, cultural worldviews (including religion) are thought to serve a compensatory function in buffering death anxiety. Consequently, threats to the validity of these worldviews produce increased death anxiety. In the opposite causal direction, increasing the salience of mortality by reminding people of their death produces compensatory increases in religious conviction.

Early findings were supportive of effects in each of these directions. Challenges to core tenets of Christian faith (e.g., the authenticity of Christ's resurrection or support for creationism) have been found to result in increased death anxiety (Friedman & Rholes, 2007; Schimel et al., 2007). Conversely, greater mortality salience in the form of experiencing the death of a loved one (but not trauma unrelated to death) predicts increased religiosity (Morris Trainor et al., 2019). The experimental induction of morality salience among believers has been found, in some studies, to produce increased religious belief (Norenzayan & Hansen, 2006; Vail et al., 2012; Jong et al., 2012). However, Jong's (2021) review of the literature indicates that these findings are not universally consistent, nor is the proper theoretical interpretation of findings always clear. For instance, should highly religious individuals be predicted to exhibit lower death anxiety as a result of a functional buffering effect, or would they be expected to show higher death anxiety, which itself motivates their greater religious conviction? More problematically, as with compensatory control theory, recent studies have failed to support some of the core predictions of the mortality salience hypothesis. Two high-powered replication attempts did not find that reminders of death produced worldview defense in the form of nationalism (Klein et al., 2022; Schindler et al., 2021), although these replication studies did not specifically assess worldview defense in the form of religiosity.

The overall relationship between religiosity and death anxiety often differs depending on how each of the two domains is defined and measured. As an example of the complexity involved in this domain, some theories, including TMT, point to dual-processing type concepts such that mortality salience may be experienced unconsciously, requiring implicit (i.e., Type 1) or indirect methods of measurement (Pyszczynski et al., 1999). Another debate pertains to the relative primacy of specifically death-related content as opposed to other related existential and epistemic needs. Scholars disagree regarding whether anxiety regarding death is actually reducible to anxiety involving other epistemic domains such as control or meaning. McGregor et al. (2001) have suggested that the worldview defense effects in reaction to mortality threats may, at least in part, represent an underlying compensatory conviction for personal uncertainty. Yavuz and Van den Bos (2009) have found that not only does the standard mortality salience manipulation also elicit a sense of uncertainty, but the latter has larger psychological effects than the former.

A similar conceptual overlap may exist in the relationship between religiosity, death anxiety, and the role of epistemic meaning. Van Tongeren et al. (2017) found that the relationship between belief in literal immortality and lower afterlife anxiety was mediated by a sense of greater meaning in life. That study also pointed to the moderating role of individual differences in religious orientation—meaning in life was only associated with lowered anxiety for those with more internalized (i.e., intrinsic) religious belief. Despite the lack of clarity in precisely determining the most fundamental or parsimonious explanation for the compensatory response to existential threats, it nonetheless appears that religion, at least in part, plays a buffering role, and that threats to both epistemic clarity and existential equanimity lead to increased belief conviction.

Nonreligious Sources of Epistemic and Existential Security

Worldviews that satisfy epistemic and existential needs are not limited to those featuring exclusively religious content. Reliance on overarching systems of stability such as secular governance, a scientific framework, and beliefs related to superstition and the paranormal, can at least partially address individuals' needs for coherent knowledge or purposeful existence. One oft-stated perspective is that nonreligious, as well as religious worldviews are ultimately motivated by nonrational, emotional needs, and that domains such as "science" or "government" are tantamount to secular religions. An alternative framing is that the presence of similar epistemic and existential components in both secular and religious worldviews has psychological centrality to motivational needs. Only specific aspects of these domains have been found to satisfy psychological needs, and they function similarly in nonreligious and religious worldviews.

Being able to rely upon functional governance shares with religion the characteristic of providing an external source of control. Not only is this relationship apparent in cross-national patterns in which greater support for government as a potential source of control is found in places where there are perceived lower levels of personal control, but experimental challenges to a sense of personal control lead to a compensatory defense of political systems (as well as belief in God; Kay et al., 2008). That is, a hydraulic relationship exists such that threats to the perceived stability of either systems of government or belief in God lead to subsequent increases in faith in the other (Kay et al., 2010). This suggests that (reminiscent of Existential Security Theory) the provision of greater stability and control by competent governance leads to a decreased need for the sense of control provided by religion. Zuckerman, Li, and Diener (2018) found that an inverse correlation existed between the provision of government services (e.g., health and education expenditures) and religiosity across nations as well as across states in the United States. Further, the same paper found longitudinal trends such that better government services in a given year predicted lower religiosity one to two years later. This was indicative of governance serving a buffering role because religiosity was only related to citizens' greater well-being when government services were low, whereas it was unrelated to well-being when services were high. In sum, having a sense of external control appears to be a fundamental need that can be satisfied by both religion and functional governance.

For many, a scientific worldview can also satisfy epistemic needs. As with the compensatory increase in religious belief resulting from anxiety-inducing threats like mortality salience, such threats also lead to increased belief in science (Farias et al., 2013). However, as with religion, the domain of science broadly defined appears to subsume some aspects that can satisfy psychological needs and others that cannot, or that may even be threatening to certain needs. For example, in contrast to the purely technical advances made by science, it is the specific belief in science as a source of social and moral progress that may provide a sense of control. Rutjens, van Harreveld, and van der Pligt, (2010) found that those exposed to conditions in which low control was made more salient were more likely to defend the ideal of human progress. However, the suitability of science in playing this role may be greater for those who are nonreligious. Rutjens et al. (2016) found that only those low in religious belief who were exposed to mortality salience reminders showed increased belief in social-moral progress compared to those high in religious belief or those not exposed to mortality salience (Rutjens et al., 2016). In fact, some aspects of a scientific worldview may be as threatening to the religious as others are comforting to the nonreligious.

The prototypical issue representing the "science versus religion" conflict has been Darwin's theory of evolution by natural selection, as evidenced by large differences in endorsement of evolution as a function of greater or lesser religiosity. However, the threat posed by evolution (or any alternative to literal creationism) may hinge upon specific components of randomness and unpredictability. Many accept the theory of evolution when framed as being teleological or guided in some way—such as theistically guided or "intelligent design" because it provides a greater sense of control and purposefulness. Rutjens, van der Pligt, and van Harreveld, (2010) found that priming a lack of control reduced people's belief in Darwin's theory evolution relative to a greater preference for theories of life that stressed the role of God as being in control or for evolution when presented as predictable and orderly. Conversely, the preference for intelligent design over natural selection disappeared when the latter was portrayed as a process with inevitable outcomes. Similarly, using a Terror Management perspective, Tracy, Hart, and Martens (2011) found that reminders of death increased acceptance of intelligent design and rejection of evolutionary theory but these effects were reversed when naturalism was presented as a source of existential meaning. This suggests the desire to find greater meaning and purpose in science is heightened when existential threats are activated, but it can be satisfied when a scientific worldview is framed as being meaningful. That said, a scientific worldview may be less appealing for those with devout religious beliefs not only because of disputes regarding content (e.g., literal interpretations of scripture) but also because epistemic and existential niches are already filled by religion.

Although less coherent and comprehensive compared to religious worldviews, some superstitious and paranormal beliefs can also satisfy some epistemic needs. Experimentally induced threats to a sense of personal control can lead to greater endorsement of such beliefs (Laurin & Kay, 2017). Similarly, the need for a sense of meaning is predictive of both religiosity as well as superstitious and paranormal beliefs (FioRito et al., 2021; Nelson et al., 2020). In sum, adherence to secular worldviews such as beliefs in government, science, or superstition appears to be an exceptions to the theory that only religion can provide a sense of meaning, control, and existential comfort. But in some aspects, they are also the "exceptions that prove the rule." In this case, that rule is that a common set of epistemic, existential, and social needs constitute the core motivations of a range of worldviews. These operate in a hydraulic, compensatory manner such that beliefs are malleable as a function of whether or not these needs are satisfactorily providing a sense of equanimity.

Conclusion

The value added by studying religion from a functional standpoint is hopefully abundantly clear. This information extends beyond theories from extant work in the Cognitive Sciences of Religion that focus on general human tendencies (e.g., anthropomorphism, agency detection, and teleology). Functional approaches demonstrate that R/S beliefs are not only produced by invariant tendencies but also are products of situational conditions (e.g., stability versus threat), as well as individual difference traits. Rather than a universal predisposition to seek human-like agency in the form of a personally concerned God, the temporal threat to an individual's equanimity increases the likelihood of creating a religious attribution. As with the other work from a social cognition perspective mentioned elsewhere in this book, a functional approach to religion provides a more specific account of religion, and most importantly in the current context, evidence of the experimentally induced malleability of belief.

The dual process perspective is also relevant to the functional approaches to religion. For example, as part of maintaining cognitive consistency, the reduction in anxiety subsequent to belief bolstering can occur at an unconscious level. That is, participants in experiments whose beliefs have been manipulated often misattribute the source of their attitude change. Consistent with frameworks regarding implicit cognition, the compensatory conviction process does not necessarily involve conscious intention or awareness (McGregor & Marigold, 2003).

This work also has implications for the philosophical debate regarding religion as a domain that uniquely satisfies epistemic and existential needs (Pargament et al., 2005). Certainly, this is true for many individuals. But many of the studies mentioned above demonstrate the interchangeable nature of epistemic and existential needs with equivalent functions performed by secular as well as religious sources. Another common philosophical stance for which the functional approach to religion has relevance is the "non-overlapping magisteria" position.

Some scholars have argued that interpretation of associations between individual characteristics and their religious beliefs is metaphysically neutral because an actual spiritual agency could account for these effects. For instance, psychologists practicing what is known as "theistic psychology" account for associations between believers' psychological characteristics and their images with God as possibly reflecting, in part, God's actual influence. O'Grady and Richards (2007) state "individuals may experience God as a compensatory figure because God really did help fill in the gaps left by inadequate parenting" (p. 190). Certainly, correlational work cannot specify the causal direction such as the associations between psychological traits based on parenting and the perceived characteristics of God. However, experimental work of the type mentioned above does provide evidence for causal origin of the association as originating with the psychological traits of the believer interacting with the social context and producing their religious beliefs. The initial motivational state of a believer, whether for social contact, consistency, certainty, or meaning, motivates them to perceive that external religious agency fulfills that need, which then forms associated externalized attributions. Thus, "I need X" becomes "God provides X" becomes "God wants or is like X."

4

Influence of the Social and Group Context

"Men create gods after their own image, not only with regard to their form, but with regard to their mode of life."

—Aristotle

Social Influences on R/S Beliefs

It scarcely bears repeating that many aspects of religion and spirituality (R/S) are socially learned and transmitted via mechanisms such as parental inculcation, vicarious exposure to groups, and cultural immersion (Kelley & De Graaf, 1997). The most robust predictors of whether someone is religious include demography, social context, and most importantly, the religiosity of one's parents (Martin et al., 2003). The extent of social influence on religious content is so pervasive that there would seem to be little benefit in enumerating different vectors of transmission. Rather, the focus of this chapter will be on how the experiential and perceptual aspects of religion are internalized from social, contextual, and cultural factors and externalized onto spiritual agents. This includes 1) the social mechanisms that influence how believers come to view religious agents as possessing certain characteristics and desires, 2) how believers come to attribute certain events to God's intentions, and 3) how believers come to feel that they are in a relationship with a person-like theistic agent (Davis et al., 2021). These types of beliefs differ from doctrinal or factual content in that they are experienced as self-evident, in accordance with naïve realism (believing that one sees the world as it actually is). To use terminology from psychodynamic theory, such content is "ego-syntonic", or consonant with one's self concept and not merely derivative of external sources. For example, rather than "I learned this religious concept in Sunday school", a fully ego syntonic belief represents personal knowledge (e.g., "I have come to know the Lord").

In accordance with Dual Processing model of cognition, the internalization of socially transmitted, relational aspects of religion involves not only Type Two processes (e.g., memorizing scripture or learning doctrines) but also Type One implicit functions (e.g., intuitions that God is watching or has certain desires). Because these processes are automatized and nonconscious, acquisition via social exposure is not always correctly recognized as the source of transmission. To use another psychodynamic term, the views of social agents are "introjected"—unconsciously internalized and adopted as one's own. This chapter will focus on the process by which social reality—religious worldviews shared within social contexts ranging from small groups to entire cultures—becomes internalized without conscious awareness. Then, as with other frameworks discussed in this book, the chapter will explore how these internalized, socially acquired beliefs are externalized as projections that involve social aspects of religion, such as beliefs about religious group identity or views of God as having social allegiances.

Group Influences and the Cognitive Sciences of Religion

The process by which religious beliefs and behaviors are socially acquired has been a central focus of the Cognitive Sciences of Religion perspective, such as the delineation of distinct functional pathways of inculcation. "Conformist transmission" is thought to rely upon the simple frequency of exposure to group members who perform actions (e.g., prayers, chants, public recitation of creeds), which determines the likelihood that they will be adopted by others (Henrich & Boyd, 1998). Religious concept acquisition is enhanced by prestige biased learning, which takes place when those modeling the beliefs and behaviors are respected as leaders or "winners" (Henrich & Gil-White, 2001). Beliefs are more likely to be internalized when accompanied by credibility-enhancing displays (CREDs)—cues presumed to reflect genuine, deep commitment such as costly ritual displays (e.g., serpent handling, fire walking; Henrich, 2009). In accordance with an emphasis on cultural evolution, explanations from the CSR perspective tend to focus on the functionality and adaptive benefits of religious practices. Commitment displays and CREDs are thought to have evolved to enable the distinction between free-riders and those with genuine beliefs and loyalties, thereby increasing group competitiveness (Bulbulia & Sosis, 2011). The beliefs of those who embody traits valued by the group or who engage in costly ritual displays are more likely to be perceived as credible information sources. The CSR approach investigates the ultimate origin of religion, including why it takes predictable, even universal forms across cultures and how social manifestations may be generated by the evolved architecture of the human mind (Gervais & Najle, 2015). For instance, the ultimate purpose of phenomena such as conformist transmission is primarily to enhance group cohesion by augmenting commitment. The CSR approach to social influence and other group processes regarding religion primarily focuses on how behaviors are imitated and interpreted by group members, and how groups transmit such practices to others.

The approaches and emphases taken by the fields of Social Psychology and Social Cognition complement CSR and related anthropological perspectives. An interpersonal social psychological approach focuses more on the contextual variation of social influences (i.e., why under these but not those conditions). As in the preceding chapter, the social cognitive perspective addresses what individual psychological motivations are functionally served (i.e., not merely promoting the group as a whole) by sharing religious belief with others (e.g., increased personal certainty and epistemic clarity) and how these factors respond to contextual changes. Additionally, a social psychological approach emphasizes individual differences, including personality and cognitive traits, that make some people particularly susceptible to social influence. Finally, and in keeping with the present themes, the social psychological approach provides a more specific focus on the process of internalization and the phenomenology of religious belief content. This will be illustrated by focusing on experiments demonstrating that social sources can influence religious belief without conscious awareness.

Conformity and Social Influence

Social interactions involve not only the rote imitation of others' behaviors, but also lead us to adopt others' perceptual or emotional experiences through the process of conformity. Several of the classic paradigms of social influence demonstrate how group conformity can lead to belief internalization. In one of the earliest experiments demonstrating conformity to group norms of perception, Sherif, (1935) used the autokinetic effect; a light pinpoint projected in a dark room that appears to move (due to eye movements and the lack of a fixed frame of reference). Participants were asked to estimate how far the light moved over the course of several sessions. When others in the room with the subject stated their answers audibly one after the next, the group members' estimates of the distance traveled by the light converged to a common figure across successive trials. In other words, the perceptions of the participants exhibited conformity with the group norm. In later experiments, when a confederate was planted in the group by the experimenter to give overestimates of the distance, the inflated estimate not only shifted the perceived group norm upward, but this norm persisted over many trials even after this confederate was removed (Jacobs & Campbell, 1961). In effect, participants' own perceptions were shaped through the process of conforming to, and internalization of, the group norm. Further, this was not perceived to be an externally derived ("ego dystonic") form of conformity ("just going along with what they said"), but rather was experienced by participants, in accordance with naïve realism, as their own subjective perception. This illustrates how R/S beliefs are best understood not as either conscious mimicry of others or as idiosyncratic ideas distinct from those of others, but as products of shared reality that have been internalized and adopted as being one's own interpretation of reality.

Perhaps the best-known series of conformity experiments was conducted by Solomon Asch (1956). In the original prototypical configuration of the study, a participant was asked to sit with a panel consisting of what appeared to be other participants, but who were all confederates of the experimenter. The task for the naïve participant was to view a series of lines of different lengths or at different angles and state which best matched the criterion. In contrast with the Sherif (1935) autokinetic effect, the correct answer in the Asch paradigm was intended to be unambiguous. The participant was always positioned to provide their answer after a number of confederates had verbally given theirs. On some trials, the confederates were instructed to give obviously incorrect answers to determine whether the actual participant's answers would be influenced. Therefore, the participants had a choice—they could either respond correctly, thereby defying the group consensus, or they could verbally conform to the incorrect norm. The results indicated that participants embedded in a group of half dozen others conformed by providing incorrect answers on three-quarters of the trials. In total, 37 percent of all responses were (incorrect) conforming.

It is common for Asch's findings to be interpreted as primarily demonstrating the power of the group norm in influencing external forms of conformity or "normative influence." That is, most participants, despite knowing full well that their perception was correct and that of the others was incorrect, felt compelled to "go along" and not stand out from the others. But the aspect of the findings more relevant to the present context pertains to another portion of participants whose subjective perceptions of stimuli changed because of the group norm. As with Sherif's study using the autokinetic effect, this informational influence was sufficiently powerful that many participants internalized the norm in a way that led them to misperceive the reality of their own eyes. That is, despite the fact the correct answer in Asch's paradigm was clear, a portion of participants disregarded this reality and privately accepted the group members' responses as their own. Even after debriefing as to the deception of the confederates, these participants often denied being influenced by the group or consciously dissembling their responses. Subsequent studies using scans of brain activity have demonstrated these effects occurring on a relatively "low" level of neural processing. For example, visual perception areas of the brain are active during conformity experiments rather than executive (i.e., deliberative) regions, suggesting that the internalized norms are not mere conscious compliance (Berns et al., 2005). Again, the group norm actually altered the perceived reality of the participant.

Social influence not only affects phenomenological sensory experiences but is also involved in processing memory and emotions at an implicit level, inaccessible to conscious introspection (Stein, 2013). One such classic experiment by Schachter and Singer (1962) served as the basis of their "two-factor" theory of emotion which posits that emotions are experienced and labeled in accordance with both physiological arousal as well as expectational sets such as social cues. Participants received injections of either adrenaline (producing a generalized state of arousal and feeling "keyed up") or a saline placebo. Some of them received accurate descriptions of the expected arousing effects but others did not receive a clear description. Then, they were placed in social contexts with confederates who displayed behaviors reflecting different emotions (e.g., euphoric versus angry). The results indicated that participants who experienced arousal without a clear expectational set tended to label their emotions in accordance with those expressed by others around them. In effect, although the physiological aspect of the emotion was identical for all participants (i.e., "aroused"), the subjective experience of the emotion was shaped by social cues. That is, even though participants' physiological experience was identical, their realities regarding this arousal were markedly disparate.

A similar demonstration of the social malleability of emotional attribution was conducted by Dutton and Aron (1974)—dubbed the "Love on the Bridge" study. Contact was made by an attractive female confederate with male participants who had just crossed over a nerve-wracking rope suspension bridge (versus, in another condition, a structurally sound bridge) and were therefore in a state of physiological arousal. After crossing their respective bridges, all participants were given the personal contact information by the attractive confederate. Results demonstrated that those who crossed the suspension bridge misattributed the correct cause of their physiological state as attraction to a confederate who chatted with them after they crossed the bridge, as evidenced by the fact that they were more likely to call the number they were given. Taken together, the results of these seminal studies in social psychology demonstrate that the labeling of one's own emotions is malleable and susceptible to misattribution as a function of social cues.

Social contexts such as groups can also shape perceived reality simply by providing consensual validation. Recall from earlier chapters that one of the responses to failed prophesy in Festinger et al.'s study was that group members sought reassurance for their worldview in the form of social support. Beyond the specific instance of disconfirmed prophetic beliefs, Festinger (1954) also theorized that people are generally motivated to seek out interactions with similar others who validate their reality, and that this is particularly the case with beliefs that have few or no external criteria to determine their accuracy. Seeking out others to provide consensual validation is not an unbiased process, but rather is directed selectively at those likely to have similar beliefs (Hampton & Sprecher, 2020). Conversely, people tend to avoid contact with those who may challenge their worldviews. Because of the lack of a clear external referent, religious and spiritual beliefs are especially vulnerable to uncertainty and disconfirmation. Therefore, many socially shared functions of religion (e.g., rituals, group recitation of creeds) exist specifically for the purpose of providing the means by which beliefs can be consensually validated (e.g., "We all believe this", "We are distinct from unbelievers"), thereby reducing uncertainty (Engstrom & Laurin, 2020).

Building on the concepts from the previous chapter, belief acquisition and internalization via cognitive dissonance reduction are processes that do not solely operate within individuals, but rather are also socially mediated. This is a framework in which an interpersonal social psychological approach can be especially useful in complementing anthropological and CSR perspectives on shared religious belief. According to the predominant view from CSR, religious ritual displays have culturally evolved primarily for the purposes of advertising one's commitment to the group or accurately distinguishing between free-riders and true believers (Bulbulia & Sosis, 2011). However, participating in activities and worship with others also validates group members' own beliefs, even if they are not demonstrating their loyalty to others or participating in commitment displays (i.e., it is not only "other-directed"). Emotional benefits can accrue in the form of dissonance reduction as members adjust their attitudes and beliefs to match a common group norm (Matz & Wood, 2005). Conversely, exposure to those who do not share the group norm raises members' dissonance and disrupts the consensually validated reality. In the same vein, recalcitrant heterodox members are often expelled from the group, relegated to the status of out-group nonbelievers. Therefore, one method of containing cognitive dissonance is to maintain strict separation of in-and outgroup members and to quickly identify potential defectors or "backsliders." Cults and sects often publicly punish, humiliate, shun, or revoke group membership from those who consistently deviate from group norms (e.g., the People's Temple group under Jim Jones). These actions are accompanied by attributions that can be used to diffuse potential threats; as mentioned in the previous chapter, dissonance is avoided by derogating the source of conflicting information (i.e., "We do not have to listen to non-group members", "Defectors are like Judas—influenced by Satan"). Failed prophesy is often attributed as being the fault of those outside the group, further accentuating the in- versus outgroup boundary (Zygmunt, 1972). Therefore, engagement in shared group activities not only fulfills the purpose of assessing genuine commitment, but also serves as a method of dissonance reduction via consensual validation ("The fact that we all agree is further evidence that our beliefs are true"). These activities increase social cohesion and the relative preference for in- over outgroup members (Legare & Wen, 2014).

Different types of groups may be relatively attractive to prospective members in different contexts as a function of the degree to which they satisfy individual members' psychological needs. One characteristic that makes certain religious groups appealing (and conducive to the internalization of normative beliefs) is the quality of "entitativity." Highly entitative groups are seen as having clear boundaries and internal structure, common goals, and internal homogeneity relative to low entitative groups, which appear to have more porous and inchoate boundaries. The degree of preferred group entitativity varies as a function of not only individual preferences but also situational needs and circumstances. As mentioned in the chapter on cognition, some people have higher needs for clear, structured knowledge, and are more likely to gravitate to highly entitative groups, whereas those with a greater tolerance for ambiguity are more likely to prefer groups that appear low in entitativity (Hogg, 2014). As predicted by compensatory models, under conditions of greater uncertainty (e.g., threats to belief), people are more likely to prefer highly entitative religious groups. This can be seen in religious groups under conditions of social, political, and economic instability. Historical data demonstrate that under such conditions, religious citizens are more attracted to strict, authoritarian churches (McCann, 1999). Similarly, in an experiment where uncertainty was primed, religious individuals displayed a preference for orthodox over moderate religious leaders (Hogg et al., 2010). One interpretation of this trend is that, when confronted by threats, the character of a group can shift to compensate by purging noncommitted members (e.g., excluding the "fence sitters"), therefore retaining only the true believers. By contrast, under conditions of relatively low threat or in which epistemic needs for certainty and control are being adequately met, less entitative (e.g., more ecumenical and accepting) religions tend to be more appealing. As such, rather than an invariant, universal phenomenon, the social acquisition of religious beliefs and subsequent internalization results from an interaction of several factors. Beliefs are more likely to be endorsed as true and easily internalized when the social context in which they are transmitted matches with believers' personal characteristics and epistemic state.

Religion and Social Conformity

In addition to religious believers adapting to social groups, some evidence suggests that traits associated with religiosity themselves promote conformity. In a series of experiments, Saroglou, Corneille, and Van Cappellen (2009) demonstrated that those with submissive tendencies were even more likely to comply with an experimenter's requests after being primed with religious concepts. Similarly, Van Cappellen, Corneille, Cols, and Saroglou (2011) found that those high in dispositional submissiveness were more likely to assimilate their perceptual estimates to those of their peers after religious priming. Taken together, these findings suggest a shared conceptual basis such that increased salience of religion leads to greater social compliance, at least for those already more prone to dispositional submissiveness.

Other research on the interaction between religiosity and individual differences also indicates those who are more religious tend to value conformity to social groups relative to those who are less religious. Similarly, religiosity, particularly fundamentalist belief, is strongly correlated with authoritarianism, a trait that emphasizes conventionalism and submission to the group (Altemeyer & Hunsberger, 1992; Blogowska & Saroglou, 2013). Longitudinal work has demonstrated a causal connection between the two constructs such that the experience of religious conversion precedes increased authoritarianism, and conversely, diminished authoritarianism precedes deconversion (Lockhart et al., 2022). A parallel pattern is found in the endorsement of personal values—desired goals that motivate people's actions, influence cognition, and serve as guiding principles regarding behavior. Religiosity is most associated with values that conserve social and individual order such as tradition (acceptance of religious customs and ideas) and conformity (restraint from violating social norms), and inversely related to valuing personal autonomy, such as in the form of self-direction (i.e., independent thought and action; Saroglou et al., 2004). Further, longitudinal analyses indicate that religious affiliation at an earlier time precedes later increases in valuing tradition and conformity as well as decreased valuation of self-direction (Chan et al., 2020). Related work in the domain of moral foundations has found that, relative to the nonreligious, religious people endorse group-binding (rather than individualizing) morality, including the prioritization of ingroup loyalty (Graham & Haidt, 2010). Such patterns of individual difference characteristics suggest that greater religiosity is causally linked with trait preferences for greater social conformity.

It must be mentioned that these patterns could just as well be characterized in the opposite sense that the nonreligious are more individualistic. One manifestation of this is the notable difficulty in organizing people into groups constituted on the basis of shared secularism—a process that is often likened to the proverbial practice of "cat herding" (Brewster et al., 2020). The nonreligious may also be distinguished in the specific aspect of informational, as opposed to normative conformity. Recall, as discussed in the Asch paradigm, that conformity in the normative sense refers to external responding, as opposed to the informational sense consisting of subjective, internal perceptual change. This distinction echoes aspects of Dual Processing models in that informational conformity occurs without conscious awareness (by definition), as the experience is processed automatically (i.e., Type One cognition) as opposed to consciously (Type Two). In an interesting example illustrating this distinction, Thiruchselvam et al. (2017) compared these two types of conformity as a function of religiosity on attitudinal judgments of facial attractiveness by measuring neural responses as well as self-reports. The Late Positive Potential, as detected by electroencephalogram (EEG) is an event-related potential sensitive to the private appraisal of stimuli. Although self-report ratings of both groups displayed the typical conformity response by shifting toward group norms, the neural responses of non-religious individuals were unaffected by informational conformity. In other words, although non-religious individuals externally conformed to the peer-ratings, their internal perceptions were less affected (i.e., maintaining their idiosyncratic perception) in contrast to religious individuals for whom both these measures coincided. This would seem to suggest that in contrast to the superficial conformity of the nonreligious (whose subjective perception is not altered by norms), the type of conformity associated with religiosity occurs at a conscious as well as nonconscious level of cognitive processing.

In sum, there is evidence that religiosity is causally linked to a greater affinity for social conformity. This has implications for the social transmission and internalization of religious concepts. Just as with the classic experiments on conformity and social influence on misattribution, the power of group influence is sufficient to alter individuals' internalized perceptions of religious and spiritual beliefs. In the following sections, the process of projecting these beliefs onto external sources will be explored in greater detail.

Culture and the Environment

In addition to the process occurring in small social groups, aspects of the cultural milieu and the physical environment can also become internalized and shape individuals' religious representations. Anthropological theories, particularly those from environmental determinist and cultural materialist schools of thought, have suggested that factors such as climate and food supply influence religious beliefs, practices (e.g., in the form of rituals and dietary rules) and images of the deity (cf. Harris, 1977). However, earlier approaches were often overly speculative rather than empirically based. More recently the "new science of religious change" approach, which utilizes a multidisciplinary framework, has provided better evidence that group-level cultural processes interact with individual-level psychological functions in shaping religious concepts (Jackson et al., 2021b). These approaches use methods that are better able to establish causal directionality such as adopting sophisticated ethnographic coding, agent-based computer modeling, time-series analysis, and most importantly, tests utilizing experimental manipulation, while simultaneously controlling for extraneous factors.

As discussed in the previous chapter in the context of the Existential Insecurity Theory, countries, regions, and states with insecure living conditions tend to feature higher levels of religiosity (Barber, 2011; Immerzeel & van Tubergen, 2013; Norris & Inglehart, 2011). Such associations are the purview of socio-ecological psychology, a discipline that studies how the objective social and physical environment affects thinking, feeling, and behaviors. Research in this area suggests that general properties of cultural religious practices tend to covary systematically with features of the local environment. For example, there is a positive association between local levels of religiosity and regional prevalence of parasitic infection (i.e., the average disease stress experienced by people; Fincher & Thornhill, 2012). One possible explanation for this is that the degree of "ingroup assortative sociality" (i.e., insularity and attenuated contact with out-group members) reinforced by religion may have evolved as an adaptation to avoid infection from novel parasites. Similarly, other anthropological work suggests that belief in specific types of deities can develop as a culturally evolved response to environmental conditions. Some cultures feature "Big Gods"— supernatural beings believed to govern all reality, intervene in human affairs, and enforce human morality, whereas others have gods of smaller scope who are relatively unconcerned about specific human needs. Studies have indicated that Big God beliefs may improve the ability of social groups to deal with adverse ecological conditions such as poor access to food and water (Botero et al., 2014). This theory has been applied to the observed geographic distribution of religiosity including the monotheistic, Abrahamic faiths emerging from the Middle East and Levant.

It is certainly true that mere associations between socio-environmental conditions and aspects of cultural religiosity do not allow us to conclude a causal relationship, particularly given the complexity of numerous cultural and environmental factors. However, longitudinal work has provided evidence of a temporal connection in several domains such as the relationship between warfare and religiosity. Specifically, there is evidence that the presence and intensity of armed conflict in a region lead to subsequent increases in religiosity (Echeverría Vicente et al., 2022; Henrich et al., 2019). In accordance with theories of existential security (as mentioned in the previous chapter), this may represent a compensatory reaction to increased fear and anxiety (Du & Chi, 2016), that also affects which specific qualities and characteristics are attributed to God. Beyond the detection of temporal connections between social conflict and religious beliefs, Caluori, Jackson, Gray, and Gelfand (2020) found that individuals exposed to experimentally manipulated conflict salience were more likely to perceive God as being punitive. This relationship is mediated via people's preference for strict social norms and strong punishments for deviations (so-called "tight" cultural norms). Further, just as priming of ecological threat increased punitive religious beliefs via support for greater cultural tightness, priming cultural tightness increased Christians' beliefs in punitive qualities of God partly because it made people more motivated to punish rule-breakers (Jackson et al., 2021a). Taken in the aggregate, such findings indicate that not only are general levels of religious participation and devotion affected by social conditions, but these conditions can induce externalized projection of specific characteristics onto God/s.

This connection between physical and social environments accompanied by attributions of specific characteristics to God is reminiscent of the sociological concept of "metaphoric parallelism," which posits that beliefs about the gods' desires are representations of social facts, such that "God's" characteristics reflect properties of the world (Winter, 1973). In an example from the physical environment, in societies where water resources are scarce, supreme deities are significantly more likely to be understood as concerned with, and supportive of, human morality (Snarey, 1996). As mentioned in the previous chapter, cultures where nurturing parenting is the norm tend to believe in deities that are more benevolent compared to cultures with authoritarian practices, which tend to have more malevolent deities (Lambert et al., 1959).

Other manifestations of parallelism include instances when communal concerns such as threats to local ecologies or to social cooperation are externalized and represented as religious concerns or "God problems" (Bendixen et al., 2021). Consistent with a projective process, for example, people living in famine-struck small-scale societies believe that God or gods are concerned with the weather and food supply (Skoggard et al., 2020). In a series of studies of the Tyvans from southern Siberia (who have a Buddhist-animist belief system), Purzycki (2016) demonstrated a correspondence between the appearance of novel social problems (e.g., alcoholism and theft) and increased beliefs that the spirits are concerned about the same moral problems. This phenomenon can be observed on a smaller scale in laboratory settings. For example, when playing an economic trust game, participants entrusting investments in others who subsequently failed to return money were more likely to make the attribution that greed angers God (Purzycki et al., 2020).

Thus, parallelism is a bi-directional process—religious beliefs are internalized from individuals' environment and social groups, and beliefs also represent externalizations of personal characteristics and priorities attributed to God. For instance, Oishi et al. (2011) found cultural differences between European Americans and Koreans in their associations of the qualities of Jesus (the former attributed more positive qualities such as "awesome" compared to those of the latter, who emphasized qualities of suffering). More significantly however, the analyses indicated that national differences in conceptions of Jesus were predicted by participants' own self-reported personality traits and happiness, and that this relationship was bidirectional. In other words, some of this effect was attributable to people projecting their own personality traits and levels of well-being onto the image of Jesus, while another portion of the effect was that they were interpreting their own personality and well-being via the culturally normative view of Jesus.

Religion as a Social Identity

Religion involves not only the endorsement of a set of related beliefs, such as those pertaining to supernatural agents or the afterlife, but it also includes a sense of belonging to a group (Ysseldyk et al., 2010). As outlined in the preceding section, work from the Cognitive Sciences of Religion has established that a substantial portion of what constitutes religion is composed of aspects that culturally evolved for social purposes, such as coalition building, shared ritual bonding, and the sanctification of group boundaries. Indeed, internalizing a specific religious social identity (e.g., "I am a member of X denomination") may be equally, if not more central to religion than belief content. For instance, some people consider themselves "culturally Jewish," or have a national identity that closely aligns with a religion (e.g., Greek Orthodox), or emphasize a strict boundary distinction between religious and nonreligious ("At least I'm not an atheist"). As religious social identity becomes internalized, people view their own self-identity as embodying characteristics of the group, in a form of self-stereotyping ("Members of X tend to value Y, so that is what I value"). This section will also demonstrate how characteristics relevant to individuals' social identity are externalized so that God is seen as possessing the same qualities. Given that topics pertaining to religious social identity (e.g., group formation, sect/ cult theories, prejudice) constitute some of the most extensively covered territory in the psychology and sociology of religion, the present material will be limited to two core phenomena: 1) How religious social identity is internalized such that self-identity reflects group identity; and 2) How those same aspects are externalized, projected, and viewed as characterizing God (see Figure 4.1).

Social Identity Theory (SIT) posits that individuals base their sense of who they are to a substantial degree upon their social and group membership, a process that protects and enhances their self-esteem (Tajfel & Turner, 1979). Because of this functional link to self-esteem needs, individuals are motivated to view themselves and other ingroup members more favorably than those in the out-group, who are often derogated. The degree to which people identify with a given group varies from person to person, which can be also seen in the case of religious identity. Whereas some individuals view their religious group membership as self-central, for others it is peripheral. Social Identity Theory has had a major impact on understanding that religious identity represents an amalgam of beliefs together with social belonging. For example, the construct of religious fundamentalism refers not only to cognitive components relevant

Social Paths of Religious Internalization to the Self and Externalization from Self Projected onto Religious and Spiritual Agents

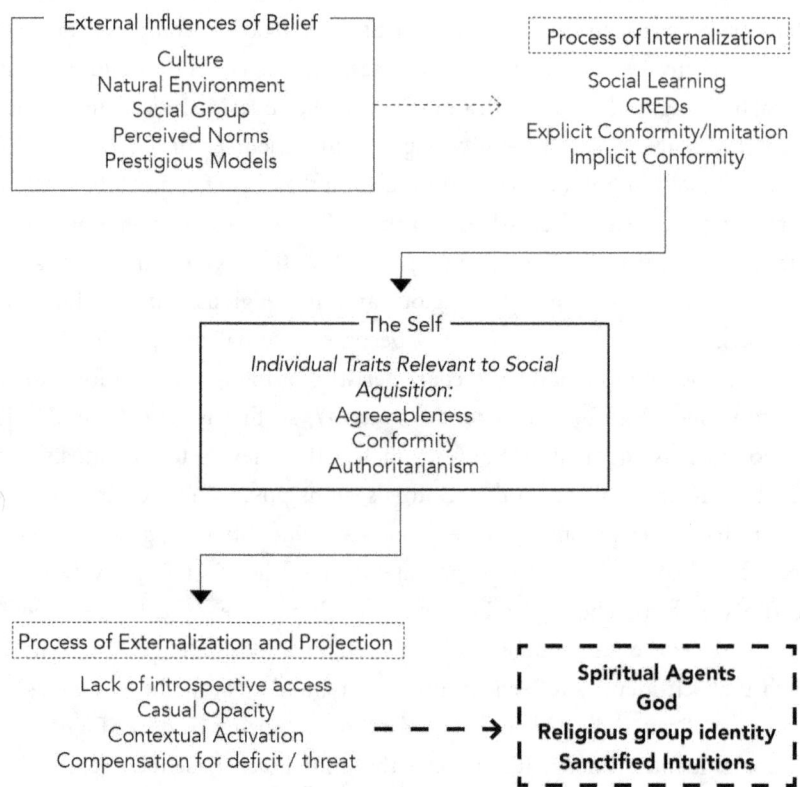

Figure 4.1 Social Paths of Religious Internalization and Externalization.
Source: Olivia Brenner.

to beliefs such as doctrinal rigidity, but also belonging aspects such as the tendency to see one's religion or denomination as having a special relationship with the divinity. Jackson and Hunsberger (1999) found that fundamentalism is correlated with religious parochialism—greater positive evaluation of fellow ingroup members (i.e., Christians and believers), and negative attitudes toward out-group members (i.e., atheists and nonbelievers). As will be seen, SIT also predicts that religious beliefs, particularly those associated with fundamentalism, increase in response to perceived threats to group identity.

Social Identity Theory has been instrumental in explaining the phenomenon of religious prejudice—the tendency to disfavor others because of their group identities, which involves not only other religious groups, but includes other forms of identity (ethnic, racial, and national). The massive literature on the religion-prejudice association is fraught with complexity but has yielded some reliable broad conclusions. One is that religiously based prejudice varies as a function of the specific target group in question. Johnson et al. (2012) found that the level of individuals' religiosity and spirituality were related to negative attitudes toward out-groups (in this study, Muslims, atheists, and gays) relative to ingroups (fellow Christians). The association also varies depending upon perceivers' specific religious dimensions or orientation. In one meta-analytic study, Hall et al. (2010) found that religious fundamentalism was related to greater religious and ethnic prejudice, but intrinsic (personally important) religiosity was negatively related to such prejudice. Another pattern, more relevant to the present topic, is that aspects of religious identity overlap with other forms of social identity (e.g., nationality, ethnicity), as well attitudes and traits that may not necessarily involve religious content (political orientation, authoritarianism). Consequently, attempts to draw direct causal connections between religiosity and prejudicial social attitudes invariably involve separating, whether statistically or through other controlled procedures, independent influences from these different constructs. Moreover, general religiosity (e.g., belief in God or intrinsic orientation) does not have the most robust causal impact on forms of prejudice and ingroup bias. Many studies indicate that the relationship between religiosity and prejudice is reduced to non-significance or even reversed when controlling for constructs such as authoritarianism (Laythe et al., 2001). Therefore, on the one hand, the relationship with prejudice can be characterized as not specifically driven by religious identity but rather by the overlap in content shared by religious identity and other constructs (e.g., ethnocentrism, fundamentalism). However, it is equally true that in practical reality, without artificial separation, religious identity does functionally overlap with other social identities such that situational activation or increased salience in one identity aspect increases the salience of others. In this case, there exist functional similarities between authoritarianism, fundamentalism, religious identity, and prejudice. This is evident in the ubiquitous instances where religious identity blends with forms of nationalist or political movements.

The shared conceptual basis of religious and other social identities can be observed in the activation of religious identity in experimental contexts, which also increases affinity for perceived fellow religious ingroup members and increased antipathy for out-group members. For example, after priming with religious words (e.g., sacred, divine) religious participants allocated more money in an economic game to ingroup members (Christians) than to out-group members (Muslims; Shariff, 2009). Similarly, Johnson, Rowatt, and LaBouff (2012) found that priming Christians with Christian religious concepts (e.g., Bible, Jesus) increased negative attitudes toward value-violating out-groups (e.g., atheists) relative to value-consistent ingroups. Further, in this study and others, the effect of the primes did not depend upon the level of participants' own religiosity, indicating that the mechanism of intergroup bias (as predicted by social identity theory) is not only the degree to which individuals personally identify with their religious group, but activating religious concepts themselves increases the salience of social identity (i.e., making people more parochial and insular) for all participants.

Such results have implications for the role played by religious concepts in shaping attitudes regarding groups that do not necessarily involve religious identity, but merely constitute different social identities, such as with racial prejudice. Johnson, Rowatt, and LaBouff (2010) found that, even controlling for individual differences in religiosity, subliminally priming white Christian Americans with religious content resulted in increased covert racial prejudice against Black people. This again implicates intergroup identity aspects of religion, such as the identification with an amalgamated construct—"White Christian Protestant"—that is made more salient by the activation of religious identity alone. Apropos to the current point, by identifying oneself with a perceived religious group and related shared values, there are "spillover" effects onto other aspects of identity, even those without any overt relationship to religious belief content. Similarly, Bloom, Arikan, and Courtemanche (2015) found that priming with religious content affected attitudes toward immigrants. Notably, this study also pointed to at least two other complicating factors. One involved the perceived in- versus outgroup similarity of the target groups. Bloom et al. found that religious priming led to differential attitudes toward various ethnic and religious target immigrant groups (e.g., religiously or ethnically similar or dissimilar) that also interacted with another factor: the specific aspect of religiosity made more salient by priming. Priming of religious social identity resulted in increased opposition to dissimilar, out-group immigrants whereas activating religious beliefs had the effect of promoting welcoming attitudes toward immigrants of the same religion and ethnicity. As mentioned above, the general construct of religion involves aspects of both belief and identity. Other work has also found differential effects of priming religious (group) components, which tend to constrain prosociality toward only the ingroup, versus priming supernatural (God) components, which enhance prosociality even toward outgroup members (Preston & Ritter, 2013). Thus, belief (i.e., in God) content is to some extent distinct from belonging (i.e., group identity) content.

Just as the activation of one aspect of social identity can also activate other unrelated identities, being threatened with stimuli unrelated to religious identity can produce a religious identity-related reaction. For example, as covered in the previous chapter, responses to mortality salience—reminders of one's own death—can result in compensatory bolstering of religious beliefs (Routledge et al., 2018). The worldview defense reaction triggered by mortality salience (as outlined in Terror Management Theory) can also include social identity components such as greater favoritism of those who share one's religious worldview along with derogation of those who do not (Greenberg et al., 1990). Other types of threats, such as social ostracism, have been shown to induce greater support for fundamentalist beliefs (Schaafsma & Williams, 2012), demonstrating the ties between social identity and beliefs.

In this manner, forms of social identity are internally represented in a way that fuses religious identity together with other identities such as nationalism or political identity, producing various amalgams of religious nationalism (for those in the United States—Christian Nationalism or Identitarian Christianism). As a result of this identity fusion, demographic and cultural changes (e.g., increased non-white immigration and political power) are perceived as religious threats, particularly for those whose religious or ethnic identity is highly self-central. The alignment between Christian identity and national identity creates a symbolic boundary (e.g., beliefs that one must be a Christian to be a "real American"), in a way that demonstrates reactivity to temporal and cultural events (Whitehead & Scheitle, 2018). As a result of these overlapping identities, identity threat in a nonreligious domain ("whites are being replaced") can trigger compensatory responses couched in religious identity language ("we are a Christian nation"). The internalization of these combined identities increases the likelihood that people will have antisocial reactions to contextual triggers such as, in the case of Christian Nationalists, perceiving themselves as victims and showing greater support for retaliatory violence (Armaly et al., 2022).

Just as religious worldviews can increase as a compensatory response to perceived threats, increases in religious and/or social identification can be malleable as well. Although it has often been assumed to be a static construct that exerts a one-directional influence on social, political, and moral attitudes, religious identity varies in strength and in alignment with other identities such as political ideology (Egan, 2020). Experimentally induced priming as well as historical events can shift individuals' religious identity and behaviors as a function of political partisanship; even at an intuitive level (Margolis, 2018).

Externalizing Religious Social Identities: "God Thinks Like Us"

Just as membership in a religious group and other social constructs associated with a religious identity are internalized and constitute aspects of the self, social identities that originate in the self can be externalized and viewed in the form of "God's" perceived identity and allegiances. In other words, "My group believes X" becomes "I believe X" becomes "God believes X." To the extent that the actual origins of the beliefs are not consciously recognized, it becomes more likely that they will be attributed to God's influence. One example of this is political orientation. As seen in many contemporary political issues, even those who ostensibly share the same religious identity may espouse vastly different attitudes associated with their political orientation. Christians, whether liberal or conservative, perceive Jesus to hold the same ideological beliefs they do. Ross, Lelkes, and Russell (2012) found that liberals believed that a contemporary Jesus would hold a liberal ideology, such as being concerned about economic inequality and the mistreatment of immigrants, while conservative Christians reported that Jesus would hold a conservative ideology, showing concern for traditional morality (issues of abortion and gay marriage). Experimental work also shows that increasing the salience of religion has a differential effect on people as a function of their political orientation. In the aforementioned study, Bloom et al., found that religious priming increased conservatives' desire for greater social distance from immigrants but had the opposite effect on liberals. In other words, the internalized constructs that form political identity (whether liberal or conservative) become amalgamated with individuals' religious identity and are externalized and perceived as coming from religious sources.

Undoubtedly, variation in views of God is also attributable to participation and membership in a wide range of religious groups, with many different interpretations, who refer to large bodies of often ambiguous scripture, all of which enables "cherry picking" based on personal tastes. As stated in the introductory chapter, different religious views could be accounted for simply by having been exposed to different information. However, there are more psychologically sophisticated mechanisms accounting for the externalization process. For one, believers also project characteristics onto God or Jesus that have little to do with socially learned content or any plausible source in current religious discussion. Jackson, Hester, & Gray (2018) asked American Christians to choose visual representations for what they thought the actual face of God would look like. The resulting perceptions of God's face were shaped by an egocentric process in that God was perceived as looking similar to the participants themselves on dimensions such as attractiveness, age, and, to a lesser extent, race. Indeed, instances where God is believed to have opinions and positions on mundane matters, including aesthetic tastes in art and music, linguistic preferences, and even favorite sports teams, are too numerous to mention, all of which clearly represent the attitudes of the believer being projected onto God. Although these examples may appear trivial, there are others in which misattributions of God's will or belief in divine sanction for our own desires and actions are far more consequential.

The Sacralization of Social Identity

One problematic consequence of the projection of social identity-related attributes onto God is that our own desires come to be seen as receiving divine support—the process of sacralization or sanctification. As described by Hall et al. (2010) in reference to the relationship between religiosity and prejudice, "the divine in religious worship is often imbued with ingroup attributes. That is, religious figures are constructed in believers' own images" (p. 134). Consider one classic illustration of how the fusion of religious and ethnic identities can become sanctified when externalized onto God. In 1966 George Tamarin asked a group of Israeli schoolchildren aged 8–14 to read a Torah passage from the book of Joshua, chapter six, describing the conflict between the Israelites and the people living in the city of Jericho. The story culminates in the Israelite army destroying the city ("… men and women, young and old, oxen, sheep, and asses, with the edge of the sword … And they burned the city with fire, and all within it …"). Tamarin then asked the Israeli children, "Do you think Joshua and the Israelites acted rightly or not?" Sixty-six percent of the children gave "total approval" for Joshua's actions; 8 percent gave "partial approval and disapproval" and 26 percent totally disapproved. One child who approved said, "Joshua did good because the people who inhabited the land were of a different religion, and when Joshua killed them he wiped their religion from the earth." Tamarin gave a second group of Israeli schoolchildren essentially the same passage, except instead of Joshua and Israel it referred to "General Lin from a Chinese Kingdom 3000 years ago"; the rest of the passage was identical. In this version, only 7 percent of the Israeli children gave total approval, 18 percent gave partial approval/ disapproval, and 75 percent totally disapproved. Though highly contrived, this example nonetheless is a stark illustration of how social identity biases combine with religious externalization to imbue conflicts with sacred qualities—"God is on our side."

The capacity of religious identity to provide a divine imprimatur for conflict has been demonstrated in small-scale laboratory tasks. Bushman et al. (2007) exposed participants to a text featuring violence, one version of which was specifically contextualized as being from the Bible, and in which God is seen supporting the violence. In a second portion of the study, aggression was measured by a task in which participants could blast a competitor with loud noise through headphones. Results showed that framing with a violent context increased the level of aggression, particularly among religious believers exposed to scripture passages in which the violence was "God-sanctioned." Similarly, Koopmans, Kanol, and Stolle, (2021) found that priming religious individuals with pro-violence quotes from religious scripture raised attitudinal support for religious violence, particularly among fundamentalists.

As with the Tamarin study, such experiments may seem artificial and irrelevant to meaningful instances of actual social conflict. However, the sacralization of social identity preferences is also apparent in real-world patterns of inter-group strife, where the infusion of religion increases the intensity of existing conflicts. There are several mechanisms that may account for this effect. One such mechanism related to a sanctification process pertains to the greater sense of moral certainty resulting from the infusion of religion. This can increase the relationship between religiosity and support for violent warfare (Shaw et al., 2011). Another mechanism is that religion is likely to add symbolic meaning to secular grievances. In contrast to psychological reactions to grievances not involving religion (e.g., boundary disputes), grievances elicited when individuals' feel they are defending their religious identity are particularly powerful. Symbolic threats (to values, norms, morals, and identity) show a closer relationship with intergroup hostility than do realistic threats (e.g., resource competition). The more closely identified people are with their religious group, the greater the likelihood of construing conflicts in terms of symbolic threat (Obaidi et al., 2018). Those with strong religious worldviews are most likely to endorse prejudice and even aggression against out-groups because of a heightened sense of threat (Goplen & Plant, 2015). Similarly, fusions between religious and other forms of social identities lead to greater likelihood of prejudice and discrimination against groups perceived as holding incompatible values (Neuberg et al., 2014). As we saw above in the case of racial prejudice, ethnic and religious identities can become fused, adding to a sacred quality to defense against threats. In the United States, conservative Christianity is particularly aligned with white racial identity and associated political views such that whites react to perceived status threats by intensifying and sacralizing their authoritarian views of social order (e.g., becoming more punitive to ethnic minorities; Perry & Whitehead, 2021).

Part Two

Misattribution of the Effects of Religion

5

Exceptional Religious and Spiritual Experiences

"Si Dieu n'existait pas, il faudrait l'inventer." *("If God did not exist, it would be necessary to invent him"). Voltaire* Epistle to the author of the book, The Three Impostors.

(1768)

This chapter represents a shift in perspective from the first four chapters. The preceding sections of the book were organized on the basis of psychological concepts (e.g., cognition, attribution theory). The second portion of the book will focus on several phenomena that are often attributed to the effects of religion and spiritual influence (i.e., exceptional experiences, mental health, morality). In each chapter, these phenomena will be viewed through the lens of social cognition. The chapters will build upon previous material, using psychological concepts to explain how R/S attributions are created.

Defining "Exceptional Experience"

Some phenomena are perceived by those who experience them as having a unique or *sui generis* quality. Various terms such as "anomalous" or "non-ordinary" have been used to distinguish these experiences from what are perceived to be more common or ordinary religious beliefs (Taves, 2009). From a psychology of religion perspective, that which is considered exceptional is defined phenomenologically by the perceiver themselves. Stated somewhat circularly, an experience is exceptional if the person experiencing it deems it to be so. There are already several influential scholarly works that broadly capture the history, nosology, and phenomenology of exceptional R/S experiences (Hood, 2001; Taves, 2009). By contrast, the present coverage will focus more narrowly on a social cognition and attributional perspective to explain how and why certain features are perceived as exceptional.

Experiences deemed exceptional are typically attributed as having high degrees of tangibility and immanence (e.g., "God feels present right here, right now"), which in turn lends a confirmatory or dispositive quality ("only God could explain this"). Rather than an exhaustive survey of all possible experiences, the central focus here will be on studies that reveal the psychological mechanisms of perceived causality. Specifically, although these experiences are attributed as originating from external supernatural agency, this represents a misattribution of secular influences originating from other sources. These can be traced back to the same causal mechanisms featured in the first portion of the book, primarily individual cognitive and personality traits interacting within cultural, social, and group conditions. Another, more practical basis for selecting the experiences featured in this chapter is that these have all received scholarly attention in a substantial body of literature and as such, the influence of social cognitive factors has already been clearly documented. The phenomena include interactive dialogical prayer, personal revelation, glossolalia (tongue-speaking), possession, and related others that feature immanent spiritual involvement.

Is the Term "Misattribution" Justified?

It is common in most social psychological accounts of religious belief in general, and those featuring exceptional experiences in particular to acknowledge the potential methodological limitations and interpretive biases of researchers. Of course, one way to minimize ostensible bias is to limit coverage to a purely descriptive approach, such as listing defining features of the exceptional phenomena. Likewise, some accounts avoid potential bias by adhering closely to the subjective, phenomenological viewpoint of those reporting spiritual experiences (i.e., "insider accounts"). By refraining from any putative explanatory framework, social science accounts of R/S experiences can avoid potential accusations that researchers are adopting an "objective" stance. This distinction is captured by the subdivision used in fields of study such as anthropology that designates approaches as Etic (outsider) as opposed to Emic (insider). Etic accounts of religious belief have been accused of question-begging because assumptions made from an outsider perspective (e.g., psychological) differ from assumptions made by those who actually experience the phenomena. Etic outsiders may simply assume that the ontological referent of religious experience (i.e., a spiritual source) is illusory, whereas insiders may regard it as ontologically real.

I believe the present explanatory approach (including the use of the term "misattribution") is justified and avoids making unwarranted a priori ontological assumptions for several reasons. First, the focus will be on research material that typically relies upon participants' own attributions in the form of self-report data, such as measures of beliefs and experiences, rather than imposing any outsider interpretation or mischaracterization. Such studies usually include dependent variables consisting of participants' degree of belief conviction, attributed images of God, perceptions of supernatural agency, and the like. Consequently, the measures of perceived experiences (e.g., "have you ever had a spiritual revelation?" or "Do you view God as personally accessible?") do not represent the imposition or mischaracterization of researchers but rather, they capture aspects of the subjective viewpoints of participants. Descriptions of numinous experiences do not require a complete phenomenological account when they can simply be stated in neutral language such as "participants attributed a higher degree of immanence to God when in condition X compared to those in condition Y." Any additional subjective attributions such as the perceived origin of the numinous experience are not necessary to make statements explaining the mechanisms influencing such experiences.

A related issue pertains to the content of experiential self-reports vis-à-vis the known impact of objective experimental manipulation. In studies of secular social cognition, it is often the case that participants' beliefs and experiences are malleable as a function of experimental manipulation, yet they are unaware of this. In other words, participants may not correctly attribute the actual source of their experiences. Most studies that feature subtle manipulations (e.g., contextual priming) followed by debriefing awareness probes, often reveal that participants were unaware of, and may deny having been influenced by the manipulation. Participants may even offer explanations for their experiences that are objectively incorrect, such as in the case of confabulatory phenomena (Nisbett & Wilson, 1977). Similarly, studies on the sensed presence phenomenon indicate that participants may attribute the external source of their feeling to an actual spiritual agent. But suppose this is only experienced by those in conditions of high expectancy (e.g., priming of spiritual concepts) and only for those who are high in certain traits (e.g., Absorption). In such cases, the participants' explanation of an actual spiritual agent is irrelevant to describing the known effect of the manipulation. This type of disjunction of self-reported mental content (subjective intentions and motivations) occurring independently of the manipulation is commonplace in experimental psychology. Therefore, it is not atypical for researchers as "outsiders" to aptly describe these discrepancies as being misattributions on the part of participants.

Misattribution of Agency or Presence

The first portion of this book focused primarily on religious and spiritual beliefs rather than experiences. Beliefs are cognitive attitudes about a given supernatural entity (e.g., "I believe God exists"), whereas a perceived experience is an attribution of contact with entities. The former is not dependent upon the latter. Many people believe that God exists without ever having experienced, say, direct revelation or hearing God's voice (Wilt et al., 2022b). One consequence of adopting an attributional or phenomenological approach to exceptional experiences ("it is spiritual if they say it is") is the difficulty in establishing criteria that clearly distinguish between experiences deemed exceptional as opposed to those deemed ordinary. A believer not normally exposed to charismatic worship who visits a Pentecostal church may describe glossolalia as exceptional in the literal sense of personally atypical, whereas a seasoned Pentecostal worshipper may encounter this on a regular basis and therefore deem it as less exceptional. One shared feature that may help define exceptionality is the perceived tangible presence of a supernatural agent (e.g., God, the Holy Spirit). Accordingly, the current focus will be on experiences in which spiritual agents are perceived to be immanent, concrete (e.g., in close "physical proximity") and—most relevant to the present topic—that involve attributions of personal interaction. In these phenomena, the believer has awareness of the thoughts, desires, and intentions of the spiritual agent. For example, interactive prayer is not directed at a distant God but is perceived as a conversational dialogue (i.e., "God talks back"). Phenomena associated with charismatic or ecstatic worship, as with interactive prayer, feature a high degree of immediacy and emotional intensity. In Christianity, groups such as Pentecostals or holiness traditions feature related phenomena that include attributed immanence or direct experience (e.g., "signs of the Spirit") such as glossolalia or possession (to be discussed below). Likewise, in Islam, traditions such as Sufism have more mystical elements with distinct patterns of ecstatic worship. Again, the present focus will be limited to attributions regarding the immanent presence of person like agents and interactive communication with such agents.

This topic has received extensive coverage by the anthropologist Tanya Luhrmann, notably in her books *When God Talks Back* (2012) and *How God Becomes Real* (2020). Luhrmann describes worshipers in the Christian Renewalist tradition, and others associated with charismatic and Pentecostal denomination—who engage in interactive prayers, including speaking to God, and receiving responses via intuitions, impressions, images, feelings, and life-events. These perceptions are not only tangible and regularly occurring (e.g., hearing God say "I will always be with you" while in the car) but also bidirectional, like a conversation between two persons (e.g., "imagine God as your best friend"). A related phenomenon is the experience of receiving personal knowledge or insight from spiritual agents in the form of revelation. For example, the Church of Jesus Christ of Latter-Day Saints ("LDS" or "Mormon") has a tradition of prophesy in which members listen for a "voice" or "whisperings" of the Holy Spirit. They may perceive their thoughts and feelings as being revelatory of divine wisdom such as personal instructions for decision-making. In psychological terms, these believers are having an internal experience, but attributing this to an external origin. These experiences may also be followed by efforts to validate the authenticity of the experience using criteria such as the believer's degree of emotionality, subjective certainty, or other tests of discernment.

Social Psychological and Cognitive Influences on Attributions of Presence

As discussed in the earlier section on attribution theory, the most robust predictors of religious attribution stem from the perceiver's background—chiefly, frequent exposure to R/S concepts that establish norms (e.g., social modeling). Experiences of immanent presence and agency are more common in some religious traditions than others. Those who are socialized in certain groups or denominations have often been exposed to family and peers also having interactions with R/S agents and have had opportunities to "practice" these experiences such as in worship. Whereas 24 percent of mainline Protestant Christians "receive definite answers to specific prayer requests" at least once a month, roughly twice as many (46 percent) members of evangelical churches report the same (Pew Research Center, 2008). In a survey of Pentecostal believers, 85 percent reported at least sometimes feeling "the unmistakable presence of God during prayer" (Poloma & Green, 2010). Similarly, roughly half (54 percent) of Pentecostals and 39 percent of Charismatics report receiving direct revelations from God (Pew Research Center, 2006). Thus, for these groups, exceptional experiences are not exceptional in the sense of being rare; they may even be commonplace.

As we saw in the earlier section on attribution theory, group differences are similarly evident in patterns of causal attributions, with fundamentalist, evangelical, and charismatic (as opposed to moderate or mainline) groups attributing a wider range of occurrences to supernatural causation. Another general pattern observed across different surveys is that, whereas references to experiences described in less tangible terms (i.e., God hears prayers, Jesus loves you) are endorsed by wide range of believers, those described in more tangible and specific terms (e.g., hearing the literal voice of God, feeling the Holy Spirit in the room) are less commonly endorsed. Clearly, one's religious background has a strong determinative effect on the likelihood of exceptional experiences, and this effect is greatest for the most concrete, dramatic, or vivid experiences.

Just as individually varying cognitive and personality traits are predictive of general R/S beliefs, these same traits are also associated with exceptional experiences. For example, as discussed in Chapter 1, perceived supernatural engagement is more common among those who have a more intuitive and experiential cognitive thinking style and less common for those with an analytic cognitive style (Wilt et al., 2022b). As documented in Luhrmann's work, two traits may have particular relevance for a range of exceptional experiences: Absorption and Porosity. Absorption refers to the tendency to become immersed in one's own thoughts and feelings and is not only associated with religiosity/spirituality but also anomalous and mystical experiences, fantasy, and trance-like states, hearing voices, and paranormal phenomena (Levin et al., 1998; Luhrmann et al., 2021; Luhrmann et al., 2010). Porosity refers to the extent to which minds and mental content are viewed as private and bounded versus publicly accessible and uncontained. Viewing the mind as highly porous entails believing that thoughts, emotions, and wishes can have tangible real-world effects, such as that others can read one's own mind or that one can make one's thoughts available to others. Luhrmann et al. suggest that societies and cultures vary in the degree to which minds are seen as porous, but individual variation in porosity also exists within societies. Absorption and Porosity are distinct and complementary constructs in that the latter refers to cognitive beliefs concerning how the mind works, whereas the former is an experiential personal orientation that influences the way that thoughts and mental events feel.

As we have seen in the earlier chapters with reference to ordinary religious belief, dispositional factors do not produce R/S attributions in isolation but rather interact with situational and contextual factors. Likewise, non-ordinary experiences are also the product of the interaction between individual predispositions and socio-cultural contexts. Luhrmann (2012) describes the ability to engage in interactive prayer as a consequence of "talent" (e.g., high in absorption), as well as "training." This training can occur via socialization within specific religious traditions (mentioned above). In the previous chapter we saw how conformity and emotional contagion effects can shape the specific construal of an aroused state via contact with others in a social group. Role theory posits that religious concepts such as stories from sacred texts or shared traditions provide models that create perceptual sets such that when a religious frame of reference is activated, there is a template for exceptional experiences (Wikstrom, 1987). For example, Christian pentecostal traditions refer to depictions in the Biblical book of Acts of early church apostles filled with the Holy Spirit as a scriptural basis for their practices. Likewise, group norms create scripts that form cognitive expectancies for beliefs and behaviors. As predicted by emotional attribution theory (Schachter & Singer, 1962), when worshipers are experiencing a state of emotional arousal, these norms have an even greater influence (Holm, 1987).

One basic mechanism of social influence is the network of associations linked to R/S concepts in believer's minds (i.e., "schema"). Activation of one concept can trigger other related concepts and change the threshold required for experiences, such as when religious believers are more likely to perceive agency after exposure to religious primes (Van Elk et al., 2016). Associations between concepts are internalized as religious schemas quite early in life, making some concepts more plausible and easily believed when they are later encountered. For instance, children aged five-to-six years old from religious backgrounds are more likely to judge a protagonist in religious stories to be a real person, whereas secular children with no religious exposure judge the protagonist in religious stories to be fictional (Corriveau et al., 2015). Therefore, even though many people regardless of their R/S orientation will encounter anomalous experiences in their lives, those from a background where interaction with spiritual agents is normative are more likely to interpret such ambiguous stimuli as religiously relevant.

As mentioned in earlier chapters, individual traits interact with social learning history, creating a potentiating effect. This explains why those high in trait absorption are particularly likely to perceive potential agents or sensed presences provided the proper conditions (Erickson-Davis et al., 2021; Maij et al., 2019). The threshold of perceptual criteria used to distinguish experiences that are merely unusual from those deemed exceptional is lower for those with high levels of these traits and with a social learning history marked by exposure to these concepts. For example, evangelical Christians report rates of hallucinations that are intermediate as compared to nonreligious controls (low rates) and those with psychosis (high rates), indicating that particular religious backgrounds can contribute to labeling a given experience as anomalous (Davies et al., 2001). The attribution of a given experience as exceptional is therefore a product of ambiguous stimuli, encountered in a situation with high arousal, by a mind prepared with a religious expectational set. The sum of these factors can increase the likelihood of mistakenly attributing stimuli as being from one source that originated from another (i.e., a source monitoring error; Bentall, 1990). Repeated misattributions also create a feedback loop in which prior beliefs establish an expectational set and later experiences further confirm this set. In the present case, beliefs about supernatural entities (e.g., "spirits are communicating with us") increase the likelihood that environmental stimuli will be perceived as spiritually relevant, which in turn shapes perceptions in a confirmatory manner, reinforcing the schematic network of beliefs in a re-iterative process (Exline & Pait, 2021).

A greater propensity to attribute exceptional experiences as a function of trait and contexts, however, does not necessarily indicate the presence of *mis*attributions. Prior work has often descriptively characterized the phenomenon of greater agency detection or sensed presences on the part of some individuals in certain contexts without taking a position either way on the actual ontological referent. Perhaps the ability of some individuals to detect agency with greater frequency than others could even represent a heightened ability—a spiritual perspicacity. For example, Barrett and Church (2013) argue that differences in agency detection between believers and atheists could just as well be interpreted as a distortion by the latter (epistemic "beer goggles" or taking a "stupid drug") rather than as over-activity or projection among the former because the reliability of the belief-forming functions cannot be independently determined. Taves (2009) suggests that observers adopting an Etic perspective have no criteria for judging whether a sensory perception authentically reproduces the source of an experience. Luhrmann (2012) describes the interactive prayer framework consisting of trait abilities refined by training as "... fully compatible with both secular and supernaturalist understandings of God" (p. 223). She states: "Does this mean that the perception of God is always no more than the imagination? No, no more than the failure to hear God's voice is the mark of someone who is not devout. If the supernatural is real, it reaches to each according to that person's skills and style" (p. 222).

However, at least two lines of evidence argue against a neutral characterization, suggesting that the term *mis*attribution is apt. First, the individual traits associated with exceptional experiences (absorption, porosity, and others), are themselves associated with biased perception, such as over-attribution, rather than perceptual accuracy. At the level of basic constructs, absorption and porosity share content with other constructs known to produce such inaccuracy. Porous ideation—the view that thoughts, wishes, emotions, prayers can have tangible effects such as being accessible to other entities—shares content overlap with measures of schizotypic ideation, hallucination-proneness, and ontological confusion. Recall from Chapter 1 that schizotypy (a trait also related to some dimensions of religiosity; Wlodarski & Pearce, 2016) refers to magical thinking, unusual experiences, and ideas of reference as well as increased attributions of mental states to God. Luhrmann et al.'s measure of porosity taps the endorsement of similar beliefs such as that spirits can read our thoughts and that one's thoughts can go out into the world. These beliefs are identical to items on the unusual perceptual experiences dimension of the Schizotypic Personality Questionnaire (Raine, 1991; "I often hear a voice speaking my thoughts aloud," "I have seen things invisible to other people," "My thoughts are sometimes so strong that you can almost hear them"). Likewise, measures of trait hallucination proneness (Launay & Slade, 1981) include item content such as "My thoughts seem as real as actual events in my life," "I see shadows and shapes when there is nothing there"). Measures of ontological confusions (Lindeman & Aarnio, 2007) assess beliefs that mental or immaterial properties can interact with the physical world resulting in objective, material outcomes (e.g., "prayers can heal physical ailments"). Therefore, porosity content overlaps with content from constructs known to produce perceptual misattributions.

Beyond shared content, experiments using objective target criteria also indicate that absorptive and porous traits are associated with perceptual inaccuracy. In signal detection terms, they do not produce "correct hits" but rather "false positives." A "false positive" in this case is perceiving a stimulus to be present when it not, as evidenced by studies that use placebo controls or random stimuli as criteria (i.e., where a correct response is a rejection). Those high in absorption are more likely to perceive signal where there is only noise (Lifshitz et al., 2019). For example, Granqvist et al. (2005) tested participants in a "God helmet" paradigm, where they wore a brain stimulation device in a study ostensibly on the "influence of complex, weak magnetic fields on experiences and feeling states." Although there was no effect of any manipulation of magnetic fields in the helmet, participants high in absorption were more likely to report sensed presence and mystical experiences. Likewise, in other studies, individuals with high levels of trait schizotypy and hallucination proneness showed greater over-detection of non-agentic objects, made more mistakes on source monitoring tasks such as misattributing internal events as being externally derived, perceived meaning in random visual stimuli, and displayed greater apophenic over-detection (Brookwell et al., 2013; Gray et al., 2011; Partos et al., 2016; Wlodarski & Pearce, 2016). Thus, traits that predispose people to exceptional experiences are associated with biased perception, not more discerning perception.

In addition to illustrating the role of trait absorption in perceptual over-detection, experimental findings such as Granqvist et al.'s helmet study also illustrate the importance of expectational and social influences that interact with traits to create misattributions. Several studies suggest that sensed presences and other agentic phenomena result from the interaction of individual traits within a context that introduces a preparatory or expectational mindset. In experimental paradigms, this can consist of procedures that provide a plausible rationale or conduit for experiences, such as the sham God helmet apparatus or virtual reality goggles. In sham God helmet conditions (i.e., essentially, a placebo with sensory deprivation qualities) a substantial proportion of participants report exceptional phenomena, including sensed presences, although some studies indicate that only those participants who identify as being more spiritual and high in absorption are particularly likely to do so (Andersen et al., 2014; Maij & van Elk, 2018; Maij et al., 2019). It appears that high absorption produces a greater responsiveness to situational cues inducing expectations of the extraordinary.

Virtual reality paradigms also provide a plausible method that successfully induces false agency detection in substantial number of participants (Tratner et al., 2020). Merely suggesting that participants are likely to encounter active agents in a virtual environment is sufficient to increase the likelihood of false detections (Andersen et al., 2019), but high absorption predicts greater immersion and higher levels of perceived "presence" while using virtual reality (Kober & Neuper, 2013). For example, in one study, the visual representation component of virtual reality enhanced participants' sense of responsive interaction with presences, but again, trait absorption was associated with an even greater sense of presence (Erickson-Davis et al., 2021). Misattributions of agency have also been produced by other paradigms providing an expectational context. Swiney and Sousa (2013) informed participants that an experimental procedure featuring a (sham) headpiece could connect their mind to that of a person in another room. The majority of participants (72 percent) misattributed agency to the other person as transferring a thought to their mind at least once, particularly thoughts of negative valence. These studies all suggest in different ways that attributions of unusual experiences are the result of situational and expectational influences interacting with dispositional predispositions in the production of exceptional phenomenology. It is noteworthy that these artificial, laboratory-induced experiences are subjectively perceived to be as robust and long-lasting as other, more spontaneous, "genuine" experiences (Andersen et al., 2014). In other words, experiences produced by manipulated expectational sets are indistinguishable from those labeled as spontaneous from the perspective of participants.

Misattributions of Personal Volition: Glossolalia and Possession

Some exceptional experiences involve attributions of alterations in personal volition (i.e., a sense of ownership) along with the additional component of perceptions of external agency. Phenomena such as glossolalia (tongue-speaking) and related spiritual signifiers (e.g., "holy laughter," "slain in the Spirit") feature behaviors that occur without a clear sense of volition; rather, causality is attributed to external agency. In the case of possession or channeling, believers perceive that their own consciousness has been displaced by an external agent, evincing a disrupted sense of personal ownership. The attribution of external agency in glossolalia and possession shares features with some interactive prayer experiences when the latter also involves subjective reductions in volitional control (i.e., a "passivity experience"). For example, Luhrmann relates the experiences of one Renewalist prayer receiving images from the Holy Spirit in which the subject reported "... my mind is just a screen that they're flashed on. So it's more like watching for the images rather than generating images, I think. Somebody else is controlling that clicker" (2012: 137). Although these phenomena have distinguishing features, chiefly in the phenomenological content of believers' attributions, the current focus will be on the key shared feature of volitional misattribution. The central question will be: When individuals experience behaviors featuring a perceived loss of volition such as glossolalia or possession, what psychological mechanisms account for the causal misattribution to an external source?

The Illusion of Conscious Will and Volitional Misattribution

Before examining evidence pertaining to the formation of volitional attributions in religious and spiritual contexts, a more fundamental issue relates to our general conscious awareness of personal ownership. Rather than dichotomous attributions to either internal or external causation (i.e., behaviors seen as being either "caused by me" or "caused by something else"), many instances represent a volitional middle ground of unclear causation. Likewise, some R/S experiences are also perceived to be a mixture of internal ("I did this") and external ("God did this") causal influences. This illustrates a hydraulic-like relationship between the degree of conscious awareness of personal volition and the attributed source of behaviors. As conscious ownership of behavior decreases, attributions to external causality increase ("If it seems like it's not me, it must be God"). This is partially attributable to the stereotypic assumptions individuals make regarding possible reasons that explain how their behavior could occur in the absence of volition. As Boyer (2013) states: "once you feel that a particular thought did not come from your own cogitations, the conjectural reflective interpretation, that it came from another agent, is considerably strengthened" (p. 353). In effect, nature abhors a causal "attributional vacuum," which becomes filled by external agency.

It is not unusual that a sense of personal ownership of our actions does not always accompany their actual causation. In *The Illusion of Conscious Will* (2017), Daniel Wegner uses a two-dimensional model to describe how the actual origin of behavior—the "doing" (as opposed to passivity or "not doing") is independent from the feeling of volition ("willed" versus "not willed"). In cases where these two coincide, one feels an intention to perform a behavior and the behavior occurs, or in the opposite case behavioral inaction or passivity is accompanied by a perceived lack of volition. However, as mentioned throughout this book, there are many instances in which something causally influences our behavior but is not so perceived. This can be seen in experiments where subliminal priming and implicit stimuli shape participants' behavior without their awareness. This "doing but not willing" is often accompanied by misattributions of causality such as confabulating an incorrect explanatory rationale (Bargh & Chartrand, 1999; Nisbett & Wilson, 1977). As seen in Chapter 1, dual processing theory explains that many, if not most of our behaviors originate in Type 1 processes and involve behaviors that are automatic, occurring without volitional, deliberative Type 2 process input. Even some actions elicited by explicit manipulation of brain functions (e.g., electro-magnetic stimulation of motor centers) can be misattributed by subjects as consciously chosen (Brasil-Neto et al., 1992). In these cases, "having behaved but not willed" produces the belief that they must have had a reason for acting.

Hypnosis is a phenomenon in which subjects perform actions in response to suggestive cues without the feeling of volition. It also illustrates another feature of the volition attribution process—a mixture of conscious and unconscious awareness constituting a continuum of ownership—one that is malleable. Wegner (2017) describes how action sequences that begin with a degree of deliberation can become automatized and thereafter perceived as being more passive. This suggests that hypnosis, rather than representing either—at one end of a continuum of consciousness—a trance state featuring no conscious volition, or at the other end of the continuum, deliberate "faking," is better understood as representing a volitional middle ground state of self-induction. The sociocognitive model of hypnosis and dissociative states (Spanos, 1994) has yielded evidence indicating that a reduced sense of volition results from an expectational set in which participants "decide" (again, with a mixture of conscious and unconscious awareness) to cede behavioral ownership to an external source (i.e., the hypnotist's suggestions).

Other instances of behaviors performed without an accompanying sense of volition include phenomena caused by the ideomotor effect involving unintentional subtle reflexive muscle movements. The facilitated communication technique was developed in 1990s to assist nonverbal patients in typing on a keyboard or letter pad. However, although many facilitators assumed that they were providing solely physical support, in fact they were inadvertently biasing the typed content by guiding the patients' arm motions (Wegner et al., 2003). Related phenomena such as Ouija boards, table turning, and channeling of spirit messages produced via automatic writing are all behaviors that typically occur on the part of those who lack a sense of volition or conscious realization that they have influenced the process. As we will see below, when individuals view themselves performing behaviors in the absence of volition, they are more likely to misattribute causation to outside agency.

Returning to R/S phenomena, Wegner suggests that behaviors such as glossolalia and possession/trance also involve a similar fluctuating sense of agency, such that initial deliberation shifts over to eventual automaticity. As with other exceptional phenomena, individual difference factors such as absorptive personality traits predispose those most constitutionally adept at "going with the flow" to perform actions or rituals with a decreased sense of volition. Indeed, self-reports from those practicing glossolalia refer to a range of volitional control. Some with a greater skill level report tongue speaking spontaneously with very little effort, while others exert a greater degree of deliberation, at least at first ("fake it til you make it"; Brahinsky, 2020). This range of volition is linked to the formation of attributions regarding the originating causal source. On the one hand, glossolalics report that their experience of speaking in tongues originates externally as a gift from the Holy Spirit. At the same time,

Brahinsky (2020) reports "nearly every person ... described a period in which they deliberately made nonsense sounds .... They 'pretended'" (p. 52). The shift from pretending or consciously producing an experience to having a "genuine" experience (i.e., attributing cause to external agency) is a process involving a mixture of predisposing traits together with social influence, producing behaviors deliberately cultivated with practice.

Glossolalia: Social Learning, Contagion, and Role Theory

Non-linguistic speech or glossolalia is often interpreted as a manifestation of spiritual presence. In contemporary western Christianity, it is commonly practiced in Renewalist, Pentecostal, and Charismatic denominations. Fifty-seven percent of Pentecostals report at least some experience with glossolalia in contrast to 25 percent of Catholics and 16 percent of Mainline Protestants (Pew Research Center, 2008). However, glossolalia also occurs in many non-Western cultures, including indigenous or Shamanic religions (e.g., "spirit language"). It is also important to keep in mind that glossolalia is not a unitary phenomenon. It can be practiced individually or (more commonly) in social contexts such as worship services. In private prayer it may be practiced at a relatively low level of emotional intensity and with a high degree of self-awareness, or it may occur in a communal setting with high excitation and relatively less awareness (Grady & Loewenthal, 1997). In contemporary Pentecostal Christianity, glossolalia can co-occur with other behavioral manifestations such as being "drunk" or "slain in the Spirit," and "holy laughter."

There are numerous aspects associated with glossolalic speech that contribute to the attributional transfer of ownership over one's actions, leading to the perception that one is speaking under the influence of external agency. As with sensed presence and interactive prayer phenomena, attributions of volitional control represent a product of individual predisposing factors, elicited by contextual circumstances, and reinforced by social learning, largely via expectational cues. In the previous chapter, social conformity influences operating within groups shape not only external behaviors, but also internalized beliefs. As with other exceptional experiences, glossolalia involves behaviors and associated emotionality spreading throughout a group in a process of social contagion.

Social contagion is more likely to occur in conditions of attributional ambiguity when individuals look to others in their social environment for cues on how to behave. Other social contagion phenomena such as mass hysteria represent secular analogues to exceptional spiritual experiences. Under certain conditions, individuals can experience unusual symptoms without any known physical explanation that spread through communities via social contact. A recent example was the 2011 outbreak of Tourette-like tics and spasms among high school students in LeRoy New York that eventually affected over a dozen people. In this cluster of cases, it is likely that some individual students initially suffered conversion disorders caused by psychological stressors that produced physical manifestations, after which the symptoms spread via mass hysteria (Bartholomew et al., 2012). A less dramatic, and more benign example of social contagion is the practice of group "laughing yoga." First started in India by Dr. Matan Kataria, this involves the use of breathing exercises to induce a contagion of laughter for the purposes of health benefits and mood enhancement. Practitioners initially exert effort to produce forced laughter, but eventually in the presence of others, the laughter becomes spontaneous. The experience becomes internalized when members report that things start to seem more amusing. Such examples illustrate that behaviors and emotions are shaped via social mechanisms without the perception of volitional control. Obviously, these non-spiritual examples of social contagion differ from glossolalia and similar behaviors in spiritual contexts in that the former do not involve causation attributed to external agency as do the latter. Those experiencing contagious laughter in yoga groups may not make any external attribution at all, viewing their behavior as a spontaneous reaction to the context, whereas worshipers engaging in "holy laughter" may perceive themselves to be passive conduits for the Holy Spirit.

The social mechanisms influencing glossolalia span a range of volitional control, from relatively automatic and implicit (e.g., conformity to group norms), to those requiring more effort (e.g., explicit imitation and training). The majority of glossolalic individuals report having first spoken in a group context rather than alone (although some subsequently go on to speak both alone and in groups; Holm, 1987). The socialization and enculturation of religious practices involve exposure to models, some of which are present and tangible (i.e., other group members), and others described in scriptural texts or oral traditions. In Pentecostal Christianity, individuals gain knowledge of Biblical stories such as the epiphany of the Apostles in the book of Acts, which provides an ur-description of tongue speaking. Role theory (Wikstrom, 1987) suggests that these "scripts" create an expectational set for subsequent experiences, providing guidelines and explanations for behavior. Individuals may consciously identify themselves with a specific role based on scripture or on someone in their group and behave accordingly. Alternatively, initiation of specific behavioral sequences may occur on an implicit level of consciousness, triggered by relatively strong "demand cues." The rituals of Pentecostal worship are replete with emotional intensity, music, dancing, singing, and other physical activities. Rituals such as "anointing," "laying on of hands," or "altar calls" serve as scripted cues that certain experiences are expected to occur (in operant learning terminology, these represent "discriminative stimuli"). As described earlier, emotional attribution theory states that the labeling of our own emotions is partly socially derived, and in that sense, is also a manifestation of social contagion. The participants in the classic Schachter and Singer (1962) experiments, were in a state of arousal (literally produced by an "adrenaline rush") and were exposed to social cues from others, leading them to attribute their own emotions in accordance with the proximal environment.

As with interactive prayer, the most relevant social factors that influence attributions of external agency in glossolalia are those that establish an expectational set. A reduced sense of volitional control can be produced by a plausible context and the expectation that behaviors will be altered by spiritual influences. This can be seen in phenomena similar to glossolalia (but lacking a spiritual contextualization) where the sense of volition can be experimentally manipulated. Phenomena such as delusions of passivity and alien control (e.g., thought insertion, alien hand syndrome) are those in which subjects perceive self-generated actions as not personally willed, but instead caused by an external source. Although these sometimes result from neurological conditions, they can also be induced by procedures featuring suggestive cues such as with hypnosis (Blakemore et al., 2003). For example, Olson et al. (2016) found that participants who were led to believe that a (mock) neuroimaging machine could read or influence their thoughts, reported feeling decreased personal control, instead perceiving that an unknown source was directing their responses. In another experiment using a moveable hand model, conditions were manipulated so that participants reported a dissociation in their sense of bodily ownership (i.e., perceiving that fake hand was their own) as well as in the sense of agency (the impression that they controlled the movements of the fake hand; Kalckert & Ehrsson, 2012). Similarly, the phenomenon of automatic writing—analogous to the verbal content in tongue speaking in the attribution that one is channeling spirits, can be induced by suggestion. Walsh et al. (2014) used a mock brain scanning apparatus in conjunction with hypnotic suggestion, leading participants to expect a loss of volition ("an engineer will insert a sentence into your mind").

This produced the automatic writing phenomenon with the combination of reduced sense of control accompanied by the attribution of volition to external control. These and other similar findings demonstrate that shifting the sense of ownership from internal to external sources can often be achieved merely by providing an expectational set with a suggestive component.

Other mechanisms contributing to glossolalia feature more explicit deliberation, including social-modeling and practice. Although glossolalia is often seen as a definitive sign of spiritual presence, the ability to produce non-linguistic speech can easily be learned by novices. Interestingly, this pseudo-speech appears to originate in the same brain regions as those involved in any other non-linguistic vocalizations (e.g., "babbling"). Using PET scans of the brains of glossolalics, Newberg et al. (2006) identified decreased activity in the prefrontal cortex, reflecting weakened executive control over vocalization. Spanos et al. (1986) trained naive college students to fluently speak in tongues using a combination of observation, direct imitation, and coached practice sessions. Part of the training protocol instructed novices to simply draw a breath and make sounds until the end of the breath. Spanos et al. found that fully 70 percent of those with minimal training could eventually produce tongue-speaking that was indistinguishable, as judged by blind raters, from that of spontaneous speakers. The socially derived nature of glossolalia is also evident in the distinct local "dialects" that are spoken in different groups and churches. Analysis of the phonological properties of glossolalia has indicated systematic variation as a function of the group into which the individual is socialized (Samarin, 1972). In this sense, the actual utterances produced in glossolalia are not themselves objectively exceptional but rather, it is the attribution of external agency that differentiates spontaneous glossolalia from deliberative speech.

Many of the same psycho-social mechanisms that produce glossolalia and related spiritual signifiers play similar roles in possession/trance phenomenon. However, the two phenomena differ somewhat in that possession includes a greater attributional emphasis on identity dissociation in which the subject's personal volition is perceived to be temporarily displaced by a specific external agent. Possession is also considered a mental illness, although diagnosis can depend upon the cultural context. According to diagnostic criteria, Dissociative Trance Disorder involves a disruption of identity and altered awareness of surroundings that is perceived as being controlled by an external supernatural power. However, the diagnosis only applies to those who experience an unusual involuntary event that is neither a regularly occurring activity, nor part of a broadly accepted religious practice. Consequently, those whose cultural traditions do not regard possession as pathological and who experience it on a regular basis would be excluded from diagnosis. Like glossolalia, possession occurs worldwide in cultures as diverse as Haitian voudou and indigenous Shaman healers, although not always with the negative connotation that possession has in the contemporary West. This ubiquity suggests that there may even be a predisposition among some to readily experience a diminishment of personal volition during rituals accompanied by an openness to perceptions of external control. Those who are particularly adept may be granted higher status as spiritual conduits.

In contemporary western Christianity, possession phenomena disproportionately appear in Pentecostal and Charismatic denominations. It often features in a constellation of broader beliefs such as "spiritual warfare" concepts in which demons are thought to be responsible for a wide range of negative effects, not limited to possession. For example, among the Renewalist interactive prayers documented by Luhrmann (2012), some considered themselves "prayer warriors" who engage with demonic agents. Spiritual warfare can involve treating victims of possession with exorcisms or "deliverance." Among members of these groups, psychological difficulties such as mental illness, immorality, or unacceptable thoughts and actions are often attributed to the influence of demons. For example, rather than personal ownership of one's anger, one could describe being possessed with a demonic rage. This type of framing again illustrates that personal volition and ownership are being externalized to outside agency. As with other forms of volition, there are blended volitional states such as when believers attribute that their own personal sin or weaknesses of faith rendered them vulnerable to demonic possession.

Also similar to glossolalia, possession is a phenomenon in which the "role" of a possessed individual is socially constructed. This occurs through a mixture of scriptural references, conformity to social models and contextual expectations, and interactive responses to suggestions from other believers, exorcists, and deliverance ministers (Spanos et al., 1985). In the latter cases, exorcists who interact with individuals possessed by demons in religious gatherings are akin to secular stage hypnotists in that they are an authoritative source of suggestive cues (Spanos & Gottlieb, 1979). Those in the surrounding social milieu provide directions and reinforcements to the possessed subject who then responds in certain stereotypical ways in conformity with this script. For example, when the exorcist "names" demons, the subject, following the script, is cued to speak with a malevolent voice or to respond with violent paroxysms.

The Compensatory Functions of Attributions to External Volition

Just as R/S beliefs perform compensatory functions in response to epistemic and existential deficits (as discussed in Chapter 3), exceptional phenomena such as glossolalia and possession can also be motivated by deficits when psychological needs are threatened. First, just as increased conviction in one's beliefs compensates for uncertainty, likewise the tangibility of exceptional experiences acts as a belief-bolstering mechanism. Much as engagement in costly rituals is self-validating ("This means I am truly committed"), so dramatic behaviors such as glossolalia serve as "bridge burning" actions (Hine, 1969). When these experiences are displayed in social settings, this adds a performative quality that consensually validates beliefs ("If we are doing these things publicly, they must be valid"). In interviews with glossolalics, Brahinsky (2020) found that many practitioners reported feelings of skepticism or ontological anxiety about their beliefs. Brahinsky suggests that the manifestation of intense bodily sensations and hard-to-deny physical experiences are intended to show that there are no plausible explanations other than the reality of the supernatural (p. 49). This functional account of exceptional experience shares features with principles of cognitive consistency, dissonance reduction, and self-perception theories. In the case of possession, if an individual has a positive view of themselves as having benign intentions ("I'm a good person," "I don't rock the boat"), any appearance of negative thoughts and behaviors ("I am enraged," "I can be fierce") produces dissonance. One way to reduce such dissonance is to deny responsibility for negative thoughts and behaviors by reassigning ownership to an external agent (Gosling et al., 2006). Socially learned scripts, such as those described above, promote a volitional transfer onto negative agents, thus reducing dissonance ("It's not my fault. A demon is causing me to have bad thoughts").

Motivational elements are also operative in the relationship between exceptional R/S experiences and some forms of psychopathology. Although the practices of glossolalia and other manifestations of spirits are not themselves necessarily pathological, evidence indicates that possession phenomena are associated with exposure to trauma (Hecker et al., 2015). One interpretation of this association is that possession represents a response to, or an expression of psycho-social distress. Anthropological and sociological theories suggest that possession/trance phenomena can reduce tension and allow those who lack social agency or power, or who are marginalized to express discontent

(Ward, 1980). In repressive environments, socially unacceptable or transgressive behaviors can be openly displayed without repercussion. As seen in behaviors generally associated with dissociative experiences (i.e., in which aspects of identity or memory are altered), the attribution of responsibility to external sources (e.g., aspects of one's personality to demonic spirits) displaces blame for negative thoughts and behaviors (Spanos et al., 1985).

Even outside of exceptional experiences, it is common for many Pentecostal Christians to attribute their negative thoughts (e.g., bad decisions, temptations) to external agents such as Satan (Ray et al., 2015). The attribution of mental illness symptoms to diabolical spirits and demonic possession is more common among those with charismatic, fundamentalist, or Pentecostal backgrounds compared to mainstream religious groups (Spanos & Moretti, 1988). The discourse and rhetoric within some charismatic churches often imply that mental illnesses are caused by not only a lack of proper faith, but also negative spiritual powers ("My doubting has provided Satan with the opportunity to strike"). Whereas those with secular worldviews may describe their symptoms as manifestations of mental illness such as depression, the same symptom pattern may be described in some religious groups as evidence of "spiritual warfare" (McCloud, 2015). Commonly used criteria for demonic affliction are indistinguishable from symptoms of mental illness, again promoting the externalization of culpability (Kraft, 2016).

Although possession/trance phenomena have been thought to represent an outlet or means of expression for those with stress and trauma, there is evidence that promoting the externalization of responsibility and volition itself can be problematic. The adoption of an attributional framework in which thoughts and feelings are porous (i.e., accessible to, or influenced by external agents) can have an over-pathologizing effect. Just as absorption and porosity lead to perceptual over-detection in which ambiguous stimuli are seen as having meaning, so individuals' internal thoughts and emotions may be viewed as having great spiritual significance. Rather than "a thought popped into my head" or "I had an emotional reaction," this may be viewed as "God was telling me something." Individuals are encouraged to view relatively benign, sub-clinical phenomena (e.g., occasional anxiety and sadness) as reflecting spiritual struggle. As a result, sexual arousal to pornography becomes attributed to "pornography demons," problems with substance abuse can be seen as necessitating an exorcism of the "demon of alcoholism," and negative feelings about a situation can reveal "spiritual darkness." Although those reporting possession phenomena may use the experience as an idiom to express distress, there is evidence that adopting this attributional framework can have iatrogenic effects on mental health. In one longitudinal study, the belief in demons was not only one of the strongest (negative) predictors of mental health but demonic beliefs at an earlier point in time predicted lower mental health later, indicating a causal influence (Nie & Olson, 2016). Likewise, if individuals are suffering from serious mental illness, external attributions can lead to an avoidance of taking personal responsibility by seeking proper professional treatment (Pietkiewicz et al., 2021).

Exceptional Experiences, Testing, and Discernment

The engagement with experiences such as interactive prayer, glossolalia, and possession is motivated by the desire for the tangible and undeniable. Such experiences play a role in public testimonies as dispositive, faith-bolstering exemplars ("One can no longer doubt," "Only God could have produced that"). Still, even fervent believers concede that there are a range of ontological interpretations for exceptional experiences. Identifying the specific meanings of inner speech and imagistic prayer, as Luhrmann (2012) describes, is something congregants "worry about, debate about, and come to different conclusions about" (p. 60). Therefore, believers have developed informal tests to help distinguish genuine spiritual content from that which is self-generated. Similarly, the process known in evangelical Christianity as "discernment" refers to the ability to distinguish between spiritual phenomena resulting from desired agents such as God and the Holy Spirit as opposed to that arriving from false, demonic spirits.

Content-based criteria are used to test whether experiential insight or messages from interactive prayer are compatible with scripture, doctrine, or orthodox teachings. Luhrmann (2012) describes how Renewalist prayers advised members to closely study the Bible to "… recognize the kinds of things God says and when he says them" (p. 159). Luhrmann's interactive prayers also looked for signs and portents in the pattern of events from their own lives. Those who strove to heighten their inner senses did not believe that life events should be dismissed as random coincidence, but instead "they could recognize that the event was something God was using to speak to them about their lives" (p. 56). These signs could include anything from a well-timed phone call, flipping to a relevant page in the Bible, sudden weeping, or seeing a full moon.

Another type of spiritually validating sign includes the physical sequelae of experiences such as bodily reactions or impressive feats. In Brahinsky's

(2020) interviews with possession/ trance phenomena believers, they reported differentiating the demonic from the secular (e.g., mental distress) by referring to signs such as vomiting, agitation when confronting the sacred, super-strength, personality changes, and the like. Alternatively, testing criteria can refer to subjective, internal experiences such as certain emotions, dream content, or peculiar thoughts. Luhrmann's prayers often prioritized images that appeared suddenly or "popped" into their heads. This is similar to criteria used among LDS/ Mormon believers seeking to validate personal revelation. The former LDS president Gordon B. Hinckley described listening to a "small still voice" (Lattin, 1997). In LDS literature and scripture this is also described as whisperings, or feelings that arrive suddenly or forcefully, accompanied by sensations of "burning in the bosom" and a peaceful feeling that serves as a further witness that what one heard is right. When uncertainty is felt regarding the validity of experiences, believers seek consensual validation from others in their group. As Luhrmann states, "… the community stood in for God when God seemed distant and unreal" (2012: 79). Proper interpretations of messages and images are discussed and debated with others in the group in a process of epistemically winnowing true from false content.

Many who use these methods of validation and testing acknowledge that the criteria are inherently ambiguous; nonetheless, the ability to successfully deploy them is viewed as a matter of skill or competence that can be honed via training. "With experience one can become more expert in applying the rules and discerning the divine presence" (Luhrmann, 2012: 60). However, despite their perceived usefulness in distinguishing that which is genuine from that which is false, these methods rely on psychological mechanisms that are inherently biased. As seen in earlier chapters pertaining to general religious beliefs, the process of attribution is beset by numerous cognitive and affective limitations on introspection. This is even more true of affect-laden experiences because of the role they play in worldview maintenance, obviously a highly motivated process. As predicted by compensatory models pertaining to the functional role of religion (Chapter 3), the greater the desire for a tangible experience, the more individuals will be convinced of the reality of their experience. Heuristics and biases, even those not involving spiritual content, are similarly affected by high levels of emotionality such as when dramatic experiences produce availability heuristic errors (i.e., more vivid experiences become more memorable) or in the case of affect bias in which feelings override rational decision-making processes (discussed in more detail below).

Even validity tests and discernment methods that ostensibly use objective criteria such as scriptural fidelity are prone to biases. As Luhrmann (2012) relates, rather than validating prayer images with a strict, literal reading of scripture (e.g., "Does it contradict the Bible?") her subjects relied on the Bible only as interpreted within their various churches. Indeed, the believers in her Bible study groups appeared uninterested in any type of higher critical interrogation of scripture (e.g., "Why was the text written this way?"). As we have seen with religious projection (Ross et al., 2012), the *a priori* psychological and ideological biases that influence attributions of "what God would say" also bias the interpretation of scripture (Perry & McElroy, 2020). Therefore, referring to texts and teachings for assistance with the discernment process is likely to devolve into a matter of interpretive subjectivity based on personal ideology or prevailing group opinion.

Likewise, another validity test that would appear to have an epistemically corrective effect is to cross check interactive prayer content with that of others in a form of inter-rater reliability. However, as mentioned earlier regarding group conformity, the mere presence of multiple others does not necessarily have an epistemically corrective effect on individual perceptions (more heads are not always better than one). Rather, the realization that one's own experience differs from that of others can elicit pressure to reconcile contradictions by bringing the former into alignment with the latter (i.e., conformity to the group norm). Because homogeneous groups can further solidify preexisting biases ("groupthink"), even obviously incorrect beliefs will perseverate when consensually validated by like-minded others. The use of groups for validating information only produces greater epistemic accuracy under specific conditions such as having a heterodox membership with a range of beliefs, or enlisting a designated (and, in this case, appropriately named) "devil's advocate" to challenge prevailing consensus interpretations (Janis, 1972).

The practice of using internal thoughts and feelings to test experiential validity is similarly fraught. Luhrmann (2012) describes the Renewalist prayers as questioning whether a given piece of content is or is not something that one would imagine anyway as opposed to something spontaneous or unexpected or determining whether the message provided a feeling of peace. As one prayer stated about the arbiter of her experiences, "I'm asking my unconscious—which is really the Holy Spirit" (p. 83). As we have seen, the malleability of subjective perceptions yields something of a moving target. If the cultivation of an absorptive and porous thinking style invites people to interpret and engage with their own inner lives and to take their intuitions and feelings more seriously, this raises inevitable tensions regarding how serious is too serious, and increases the risk of over-interpretation.

Misattribution of Conversion Experience

Indicators of validity and discernment criteria include not merely temporally brief, specific experiences, but also the broader role played by R/S within a life narrative. The use of personal conversion narratives as evidence for the genuineness of spiritual experiences has deep historical roots. Some of the earliest research in the field of the psychology of religion focused on conversion experiences, including the most dramatic type known variously as the "sudden," "crisis-driven," or "emotional" conversion (Clark, 1929; James, 2003; Starbuck, 1899). The essential features are familiar to many religious groups, containing elements of salvific "Amazing Grace" or "born again"—type experiences. Features include a history of pre-conversion problems such as sinful lifestyle, psychopathology, substance abuse, or a sense of existential meaninglessness. Next, a "turning point" is encountered, or a "hitting bottom" occurs where no earthly solution has successfully alleviated the downward spiral. Then, spiritual powers intervene, followed by the convert undergoing a radical transformation. Such narratives are often publicly shared, constituting the core currency and testimony of believers' faith.

As with other exceptional experiences such as interactive prayer, glossolalia, and possession/trance phenomena, references to conversion experiences as evidential of external agency represent a misattribution of internal psychological dynamics to an external source. It first must be said that objectively substantiating conversions as misattributions is more difficult than the abovementioned exceptional experiences due to the difficulty in conducting controlled testing of contributing factors. There are obvious methodological and ethical issues raised by subjecting beliefs of personal transformation to experimental manipulation. However, several lines of indirect evidence demonstrate that known (non-supernatural) temperamental, situational, and motivational factors predictably influence the external misattribution of conversion experiences. As with other exceptional experiences, those whose personality is marked by traits such as absorption-like hypnotic susceptibility show particularly high likelihood of undergoing intensely emotional religious conversions (Gibbons & De Jarnette, 1972). The substantial influence of background exposure is also observable in the over-representation of certain denominational traditions among converts. In fact, a majority of members of Evangelical Protestant and historically Black Protestant denominations claim that they have had a "born-again experience" compared to a minority of mainline Protestants and Catholics. However, the use of survey items regarding these issues is questionable because many who self-report a born-again experience also claim this term as their group identity (Smidt et al., 2017). In other words, the application of such terms for the purposes of identifying those who have had actual conversion experiences approaches the tautological when used within groups defined by those same concepts. Therefore, caution is warranted when interpreting responses from born-again Christians to questions such as "have you ever had a born-again experience?"

As mentioned in Chapter 3, perhaps the strongest causal evidence of predisposing influences on religious conversion experiences is derived from attachment theory. Experiences of sudden, intense religious changes in response to emotional turmoil are more common among those who also report earlier parental rejection and insensitivity (Granqvist et al., 2007). Research substantiating a connection between religious conversion experiences and attachment-based compensatory predictors is particularly impressive because it includes not only experimental data but also longitudinal relationships between early-appearing traits and later increases in religiosity. For instance, high emotional reactivity at four months of age is predictive of increased religiosity in adolescence (Kagan & Snidman, 2005). Those with insecure parental connections in childhood are more likely later in life to have born-again, emotionally based conversion experiences (Granqvist, 2020). Also, activation via subliminal priming of attachment needs increases believers' views of God as a proximal, available "secure base" figure (Birgegard & Granqvist, 2004). This evidence suggests that emotional conversion experiences are a product not only of life crises, but are also influenced by fundamental traits (i.e., temperament) that substantially precede the conversion experience. This has clear implications for the interpretation of self-reported narratives, which often refer only to proximal circumstances.

As mentioned, conversion stories, which often serve as public testimony regarding the validity of spiritual agency, often feature standard themes. These narratives typically consist of a U-shaped arc with an initial downward trajectory associated with sinfulness or distress that culminates in a crisis and spiritual turning point, followed by an upward trajectory in which relief and peace predominate (Halama, 2015). Among the Renewalist interactive prayers, Luhrmann noticed these crisis-themed stories "... often acquire a local sameness, so that any church seems dense with the same kinds of personal struggles" (p. 7). Conversion narratives overlap with those in spiritually based Twelve-Step recovery groups such as Alcoholics Anonymous, where former addicts relate stories of "hitting bottom" in an arc of fall and redemption (McIntosh & McKeganey, 2000).

Religious role theory is particularly applicable in such cases because of the influence of conversion stories found in scripture or among historical figures. In Christianity, the Biblical Saul/Paul conversion on the road to Damascus story is so influential as to have achieved eponymous status as the "Pauline conversion." Paul's story constitutes an ur-role, containing key features of prior sin and difficulty, sudden dramatic intervention of the divine, and subsequent radical life transformation. Other well-known biographies follow this script, including those of Saint Augustine, Leo Tolstoy, and modern figures such as Malcolm X and George W. Bush (the latter pertaining to his recovery from alcoholism, not his political career). Obviously, given the inherently subjective nature of the conversion process and the reliance on retrospection, it is difficult to apply experimentally controlled methods of scrutiny. However, empirical evidence indicates that, rather than being a result of external spiritual forces, the remarkable similarities among narratives are derivative of underlying psychological motivations.

Conversion narratives are produced by the retrospective re-working of memories that harmonize individual experience with the expected role. In their analysis of narratives, Snow and Philips (1980) found that converts retroactively perceived their lives as being more different pre- versus post-conversion than was actually the case. Encouraged by their religious or social communities, converts amplified evidence of dissatisfaction or crisis to provide a firmer justification for the culminating event. Indeed, a similar observation was made over a century ago by Pratt (1920) "… at least nine of out every ten 'conversion cases' reported in recent questionnaires would have no violent or depressing experience to report had not the individual in question been brought up in a church or community which taught them to look for it if not to cultivate it" (p. 153).

More relevant to the psychological dynamics, many of the reported difficulties involving sin and distress appear to involve reinterpretations caused by the conversion itself, not objective prior problems. Rather than major turning point events such as crime, addiction, and failure, Snow and Philips found that many converts actually referred to inconsequential moments that were subjectively imbued with significance only post-conversion. Additionally, many such events occurred after the establishment of the new religious worldview and were thus more accurately considered artifacts of the conversion process, as opposed to precipitating conditions. Consequently, Snow and Philips conceptualized the standard conversion narratives as a *post hoc* reconstruction. This is related to issues regarding the relative depth versus superficiality of conversion-linked personal change. Paloutzian, Richardson, and Rambo (1999) subdivided domains of potential personality change resulting from conversion experiences, finding that the most basic personality levels (e.g., "Big Five" traits) exhibit no or minimal change, whereas midlevel functions (e.g., attitudes, feelings, behaviors) showed more significant change, and self-defined functions (purpose, meaning, identity) the most profound changes. This indicates that the "radical" changes reflected in conversion narratives are confined to individuals' perception of their life narratives rather than existing at the level of deep personality, which is relatively fixed in adults.

Narrative re-working is not unique to religious subcultures but rather is motivated by (secular) needs for consistency. It is common for individuals, regardless of their religiosity, to report that their "old self" was an entirely different person (Libby & Eibach, 2002). This discrepancy acquires an upward directional arc as people disparage their distant past selves relative to their current self, going from "chump to champ" (Wilson & Ross, 2001). One reason for this is that we are motivated to enhance our current self-esteem, a process that can be achieved by downward comparison such as finding an inferior exemplar with whom to draw a contrast ("I'm better now compared to what I was then"). That is not to say that past traumas were nonexistent or fabricated in religious converts. Rather, in instances where people have suffered a negative life event, the perception of post-trauma improvement partly reflects a motivated illusion that provides compensatory coping support (McFarland & Alvaro, 2000). The process of enhancing one's current status motivates an illusory feeling of growth following past problems; in effect: "My life was bad, so there must have been improvement."

The compensatory need to reduce cognitive dissonance and maintain consistency also explains why earlier versions of the self are derogated in the conversion narrative. Creating a greater psychological distance from the past provides reassurance, removing doubts that one's current self, beliefs, and worldviews, are correct and inevitable. This retrospective reworking of personal narrative also involves biased memory recall that harmonizes a perceived past with current implicit ideas about our self (e.g., "I'm currently a good Christian, so I must have turned my life around"; Ross, 1989). As mentioned in the introductory chapter regarding introspective illusions and dual processing theories, this retrospective re-working of life narratives occurs unconsciously. In the case of sudden religious conversion, the degree of retrospective perceived change is dramatically amplified relative to more typical life narratives. It is the nature of compensatory processes that the greater the psychological motivational state, the more dramatic the narrative changes needed to provide contrast. In sum, rather than attributable to the mere vicissitudes of memory, narrative accounts of conversion experiences are systematically biased, with the result that their accuracy is limited by the current motivational state of the believer.

The Role of Cultivation Techniques in the Misattribution of Experiences

The malleability of memory in conversion narratives is related to a broader issue pertaining not only to retrospective bias, but also the perceptual distortions inherent in the types of religious experiences mentioned in this chapter. This issue involves the impact of techniques used to cultivate and enhance exceptional R/S experiences. Luhrmann and Weisman (2022) describe religious settings that serve as cultural invitations to conceptualize the mind-world boundary as porous. Cultivation involves learning to adopt an immersive orientation toward inner experience. As described earlier, this is achieved by taking one's inner sensational world more seriously, treating thoughts, images, and sensations as more meaningful, expanding them to make them more vivid, and deliberately blurring the line between what is attributed to internal, as opposed to external causes. Luhrmann describes the Renewalist prayer group leaders as encouraging congregants to adopt a play-like (ludic) mode of pretending as if God is present and engaged in conversation. It is also common within Pentecostal subcultures to prioritize the meaning of inner experiences such as dreams (suggested to be conduits for the Holy Spirit), and bodily sensations (arousal, rapid breathing, sweating, shaking), which likewise represent His presence. The contents of thoughts and images generated by cultivation are shared and their meaning discussed with others in the group. Practitioners who adopt these methods are said to be rewarded with sharper mental imagery (Luhrmann & Weisman, 2022).

However, these techniques and similar others used by believers to promote R/S experiences are identical to techniques used in controlled experiments known to produce false memories and images. These include the elaboration and enhancement of vivid detail in mental images, the use of suggestive and authoritative cues, and social/consensual validation of resulting material. For example, the encouragement of imagination alone, even without any additional suggestive procedure, is known to increase participants' degree of conviction and memory for events that never occurred (Mazzoni & Memon, 2003). The combination of repeated imagination trials, vivid images, and encouragement of high perceptual detail is known to produce elaborate false memories and confusion regarding what actions an individual performed (Thomas et al., 2003). More problematically, things that implicitly "feel true" can coexist with things that are acknowledged as not true. Asking participants to imagine a bogus event increases its implicit truth value, even while they are explicitly aware of its untruth (Shidlovski et al., 2014). Thus, the adoption of a "play-like" or "as if" attitude to one's beliefs and images and placing them in an epistemological gray zone between real and not real can have serious consequences.

Some of the most dramatic studies featuring techniques geared toward enhancing the experiential mode involve the implantation of false memories. Shaw and Porter (2015) recruited college students for a study ostensibly regarding their childhood memories, in the process receiving permission to ask their parents for corroboration. The students were told that their parents described them having been in a fight so severe that the police were called (a falsehood) along with several other memories that were true. Not surprisingly, many students could not recall the nonexistent fight. The researchers then engaged the students in subtle forms of implied social pressure ("Most people are able to retrieve lost memories if they try hard enough"), along with suggestive retrieval techniques (guided imagery) over the course of several sessions. Based solely on the techniques of social cues and the encouragement to generate imagery, three-quarters of the students eventually reported recalling (false) memories of committing a crime. Some students even elaborated further by generating confabulatory memory detail of the fight (e.g., "She must have pushed me first"). These results and those from similar studies demonstrate how an externally existing narrative account (i.e., "your parents said …") can easily become internalized in the form of a false memory. By cultivating the imagination of what something *could* have been like, images become more vivid of what it *would* have been like, eventually becoming incorporated into false memories of what it *was* like. This has clear implications regarding techniques promoting elaboration of imagistic R/S content.

The use of bodily reactivity and physical sensations as guides to the veridicality of experiences is similarly problematic. Popular stereotypic notions about the validity of physical reactivity and sense memory also lead to misinterpretations. It is a common truism that the strength of emotionality evoked by an experience or memory is an indicator of the validity of the experiences (e.g., "I wouldn't be having this strong of a reaction if there wasn't something meaningful about the experience"). This is incorrect. Likewise, the notion that "the body keeps the score" (Van der Kolk, 2014) by retaining physical symptoms of trauma, even in the absence of explicit memories, is incorrect. For example, those who mistakenly believe they have been traumatized have emotional and psychophysiologic responses to cues that are indistinguishable from those who actually did suffer a trauma such as PTSD (McNally, 2005).

Despite their use as validation for spiritual insights, images and memories derived during sleep states (e.g., dream interpretation) are similarly unreliable. Those who suffer from hypnogogic and hypnopompic (liminal sleep onset) dreamlike fantasies sometimes interpret these as indicators that they were victims of trauma (alien abduction, Satanic rituals). The practice of dream interpretation can also lead to apophenic over-reading of meaning. In one study, participants provided with (bogus) dream interpretations indicating they may have been victims of bullying before the age of three were more likely to produce false memories and beliefs about the pseudo-event (Mazzoni et al., 1999). Finally, expectancies can distort the interpretation of life events in a top-down process of confirmation bias. Events are more easily implanted as false memories when they are congruent with a person's preexisting attitudes or they promote feelings of familiarity, which interferes with source attributions, leading what "feels true" to become what "is true" (Frenda et al., 2013). In sum, the enlistment of cultivation techniques that amplify absorptive and porous cognitive processes does not lead to greater perceptive accuracy or sharper images but rather encourages perceptual over-confidence without greater accuracy. The use of experiential enhancement techniques employed in hypnosis also produces similar overconfidence (Erdelyi, 1994). As a result of such cultivation of perception, mundane experiences originating from known psychological processes can acquire an enhanced "special" quality and are deemed exceptional.

Conclusion: Exceptional Experiences, Dual Processing, and Misattribution

The use of techniques to cultivate spiritual experiences, and the application of tests to validate those experiences are analogous to Type 1 and Type 2 modes of cognition, respectively. Adopting an absorptive/porous mindset with an aim toward enhancing experientially based content is tantamount to amplifying

Type 1 intuitions ("trust your feelings," "treat your images as real") and the attenuation of analytic Type 2 processes. As stated in Chapter 1, Type 2 processes can often suppress or correct intuitive responses (e.g., "Wait, first think of alternative explanations," "be careful of heuristics and biases"). However, as we saw in Chapter 1, merely having Type 2 analytic capacity is necessary but not sufficient for belief updating. First, one must be motivated and willing to deploy Type 2 thinking (Risen, 2016). Also, the use of discernment tests based in Type 2 cognition comes with their own distortions and biases inherent in that mode, such as motivated reasoning and selective skepticism.

Rather than a "corrective" dual processing account in which discernment tests validate the meanings of R/S experiences, Type 2 processes give an illusory sense of pseudo-validation in accordance with the introspective illusion (i.e., "Because I have tested the insights gained from my spiritual experience, this confirms that they are genuine"). As described by Kahneman (2011), when T2 asks an empirical or analytic question, T1, yielding the only type of output of which it is capable of producing, substitutes a response to an easier question. An individual may be consciously aware of skeptically asking "What is the evidence that I really experienced the Holy Spirit?", but their cognitive process will be biased by an intuitively based answer such as "I had a strong feeling of His presence." This answer is misattributed by T2 as constituting a reliability check because explicit beliefs justify and rationalize intuitive beliefs (Baumard & Boyer, 2013b).

As Boyer (2013) writes of Luhrmann's interactive prayers, not all dual process effects are in the direction of T1 to T2 (initial intuitions validated by analytic cognition). Rather, reflective thoughts can sometimes guide the perceptions of specific intuitions. In these instances, the reflective beliefs from T2 exert a top-down interpretive bias. Boyer suggests that the interactive prayers' reflective beliefs about experiences (e.g., expectations, knowledge of signs of the Holy Spirit) are used to calibrate mental systems "… until this conceptual description fools, so to speak, their perceptual systems" (p. 353). Even relatively low-level perceptual processes such as seeing patterns in ambiguous visual images are biased by top-down motivational and expectational states, with the result that we literally "see what we want to see" (Balcetis & Dunning, 2006). Therefore, exposure to socially learned cues, suggestions, and expectations guide the interpretation of exceptional experiences, resulting in their misattribution to external spiritual sources.

6

Mental Health

"The more I study religions the more I am convinced that man has never worshipped anything but himself." - *Richard Francis Burton,* Book of The Thousand Nights And A Night Terminal Essay: Social Conditions, fn. 13.

(1885)

Religion and spirituality (R/S) are widely believed to have positive effects on mental health and well-being (Koenig, 2018). Therapeutic practices that involve R/S components include collective worship, ritual engagement, prayer, yoga, meditation, and others. Engagement in religious communities is said to be associated with numerous aspects of "human flourishing," including mental well-being, happiness, and life satisfaction (Vanderweele, 2017). Religious and spiritual ritual practices have been found to elicit positive emotions, such as awe, gratitude, and love (Van Cappellen et al., 2016). Those who engage in R/S behaviors typically self-report favorably about subsequent benefits. These findings have led researchers and therapists to theorize that R/S treatment components are unique or superior to secular practices and treatments. Some scholars argue that R/S involve "sacred" elements such as coping resources irreducible to secular mechanisms (Wong, Pargament, & Faigin, 2018). Spiritual elements are interwoven with many standard secular practices such as psychotherapy. One of the most familiar examples of such integration is the Twelve-Step approach to addiction (e.g., Alcoholics Anonymous), the spiritual mechanisms of which have been suggested to produce benefits unattainable through secular alternatives (Pargament, 2002). The body of scientific literature connecting R/S practices with salubrious outcomes, including scholarly journals devoted exclusively to these topics, is so extensive that the beneficial effects of R/S, are for many, beyond debate.

Misattribution and the Belief-as-Benefit Theory

The assertion of R/S-specific therapeutic effects on well-being has been referred to as the "Belief as Benefit" theory, which emphasizes the presumed impact of factors such as personal convictions (Schuurmans-Stekhoven, 2013b). As will be demonstrated in this chapter however, practices associated with R/S typically contain multiple components, only a portion of which specifically feature R/S content. These components include transcendent concepts with no secular equivalent (e.g., "sacred," "sanctified"), such as belief in God or a higher power, and attributions to the literal intervention of supernatural spiritual agents. However, as seen in Figure 6.1, when determining causality, any

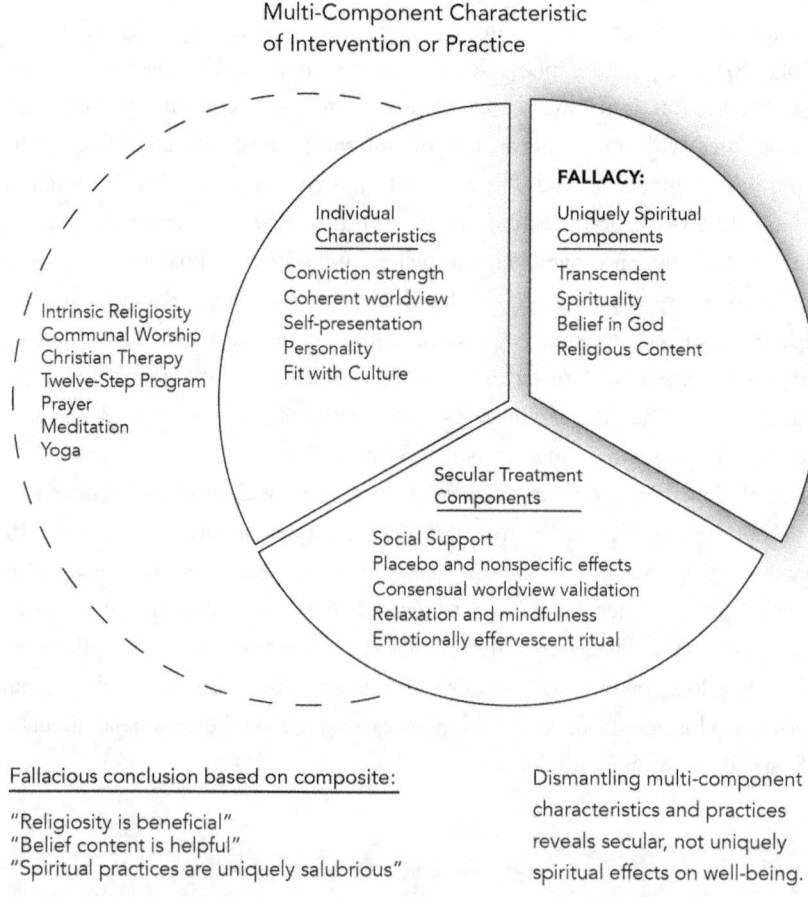

Figure 6.1 Transitive Fallacy of Composition. Source: Olivia Brenner.

theory attributing positive outcomes solely to R/S mechanisms, while not fully controlling for other potentially active components risks committing a fallacy of composition (i.e., substituting a whole for a portion). When individuals engage in a practice or therapy and subjectively perceive that their own well-being has improved, it is possible that they are misattributing the causal source of improvement. Often, the actual mechanism of treatment effect may not even be apparent to the individual.

This chapter differs in emphasis from the preceding ones in focusing not only on the subjective attributions made by believers themselves, but also on the causal inferences made by third parties such as therapists, practitioners, and researchers. The previous chapters provided examples in which an effect produced by a known psychological mechanism, whether internal (e.g., cognitive bias) or external (e.g., social role cues) was misattributed by a believer to R/S agency ("I am experiencing the effect of the Holy Spirit"). Such a mistaken assignation of causality can also occur when others infer that believers or those utilizing R/S practices have experienced improved well-being because of those practices. Improvement may be seen as stemming from one source ("Her spiritual practices have paid off") when in fact the change is caused by a different source (e.g., perhaps those who engaged in nonspiritual therapy also improved). The present chapter will describe instances where changes in well-being known to be caused by non-R/S sources are misattributed to R/S sources.

Misattributing Sources of Well-Being

If someone engages in a practice, experiences changes in well-being, and views the latter as being caused by the former, in what sense could this be inaccurate? What reason would there be to not consider the subjective report of the beneficiary themselves as the most accurate account for the actual agents of change? There are numerous situations in which subjective reports of sources of change should not be accepted at face value but, at most, viewed as provisional until validated through objective means. As an analogy, consider practices categorized as "alternative medicine" in which someone seeking symptom relief (e.g., arthritic pain): (1) engages in a type of therapy (e.g., herbal medicine, a copper bracelet), (2) reports a beneficial outcome (e.g., pain relief), and 3) attributes this amelioration to the intervention ("The herbs/ bracelet are weaving their magic"). Several competing potential mechanisms of causality must be ruled out prior to concluding that the intervention itself was the actively efficacious component. Misidentifications of therapeutic efficacy are difficult to detect outside of controlled settings such as the use of randomized, double-blind placebo control research designs.

The misattribution of improvement first requires a brief detour away from the topic of R/S to the broader issue of how well-being effects are correctly attributed to specific sources in any type of secular treatment intervention. The scientific approach to outcome research involves the control and elimination of various potential alternative ("spurious") sources of improvement. Perhaps the most widely known spurious source is the placebo effect—improvement resulting from the anticipation of an effect such as positive expectations, rather than any active component of an intervention or practice. (It can be argued that some placebo responses do activate physiological mechanisms, such as the classically conditioned release of endorphins, however even these are not caused by the inert treatment but rather the expectational association). Placebo effects are operative not only in the familiar examples of the inert controls in pharmacological trials (e.g., "sugar pills"), but also in non-medical interventions such as talk therapy. The latter instance involves a greater level of complexity than pharmacology trials because of the difficulty in identifying proper comparison conditions that are truly inert. For instance, even nonspecific aspects of therapy can be beneficial to the patient (e.g., talking with an accepting, genuine person). The general principle, however, is that any treatment used as a comparison to one with a presumed causal mechanism must be similar in every respect except for the specific efficacious component being evaluated. This is the principle of the "dismantling" study design.

Early efforts to establish the effectiveness of psychotherapy essentially consisted of collections of case reports (e.g., Freud's account of "Anna O."), in which it was simply assumed that patients' improvement was attributable to the treatment method being utilized (in this instance, psychoanalysis) and to the efficacy of specific techniques (e.g., interpretations of transference). However, these methods lacked basic control conditions such as comparisons with patients not receiving any active treatment. Starting in the mid-20th century, more systematic examinations of therapy outcomes yielded results that revealed the necessity of incorporating more sophisticated methods of assessment. Not only does psychotherapy involve potential placebo effects in which patients experience improvements merely by anticipating positive changes, but some patients improve over the course of time with no intervention at all ("spontaneous remission"; Eysenck, 1952). Other studies found that the success of therapy depended to a greater extent on nonspecific factors such as the formation of a working alliance with the therapist, rather than on the specific orientation or technique utilized (Strupp & Hadley, 1979).

It is now recognized that psychotherapy, and indeed any practice thought to have psychological benefits, contains a mixture of effects including the presumed active component or method being utilized, together with other influences that could also contribute to improvement. Often, methods previously thought to constitute the efficacious components, when evaluated in isolation from other effects, have been revealed to be inert. Consequently, proper treatment studies must decompose the process into separate components, allowing the independent examination of potential mechanisms. This is difficult given the number of elements involved in treatment. Patients are exposed to a specific method based on a coherent theoretical rationale (e.g., psychodynamic, cognitive behavioral) and utilize specific techniques based on that method (e.g., relaxation training). They are also exposed to nonspecific effects of the sort inherent in any therapeutic involvement (Hubble, Duncan, & Miller, 1999). These include supportive conversations, the process of self-disclosure, receiving any coherent explanation for problems, and forming a working alliance, among others. Therapy also involves improvements attributable to influences from outside the sessions themselves associated with anticipating, seeking, and receiving help (e.g., expectation/ placebo, spontaneous symptom remission over time, regression to the mean). Without properly designed studies to control for these components, it is not possible to conclude that any one mechanism is responsible for improvement, even when patients are engaged in treatments with an explicitly stated rationale using obvious techniques (e.g., "Depression will be diminished by correcting negative thoughts"). As with other processes discussed in this book, errors of causal attribution are not consciously evident to patients and practitioners. Symptom improvement caused by one or more nonspecific sources, can be unconsciously misattributed to other components and is not likely to be detected outside of controlled settings.

Parties other than the recipient of therapy, such as therapists and researchers, can also be mistaken regarding the source of any improvement. Just as studies must control for the expectations of the patient, the necessity of the familiar "double blind" design is predicated on the possibility that therapists and researchers are also biased by expectational effects, perhaps anticipating and seeing change when none occurs. Properly double-blinded psychotherapy research requires that the therapy sessions be conducted by clinicians separately from others who record the clients' outcomes, to objectively track changes in symptoms. Without such controlled conditions, therapists may incorrectly assume that their patients are benefitting from treatments when that is not the case, or that patients are changing for one reason when change is attributable to others.

Lilienfeld et al. (2014) described these treatment provider sources of error as "causes of spurious therapeutic effectiveness" (CSTEs)—resulting from inferences about the effectiveness of treatment made on the basis of informal clinical observations. Several CSTEs are identical to the types of motivated attributional biases mentioned in previous chapters, including effort justification and cognitive dissonance reduction. In such cases, both therapist and client presume that their engagement in treatment must have produced beneficial outcomes (e.g., "My client has been doing a lot of hard work, therefore they must be getting better"). Other biases affecting both therapists and patients include naïve realism ("I can see the change with my own eyes") and the *post hoc ergo propter hoc* (after this, therefore because of this) fallacy ("I did my therapy homework, and I feel better, so it must have worked"). Several biases involve inevitable selective information gathering biases or "cherry-picking" that occurs outside of controlled studies. These include confirmation bias, illusory correlation, and motivated reasoning (e.g., "This has worked for every person who has really tried"). In sum, without proper dismantling controls enabling the detection of potential confounds, misattributions of therapeutic effect are inevitable.

Religiosity/ Spirituality, Placebos, and Aspirational Self-Presentation

Returning to the question regarding the beneficial effects of R/S components, the appropriate scientific stance toward such claims should be the same as in any secular treatment evaluation method, including the evaluation of competing mechanisms that could account for improvement. Just as the factors mentioned above make it difficult to unambiguously link treatment improvement to specific secular treatment practices, the same spurious factors are operative in R/S practices. Regarding the placebo or expectational effect, many individuals employ R/S techniques and behaviors and perceive those practices as beneficial, but under controlled conditions it can be determined that placebo effects are responsible for salubrious outcomes. For example, Jegindø et al. (2013) examined the efficacy of prayer for reducing pain. Results indicated that among those who experienced mild electrical stimulation, religious participants who prayed indeed experienced the shocks as less painful relative to the nonreligious. But consistent with a placebo effect, the analgesic effect for both religious and nonreligious participants was attributable to their prior expectations of efficacy rather than any intrinsic property of the prayers (Jegindø et al., 2013). Religious and spiritual placebo effects have been found using numerous methods such as those described in the previous chapter, including the sham "God helmet" paradigm that produces attributions of exceptional experiences via suggestibility. In another example similar to a basic pharmacology trial, Schienle, Gremsl, and Wabnegger (2021) found that, compared to participants who were given labelled tap water to drink, those given tap water labelled "Lourdes water" (said to be from the curative sanctuary site), reported increased intensity of pleasant bodily sensations (e.g., warmth) and emotions (e.g., gratitude). In sum, as with other alternative medicine methods, many individuals with R/S beliefs engage in R/S practices such as prayer, meditation, communal worship, and the like, and often report increased well-being, but this does not necessarily indicate that the practices themselves contained any active beneficial component beyond placebo effects.

In the preceding chapter on exceptional experiences, effects attributed to external spiritual sources were described as generating expectational sets, based on social learning, internalized in the form of roles and scripts, and elicited by contextual cues (e.g., "This is what will happen to me"). In accordance with a socio-cognitive model (Spanos, 1994), the mechanisms of suggestibility and placebo responses are also operative when believers informally engage in R/S practices (e.g., prayer, worship) that are accompanied by nonspecific therapeutic elements ("Here is what I can expect to happen when I worship"). Religious and spiritual beliefs and practices are stereotypically associated with expectations of well-being (e.g., enhanced mood, happiness, and elevated emotions). As with any other secular treatment expectation, R/S believers feel that they should experience greater well-being by, for instance, engaging in communal worship, meditation, or prayer.

Moreover, in accordance with the Belief as Benefit theory, aside from R/S practices, simply being religious or believing in God is associated with general expectations of well-being (and conversely, not believing in God is presumed to be linked with negative emotional sequelae). In this sense, greater well-being constitutes an internalized social desirability stereotype. Reports of increased well-being are particularly common in contexts with greater prevalence of a shared belief in the benefits of religiosity, where this stereotype is more prevalent. This can be seen in cross-national comparisons in which religious people are happier and more satisfied in countries where religiosity is normative and secularism is discouraged (Stavrova, Fetchenhauer, & Schlösser, 2013). This "culture-fit" or "social value" effect will be discussed in greater detail below.

The system of beliefs shared within some R/S groups may place particular emphasis on well-being and happiness in the form of an aspirational stereotype. For example, as practiced in the United States, contemporary Christianity often focuses on presumed beneficial aspects of R/S, while downplaying difficult aspects of belief, which in some subcultures takes the form of a "prosperity gospel" (e.g., "God wants me to be happy and successful"; "Name it and claim it", etc.). Stereotypes such as "Christians are happier than other people" are internalized, establishing a specific way of processing, thinking, and talking about one's emotions. For many in subcultures such as those interviewed by Wilkins (2008), the happy believer stereotype was essentially compulsory, representing not only a sign that a believer is "right with God" but also constituting a precondition for group membership. This can be problematic in instances where psychological distress manifests as disappointment in God, or in projected feelings of being abandoned by God (Sherman et al., 2021).

Higher levels of well-being, self-esteem, and positive emotionality associated with R/S belief are produced by a self-enhancement tendency. This is when individuals are motivated to have overly positive views of themselves in domains that are central to their self-concept, as observed in biased presentational response styles such as inflated reports of well-being (Sedikides & Gebauer, 2010). Belief in the desirability of specific emotions on the part of believers influences the likelihood that they will experience those emotions. For example, by experimentally increasing the salience of believers' specific religious identity, Kim-Prieto and Diener (2009) elicited self-reports of whatever emotional experiences (e.g., love as opposed to shame) valued by their particular faith identity relative to other faiths. The effect of R/S on emotional enhancement can also be seen in studies of affective forecasting – predictions of future emotional experiences. When Carlson et al. (2022) asked students to predict how they might feel about receiving a low grade in class, religious students were more likely than the nonreligious to predict that they would still feel relatively happy (although religiosity failed to predict actual happiness upon receiving a low grade). Further, Carlson et al. found that the greater level of life satisfaction reported among religious participants was statistically accounted for by their level of self-enhancement. These findings suggest that greater well-being found among the religious reflects, in part, an internalized aspirational stereotype - how they think they should feel, or ideally want to feel, as distinct from how they actually do feel. It should be stated that even if a portion of greater well-being is attributable to such self-report biases, this does not necessarily indicate that the entirety of the religiosity-well-being relationship consists of enhanced responding. However, it does indicate that expectational, presentational, and self-enhancement effects can contaminate and invalidate self-reports of well-being. Studies purporting to identify salubrious R/S effects must demonstrate that effects persist after controlling for these confounding influences. Also, it should be recognized, in accordance with dual processing theories, that stereotypic enhancement effects occur via Type 1 processing and are thus largely unconscious. Consequently, individuals cannot "think their way out" or use their conscious introspection to correct for these biases.

Spirituality and Well-Being

It is common not only for individuals to attribute their mental health to their spirituality but also for practitioners and researchers to attribute the well-being of patients and participants to spirituality as well. However, it has been difficult to objectively establish the causal role that spirituality plays due to the vagueness and breadth of the construct and the resulting overlap with other constructs. Confirming a unique causal role for spirituality requires that it be conceptualized and measured distinctly from other beliefs and traits. But associations between greater well-being and higher levels of spirituality are artificially inflated by conceptual overlap between the two domains (Koenig, 2008). Some widely used measures of spirituality incorporate content blended with well-being, including items such as: "I believe there is a larger meaning to life," and "I feel an emotional bond to all humanity" (Garssen, Visser, & de Jager Meezenbroek, 2016). Other "spiritual" dimensions refer to feelings of connection with oneself, with others, or with nature (de Jager Meezenbroek et al., 2012). This criterion contamination inflates the role in positive outcomes attributed to spiritual beliefs because of the tautology involved in using the combination of spiritual-well-being content to predict well-being.

A similar conceptual blurring occurs when spirituality is defined in such a way that it conflates transcendence (i.e., references to the supernatural) with non-transcendence (e.g., something "greater than the self", "connected to others", "cherished", "giving something back to my community"). This expansive conceptualization allows for a "nontheistic spirituality" in which beliefs may or may not refer to supernatural concepts, or God, but rather involve content that even metaphysical naturalists could endorse (Garssen et al., 2016). The promulgation of such an expansive definition of spirituality is not itself inherently problematic, however it can lead to at least two interpretive problems. The first is that the conceptual expansion renders spirituality meaningless by overinclusion, subsuming believers across the entire range of meta physical beliefs from religiosity to atheism (again, united by a shared endorsement of well-being linked statements). Metaphysical naturalists such as atheists and agnostics who happen to report positive but non-transcendent characteristics are grouped with those believing in concepts transcending the naturalistic, begging the question "What well-adjusted person is *not* 'spiritual'?"

The second problem pertains to measures of spirituality used to predict well-being. Well-adjusted individuals, regardless of their belief in metaphysical naturalism, will tend to endorse blended content on such measures, leading to the misattribution that spiritual individuals have greater well-being because of their transcendent beliefs. Conversely, metaphysical naturalists and atheists who reject transcendent content are indistinguishable from those who also reject the blended well-being content, with the result that nonbelief appears to be associated with lower well-being. For example, the armed services have used a mental health screening instrument as part of the Comprehensive Soldier Fitness program that includes a spiritual dimension (Pargament & Sweeney, 2011). Well-adjusted nonreligious test-takers who reject only the transcendent content are scored as being not spiritual and thus receive feedback from the interpretive program such as "you may lack a sense of meaning and purpose in your life" and "improving your spiritual fitness should be an important goal" (Hagerty, 2011).

Conceptual blending also contributes to the misinterpretation that transcendent spirituality adds unique qualities to the prediction of well-being beyond general secular indices. For example, Pargament et al. (2005, pp. 669–70), referring to the findings of Emmons, Cheung, and Tehrani (1998), suggested that spiritual strivings share a closer relationship than non-spiritual strivings with measures of well-being. However, Emmons et al. (1998) coded strivings as "spiritual" or "self-transcendent" even when the content did not refer to metaphysical transcendence, such as striving to: "be humble", "live life more simply" (p. 403), "immerse myself in nature and be part of it" or "approach life with mystery and awe" (p. 409). This type of content could be endorsed by well-adjusted atheists as well as theists. In fact, when treated as separate predictors, transcendent content such as on the Daily Spiritual Experiences scale (e.g., "I feel God's presence") adds little unique variance to nontranscendent content ("I feel a selfless caring for others") in the relationship with well-being (Hammer & Cragun, 2019; Piedmont, 2004; Schuurmans-Stekhoven, 2013b). Such findings illustrate how the conceptualization and measurement of spirituality can lead to the erroneous conclusion that predictors of well-being are transcendent or beyond the secular.

Dismantling Spiritual Versus Secular Interventions

Similar problems with conceptualization and assessment of spirituality can affect the interpretation of research on therapeutic interventions. When techniques contain blended R/S and secular content, one cannot determine which is the actual source of effect without further decomposition. As mentioned above, outcome studies that merely contrast a given intervention with no treatment at all are not equipped to distinguish between the multiplicity of potential components, including nonspecific effects. Improvement that occurs after engagement in treatment does not constitute evidence of the efficacy of any specific component (the *post hoc ergo propter hoc* fallacy). The process of disaggregating treatments into different components often reveals that methods previously thought to be uniquely efficacious are inert. One relevant secular example of this is in the domain of treatment for Post-Traumatic Stress Disorder. For decades, the treatment of choice for anxiety disorders has been exposure therapy, based on cognitive-behavioral and social learning principles. This consists of encouraging patients to confront, whether mentally or physically, the source of their anxiety, while preventing avoidance of the feared stimuli, so that habituation can occur. Eye Movement Desensitization and Reprocessing (EMDR) therapy has been suggested by some advocates as a superior alternative to exposure (Shapiro, 1989). This method is based on the theory that anxiety reduction is optimized when clients visually track moving objects (e.g., a therapist's finger) during the recall of traumatic memories. Proponents attribute the benefits of EMDR to the activation of unprocessed memories in the brain. However, dismantling studies have failed to demonstrate that eye movements improve the efficacy beyond the more parsimonious component contained within the EMDR process (i.e., recalling memories with or without eye movements; Powers, Halpern, Ferenschak, Gillihan, & Foa, 2010). It is important to emphasize that patients in EMDR do typically improve compared to those receiving no treatment, which leads patients and therapists alike to attribute their improvement to the eye movements. However, dismantling comparisons demonstrate that this is a misattribution. The exposure component is the active ingredient, whereas the eye movements are superfluous.

This example is analogous to the misinterpretation of putative R/S mechanisms in other forms of treatment. Practices such as meditation, yoga, and prayer are typically classified as being spiritual in their essence. This is clearly apt in the sense that the history and rationales are spiritual (i.e., the stated basis by which they are thought to work) as well as in the attributions of practitioners and patients. However, from an objective perspective, and from the perspective of a dismantling approach to isolating active mechanisms, it is unclear whether the active components of these therapies are spiritual in a transcendent sense. For example, despite often including an (eponymous) transcendent rationale, the efficacy of Transcendental Meditation is due to a range of components such as relaxation, exposure-based habituation, and cognitive decentering (e.g., noticing wandering thoughts in a non-judgmental manner). Secular versions of meditation (e.g., mindfulness and acceptance-based therapy) are equally effective to transcendent versions in buffering stress and improving well-being (Vøllestad, Nielsen, & Nielsen, 2012). Similarly, the practice of prayer is viewed as quintessentially spiritual in its mechanism (i.e., transcendent contact) as well as its clear historical derivation. However, aside from differences in the target or intended recipient of prayer (i.e., external supernatural agency), other components of prayer practice are secular, including self-talk and self-disclosure, along with nonspecific placebo effects. More importantly, from an empirical perspective, these secular components, which are present in any other form of meaningful communication, yield mental health and coping benefits equivalent to religious forms of prayer (Belding, Howard, McGuire, Schwartz, & Wilson, 2010; Black, Pössel, Jeppsen, Bjerg, & Wooldridge, 2015). One reason that R/S believers are biased toward viewing prayer as effective is because they use different epistemological standards for evaluating spiritual practices, holding these methods to a lower standard of evidence than secular-based methods (McPhetres & Zuckerman, 2017). In sum, the fact that these practices are referred to as spiritual, or exist in spiritually framed versions of secular practices, does not necessarily mean that the spiritual components are efficacious in a causal sense.

Often, studies have been referred to as demonstrating that unique benefits derive from R/S as opposed to secular elements, but these almost always involve comparisons that are not truly equivalent. In a series of studies on the use of meditation for pain tolerance, Wachholtz and Pargament (2005; 2008) reported that spiritual meditation was superior to other secular forms in increasing tolerance. In the treatment protocol of this study, mantras were suggested for participants in the different conditions such as spiritual meditation ("God is love" and "God is peace"), internal secular ("I am content" and "I am joyful") and external secular ("grass is green" and "cotton is fluffy"). Based on the content alone, it is questionable that these represent semantically equivalent comparisons. These studies also reflect the above mentioned problem of conceptual blending and how it can lead to erroneous conclusions about which components are responsible for well-being. Wachholtz and Pargament (2005), suggest that secular meditation techniques must actually contain some elements of spirituality ("spiritual meditation in secular clothing" p. 381) because participants who engaged in them experienced increases on the Daily Spiritual Experiences measure. However, as mentioned above, measures such as the DSE contain a blend of transcendent and non-transcendent content; increased scores are not necessarily indicative of increased transcendence.

Likewise, in the previously mentioned study by Jegindø et al. (2013), which found that religious prayer resulted in lower pain intensity for religious participants, this condition was instructed to direct their prayer to God, whereas those in the "secular prayer" condition were told to direct theirs to "Mr. Hansen"—another comparison of dubious equivalence. Instead, a dismantled meditation version that would be more comparable to a religious practitioner contemplating "God is love" could be for a secular practitioner to contemplate an admired secular figure, perhaps one considered to be a worthy exemplar, rather than referring to their own emotions or something semantically neutral. When outcome studies directly match secular interventions to R/S ones in every aspect except for the transcendent component, results indicate few meaningful differences. For example, meditation techniques, whether secular (e.g., focusing on the present moment), or spiritual/ transcendental (e.g., breathing process interpreted in spiritual terms, framing the process as sacred) have equivalent effectiveness on pain tolerance (Feuille & Pargament, 2015).

Attempts have also been made to integrate R/S elements into existing secular forms of therapy to better accommodate patients who have R/S worldviews by framing content to be more familiar and compatible with their beliefs (Carlson & González-Prendes, 2016). An accommodating rationale is certainly appropriate for the purposes of increasing retention and engagement of religious patients. Matching clients to their preferred treatment methods has been shown to produce superior outcomes and decreased patient attrition (Delevry & Le, 2019). Indeed, in a review comparing religious versus secular approaches to treating depression, Marques et al. (2022) found that religious patients improved to a greater degree in the religious versions of the treatment methods. However, the results on religiously based interventions in this evaluation were mischaracterized as providing "superior effects." A successful matching of religious patients to R/S forms of therapy does not constitute evidence of generalized superiority or uniqueness of the R/S mechanisms, nor even that the R/S components had any effect at all.

Some reasons for why such erroneous conclusions have been drawn regarding the unique efficacy of R/S forms of treatment are methodological. In the majority of studies to date, participant samples (reflecting the populations from which they were drawn) have been overwhelmingly religious. Clearly the absence or exclusion of the full range of religiosity among participants limits the degree to which implications can be extrapolated regarding whether R/S treatment methods themselves are generally efficacious. For example, Abu-Raiya and Pargament (2015; p. 30), referring to data from Tix and Frazier (1998), suggested that R/S variables such as religious coping methods have a direct effect on health and well-being or are mediated by other spiritual specific religious beliefs (e.g., in life after death). The latter study did indeed find that religious coping predicted life satisfaction, however, Tix and Fraser themselves mentioned that their samples consisted of very few non-religious participants (less than 9% unaffiliated), stating "the generalizability of our findings may be limited to religious individuals coping with stressful circumstances" (p. 420). To make an efficacy claim regarding R/S-specific, relative to secular methods based upon such findings is apt only in the limited sense of "efficacy of R/S therapy for R/S participants," but does not represent superiority to secular methods or unique efficacy in general. By way of analogy, if a study had the opposite composition—overwhelmingly secular and atheistic with a small minority of religious participants—any claims of general inferiority of the use of R/S specific treatment methods would also be clearly inappropriate (i.e., "Christian practices are ineffective because they did not work for atheist patients"). Religious and spiritual practices are, in fact, counter-indicated within such secular patient samples. Speed and Fowler (2021) found that, although religious attendance, prayer, meditation, and religiosity had positive overall relationships with health outcomes, these relationships were absent among those without a religious affiliation or who were not spiritual. That is, behaviors such as religious attendance, often associated with benefits for R/S believers, are unrelated to the well-being of nonbelievers and the unaffiliated (Speed & Fowler, 2017).

Studies showing improved well-being for those receiving specific versions of a treatment method can be misattributed as being due to one portion or version of the specific treatment method (e.g., religious cognitive-behavioral therapy) rather than properly attributed to the actual efficacious portion (cognitive-behavioral components). Just as with the above mentioned dismantling example of EMDR versus simple exposure therapy, the improvement of patients receiving EMDR does not itself constitute evidence that "EMDR works." If eye movements do not result in greater efficacy than the simple exposure component, it is problematic to suggest that the former is somehow the active component. Likewise, when outcome studies have dismantled the components, including R/S-related ones, the active, efficacious elements of treatment are almost always found to be secular components. For example, in a meta-analysis, Worthington, Hook, Davis, and McDaniel (2011) found that, when matched in every other respect (i.e., dismantling design), there was no evidence that adding R/S components to secular therapies led to superior outcomes, even for clients with R/S beliefs.

In fact, the Worthington et al. (2011) analysis also demonstrated another methodological problem that can give the illusion of unique R/S efficacy—the use of R/S specific outcome measures. Their results indicated that patients in R/S psychotherapies outperformed patients in alternate psychotherapies, but only on spiritual outcomes (e.g., spiritual well-being), rather than objective psychological outcomes (e.g., level of depression). As with other measures of spirituality, the use of spiritual outcome indicators leads to the inability to distinguish changes in the spiritual portion from those in the actual well-being portion. In another example featuring a series of several studies comparing a secular version of Cognitive Behavioral Therapy (CCBT) with a religious version (RCBT), Koenig and colleagues found limited evidence of differential effectiveness. For example, in Koenig, Pearce, Nelson, and Erkanli (2016), RCBT was indeed more effective than CCBT in increasing daily spiritual experiences (again, the DES measure contains the same blended/nontranscendent content mentioned previously). However, contrary to a matching effect, other studies in these authors' series found that the type of CBT received did not moderate patient outcomes, even on quasi-spiritual outcome variables. Secular and religious CBT were equally effective in decreasing spiritual struggles (Pearce & Koenig, 2016), and increasing generosity (Pearce et al., 2015). More to the present point, aside from R/S-related outcome measures, Koenig et al.'s (2015) parent study indicated that for religious patients, religious and secular versions of CBT were equally effective on the objective outcome of depression severity.

The type of therapy arguably most associated with R/S content is the Twelve-Step treatment approach for addiction, commonly found in programs such as

Alcoholics and Narcotics Anonymous. Twelve-Step (TS) methods prominently feature spiritual concepts (e.g., a Higher Power) as playing not only an etiological role in addiction (e.g., references to "psycho-social-spiritual" disorders) but also in the mechanisms of therapeutic change. Many scholars refer to TS/AA treatments as some of the best examples of spirituality producing benefits unattainable through secular alternatives (Pargament, 2002). However, although there is a massive literature demonstrating that, generally, participation in TS/AA programs can be associated with salubrious outcomes, the same confounding factors complicating other R/S research also affect the interpretations of this literature. For example, studies have been limited by the conceptual blurring problem in which treatment combines transcendent (e.g., private prayer, spiritual experiences) and nontranscendent (forgiving oneself, finding purpose in life) content, making it difficult to identify the efficacious mechanisms. Consequently, studies differ regarding which components are predictive of problematic drinking (Robinson, Krentzman, Webb, & Brower, 2011).

As in other studies of R/S treatments, when spiritual mechanisms appear to be mediating positive changes it is often because they are studied in isolation to address narrow research questions (e.g., "Does spirituality contribute to change"), whereas when they compete with other explanatory variables (e.g., "Does spirituality contribute to change *beyond secular mechanisms*"), their importance diminishes (Kelly, 2017). As examples of the latter dismantling approach, studies have indicated that components such as group engagement and social support play the primary role in actual drinking reduction, with spiritual beliefs contributing minimally (Kelly, Hoeppner, Stout, & Pagano, 2012; Tonigan, Miller, & Schermer, 2002). One beneficial implication of this is that clients' spirituality or beliefs in God play relatively unimportant roles in deriving TS/AA-related benefit, thus expanding the applicability of the method to more potential clients (Tonigan, Miller, & Schermer, 2002; Tonigan, 2007). However, it calls into question the putatively spiritual mechanism of change. In a review featuring simultaneous comparisons of secular and spiritual mediators, Kelly (2017) concluded that the most important mechanisms of change in TS/AA methods included facilitating social networking and increasing clients' self-efficacy for maintaining abstinence.

To summarize, the present point is not only that R/S components do not add superior or unique efficacy to secular alternative practices and techniques, but that, taken as a whole, these results provide no evidence that improvements experienced by patients are objectively caused by R/S components at all. Although patient retention and engagement can be improved by offering R/S versions of treatments that better accord with patients' beliefs, there is no evidence that these elements contribute any unique therapeutic mechanism. Rather, the improvements in well-being are produced by secular components but are misattributed as stemming from R/S mechanisms. Therefore, a limited characterization such as "R/S believers can experience equal benefit from, or are more comfortable with, treatments utilizing R/S versions of concepts" is accurate. But it is problematic to expand this as having any implication that R/S components themselves are efficacious.

Individual Traits, Worldview Conviction, and Cultural Fit

We have seen that disaggregating the amalgamated construct of spirituality reveals effects attributable to both non-transcendent and transcendent content. Similarly, other constructs have often been confounded with R/S specific effects. Some of these involve individual difference traits such as personality and demographics. As mentioned above, because of cultural and self-enhancement biases, dispositional factors such as happiness, emotional stability, and optimism are stereotypically presumed to be associated with R/S beliefs. Consequently, their effects can be confounded with those from R/S, with the result that positive well-being states are misattributed to R/S beliefs. However, personality traits are developmentally prior and have a more substantial impact on religiousness rather than vice versa (Saroglou, 2010). For example, the link between religiosity and self-esteem is fully reducible to nonreligious variables such as dispositional optimism (Abu-Raiya et al., 2021).

Because the broad constructs of religiosity and spirituality include not only belief components, but also aspects of social-cultural identity (e.g., denominational membership) and group behavior (e.g., communal worship), these latter factors can also be confounded with the R/S belief content. One way to conceptualize these as distinct components is by using the alliterative categories of Believing, Belonging, and Behaving (Marshall, 2002). It is common for scholars to make distinctions between the relative influence of religious belief (e.g., importance of faith) as opposed to religious behaviors (e.g., worship service attendance). Less frequently distinguished, however, are the R/S versus secular versions of these same factors (i.e., determining the relative influence of R/S social bonding versus secular social bonding). Such distinctions raise the familiar issues of conceptual blending. This section will discuss examples in which well-being effects are attributed as being caused by the R/S belief component when in fact they derive from other sources.

One crucial epistemological distinction within the construct of beliefs involves separating effects relating to the content of beliefs (i.e., what one believes *in* or the metaphysical stance of religious or secular views) from the confidence in, or coherence of these beliefs. Previously, findings that religiously identified individuals experience greater well-being and life satisfaction compared to the unaffiliated have been interpreted as demonstrating the salubrious effects of having religious beliefs (as opposed to not believing). Such interpretations have implied something akin to a dose-response relationship in which positive effects on well-being increase in a linear manner ("more belief is better—less is worse") as a function of the personal importance of a religious identity (Green & Elliott, 2010).

However, these findings are being reinterpreted in light of the recognition that the measurement and conceptualization of religiosity has conflated the content component of beliefs (what one believes in) together with strength of conviction of those worldviews (i.e., how strong or coherent are one's beliefs in any worldview). (See Figure 6.2 depicting the full continuum of religiosity.) One such methodological practice contributing to this conflation is the use of overly broad categories for those lacking a religious affiliation (or the "Nones") in comparison with other religious denominations (e.g., Evangelical Protestant, Jewish, etc.). Similarly, continuous measures have been used to distinguish degrees of religiosity, such as those at the high end (e.g., highly intrinsic or those endorsing "religion is very important") from those at the low end of the same continuum (low intrinsic, "not at all important"). This is problematic because these comparisons are, in effect, between committed religious believers at one end, versus weak or indifferent believers combined with confident nonbelievers at the other end. Similarly, self-identity categories such as the Nones or unaffiliated represent an amalgam of the religious-but-unaffiliated together with secular unaffiliated, agnostics, and atheists. Rather, most unaffiliated individuals and "low intrinsics" are not atheists; just as uncertainty or indifference to R/S beliefs is not tantamount to strongly convicted disbelief (Pew Research Center, 2012).

The measurement conflation of these groups has implications for the interpretation of the religiosity—well-being relationship. As with the blended measures mentioned earlier, the use of combined categories makes it impossible to determine whether well-being is related to R/S beliefs and affiliations as opposed to individuals' level of belief convictions (or affiliation with any equivalent social group, a topic which will be explored below). The necessity of making such distinctions has become increasingly evident in light of recent empirical studies using the full continuum of belief analyzed for quadratic effects.

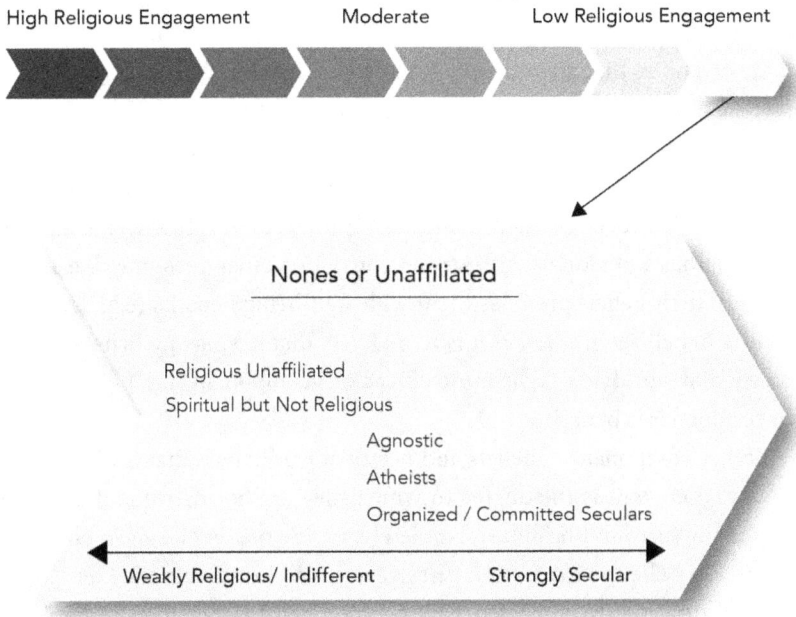

Figure 6.2 Religious Continuum. Source: Olivia Brenner.

There is evidence of a curvilinear relationship between religiosity and well-being when the former is measured, at one end of the dimension, as confident religious belief, through uncertainty or indifference, to confident disbelief (e.g., atheism) at the other end of the dimension. (Another way to describe this could be a linear relationship between worldview conviction and well-being—strong conviction in any belief system at one end versus uncertain or indifferent at the other.) For example, weakly religious individuals have significantly lower life satisfaction than highly religious individuals (Pöhls, Schlösser, & Fetchenhauer, 2020). Likewise, both strong religious believers and convinced atheists have greater well-being relative to the unsure and indifferent (Galen & Kloet, 2011a). One meta-analysis found that the strength of belief, whether atheistic or religious, moderated the relationship between belief itself and psychological health (Weber, Pargament, Kunik, Lomax, & Stanley, 2012). When measured as nominal categories, those who self-identify as spiritual have higher rates of psychopathology relative to those identifying as both religious and spiritual as well as neither religious nor spiritual (King et al., 2013). In sum, these results are inconsistent with a belief as benefit or linear dose-response relationship between R/S and well-being.

Although these curvilinear effects only represent one portion of the voluminous religion-well-being research literature, this is primarily due to the paucity of studies that are properly designed and analyzed in a manner that can detect such effects (e.g., unconfounding low from firm nonbelief, statistically analyzing a quadratic effect). However, the increasing reports of this effect suggest that a reinterpretation of the causal mechanisms pertaining to R/S and well-being is in order. Another implication apropos to the present chapter is that many religious individuals with strong convictions may presume that the R/S content of their beliefs provides them with well-being benefits (e.g., "My belief in God is beneficial"), whereas it is more likely that having any firm conviction in a coherent worldview is the more efficacious component (i.e., holding beliefs with confidence is beneficial).

Another component of beliefs and personal worldviews that is distinct from their actual content is the degree to which they are normative and align with others in the surrounding cultural milieu (e.g., proportion of a given population who are R/S believers across countries, states, and local regions). For example, the belief of a highly convicted Evangelical Christian residing in rural areas of the United States constitutes a better "fit" compared to similar beliefs of the same individual residing in an urban coastal location (or residing in the United States compared to Denmark). From this perspective, the degree of R/S belief is a proxy for communal normativity. Depending on the location, a given individual could be a "joiner" whose beliefs are consensually validated, or they could be a "deviant" whose beliefs are rejected by others. The concept of culture-fit is similar to the curvilinear effect in that, whereas previously R/S has often been interpreted as promoting a generalized beneficial well-being effect, this has overlooked the degree to which the relationship varies as a function of cultural normativity. Numerous recent studies have found that the relationship between well-being and religiosity is, on average, greater in countries, states, and city regions where religiosity is the norm, whereas this is not the case where secularity is the norm (Diener, Tay, & Myers, 2011; Gebauer et al., 2017a; Stavrova et al., 2013). This also applies to more circumscribed contexts such as within families. Adolescents' mental health, rather than simply being a function of their religiosity, is contingent upon whether they share the religious views of their parents (Kugelmass & Garcia, 2015). Thus, greater well-being is a product of the contextual match itself, rather than a property of R/S belief.

As with similar concepts mentioned above, it is possible to aptly characterize a R/S–well-being relationship in a narrow sense such as "R/S beliefs are associated with well-being in contexts where the former is the norm." However, a more accurate characterization is that any worldview beliefs are conducive to well-being if they are confidently held and consensually validated in the surrounding cultural milieu. Well-being is an outcome of general confidence, commitment, and clarity of worldviews normative within a given context rather than an effect caused by R/S itself.

Social Embeddedness

The link between well-being and R/S is generally most apparent when the latter is conceptualized in the communal sense (i.e., the belonging and behaving functions of religion) rather than belief alone. Communal religion typically involves regularly engaging in collective activities such as group rituals with others who share similar worldviews, often in an emotionally enhanced context. Longitudinal studies indicate that religious service attendance is associated with a range of beneficial mental health outcomes, such as lower rates of depression (Garssen, Visser, & Pool, 2021). Efforts to identify via dismantling the most beneficial elements of R/S as it is practiced communally have pointed to factors such as increased social contact, social support, and positive social modeling opportunities. For example, the social networks of frequent church attenders are denser relative to nonattenders (Ellison & George, 1994). The relationships between the believing aspects of religion (e.g., perceived importance) and mental health have also been found to be largely attributable to the overlap between believing and belonging aspects such as social and emotional support (Hovey, Hurtado, Morales, & Seligman, 2014; Salsman, Brown, Brechting, & Carlson, 2005). In fact, when the social relationships and support associated with collective religious engagement are taken into consideration (i.e., statistically separated), the relationship between belief in God and well-being is substantially diminished or disappears completely (Greenfield & Marks, 2007; Lim & Putnam, 2010). Comparisons between religious and secular group members, when controlling for frequency of group attendance and social contacts, indicate that belief in God adds little to the prediction of well-being (Galen & Kloet, 2011b).

Some scholars have taken a different tack from the Belief as Benefit hypothesis by positing that the combination of R/S beliefs together with social elements constitute a unique amalgam having a salubrious impact on well-being, without secular equivalent. It is argued that that it is reductionist to decompose communal R/S elements into more basic, secular components (Wong, Pargament, & Faigin, 2018). Controlling for the social components of enacted religion would "be like studying the effects of a hurricane while controlling for the wind, rain, and storm surge" (Myers, 2012: 915). The term "religious engagement" has been used to refer to the combination of strong belief with communal involvement. Likewise, others have indicated that it is specifically the emotional effervescence involved in the collective religious rituals that produce positive emotional states such as awe, collective uplift, and flow (Van Cappellen, Toth-Gauthier, Saroglou, & Fredrickson, 2016).

The empirical validation of these uniqueness arguments hinges upon identifying the various components of collective religiosity and comparing them with secular versions that are identical in every respect except for the transcendent R/S elements. Recent studies have attempted to close this gap by examining the well-being effects of participating in communal secular behaviors. Wlodarczyk et al. (2021; Study 1) found that perceived emotional synchrony was higher among those attending religious Sunday Mass than those participating in "secular Sunday activities." However, this is something of an invidious comparison because the secular activities included informal events such as family meals or playing cards with friends. By contrast, in their Study 2, Wlodarczyk et al. studied the effects of participating in the Tamborrada, in Basque country, Spain, a non-religious communal folk activity with affectively loaded rituals. The results indicated that the participants experienced increased well-being such as greater perceived emotional synchrony and meaning of life.

Rather than defining secular social activities as merely anything lacking religious content (e.g., science lectures, sport events), a closer analogue to collective religious participation is to study groups organized around an affirmative and coherent shared secular worldview. In one such study, members of churches were compared on various well-being measures to members of a secular humanist group (the Center for Inquiry). The results indicated that any differences in well-being diminished or disappeared entirely when controlling for effects of frequency of group attendance and demographics traits (Galen &

Kloet, 2011b). However, groups formed on the basis of secular worldviews may still lack some of the emotionally rich and ritualistic components of collective R/S worship such as synchronized activities, uplifting communal music, or socially supportive interactions.

The Sunday Assembly movement involves secularly oriented collective gatherings intentionally modelled on some aspects of religious services but with the religious content removed. They combine elements of communal rituals, prosocial message content, music, and humor. The Sunday Assembly mission statement (with the motto: "Live Better, Help Often, Wonder More") emphasizes that the focus is on personal growth and communal prosociality rather than merely the absence of, or opposition to, organized religion. As such, they more closely approximate communal religious gatherings while differing in the metaphysical belief component. In a comparison of those attending Christian church rituals with those attending Secular Sunday Assembly, Charles et al. (2021) found that, although these groups differed in terms of the members' characteristics and typical length of attendance, in other respects the social bonding effects from the rituals were comparable. For both types of groups, the activities increased positive emotions and reduced negative ones. Similarly, in a longitudinal study, Price and Launay (2018) found that Sunday Assembly attendees experienced improvements in their well-being, primarily due to the small-group activities and informal socializing components. Aside from secular communal engagement, there are also secular contexts that can induce many of the positive emotional states thought to be associated with purely spiritual settings. Experiments have indicated that exposure to natural grandeur also produces feelings of awe and similar beneficial effects (Piff, Dietze, Feinberg, Stancato, & Keltner, 2015; Prade & Saroglou, 2016). Likewise, in another study, positive emotions and "flow" were equally present for those engaged in nonspiritual social activities as well as those attending Catholic mass (Rufi, Wlodarczyk, Páez, & Javaloy, 2016).

In sum, earlier studies that appeared to indicate well-being advantages for members of religious groups were often interpreted as reflecting direct causal benefits of R/S beliefs. However, increasingly sophisticated dismantling comparisons have revealed numerous separable components associated with R/S beliefs and practices, only some of which are inherently transcendent or unique. Engaged religious attendance and worship reflects a number of components including: Belief in God, strong worldview conviction, operating in a group of other supportive believers, engaging in formal collective rituals featuring emotionally laden behaviors, with ancillary informal social activity and interactions. Although cumbersome, such a characterization illustrates that only the first portion of these elements (i.e., beliefs in a transcendent deity) involves elements that cannot be derived from secular contexts. Further evidence is needed to substantiate these findings, but the trend observed in the pattern of research findings represents one of a continual erosion of the hypothesis that R/S beliefs have unique benefits. Rather, the closer the secular analogue is to the prototype of religious engagement the more indistinguishable are any effects on members' well-being.

Conclusions

Interpretations of the relationship between spirituality and well-being have tended to follow certain patterns. As we saw throughout the chapter, based on the massive literature connecting the two domains, an initial conclusion that the effects of R/S produce benefits in well-being would seem warranted. However, much of this evidence has undergone what might be called interpretive creep, in which modest associations or instances of correlations have been characterized as consistent with a causal assumption without first eliminating competing secular explanations. One way to illustrate this is to arrange the types or degrees of association in an ordinal pattern that reflects a trend starting with more limited levels (e.g., association, correlation), followed by increasingly exclusive, causal framing.

Levels of description

1) Parallel: R/S versions as alternative versions of secular concepts (religious Cognitive Behavioral Therapy, positive religious coping, religious social groups).
2) Parochial: R/S versions operating among R/S believers, excluding the nonreligious (e.g., prayer use among the devout).
3) Indirectly causal: R/S components influencing outcomes indirectly via secular mediators (e.g., church attendance boosts social support, in turn increasing well-being).
4) Unique: R/S concepts existing or functioning differently for R/S believers (e.g., "religious worldviews provide more meaning for believers compared to their other secular worldviews").
5) Directly causal: R/S beliefs themselves responsible for differences between believers and nonbelievers (e.g., Belief in God increases subjective well-being).

6) Superior: R/S component more effective than the secular version for everyone; unique content is inaccessible to the nonreligious (Transcendent or sacred beliefs and practices).

In this chapter, we have seen instances in which the interpretation of a given result or observation, although valid at a lower, non-causal level, "creeps" upward, with the resulting description matching a higher level. For example, the finding that therapies containing religious content provide the same benefits for religious participants as does secular therapy for nonreligious participants is instead framed as "Religious practices are beneficial," or even "Religious practices are more beneficial." Likewise, improvement *after* using a religious practice or technique is described as improvement *because* of such a technique. The use of more conservative scientific standards is needed to properly interpret such findings. Practices cannot be characterized as uniquely beneficial, or even considered as possessing any active efficacious component, unless they are shown to be superior to a fully controlled equivalent. Rather than constituting reductionism, this type of dismantling rationale is in accord with standard Empirically Supported Treatment approaches to outcome evaluation (Tolin et al., 2015).

Another implication of such findings that is consistent with the material throughout this book, is that subjective attributions of efficacy are not necessarily accurate. If an individual engages in a R/S practice and attributes their improved well-being to the practice, this self-report can be erroneous. There are numerous reasons for this, including that, in accordance with dual processing theory, we lack introspective access into many mechanisms of psychological well-being. Improvements occurring after engagement in therapy practices are often attributed to the specific method of treatment when in fact they were produced by other sources. Just as it is now widely recognized that the improvement of patients engaged in specific types of therapy (e.g., psychoanalysis) may occur for reasons other than the stated treatment rationale (e.g., the reworking of internalized parental representations), so the improvement of practitioners of R/S methods is not necessarily attributable to spiritual mechanisms. The only way to determine whether the attributions of the mechanisms of change are accurate is to use fully matched control conditions, dismantling all spurious influences except for the R/S components (as illustrated in Figure 6.1).

7

Morality and Prosociality

"The savage man has a savage God; the cruel man has a cruel God; the effeminate man has an effeminate God; while the good man lifts up holy hands to a God who rewards goodness."
—Herbert A. Youtz American Journal of Theology (1907)

Just as religious and spiritual (R/S) effects are mistakenly presumed to be uniquely operative in the domains of exceptional experiences and mental well-being, moral attitudes and behaviors are similarly misattributed as resulting from R/S effects. Within the morality literature, two distinct, yet overlapping misattributions are frequently made, sharing common psychological origins but differing in their manifestations. One is the assumption that R/S belief has a general moral enhancement effect. The other assumption is that morality originates in R/S sources that are unique and irreducible to secular influences. In this chapter, I will demonstrate that the perceived association between R/S and morality constitutes a general stereotype that influences numerous psychological processes, such as impressions formed of others, judgments of one's own actions, and attributions for our moral motives. This stereotype is not only internalized, affecting subjective perceptions of morality, but it also leads R/S believers to externalize the presumed causality for their moral behavior, and to attribute transcendent influence. However, before describing such a process, it is necessary to first clarify and distinguish basic terminology and concepts.

Morality, Prosociality, and Altruism

Morality is a broad concept involving prescriptive norms (e.g., how one ought to behave), attitudinal judgments (e.g., approval or disapproval), and behaviors. Characteristics associated with morality include social manifestations (honesty and helpfulness), as well as ascetic or "traditional value" domains such as eschewing hedonistic behaviors (drug use, non-traditional sexuality). A related concept is prosociality—behavioral dispositions and actions that benefit others, whether in the form of planned behaviors (e.g., charitable donations), spontaneous assistance (bystander helping), or other-oriented traits (e.g., agreeableness, warmth, trust). While morality and prosociality often overlap, some behavior may be morally motivated without necessarily being prosocial, such as the retributive punishment of perceived wrongdoers. Altruism refers to a specific type of prosociality that benefits others, but enacted at a personal cost, such as self-sacrificing behaviors. Prosocial actions are not necessarily altruistic (e.g., making a charity donation because it yields a tax write-off). The literature referred to in this chapter will include all three of these concepts. For the sake of brevity, the broad term of morality will be used except in cases where more specific distinctions are relevant.

Religion/Spirituality and Moral Enhancement

The concept of morality is commonly associated with religion to such a degree that the terms are often used synonymously (e.g., "She is a good churchgoing woman"). A survey in the United States found that 42 percent of respondents believed that it is necessary to believe in God to "be moral and have good values" (Pew Research Center, 2017). Notably however, responses to such questions vary widely as a function of the respondent's religious identity: 85 percent of those who were religiously affiliated, compared to only 45 percent of the unaffiliated, stated that belief in God was necessary for morality. The association of religion and morality is found not only among the general public, but also among many scholars. For instance, in *Who Really Cares: The Surprising Truth About Compassionate Conservatism* (2006), public policy analyst Arthur Brooks points to the higher levels of charitable donations and volunteering engagement among those with more frequent church attendance. Likewise, sociologists David Campbell and Robert Putnam, in *American Grace: How Religion Divides and Unites Us* (2010), argue that religious Americans are "better neighbors" as evidenced by their prosocial engagement in their communities. Because psychological assessments of religious individuals indicate that they possess more agreeable and conscientious traits, they have been described as being generally "nicer" individuals (Saroglou, 2002).

Many scholars interpret correlations between measures of religion and morality as the former causing the latter. As in the previous chapter on well-being, the presumed mechanism of this relationship is based on versions of a "belief as benefit" hypothesis. Specifically, this premise suggests that unique moral enhancements result from belief in God, such as via the inculcation of transcendent values and sanctified precepts. Religion is argued to have an indirect effect on strengthening morality and self-control by promoting prosocial norms (Myers, 2012), incentivizing participation in rituals, and exposure to religious institutions and pedagogy (Marcus & McCullough, 2021). Engagement in the social aspects of religion is thought to boost group cooperation and cohesion, lending transcendent support to the creation of a "moral community" (Graham & Haidt, 2010). Perspectives from the Cognitive Sciences of Religion emphasize the cultural evolution of "Big God" concepts—socially shared beliefs in omniscient agents that promote moral behavior via supernatural monitoring enforced by punishment (Norenzayan, 2013; Purczycki et al., 2016). Although most scholars concede that secular prosociality and morality can exist outside an R/S motivating framework, some still reserve special "unique" R/S origins for particular aspects of morality. Religious influences are argued to support altruism, such as the prioritizing of others in a way "demonstrably superior to unbelief" or naturalistic sources (Clark, 2014: 161). Believers' experience of moral intuitions that prompt altruistic behavior are said to reflect the spiritual presence of a theistic God (Slife et al., 2012).

In this chapter, I will argue that theories regarding the morally enhancing effect of R/S and the belief in external derivation from transcendent sources represent misattributions of nonreligious psychological processes. This will be demonstrated by first identifying the naturalistic, secular factors most influential on morality. Then, I will describe how these effects, rather than being correctly recognized as secular in origin, are externally misattributed as being R/S in origin. Further, I will describe how a shared cultural belief in the influence of R/S on morality constitutes a ubiquitous social stereotype that is internalized by believers (and in some cases, by nonbelievers as well), which has wide-ranging effects, such as biased impression formation of others and personal self-enhancement effects (e.g., "Holier than thou"). Finally, I will illustrate how the endorsement of this stereotype leads to source errors in the form of externalization and projection of moral enhancement, creating the misattribution of morality as deriving from external spiritual sources. These theories will be examined starting with a critical review of the literature on religion and morality.

Morality and Prosociality: R/S or Spurious Influences?

Despite the sizable literature pertaining to the relationships between forms of R/S and types of morality/prosociality, interpretations are often biased by the same set of spurious influences as those mentioned in the previous chapter on well-being. In general, characterizations of R/S belief as benefit theories represent a failure to consider alternative influences. One of these is the failure to distinguish the effect of endorsing specifically R/S concepts (e.g., belief in God) from firm overall convictions or worldviews. This conflation is most evident in the frequent use of measures such as the importance of religion, intrinsic religiosity, and religious attendance and the assumption that these measures have equal validity for the nonreligious as well as the religious (see Figure 6.2 in the preceding chapter). More specifically, this practice makes no distinctions between weak, indifferent R/S views ("Not particularly religious"; "Do not attend church") and confident secularism ("Absolutely sure there is no God," "Secular humanist"). Metaphysical indifference or the absence of religious attendance is not equivalent to strongly convicted beliefs and affirmative secular involvement. Similarly, religious belief and religious belonging are distinct constructs. Therefore, any apparent differences in morality between groups as a function of frequent as opposed to infrequent religious attendance do not solely reflect the effect of belief in God.

A related spurious effect commonly occurring in research is the use of intrinsic religiosity to represent religious belief in the aggregate. Intrinsic religiosity (IR) refers to a motivation for and commitment to religious belief as being personally important, as measured by items such as "I try hard to live all my life according to my religious beliefs" and "My whole approach to life is based on my religion" (from the Revised Intrinsic/ Extrinsic Religiosity Scale; Gorsuch & McPherson, 1989). Measures of intrinsic religiosity often show stronger associations with constructs such as morality, prosociality, and well-being compared to those of other religious measures such as belief in God, or religious attendance (Ward & King, 2018). This is due to the multi-dimensional nature of IR, which includes belief content along with motivation and commitment. For example, a given individual may believe in God and attend religious services without having high intrinsic belief; conversely an atheist may have beliefs characterized by high intrinsic motivation and commitment, but to a secular/humanist worldview. Therefore, any interpretation of an association between intrinsic religiosity and a given domain as representing an effect of religious content (e.g., "belief in a monitoring God," "commitment to religious principles") requires further inspection to determine what factors are responsible for the relationship.

When the literature is examined with these distinctions in mind, prosocial effects often attributed to R/S beliefs are driven primarily by social engagement and group membership. In accordance with the general primacy of situational influence (as emphasized by social learning perspectives), the most relevant factors promoting prosociality are contextual rather than dispositional. Members of religious organizations are exposed to positive social norms and provided with opportunities to engage in prosocial behaviors (Bekkers & Schuyt, 2008; Campbell & Yonish, 2003). Perhaps not surprisingly, individuals who are members of groups that feature easily accessible, structured opportunities for engaging in volunteering and frequent requests for donations tend to report higher levels of such behaviors. Charitable giving and volunteering found among religious attenders is also a product of factors such as social networking, and engagement in informal fellowship activities (Becker & Dhingra, 2001; Merino, 2013). When these social and group factors are controlled, religious beliefs do not add significant variance to the prediction of prosocial behaviors (Galen et al., 2015). Likewise, in a computer modeling study using data from the World Values Survey, prosociality was more related to group affiliation and social networking than to worldview beliefs, whether religious or secular (Galen et al., 2021). In contrast to the influence of group membership and attendance, Putnam and Campbell (2010), stated that, "religious beliefs ... turn out to be utterly irrelevant to explaining the religious edge in good neighborliness" (p. 465). Despite often being described as the unique benefit of R/S engagement, group-based influences on prosociaity are equivalently derived from secular (e.g., Sunday Assembly organizations) as well as religious groups. Although members of religious groups may subjectively attribute beneficial aspects to their religion, the functional mechanisms are essentially secular.

In addition to contextual influences, prosociality is also associated with dispositional traits. This relationship is often misconstrued as religious belief exerting a positive influence on personality (e.g., "making people nicer"). Rather, it is better understood as a cultural adaptation of pre-existing traits (Saroglou, 2010). First, the chronological relationship involves personality traits influencing subsequent religiosity as well as the opposite causal direction (Entringer, Gebauer, & Kroeger, 2022; Heaven & Ciarrochi, 2007; McCullough et al., 2003). Second, as was described in the previous chapter regarding well-being, the culture-fit model reveals that the relationship between prosocial traits and religiosity varies as a function of the value or normativity of religion within a given milieu. Communal personality traits such as morality, warmth, and altruism are positively associated with religiosity in predominantly religious countries but are not associated within secular contexts (Ashton & Lee, 2019; Gebauer et al., 2013).

Other cultural factors moderating relationships with religiosity and prosociality involve the overall level of social development. Religiosity is more prevalent in countries with difficult living circumstances (e.g., low life expectancy, hunger) and the relationship between religiosity and positive outcomes (e.g., social support, well-being) is largely confined to these countries (Diener et al., 2011). Likewise, at lower levels of national development, religious individuals tend to show greater disapproval of civic immorality (e.g., theft, violence) relative to secular individuals, but with greater development, this gap converges and even reverses such that in highly developed countries those who are secular display greater civic morality attitudes (Hildebrandt & Jäckle, 2020). Aside from overall levels of religiosity, the degree to which religion is socially enforced (as opposed to freely chosen) also appears to moderate this relationship. Stavrova and Siegers (2014) found that there was little relationship between religion and a range of prosocial behaviors in countries with strong social enforcement of religion (e.g., Georgia, Indonesia) as opposed to those in which religion is a matter of personal choice (e.g., Scandinavian countries). This may represent the artificial restriction of religious effects in contexts featuring social imposition. Viewed in the aggregate from the perspective of religion-as-social value or culture-fit models, the hypothesis of a simple causal relationship such as "religion leading to prosocial traits" is not supported. Rather, religion appears to function as a proxy construct, representing the degree to which individuals' worldviews match their adaptation within a specific cultural milieu.

Moral Foundations and Prosociality

The broad constructs of morality and prosociality subsume numerous attitudes and behaviors. One of the most influential models to elucidate the basic substrate of morality is Moral Foundations Theory (MFT; Graham & Haidt, 2010). Based on social-intuitive and evolutionary theories of morality (discussed in greater detail below), MFT suggests that there are at least five domains of moral concern: (1) Care, (2) Fairness, (3) Respect for authority, (4) Loyalty to ingroup, and (5) Purity/sanctity. Reduced even further, the first two areas of concern together constitute "individualizing" morality, based on the "ethics of autonomy." Those who emphasize individualizing morality believe that people ought to be allowed to behave as they choose, as long as they do not harm others or act unjustly. By contrast, the latter three domains reflect "binding" concerns. This view prioritizes so-called traditional moral values such as preserving the cohesiveness of the family or small group. Those who are who are highly religious and ideologically conservative tend to value all moral foundations roughly equally (i.e., both individualizing and group-binding morality), whereas those who are less religious and/or politically liberal tend to exclusively emphasize the individualizing foundations, rejecting notions of authority, group loyalty, and purity (Graham & Haidt, 2010). Put differently, because most people largely agree in emphasizing the morality of care and fairness, individualizing foundations are not strongly related to religiosity. By contrast, those high in religiosity and conservatism take into consideration binding foundations, which tend to be rejected by the nonreligious (Ståhl, 2021).

This concurs with observed patterns in that religious and nonreligious individuals do not greatly differ regarding communal behaviors such as honesty, or universally condemned behaviors such as violence (i.e., the "lie, cheat, steal, and kill" varieties), whereas attitudes regarding ascetic morality are significantly related to religiosity (Weeden & Kurzban, 2013). Moral reactions most strongly diverge as a function of religiosity in sexual and reproductive domains—homosexuality, prostitution, birth control, abortion, extramarital affairs, and casual sex (Moon et al., 2019). These correspond to the MFT domain of purity/sanctity.

The selective emphasis found in religious morality toward group-binding and asceticism rather than universal considerations of care and fairness provides context for the attributed source and motivation of morality. Behaviors such as higher levels of charitable donations and volunteering on the part of the religious are often characterized as motivated by a generalized concern for other people. However, a greater complexity in motivating influences emerges when the identity of the targets or intended beneficiaries of prosociality is considered. Some people prefer to direct their prosociality primarily toward those proximal to themselves (i.e., family, friends, local church community) rather than outgroup members, suggesting a prioritization of the ingroup, rather than acting out of general care. A similar moral rationale characterizes nepotism, which does not involve universal helping behaviors but rather those that promote kin over strangers. Such behaviors are better characterized as motivated by group parochialism.

Parochialism and Trust

Behaviors expressed selectively, such as directed at targets within ones' own group rather than universally to in- and outgoup members alike, are referred to variously as minimal prosociality, parochial altruism, or simply parochialism (Choi & Bowles, 2007; Saroglou, 2006). Although the tendency to favor similar others is a nearly universal bias, it also differs in degree between individuals, groups, and cultures. This can be represented by the relative discrepancy or "gap" between prosociality directed to ingroup members (e.g., friends, co-religionists, or similar others) versus outgroup members (strangers, those with differing religions or ethnicities). Such parochial gaps also vary as a function of religiosity. Although studies have reported greater engagement in volunteering on the part of religious individuals, this is ambiguous from the perspective of parochialism. A substantial proportion of volunteer work is on behalf of religious organizations (e.g., church based) or groups directly benefitting religious causes. Many studies that distinguish types of volunteering find that religiosity is associated with more volunteering for beneficiaries that affirm religious values but not for secular causes (Lam, 2002). Likewise, those who are religiously affiliated are less likely to volunteer for groups in which their religion constitutes the minority (Storm, 2015). By contrast, those who are unaffiliated volunteer at equivalent or greater rates than the religiously affiliated when the type of volunteering is generalized and not via a religious organization (Cragun, 2014). Thus, religious effects on volunteering are weak to nonexistent in general community contexts when the beneficiaries are not identifiably religious (Low et al., 2007; Monsma, 2007; Wang & Graddy, 2008). This suggests that religiosity is more predictive of where and why people volunteer for certain causes rather than on whether or not they volunteer (Borgonovi, 2008; Galen et al., 2015). Charitable giving follows a similar pattern in that higher levels of religiosity are associated with greater ingroup exclusivity in donations. In one longitudinal study, religious attendance and belief in divine moral authority predicted later charitable behavior only directed toward the local religious group whereas other aspects of R/S beliefs and teachings were unrelated to charity (Reddish & Tong, 2021).

A similar pattern is seen in regard to interpersonal trust—a general indicator of prosociality also constituting a facet of the "Big Five" personality trait of agreeableness. One of the most consistent markers of highly functional societies is the high level of mutual trust citizens have in one another (Delhey & Newton, 2005). The higher level of trust reported by religious individuals has been presented as evidence for the belief-as-benefit theory. Putnam and Campbell

(2010) attribute their finding that religious people are "more trusting of just about everybody than are secular people" (p. 460) to their spending more time with other trustworthy people or "… because their faith encourages them to look on the brighter side of things." Indeed, from a cultural anthropology perspective, it has been suggested that one of the culturally evolved functions of early proto-religions was specifically the promotion of social trust, allowing small-scale societies to "scale up" by making interactions with strangers (e.g., market based trade) less fraught (Norenzayan et al., 2016). Such theories suggest that belief in supernatural monitoring contributed to trusting interactions because it reinforced the presumption that others also believe that they are being monitored ("watched people are nice people"). This implies that atheists are not to be trusted because they are perceived to lack this constraining belief (Gervais et al., 2011).

However, as with parochial morality, the characterization of religiosity as instilling generalized trust is qualified by factors such as the specific aspect of religion (e.g., belief in God versus fundamentalism) and the intended reference person or group ("trust in whom?"). Putnam and Campbell state: "Religious Americans are more trusting and (perhaps) more trustworthy" (p. 458), but those authors contrast, for example, the effect of fundamentalist beliefs on trust (negative) with those of religious attendance (positive). In fact, many studies have found that while social forms of religiosity predict greater trust, individual forms of religiosity predict lower trust (Valente & Okulicz-Kozaryn, 2021). When social aspects of religion such as group attendance are held constant, beliefs themselves are often unrelated, or even negatively related, to generalized trust and volunteering (Loveland et al., 2017; Welch et al., 2007).

The key to explaining this paradox is found in the identity of the recipient of trust. Across countries and states, the general negative relationship between trust and religiosity becomes stronger with increasing contextual religious diversity (Berggren & Bjørnskov, 2011). As with parochialism, it is common to display greater trust toward those who are familiar as opposed to strangers, outgroup members, or people in general. However, people vary in the degree of "radius" between their trust in strangers versus in familiars. Those with a relatively broad radius of trust make few distinctions between familiars and strangers, largely because they see no reason to distrust the latter group. By contrast, those with a smaller radius of trust are more suspicious of those outside their immediate sphere and are characterized as insular or clannish. In this sense, as with nepotism, the "effect of religion" does not increase overall trust, but rather it changes the radius by focusing trust toward the ingroup while decreasing trust in the outgroup.

This is best illustrated by experiments using economic exchanges in settings that allow for the control of the group identities of the partners. In a familiar pattern, participants who are religious do tend to be more trusting in their economic offers to partners, but this is typically contingent upon the partner's identity as a potential fellow ingroup member (Galen, 2012). For example, Thunstrom et al. (2021) found that religious people trust those of higher religiosity more, but only if they share the same religion (e.g., Christians trust Christians more than they trusted Muslims and nonbelievers). Those who are nonbelievers tend to display trust in a less contingent manner (i.e., greater trust in people in general; Galen et al., 2022; Nezlek, 2022).

Just as religious belief subsumes different strains that evince opposing relationships with prosociality (e.g., emphases on salvation versus on social justice), religious group membership also subsumes components with paradoxical effects on prosociality. That is, religious organizations enhance social networking opportunities but exert a homophilizing effect that limits contact with those outside the group. This narrows the radius of trust, decreasing tolerance for outsiders (Galen et al., 2021). In sociological parlance (Putnam, 2000), religious believers tend to exhibit more bonding social capital (closed networks consisting of those from the same background), whereas nonbelievers tend to exhibit greater bridging social capital (i.e., contact between diverse social groups).

Religious homophilizing can also present interpretive problems in that the referent of trust is often not specified on surveys and questionnaires. For example, an item on the World Values Survey asks: "Generally speaking, would you say that most people can be trusted?" Because more religious individuals, particularly those with sectarian allegiances (e.g., fundamentalist), have relatively narrower radii of contacts, their reference group ("most people"), on average, consists of those similar to themselves as opposed to the reference group for the nonreligious for whom "most people" includes more dissimilar others (e.g., the concept "others" differing in a rural village versus London). Therefore, R/S believers may report that they trust others, but their social networks of others consist primarily of people similar to themselves rather than strangers (Nezlek, 2022). Consequently, the negative effects of religiosity on generalized trust may be even greater than previously suggested, when taking into consideration existing differences in social networks as a function of religiosity.

Examined in the aggregate, the pattern of prosocial attitudes and behaviors yield several conclusions regarding the role of R/S influences and motivating factors. What has often been interpreted as enhancing effects of religion on morality and prosociality (e.g., greater cooperation and niceness) may mask group-binding or parochial effects (McKay & Whitehouse, 2015). At higher levels of religiosity, prosocial behaviors are increasingly moderated by factors such as the identity of the targets and the degree of pluralism or homophily in the social milieu (e.g., channeling of volunteering and charity to religious, rather than secular sources). When viewed from a pluralistic or universal perspective, the primary motivation associated with most forms of R/S is not the promotion of general welfare, but rather of ingroup interests and cohesion. Stated differently, the same forces that make religious groups cohere (binding and bonding) also lead to parochialism. As described by Norenzayan: "a religious community would not be a cooperative community if there were no social boundaries" (2013: 160). However, this motivation may not be consciously recognized. Viewed from the subjective perspective of an ingroup member, what is salient regarding prosociality may be simply that one is engaging in it (e.g., donating and volunteering) rather than any awareness of selectivity. Consequently, believers attribute their motivation to altruistic benevolence while being unaware of selective or biased aspects.

Just as moral or prosocial motivations can only be properly assessed by distinguishing the identity of the target recipient, comparisons between different methods of assessment can reveal motivating factors. A substantial proportion of the research literature is based upon self-report measures (e.g., personality inventories, hypothetical actions) rather than observed behavior (e.g., bystander assistance paradigms). This is relevant because the association between R/S and morality/prosociality tends to be greater when assessed via self-report rather than actual behaviors. Religious people self-report on personality measures such as agreeableness that they are more trusting of people, but they are not behaviorally more trusting of strangers in economic exchange games (Galen et al., 2022). Likewise, religious individuals are more likely than the nonreligious to report that they value honesty and that they do not cheat. However, there is little or no relationship between religiosity and actual behavioral honesty (Williamson & Assadi, 2005). Similarly, in the domain of retributive aggression, those who are high in intrinsic religiosity report that they are less vengeful, but this is unrelated to actual retaliatory behavior (Greer et al., 2005; Leach et al., 2008).

A related distinction pertains to the relative degree of self-initiation or planning, as opposed to spontaneity in the measure of prosociality. Behaviors such as charitable giving and volunteering are quintessential examples of planned prosociality in that they are self-initiated and targeted. By contrast, social psychological experiments often consist of surreptitiously observed behaviors in ambiguous contexts where participants are blind to the purpose of the study.

One major advantage of conceptualizing morality based on spontaneous helping is the reduced influence of self-presentation or expectational sets in which participants conform their responses to how they should behave. Evidence cited in support of theories of religious prosociality tends to consist primarily of planned, non-spontaneous actions (e.g., charitable giving) and self-reported measures (e.g., "How often have you helped a stranger?"). However, dispositional religiosity effects tend to be weak to nonexistent in spontaneous tasks. Everyday behavioral interactions in secular contexts such as blood donation, financial transactions, tipping, or anonymous payment on the honors system do not show a religious prosociality effect (Gillum & Masters, 2010; Grossman & Parrett, 2011; Pruckner & Sausgruber, 2008).

The measures perhaps most diagnostic of spontaneous prosocial tendencies are studies of bystander assistance, such as the classic "Good Samaritan" experiment (Darley & Batson, 1973) in which naive participants were observed as they walked past a "victim," providing an opportunity to help. The results revealed a substantial impact of contextual factors (e.g., whether the participant was in a hurry) but few differences as a function of religiosity. Subsequent experiments by Batson and colleagues (e.g., Batson et al., 1989) systematically varied spontaneous helping scenarios to discern the underlying motivations and their relationship with religious orientation. Batson et al. concluded that greater intrinsic religiosity was associated with the motivation to appear helpful (to others, to God, to themselves), and to project a prosocial image (i.e., "reward-based helping"). By contrast, participants with a Quest religious orientation (low in fundamentalism, open-ended) were motivated to help because of genuine empathy, based on the stated needs of the victim ("empathy-based helping").

By examining the aggregate patterns across different conceptual formats (i.e., self-reported versus behavioral; spontaneous versus planned), a coherent picture emerges of how R/S does and does not play a role in morality and prosociality, and more importantly of the inferred motivation behind the patterns. Religious moral motivations appear to be more deliberative, such as prioritizing the ability to select particular beneficiaries. By contrast, the role of religiosity is reduced in diverse contexts and spontaneous situations that would make it difficult to engage in selective prosociality. A related situational feature is that religiosity, when operationalized as a stable trait (e.g., intrinsic orientation), is often unrelated to prosociality unless contextual salience is increased, such as by experimental priming or moral identity threats (Ward & King, 2018). This suggests that R/S belief functions more as a set of associated concepts associatively linked by stereotypic content, requiring activation.

Stereotypes of Religious Morality

The extant evidence suggests that the R/S belief-as-benefit hypothesis is not supported in any general sense and calls into question the accuracy of self-attributions regarding moral motivation (e.g., "My greater morality is derived from R/S sources"). Nonetheless, there exists a widespread belief to the contrary, particularly among the devout. Roughly half of Americans who are religiously affiliated believe that it is necessary to believe in God to be moral (Pew Research Center, 2017). Many social science researchers also support the religious prosociality hypothesis. This belief in the moral benefit of R/S constitutes a general social stereotype, manifesting in numerous ways. The following section will focus on two: Biases in the formation of impressions of others, and the discrepancy between individuals' self-perceived versus actual morality.

Firstly, when forming impressions of others, targets depicted with a religious identity are rated by participants as being more moral and as possessing enhanced prosocial personality traits (e.g., agreeableness) relative to ostensibly nonreligious targets (Galen et al., 2014; Galen et al., 2011). Although endorsement of this stereotype is particularly strong among the highly religious (Ward & King, 2021), some studies suggest that even the nonreligious attribute, to some extent, greater morality to religious targets (Gervais et al., 2017). Conversely, the nonreligious, particularly atheists, are thought to be untrustworthy, although there is some evidence that negative moral stereotypes regarding atheists can be diminished by reminders of counter-stereotypic information, such as that they can have a moral system and be concerned for others (Mallinas & Conway, 2022).

Just as impressions of others' morality are stereotypically biased, individuals' attributions regarding their own morality are influenced by a "better than average" bias (Tappin & McKay, 2017). This is enhanced among those who are high in religiosity in a "holier than thou" effect, such as seeing themselves as being more adherent to biblical commandments than others (Eriksson & Funcke, 2014; Rowatt et al., 2002). The discrepancy between views of one's own, versus others' morality appears to exist, not because others' morality is underestimated, but rather because believers' own morality is overestimated (Epley & Dunning, 2000). The gap in accuracy between moral ratings of self, versus others is due, in part, to different methods used to make two types of judgments. In accordance with dual processing theory, people tend to evaluate their own behavior based on idiosyncratic information such as their intentions and presumed personality traits, leading to biased moral estimates (e.g., "I am a nice person so I would not administer shocks to someone"). By contrast, views of others' morality are based on objective base rate information (e.g., "Others will conform to the situation"), producing predictions that are unbiased by personal introspection and introspective limitations (Wilson, 2002). The endorsement of a religious morality stereotype is one type of bias that contaminates self-ratings in the manner of a transitive inference: "I'm religious, and religious people have moral qualities, therefore I must have these qualities."

This process provides a more complete explanation of the findings in the previous sections (e.g., self-report versus behavioral outcomes). The application of the religious morality stereotype to oneself inflates estimates on self-report measures of prosociality (e.g., hypothetical predictions) as opposed to behaviors observed in controlled experimental contexts (Galen, 2012). Moral domains consisting of behaviors stereotypically associated with religious teachings lead religious individuals to report that they engage in these behaviors to a greater extent. Values that are stereotypically associated with religion can also lead to congruence fallacies. Specifically, religious individuals report that, when they engage in moral behaviors they are motivated by their religion, such as: "When I'm forgiving, it must be because my religion has taught me forgiveness."

These biases also contribute to divergences between general endorsement of moral values in the absence of specific behavioral enactment of those values. For instance, while religiosity is associated with higher self-reported trait forgiveness (e.g., "how forgiving are you?"), it is not substantially related to measures of forgiveness for specific transgressions (Brown et al., 2007; McCullough & Worthington, 1999). A similar pattern can be observed in behaviors inversely related to forgiveness. Specifically, greater religiosity is correlated with lower self-rated retaliatory aggressiveness; but behavioral measures of aggression are unrelated (Leach et al., 2008).

Several theories have been offered to explain this "religion-forgiveness discrepancy," including the introduction of response bias based upon the method of eliciting examples of past forgiveness. Tsang, McCullough, and Hoyt (2005) suggest that asking people to generate examples of past transgressions can attenuate the extent to which reports of forgiveness correlate with religiosity. Offenses that have been forgiven may be more difficult to remember (i.e., those who are truly forgiving are less able to recall having been wronged because they "let it go"). When more restrictive recall procedures were used, Tsang et al. identified a small but significant relationship between religion and transgression-specific forgiveness. However, the most robust influence on the religion-trait forgiveness discrepancy is simply the degree to which more religious individuals believe that they should be more forgiving (i.e., a stereotypic effect). As with other relationships with religiosity, biases such as parochialism influence the selectivity of forgiveness. Shared ingroup loyalty (e.g., common membership in the same church shared by perpetrator and victim) leads to increased forgiveness, relative to outgroup offenders (Greer et al., 2014). In sum, stereotypic content held by highly religious individuals regarding moral values results in inflated self-reports of being more forgiving in the abstract, whereas religiosity is unrelated to specific instances of forgiving transgressions.

Similarly, the trait of humility also reflects a religious value-behavior discrepancy. Humility is an other-focused interpersonal stance, marked by the inhibition of selfish motivations (Davis et al., 2017). Humble individuals are down-to-earth, low in self-focus, with a realistic view of themselves (Rowatt et al., 2014). As with other moral values conceptualized as traits, R/S is presumed to lead to greater humility because some religious content emphasizes it as a virtue. Nonetheless, the literature has indicated weak and inconsistent evidence that R/S increases humility, an effect largely attributable to conceptual and definitional issues. (Davis et al., 2017).

One such issue is related to definition of humility itself, which includes a lack of arrogance and awareness of one's limitations. These qualities make it difficult to measure trait humility because those who are genuinely humble will downplay their own humility. In contrast, narcissists may "humble brag," rendering self-assessments—consisting of items such as "I am a humble person"—of dubious validity. Likewise, asking people to report their degree of self-awareness is conceptually problematic, just as with any other self-reflective cognitive processes such as the Dunning-Kruger effect, which stipulates that unskilled people are unable to accurately assess the extent of their own incompetence. Similar to other stereotypic spiritual values, greater religiosity is associated with greater self-reported humility. In a series of studies, Van Tongeren et al. (2018) found that the religious report greater strivings to act humbly and a greater desire to be described as humble. The authors also found that experimentally priming humility decreased hypothetical intentions to behave defensively in retaliation to criticism among religious participants and an increased tendency among nonreligious participants. However, the overall pattern did not indicate greater state-humility among the religious (i.e., the lowest level of retaliatory intention was found among nonreligious participants who were neutrally primed).

One method used to circumvent the limitations of self-report measures is to cross-validate them with peer ratings. Rowatt et al. (2014) found that greater self-reported humility among the religious was ostensibly validated by peers. However, these peer reports were completed by friends and acquaintances who were not blind to the religious identity of the target individual. Given the ample evidence of biased impression formation (mentioned above) of the morality of religious targets, peer reports of moral values, including humility, essentially represent the same phenomenon. Rather, the measures least likely to be contaminated by stereotypic effects feature comparisons between ratings of the self on specific traits ("How humble are you?") compared to ratings of others ("How humble is the average person?"). As mentioned above, these self-other comparisons (e.g., Eriksson & Funcke, 2014) suggest a religious better-than-others effect, not humility.

In sum, self-rated moral value traits exhibit a misattribution of morality effect consistent with a process in which stereotypic activation increases the tendency to focus on expected content (e.g., how one ought to behave). A portion of this response bias derives from an internalized general social stereotype of religious morality, which is enhanced among the highly religious. Consequently, veridical moral indicators are unlikely to be assessed and reported in an unbiased manner, thus requiring controlled conditions for assessment. Ideally, studies should compare self-reports to more objective assessments of spontaneous behaviors in low-demand settings.

Stereotype Internalization

Taken in the aggregate, patterns of moral and prosocial relationships with R/S suggest a common underlying explanation: The influence of R/S believers' internalized self-stereotype of morality. According to self-categorization theory, self-stereotyping occurs when people make inferences about themselves based on the stereotype of the group to which they belong. As stated earlier, there is a transitive process by which individuals extrapolate their moral standing from their group identity: "I'm religious. Religious people are more moral because their beliefs and teachings promote morality. Therefore, my level of morality is greater due to the influence of my religiosity." As reflected in survey data mentioned at the beginning of the chapter, the religious prosociality hypothesis posits that specific R/S practices are believed to be conducive to greater morality; however, the link between religiosity and moral self-image may be more parsimoniously explained by self-stereotyping (Ward & King, 2021). Eriksson and Funcke (2014) found that more religious people judged both themselves and their ingroup particularly high on warmth (the better-than-average effect). They also judged the average religious in-group member (a prototype exemplar embodying the group stereotype) even more favorably than themselves. This also explains biases in impressions formed of outgroup members. In Galen, Williams, and Ver Wey (2014), the degree to which religious targets were rated as being more moral and agreeable relative to nonreligious targets was mediated by participants' endorsement of negative stereotypes regarding the morality of the nonreligious.

A similar phenomenon can be observed in meta-stereotypes held by both religious and nonreligious individuals. Meta-stereotypes refer to group members' beliefs regarding how they are perceived by others (i.e., "how we think you think about us"). Saroglou, Yzerbyt, and Kaschten (2011) found that believers and non-believers largely agree that religious people are seen as being high in prosociality and low in hedonism and impulsivity, while the nonreligious are viewed as exhibiting the opposite pattern. The awareness of meta-stereotypes is manifested in patterns of behavior such as favoritism based on positive views of fellow ingroup members. As previously discussed, religious people are presumed to be more trustworthy as observed in economic exchange experiments in which people forward more money to religious partners (illustrating the principle: "trust people who trust in God"; Norenzayan, 2013). This may reflect the presumption that others who believe they are being supernaturally monitored are deterred from cheating ("watched people are nicer people"). This stereotype is particularly endorsed by highly religious individuals. Although religious partners are trusted more by most people in general (i.e., a stereotype effect) they are especially trusted by other religious people (an ingroup favoritism effect; Galen et al., 2014; Tan & Vogel, 2008).

Self-categorization theory stipulates that the qualities that any given person sees in themselves are deduced from the perceived group stereotype. In the present case, religious individuals have a high self-image of morality because they have internalized the stereotype of their religious ingroup, which is one of high morality (Ward & King, 2021). This is not the only possible explanation for the correspondence between individuals' views of their own morality and their views of other group members' morality. It is theoretically possible for the causal direction to run in the opposite direction—that views of the self are projected onto the group (van Veelen et al., 2016). This self-anchoring theory, when applied to religious morality, would suggest an inductive process by which religious individuals hold favorable views of their own morality that are then seen as characterizing their favored group ("I am moral. Therefore, my religious group is moral too"). However, Eriksson and Funcke (2014) argued against this view because religious participants did not view themselves as superior in all domains or compared to all people (including ingroup members) but rather only in the stereotypic-relevant domain (i.e., warmth) and only when in comparison with those outside their religious ingroup.

Self-stereotyping can also involve compensatory motivations such as when individuals are threatened by the prospect of failing to embody characteristics of their group stereotype. Burris and Jackson (2000) exposed participants to (false) feedback suggesting they were low in helpfulness (disconfirming their prosocial stereotype). The results indicated that high-intrinsic religious individuals increased their religious self-stereotyping by enhancing their ratings of the subjective importance of their religious group when exposed to this threatening feedback. This points to a motivated defense activated by stereotype-disconfirming information. Other evidence also suggests that internalized religious stereotypes can elicit a defensive reaction in response to perceptions that others hold negative views of one's religious group. Palasinski and Seol (2015) found that Catholic Christians were more likely to offer help to a religious outgroup (a mosque) after being told that Catholics were viewed by others as intolerant, reflecting a motivation to counteract negative stereotypes.

Religious Self-Enhancement

The existence of stereotypes regarding religious morality and their observed effects (e.g., discrepancies between self-report and behavior) is most parsimoniously explained by Religious Self-Enhancement (RSE) theory. As with other epistemic and existential needs (see Chapter 3), humans are motivated to maintain a favorable self-image, leading them to present enhanced versions of themselves. One manifestation of RSE is within the domain of religion itself, in which believers attempt to present a favorable image of their own religious attitudes and behaviors. This can be observed, for example, in self-reported measures of the frequency of church attendance, which are inflated compared to reports from other sources such as momentary time diaries, peer reports and behavioral records (Brenner, 2011). In accordance with social value theories of religious norms, the RSE varies as a function of the normative importance of religious identity across societies, yielding a wider reporting gap in the United States than in Europe. Similarly, in the Muslim world, the overreporting of prayer is associated with the relative importance of individuals' religious identity (Brenner, 2014). Methods of assessment that accentuate the salience of religious identity, such as asking people to self-report on measures or interviews, tend to result in over-reporting of attendance (Brenner, 2012) compared to open-ended measures featuring lower salience such as time diaries ("What did you do Sunday?"), which are less reactive to self-presentation biases. Religious self-enhancement can also be seen when responses are made under bogus pipeline conditions (i.e., using a physiological device to convince participants that their "real" responses can be detected, thereby discouraging self-presentation strategies). Jones and Elliott (2017) found that, relative to responses made in bogus pipeline conditions, intrinsic religiosity and spiritual experience reports were higher under normal (non-pipeline) conditions, indicating the presence of a socially desirable response set. In sum, the influence of RSE reflects individuals' motivation to present themselves in accord with a stereotypic identity of "a good religious person."

Religious Self-Enhancement of Morality

The specific method of self-esteem enhancement is largely determined by one's culture. In materialistic or individualistic cultures, efforts to enhance self-esteem are likely to involve the accumulation of resources and personal achievements, whereas those in collectivist cultures acquire esteem by promotion of one's family or group (e.g., being a "team player"; Markus & Kitayama, 1991). Social cognitive biases are also motivated by self-esteem needs, including those heuristics promoting a more favorable view of the self (e.g., self-serving attributions, confirmation bias, downward social comparisons with inferior others). The tendency to self-enhance is an early-appearing basic motive (akin to personality traits), of which religiosity is one possible expression. Indeed, religiosity itself can be conceptualized as a culturally contextualized method of self-enhancement (Sedkidies & Gebauer, 2010). Religion-as-social-value and culture-fit theories demonstrate that various traits often described as being products of religious belief (e.g., agreeableness) are instead religious manifestations of more fundamental underlying traits (e.g., communal personality types) expressed in accordance with cultural norms. Those who live in a predominantly religious milieu enhance self-esteem through religious engagement, as can be seen in the greater correlation between self-enhancement and religiosity in such milieus (Eriksson & Funke, 2014). Enhancement is most likely to occur on dimensions perceived as central to the self and, according to self-categorization theory, prevailing group norms determine what is considered self-central. Therefore, given that the stereotypic group norm for religious people includes high levels of morality and prosociality, religious people are most likely to self-enhance on those dimensions.

Self-enhancement phenomena have most commonly been explored in the scientific literature using self-report measures of socially desirable responding, impression management, and self-deception (i.e., attempting to "look good"; Paunonen & LeBel, 2012). Although religiosity is associated with higher scores on measures of self-deception and impression management (Leak & Fish, 1989), there has been a long-running debate regarding the proper interpretation of this effect as either representing enhancement biases or veridical prosociality. For instance, Trimble (1997), argues that the higher scores on standard social desirability scales result from content overlap in which intrinsically religious people actually do perform the sorts of actions featured on such scales (e.g., morality, self-restraint). The personality trait of agreeableness (discussed earlier because of its association with religiosity) is also the "Big Five" trait most closely related to socially desirable responding because of the nature of its content (i.e., warmth, trust). People attempting to appear moral or who are instructed to simulate a positive response set specifically self-enhance on facets of this trait (Furnham, 1997; Paulhus & John, 1998). This susceptibility of agreeableness to self-enhancement can also be observed in the greater discrepancy between self- and peer ratings, in comparison to other Big Five traits (Ludeke & Carey, 2015). Ludeke and Carey (2015) found that the association between religiosity and inflating self-rated agreeableness was fully mediated by the degree to which religious individuals saw value in this characteristic and attempted to selectively enhance it. Conversely, when using measures that are more ecologically valid than self-reports (e.g., reports of moral acts on momentary time diaries) this relationship disappears. Specifically, Hofmann et al. (2014) found no link between religiousness and agreeableness-related behaviors, indicating that religiously related enhancement is a product of self-report bias. Similarly, a recent meta-analysis concluded that the relationship between standard measures of socially desirable responding and prosocial behaviors in experimental settings (i.e., economic games) was essentially zero (Lanz et al., 2022). Realistically, the "substance versus style" debate is not likely to be satisfactorily resolved solely via the use of SDR inventories. Given the limitations of self-report measures, a conservative conclusion may be that the religious are prone to (1) represent themselves in socially desirable ways and are (2) more likely to enhance on those traits most closely associated with self-central, stereotypical values (Ludeke & Carey, 2015).

Some measures offer more objective conceptualizations of self-enhancement compared to the standard inventories of socially desirable responding. In a series of studies, Gebauer, Sedikides, and Schrade (2017) demonstrated that religious individuals self-enhance in three major domains: Better than average ratings, knowledge overclaiming, and grandiose narcissism. As mentioned above, religiosity is predictive of a greater gap between self-rated morality and their views of others' morality (Eriksson & Funcke, 2014; Rowatt et al., 2002). More specifically, Gebauer et al. (2017) found that Christians exhibited a better-than-average effect on their ability to live up to Christian commandments of faith (e.g., "have no other gods before me") and communion (e.g., "honor thy mother and thy father"). Christians also displayed enhancement on measures of knowledge overclaiming, which assessed participants' reported familiarly with concepts both real (e.g., the Ten Commandments) and fictional (e.g., "the story of Jesus and the golden goblet"). Christians overclaimed knowledge to a greater degree than did nonbelievers, especially in self-central domains such as (nonexistent) Biblical concepts. Gebauer et al. (2017b) also found a large relationship between religiosity and narcissism in its communal form (e.g., "I am the most helpful person I know"), which, although unrelated to objective prosociality (Nehrlich et al., 2019), is self-central to religiosity. In similar work, content reflective of an inflated moral self-image (e.g., "I always live up to my moral aspirations," "I am a more moral person than my peers") is also correlated with religiosity (Ward & King, 2018). In sum, such findings support the religiosity-as-self-enhancement hypothesis, contradicting the notion that R/S promotes greater humility.

In addition to these associations with general religious belief, there is evidence that engagement in specific spiritual practices may also potentiate enhancement tendencies. Vonk and Visser (2021) identified a form of spiritual narcissism by comparing self-ratings and other ratings on a range of spiritual skills (e.g., "I am aware of things that others are not aware of"). These authors found that responses from those attending "energetic training centers" (purporting to develop paranormal skills such as aura reading and past life regression) reflected a sense of spiritual superiority and supernatural overconfidence compared to those training in secular mindfulness techniques. Similarly, both yoga and meditation practices increase practitioners' self-enhancement tendencies on measures of communal narcissism, better than average comparisons, and self-esteem (Gebauer et al., 2018). These results suggest an association between the motivation for the ostensible acquisition of spiritual skill sets and self-enhancement.

Summary of Self-Enhancement and Religious Moral Stereotyping

A summary of the extant information in the chapter indicates that religiosity and spirituality are most clearly associated with greater prosociality on attitudinal measures and self-reported behaviors of a planned nature, particularly content that is susceptible to self-enhancement tendencies. The central construct linking these patterns is the internalization of a stereotype of religious morality. However, because people are unaware of self-stereotyping in the process of self-enhancement, this leads to a paradoxical outcome. The more motivated people are to be moral, the more vulnerable they are to biases of self-enhancement (Ellemers, 2017: 33). Stated differently, to the extent that a stereotype of religious morality is self-central, individuals are unaware of their tendency to unrealistically enhance in that domain. Notably, Gebauer et al. (2017b) found that religious self-enhancement differs from other psychological motives in a pivotal way: Although Christian participants claimed that their religiosity satisfied a range of motives (e.g., safety and security, meaning in life, calmness about death), they explicitly denied that their religion satisfied self-enhancement motives (i.e., that it would yield superiority over nonbelievers). As mentioned earlier, explicit religious content is often perceived to encourage humility, but it appears to exert the opposite effect at an implicit level. This illustrates the central paradox that, although religious individuals self-enhance on the domain most central to their identity (i.e., morality), they specifically deny that their religion contributes to moral enhancement and are consequently less aware of the actual enhancing effects, leading to a moral "blind spot bias."

Secular Mechanisms for the Misattribution of Greater Morality

As described in the preceding sections, internalized stereotypes of morality promote an enhanced sense of moral identity in the absence of corresponding high levels of behavioral morality. This disjunction or gap is amplified as a function of greater religiosity. In the following section, the causal mechanisms and consequences of this gap will be explored.

The literature on secular morality has identified various methods by which moral inconsistencies remain unrecognized or are rationalized so that an inflated moral self-image is preserved. Numerous enhancement mechanisms rely on automatic and unconscious motivated processes (e.g., biased memory, selective attention, self-serving attributions; Hepper et al., 2010). For example, individuals can selectively attend to abstract moral values, emphasizing hypotheticals (e.g., plans, desires), rather than concrete, observable behaviors (Kruger & Gilovich, 2004). By adopting a distal temporal focus, people can recollect instances of past behavior or create forecasts of future intentions (the "should" self), allowing morality to be construed based upon expectations and ideals rather than specific proximal behaviors (Tenbrunsel et al., 2010). Similarly, the holier-than-thou effect also derives from individuals' tendency to overestimate the degree to which their behavior is influenced by moral sentiments and intentions, while underestimating self-interested motives (Epley & Dunning, 2000). This represents the classic bias identified by Tversky and Kahneman (1982) in which people tend to make predictions biased by an internal approach—a reliance on idiosyncratic information derived from introspection rather than more valid objective base-rate information. Therefore, one general secular explanation for the existence of an unrealistically high moral self-image is that it is maintained via motivated cognition consistent with self-stereotyping.

The existence of a gap between moral self-image and behavior often involves a conflict between the desire to appear moral versus the desire to avoid costs incurred by foregoing benefits or having to engage in self-sacrificing behavior. This is exemplified by the phenomenon of moral hypocrisy, in which self-serving motivations must be rationalized to maintain a facade of morality (thereby deceiving oneself as well as to others). In a series of studies (Batson et al., 1997; Batson et al., 1999b; Batson et al., 2002) Batson and colleagues identified several ways in which individuals maintained the appearance of honesty while benefitting from dishonesty. A paradigm was used in which participants could assign two tasks, one to themselves and the other to a (fictitious) partner. The tasks consisted of one clearly preferable option (an interesting task that could earn prize money) versus an undesirable option (a boring task earning nothing). The variables of interest consisted not only of which task would be assigned but also the methods by which participants justified their allocation decision. The researchers identified dispositional and contextual factors predictive of whether participants would act fairly and in accordance with their stated moral principles. Across several study iterations, there was a consistent discrepancy between the method identified by participants as being most fair, and the decision method that they actually used. The hypocrisy phenomenon manifested in the justifications used by participants in attempting to appear fair, while keeping the preferable task to themselves.

Batson and colleagues observed several patterns of moral rationalization in which participants took advantage of the "wiggle room" created by ambiguities that allowed a failure to act in accordance with stated principles. In several of the study variations, participants were informed that they could choose to allocate tasks by flipping a coin. However, for many participants, the coin flip did not produce consistently fair results (equal outcomes in assigning the desirable task to the partner or themselves). Rather, the coin merely provided justificatory cover in that they could point to their decision to flip as evidence of their fairness, but subvert this by fudging the results of the flip (e.g., "That was a practice flip," "Best out of three" or "Did I say heads? I meant tails").

A consistent pattern in these studies was the failure of self-reported morality measures to meaningfully predict behavioral outcomes. Although higher scores on some measures (e.g., trait social responsibility) predicted the likelihood of choosing the fair coin flip method of task allocation, they were largely uncorrelated with fudging the flip (versus making a fair assignment). Batson and colleagues also noted that discrepancies between moral standards (e.g., "I should be fair") and behavior (i.e., "I'm taking the desirable task") could be resolved via several routes, such as disattending to contradictions between standards and behavior. Similar methods have been observed by other researchers, such as motivated forgetting of standards after engaging in unethical behaviors (Shu & Gino, 2012). These patterns parallel behavior-induced attitude change found in self-perception and cognitive dissonance phenomena in that standards are relaxed to align with behavior, making cheating more acceptable (Shu et al., 2011). The motivated cognitive processes that function to minimize the gap between unethical behavior and moral self-image often rely, at least some degree, on self-deception. Batson et al. (1999b) found that making participants more aware of themselves by placing a mirror in the room had some limited effect in decreasing self-deception and increasing honesty. However, even under awareness conditions, fair task assignment was unlikely if the expected standards of behavior were left unclear due to vague instructions (i.e., "the decision is up to you") as opposed to specified ones ("most people flip a coin"). Rather, as with dissonance-driven attitude change, even self-aware participants could simply redefine fairness standards to match their behavior by justifying how keeping the desirable task was really the right thing to do. In other words, mere self-awareness, in the absence of clear expected standards, did not increase honesty.

These results have implications for other theories of putative morality-enhancing factors such as the presence of a social audience or supernatural monitoring. Without clear objective standards, the mere perception of being watched (i.e., by God/s) will not increase moral outcomes if attention is not also drawn to a clear standard for moral behavior ("God wants me to abide by the coin flip") that leaves less room for rationalization (e.g., "God wants me to benefit"). Subsequent studies have also demonstrated that self-deception (i.e., the inverse of self-awareness) serves to render moral gaps less noticeable and is more likely to take place when the hypocrisy is subtle rather than blatant. Small amounts of dishonesty allow self-serving behaviors to occur without major adjustments to one's moral self-concept required by excessive dishonesty (Mazar et al., 2008). Rather, motivated reasoning biases operate optimally in conditions subtle enough to allow plausible deniability.

There are other ways in which a gap between a high moral self-image and actual behavior can be reconciled without changing behavior. According to self-affirmation theory (Steele, 1988), when people experience a threat to one aspect of their identity (e.g., having acted selfishly) self-esteem can be preserved by bringing to mind strengths in other domains (e.g., being personally abstemious with substance use). Similarly, people egocentrically play to their strengths by redefining whatever matches their own traits or skill sets as being more desirable (Dunning et al., 1991). Therefore, failures to act prosocially (e.g., being kind) can be "offset" by focusing on other moral assets such as ascetic "personal morality" qualities.

The relationship between one's moral self-image on the one hand, and moral behavior on the other can also function in a hydraulic or compensatory manner, as with other psychological needs that maintain self-esteem (see Chapter 3). Acting virtuously or merely imagining engaging in prosocial behaviors can license moral laxity (Merritt et al., 2010). For example, Khan and Dhar (2006) found that those who imagined engaging in volunteer work showed a subsequent preference for a luxury good item; and those imagining helping another student were more likely to keep money for themselves rather than donating to a charity. One explanation for moral licensing is that good deeds establish moral credits, much like a bank account, that can be drawn upon to purchase the right to do bad deeds. Alternatively, a self-attributional perspective suggests that present behavior is viewed through a lens of past moral credentialing such that individuals conclude that if they have previously shown themselves to be moral, this standing leaves them free to behave as they wish. Moral credentials appear to be fungible in many ways, such as being vicariously acquired. For instance, those who are told that their ingroup was more moral than others or that members of their group behaved in a nonprejudiced way experience an inflated moral self-concept that can subsequently license greater prejudice (Kouchaki, 2011).

Likewise, when people anticipate that they may do something immoral or will be tempted in the future, they strategically attempt to stockpile moral credentials so that they will be more impervious to guilt (Merritt et al., 2012).

Compensatory moral motivation can function in the opposite direction as well, such as when earlier transgressions can increase later efforts to restore a damaged self-image. In a series of studies on moral compensation reminiscent of a "Lady MacBeth effect" ("out damned spot!"), Zhong and Liljenquist (2006) found that recalling an occasion when one acted immorally led to metaphoric as well as literal attempts at cleansing. Participants who contemplated past unethical deeds later displayed a greater affinity for cleaning products, as well as the desire to engage in prosocial action (i.e., to alleviate guilt). Further, this needs to compensate after immoral recall could be metaphorically wiped away, by allowing participants to clean their hands, reducing not only the threat to their moral self-image but also their compensatory motivation to perform volunteer work. Both moral licensing and compensation are dependent upon a sense of moral self-worth, such that those whose moral traits are subjectively perceived to be highly important will experience a greater motivation to compensate for misdeeds and to relax their standards after earning moral credentials in ways that align with their self-concept (Mulder & Aquino, 2013). As with most of the other mechanisms discussed, these processes operate largely unconsciously and out of awareness.

Religious and Spiritual Misattributions of Greater Morality

Many secular mechanisms that maintain or rationalize a gap between moral self-image and actual behaviors have R/S "versions." In other words, R/S terms and concepts serve psychological functions in a manner analogous to secular ones. For example, the tendency to overclaim moral virtues (e.g., humility, forgiveness) is a nearly universal self-serving bias. Methods of self-enhancement and rationalization can include secular (e.g., "Mother raised me to have more humility than everyone else") or religious (e.g., "My religion teaches humility") content. Likewise, moral licensing can be achieved via secular means ("I already gave to charity at the office") as well as religious ("I already gave to charity at church"). However, the wider self-report versus behavior gap in religious people suggests that some R/S mechanisms function to protect, enhance, and rationalize morality even more effectively than secular counterparts. In other words, the stereotypic association between R/S and morality produces greater motivation to deploy R/S rationalization methods in comparison to secular counterparts. The following section will present evidence of not only R/S misattributions of morality (or rationalizations of immorality) but also evidence of these R/S-exacerbated effects.

As described in Chapter 2, many causal attributional biases (e.g., Just World Belief, System Justification, victim blaming) have R/S versions (e.g., divine punishment, God's will). These R/S attributions involve content that amplifies existing secular biases, such as religious beliefs that promote victim-blaming attribution. For instance, Lea and Hunsberger (1990) found that those high in Christian orthodoxy showed greater levels of victim derogation after being reminded of their religion. Viewed from the perspective of the moral biases mentioned earlier in the present chapter, there is evidence that R/S concepts exacerbate such phenomena, including ingroup favoritism, impression formation, and self- versus other rating, by contributing to greater attributional biases (e.g., the holier-than-thou effect). In instances of impression formation biased by the target's social identity, outgroup members, particularly those who challenge or violate religious values, are viewed as less moral (or are literally demonized) in comparison to religious ingroup members (and by extension, the self) in accordance with stereotype effects. Religious and spiritual concepts can provide attributions that such individuals are reaping karmic moral payback or divine punishment. Feelings of schadenfreude can be justified by projecting the perceived deservingness and subjective wish for retribution externally, such as viewing misfortune as punishment stemming from God's will rather than our own wish-fulfillment (Portmann, 2000). These attributional examples from Chapter 2 demonstrate how R/S content can contribute to biased processing of moral content.

Moral licensing effects, in which earlier virtue can lead to later misdeeds, and vice versa in the case of moral compensation, have clear religious analogues. Post-misdeed guilt elicits a dissonance-driven desire for alleviation (e.g., confession, prayer), motivating compensatory rituals of moral cleansing (ablutions, absolution, penance). Even beyond specific misdeeds, R/S beliefs can contribute to licensing effects by promoting enhanced moral credentials, acquired vicariously via association with a religious group identity. As will be discussed in greater detail later in this chapter, this process contributes to attributions that the believers' own morality aligns with or represents a manifestation of the divine will.

Misattribution of Moral Content

The preceding sections described how people can misperceive the overall level of their own morality. Similar misattributions are made regarding the source of morality, including the reasons behind one's moral reactions. Just as the discrepancy between our perceived moral virtue vis-à-vis our behavior can be processed in a biased manner (e.g., minimized, rationalized, or justified), the attributed origins and content of our morality can be biased as well. Our ability to accurately introspect upon the origins of many of our mental experiences is limited, and in some cases, nonexistent (i.e., causal opacity). This lack of introspective awareness can lead to mistaken beliefs that our moral attitudes and reactions derive from R/S sources when this is not the case.

For many years, the study of morality was dominated by cognitive approaches, notably Kohlberg's (1976) stages of moral development model. As assessed by the Defining Issues Test (Rest et al., 1999), judgments of the correct course of action in particular situations were thought to be shaped and constrained by cognitive development and reasoning abilities. For example, the "Heinz and the expensive drug" dilemma features a man who needs to obtain a drug to save his wife, but he cannot afford to purchase it from a wealthy man. Kohlberg suggested that moral judgments regarding such dilemmas could be made, for instance, at a conventional level of development, based on social rules and laws (e.g., Heinz should not steal because that is illegal). Others reasoning at a post-conventional level may conclude that the preservation of human life represents a principle that transcends laws based on social convention, and therefore could justify stealing the drug. According to Kohlberg's model, such moral reactions are products of cognitive judgments, and at a more fundamental level, reason drives affect. However, in the past two decades, there has been a shift in conceptualizations of morality toward a greater emphasis on affect-driven, evolutionary-based process that function independently from, or even in opposition to, rational cognition. Perhaps the most influential such theory is Haidt's (2001) Social Intuitionist Model, which emphasizes the primacy of initial emotional and physiological responses. For instance, Schnall et al. (2008) found that inducing the feeling of disgust increased the severity of participants' moral judgments, even in situations with no direct connection between the emotion and the moral content being evaluated.

Further, Social-Intuitional models assert that because morality originates with prepotent, emotional responses, we are not always able to articulate rational reasons for our reactions. Haidt, Bjorklund, and Murphy (2000) have described those unable to rationally justify their moral reactions as being "morally dumbfounded"; often responding with variations of: "I know it's wrong, but I just can't come up with a reason why." Further, this suggests that not only are moral reactions based in affective intuitions (e.g., disgust), but that subsequent analytic judgments are created *post hoc* as justifications or rationalizations of affective responses. Haidt, Bjorklund, and Murphy (2000) found that, when confronted with factual or logical flaws in their accounts of moral reasoning, participants often searched for a different rationale and simply persevered in their original response.

The process of experiencing a moral intuition or affective reaction in the absence of conscious access may promote the generation of alternative plausible explanations (Cushman et al., 2006). In accordance with dual process accounts, when behavior is unexpectedly activated without accompanying conscious awareness an explanatory vacuum is created (Bar-Anan et al., 2010). Just as nature proverbially abhors a vacuum, the lack of awareness of our moral reactions is accompanied by negative affect, increasing the motivation to explain the behavior by creating confabulations or rationalizations that fill in the blanks (Gantman et al., 2017). The phenomenon known as casuistry refers to specious reasoning offered as justification for questionable behavior. For example, those who are biased toward favoring male job candidates can instead justify their selection as being based on educational qualifications that happen to also favor the male candidates (Norton et al., 2004). Casuistry involves not only strategic motivations such as the effort to appear (to others) as unbiased, but also self-deceptive components such as rationalizations that provide reassurance of moral rectitude. In essence, casuistry involves an attributional error in which individuals perceive their actions as being motivated by one set of features of a given situation when in fact they are actually motivated by other (self-serving) features.

People can also misattribute which domain or type of moral foundation is influencing their attitudes on a given issue. Koleva et al. (2012) found that individuals' stance on abortion, despite being framed in terms of harm prevention (e.g., protecting innocent life), was better predicted by their endorsement of the purity moral foundation (i.e., concern for violations of traditional sanctity values). Similarly, liberals' stance on gay marriage, often framed as motivated by fairness concerns (e.g., all consenting adults should have equal rights) is also better predicted by their (low) prioritization of the purity foundation. As mentioned earlier in the chapter, R/S moral attitudes are primarily distinguished by ascetic stances on sexuality, reproduction, and personal restraint (Moon et al., 2019). These examples illustrate that R/S believers, in accordance with stereotypic beliefs, may misattribute their reaction as representing general moral rectitude and communal prosocial attitudes, when in fact their moral reactions derive from more limited, narrower domains.

Conscious explanatory accounts that function to fill the introspective vacuum left by moral dumbfounding stem from a number of influences. These rationales consist of stereotypical content, social enhancement, and other justifications regarding why something should be seen as morally right or wrong. Content misattributions also occur in the absence of awareness of situational influences. Just as participants in social psychology experiments confabulate incorrect explanations for their behaviors (Nisbett & Wilson, 1977), prosocial helpers often formulate dispositional reasons for helping ("I was raised to care about those in need") when in fact they are influenced by contextual parameters. Likewise, when asked to explain engagement in helpful behaviors, an R/S believer may provide a religious rationale such as "my religion emphasizes kindness" whereas the actual motivation for the behavior may have been contextually based (e.g., not being in a hurry) or produced by unrelated heuristics (e.g., noticing an ingroup member who needs help).

A contributing factor to misattributions of R/S content is that "religion" is not a unitary construct. As discussed earlier, beliefs (e.g., in Gods), belonging (social identity), or behaviors (group worship, rituals) are not synonymous, and often differ in their relationship with moral constructs. Anthropological and Cognitive Science of Religion perspectives demonstrate that, on the level of ultimate function, phenomena subsumed within the general category of religion represent distinct constructs with independent origins. This multi-dimensionality contributes to source misattribution in that individuals may believe that their morality is influenced by one aspect of religiosity, when in fact they are influenced by another facet. For example, R/S content originating from social exchange intuitions ("God wants me to follow the golden rule") is functionally independent from R/S content generated by group binding and coalitional intuitions (e.g., "God favors our group consisting only of true believers"). As a result, this person may attribute their honesty and fair play to prosocial tenets of faith, when in fact, their actions are motivated by coalitional preferences, accompanied by parochial qualities.

Patterns of R/S source misattribution can also be observed by psychometrically deconstructing multi-dimensional religious inventories. Such analyses reveal that responses regarding individuals' valuation of their personal salvation (vertical faith prioritizing a relationship with God) are unrelated to their valuation of altruistic concerns, which are more closely related to humanitarian values (horizontal faith; Ji et al., 2006). This distinction is also reminiscent of the classic finding by Rokeach (1969) in which religious individuals who valued personal salvation were more likely to be racist and oppose social equality, whereas those whose religious values prioritized forgiveness were more supportive of social justice. Likewise, because intrinsic religiosity shares variance with authoritarianism, relationships with prejudice often change substantially, or reverse in their directionality depending upon whether such constructs are statistically distinguished (Tsang & Rowatt, 2007). As depicted in the Biblical parable of the Good Samaritan, an individual dwelling upon salvific religious concerns (e.g., personal moral purity, being in good standing with their group) may be deterred from an emphasis on other aspects of religion, such as empathy for others.

The multi-faceted nature of religious constructs has implications for the misattribution of content, due to the possibility of misperceiving which factor is influencing one's morality. In the case of ingroup favoritism and prejudice, religious individuals may selectively refer to one subset of R/S influences and deny others. The Justification-Suppression model of prejudice (Crandall & Eshleman, 2003) posits that there are competing forces involved in the formation and expression of social attitudes. Prejudice originates in deep-seated evolved tendencies to feel antipathy toward others who are different. Given the social sanctions against such raw prejudice, the expression of these attitudes is filtered and adjusted by processes that, alternatively, can suppress antipathy (e.g., empathy, humanitarian values, social desirability), or justify it by using more acceptable framing (e.g., social dominance or authoritarian values). Consequently, expressed prejudicial attitudes represent the product of a multiplicity of influences working at cross-purposes at an unconscious level. This results in observed patterns where prejudice may be implicit (e.g., microaggressions) and not consciously recognized. There are religious versions of these various components such as prejudice-suppressing factors (e.g., "Jesus said to love your neighbor"), as well as justificatory factors (e.g., "Jesus said sinners will be punished"). However, because of the stereotypic religious emphasis on prosocial elements, believers may self-report being influenced only by the former ("My religion makes me empathic"), while denying the latter ("They live a sinful life"). As a result, belief in R/S content attenuates the conscious recognition of bias (as observed in discrepancies between self-report versus behavioral measures) because the prejudice is hidden by justificatory rationalizations.

This is exemplified in the instance of religious antipathy toward homosexuals, often justified by invoking the concept: "Love the sinner but hate the sin." Batson et al. (1999a) used an experimental paradigm that assessed selective engagement in prosocial helping. Religious participants could earn money for two other students by engaging in tasks, dividing their time between the two according to their own preferences. Thus, rather than expressing antipathy directly, prejudice could be inferred from preferential helping—selectively performing tasks for one person rather than another as a function of the identity of the "helpee." In one condition, one of the two students being helped was identified as gay, whereas in the other condition both were presumably straight. Results indicated that participants higher in intrinsic religiosity spent less time helping the gay student, even when this help would not have promoted homosexuality, indicating that religiosity predicted greater antipathy toward the "sinner" rather than just the "sin." More to the present point, participants were questioned in the debriefing phase regarding the basis for their time allocation between the two students. Those high in intrinsic religiosity did not describe their division of time spent helping as driven by overt antipathy to gays (i.e., they did not state "I didn't help the student because they were gay"), rather they could preserve a facade of even-handedness by rationalizing their choices ("I wanted to be fair by helping both of them equally"). Other similar work has also found that the association between religious attendance and antigay bias is attributable to belief in the sinner–sin religious justification, indicating that, in accordance with a justification-suppression model, this concept functions to legitimate antipathy toward gays while preserving a facade of morality (Hoffarth et al., 2018).

A similar disjunction occurs in "moral incongruence" phenomena in which believers struggle with aligning their behaviors with their stated values. For example, although consumption of pornography is viewed as morally wrong by the vast majority of religious individuals, the actual relationship between religiosity and pornography consumption is more tenuous, suggesting that many believers have difficulty "practicing what they preach" (Perry, 2018). In many ways, moral incongruence shares much in common with the psychological dynamics of other inconsistency phenomena such as cognitive dissonance. In the case of incongruence between religious disapproval of pornography and actual consumption, believers' responses resemble compensatory phenomena mentioned in Chapter 3. MacInnis and Hodson (2016) found that those high in religiosity who also reported viewing sexual content on the internet were likely to report not only strongly negative views (e.g., that pornography was even worse than racism or gun violence), but also that they were "monitoring society's immorality," suggestive of attempts to rationalize incongruent behavior.

Rationalization of Immorality and Divine Projection

In the preceding section, we saw how the causal opacity of moral reactions contributes to misattributions, rationalizations, and justifications. The internalization of moral stereotypes that produce an enhanced moral self-image can contrast with actual immoral behaviors, leading to attempts to rationalize or justify these gaps. Because moral standards are malleable, non-prosocial or antisocial behavior can be re-construed as being moral using R/S forms of rationalization. There are a variety of secular justifications for self-serving behaviors, such as minimizing or ignoring detrimental consequences for victims of aggression. Bandura (1991) points out however, that rather than merely reflecting moral disengagement (i.e., refraining from construing a situation in moral terms), antisocial behavior itself can be produced by the motivation to achieve an alternative set of desirable moral goals. For instance, rather than emphasizing the value of empathy for victims of aggression, one can instead moralize obedience to authority, enabling an "I am a good soldier who follows orders" rationalization (Tsang, 2002). Some of the most common rationalizations of immorality involve moral exclusion, in which the targets of immorality are viewed as different or inferior, therefore justifying the use of different standards of moral consideration. Identity-based distinctions enable rationalized immorality via the use of hypocritical standards, as observed when transgressions committed by us and our fellow ingroup members are seen as more acceptable than the same actions committed by outgroup members (Valdesolo & DeSteno, 2007). This permits the illusion that we are focusing solely on someone's moral or immoral actions, when in fact we are also taking into account their in- versus outgroup status. For instance, unethical behavior is "socially contagious" in that immorality performed by ingroup members is more acceptable than when performed by outgroup members.

Religious and spiritual versions of these secular mechanisms similarly promote rationalized immorality. Actions can be re-categorized to be consistent with, or justified by religious standards, such as believing that one's morality is derivative of doing God's will (*Deus vult*). Some R/S mechanisms legitimating immorality are not misattributions per se but are derived from content such as scripture and teachings. As with any other socio-cultural worldview with deep historical roots, R/S is associated with a body of texts and teachings constituting a mixture of prosocial and antisocial content. Therefore, some justifications for immoral behavior are produced by enacting that portion of religion featuring antisocial content. For instance, exposing people to legitimations of violence in religious scripture increases their support for violence (Koopmans et al., 2021). Likewise, Bushman et al. (2007) found that exposure to scripture featuring violent themes led participants to display greater behavioral aggression, particularly when the passage was presented as being from the Bible or mentioned God. The universal tendency toward confirmation biases can shape individuals' selection of specific types of R/S texts or doctrines resulting in cherry-picking of justificatory content. Believers high in religious fundamentalism display greater recall of religious content than those low in fundamentalism, while also exhibiting biases of overinclusion or false positives, generating content more conducive to their belief schemas (Galen et al., 2009). A conservative Christian may be more likely to misattribute scripture with judgmental themes as being Jesus's words (i.e., a source monitoring error). For example, a judgmental passage ("If a man also lie with mankind, as he lieth with a woman, both of them have committed an abomination"—Leviticus 20:13) could be misattributed to Jesus, whereas nonjudgmental content (e.g., "Judge not, that ye be not judged"—Matthew 7:1) may be forgotten.

Effects of R/S on rationalized immorality can also occur indirectly rather than via specific belief content. As mentioned in Chapter 4, religiosity exacerbates and sanctifies inter-group strife via the encouragement to act upon perceived sacred values (Neuberg et al., 2014). Disagreement regarding religious values contributes to the derogation of outgroups, particularly those with worldviews seen as foreign or threatening (Goplen & Plant, 2015). As with moral exclusion, these value-violating outgroups are seen as legitimate targets of aggression. In one experiment, those with higher levels of religiosity expressed greater behavioral aggression by allocating larger amounts of hot sauce for gay participants to consume compared to non-gay participants (Blogowska et al., 2013). Also, higher levels of moral certainty (correlated with higher levels of religiosity) exacerbated the relationship between religiosity and support for violent warfare (Shaw et al., 2011). More specifically, a greater endorsement of moral foundations related to purity and sanctity is associated with increased dehumanization and prejudice toward sexual outgroup members. In another study, priming with religious content led to increased sanctity values and a corresponding increase in prejudice toward sexual outgroups such as sex workers (Monroe & Plant, 2019).

One form of rationalized and self-deceptive immorality that may be particularly linked to R/S is the use of self-serving attributions in the context of passive immorality. Such instances involve personal benefit that occurs from accepting the status quo and allowing events to occur (i.e., acts of omission), rather than active immorality (acts of commission). For example, Von Hippel, Lakin, and Shakarchi (2005) devised a study in which participants were rewarded for correctly solving math problems on a computer with a programming glitch that displayed the correct answers after an interval unless the participant hit the space bar. Perhaps not surprisingly, rates of cheating tended to be higher in such passive conditions because participants could justify to themselves that it was unintentional (e.g., being "unable" to hit the spacebar in time to avoid seeing the correct answer).

There is evidence that the tendency to rationalize self-serving, passively immoral behaviors is potentiated when individuals make divine causal attributions. In a series of studies, Jackson and Gray (2019) identified a pattern more prominent among those who believed specifically in an interventionist God (e.g., making attributions such as "God's will is at work" or "God does X to help"). In situations where no active human agency was present, those who believed in an interventionist God were more likely to see passive immorality as permissible. Rather than in the case of active, agentic immorality, such as stealing someone's wallet, passive immorality could involve simply finding the wallet on the sidewalk and keeping the money, allowing the believer to feel justified because this was "part of God's plan." This attribution could be seen as an externalized version of the self-stereotyping effect in which one presumes that one's actions must be moral based on the belief that one personally embodies an enhanced moral stereotype. Also important, in terms of establishing causal directionality, Jackson and Gray found that contexts featuring passive immorality were more likely to lead to the generation of divine attributions for highly religious participants. This indicates that the act of construing events as occurring without any evident human agency may promote the assignment of causality to God's will. Further, religious participants in these studies who imagined past passive immorality (e.g., failing to stop something from occurring that benefitted them, despite it having a negative impact on others) made more divine attributions and rated their (in)actions as more permissible. These results indicate that when believers engage in morally questionable actions and incur no apparent consequences such as divine punishment (i.e., consistent with the belief that everything happens in accordance with God's will) they may interpret this as tacit approval or divine imprimatur (e.g., "It wasn't wrong, otherwise God would not have allowed it"). This phenomenon aligns with other work suggesting that viewing God as accepting of events may promote immoral behavior. DeBono, Shariff, Poole, and Muraven (2017) found that Christians instructed to read and write about a forgiving God stole more money and cheated more on a math assignment than those who read and wrote about a punishing God. These effects add further texture to understanding the implications of an attributional mindset associated with having R/S versions of Just World and System Justifying beliefs in which "things are the way they are because it is God's will." In essence, the construal of one's own motivation or behavior as something that God allows can provide a rationalization for immorality.

As mentioned in Chapter 2, externalized R/S attributions not only involve benevolent agents such as God but may invoke specifically negative agents such as Satan or demons seen as responsible for our immorality (Ray et al., 2015). By doing so, believers can accept credit for prosocial actions, while blaming antisocial behaviors on these malevolent agents, or personifying them as being in conflict (the proverbial angel on one shoulder and the devil on the other). This allows the construal of one's own immoral tendencies as attributable to negative R/S agency. For instance, in 2021, after striking comedian Chris Rock on stage, actor Will Smith used attributional language in his Oscar acceptance speech that was both religiously self-aggrandizing (e.g., "I am overwhelmed by what God is calling on me to do and be in this world") while also externalizing responsibility for his aggression ("At your highest moment, be careful. That's when the devil comes for you.").

Because of their self-serving nature, these forms of immorality rationalization are tantamount to any other similar processes in which internally originating components are projected externally as derivative of R/S agency. At the most basic level, this is observed in the alignment between our own moral (and immoral) attitudes with those of "God." Believers display this Self-God overlap on a range of traits. This is particularly true of the highly religious, who view almost every positive adjective that is characteristic of themselves as characterizing God as well (Hodges et al., 2013). Although egocentric attribution also applies to non-R/S social relationships, people are even more likely to believe they share attitudes and moral values with God than they are to believe they share these with other people (Epley et al., 2009). Likewise, conservative and liberal Christians alike characterize Jesus as sharing their own socio-political views, with the most religious displaying a very high Self-God correlation ($r = .76$; Ross et al., 2012).

Perceived Self-God similarity, however, is not a perfect alignment. Some scholars have focused on differences in the attributed Self-God "gap" as contradicting a projective hypothesis. Smith et al. (2022) demonstrated that believers think that, compared to how they themselves view religious outgroup members, "God" views those people as more humanlike (put differently, God is seen as dehumanizing outgroup members to a lesser extent than does the believer). Further, Smith et al. found that when believers adopted "God's perspective" this had the effect of reducing outgroup dehumanization, indicating that self and God views were not identical. However, the attributed ordinal pattern of dehumanization was still the same in that ingroup members (fellow Christians) were rated by both self and by "God" as most human like, and outgroup members (Muslims, atheists) were rated by both as least human like, albeit with "God" demonstrating a more humanizing tendency across categories. As Smith et al. (2022) state: "… God is viewed as parochial, albeit less parochial than the self." These results are similar to the attributions of sociopolitical views from Ross et al. (2012) in which "Jesus' views" were perceived to be more moderate than those of the participants themselves (i.e., with liberals characterizing Jesus as somewhat less liberal than themselves and conservatives characterizing Jesus as somewhat less conservative than themselves). However, just as with Smith et al., Ross et al. found that this effect was much smaller than the projective effect (i.e., liberals attributing liberal views to Jesus and conservatives attributing conservative views to Jesus). Stated more generally, of the two effects, the differences between self and God attributions are less consequential than the overall projective effect of ones' general moral views being attributed to God. In essence, although you and God may disagree on some details, God still thinks like you, while perhaps being somewhat kinder.

The rationalization of immorality by means of projection is most clearly seen not merely in attributions of God's approval of attitudes and behaviors, but also in demonstrations that the causal direction leads from self to God. Changes in individuals' own moral needs and motivations influence how "God" views those issues. Epley et al. (2009; studies 5 and 6) manipulated participants' beliefs on specific moral issues (by exposing them to strong versus weak arguments or by having them deliver a speech), resulting in subsequent shifts in their ratings of "God's view" on those same issues. A similar projective effect was mentioned in Chapter 4; Purzycki et al. (2020) found that participants playing an economic trust game whose partners failed to return money were then more likely to make the attribution that greed angers God. Likewise, the material in Chapter 4 also suggested that attributions of God as being more accepting of aggression are shaped by environmental and cultural factors. Experimentally induced priming of conflict salience or cultural tightness themes leads people to perceive God as being more punitive (Caluori et al., 2020; Jackson et al., 2021a). Therefore, across a range of methodologies, such studies support the existence of a projective process in which alterations in individuals' moral priorities are externalized in the form of attributions that God has similar moral views.

In the case of projected rationalizations of immorality, believers' attitudes or behaviors that may contradict their self-stereotype of morality represent potential sources of dissonance, except when they can be justified by attributing them as consistent with God's approval. This interpretation is suggested by several of the studies described earlier. For instance, the pattern noted by Jackson and Gray (2019) of divine attributions being especially common in harmful situations lacking a responsible human agent, is consistent with a motivated tendency to create attributions of God as allowing what would otherwise appear to be self-serving. Aside from the experimental induction of projective attributions that rationalize immorality, the most informative studies are longitudinal methodologies in which believers' psychological states at an earlier point in time predict their views of God at a later point in time. In one such example, Shepperd et al. (2019) found that higher levels of adolescents' aggressive behavior predicted decreased belief in a loving God; likewise, earlier benevolent behavior predicted increased belief in a loving God and decreased belief in a punitive God. These patterns indicate that at least some variance in attributions of God's qualities originates with individuals' own behaviors and attitudes. More to the present point, these qualities include attributed traits that function to legitimize potentially problematic behavior, such as beliefs that God approves of aggression or punitiveness.

Summary

Attempts to draw simple conclusions regarding the role of R/S in morality and prosociality are limited by complexities and qualifications in these domains. Nonetheless, some general patterns are discernible. Religiosity and Spirituality are associated with:

- Greater prosociality on self-reported versus behavioral measures.
- Greater planned versus spontaneous behavioral prosociality.
- Closer positive associations between morality and religiosity in religiously normative, compared to secular social milieus.

- Higher levels of self-enhancement such as socially desirable responding, better-than-average ratings, communal narcissism, and knowledge overclaiming.
- Greater endorsement of a religious morality stereotype among believers.

Implications for Theories of Supernatural Monitoring and Punishment

These patterns have implications for theories (articulated in the Cognitive Sciences of Religion) that morality is shaped by belief in supernatural monitoring and punishment. The sense that one is being watched and morally held to account can be conceptualized as something akin to a self-awareness induction (e.g., a mirror) in that one is made more self-aware of one's actions by believing that God is watching. However, we have seen that self-awareness is insufficient to produce generalized prosociality in instances where the expected course of action is not clear. For instance, when presented with an opportunity to either help or punish an outgroup member or value violator, which course of action does God want an R/S believer to follow? The recategorization of such situations from immoral to moral (i.e., "God wants me to harm the wrongdoer") renders any notions of supernatural punishment irrelevant because those who believe they are enacting God's will likely expect to be rewarded for doing so, not to be punished. Similarly, in the case of passive moral opportunities (e.g., picking up a lost wallet in the street), a "watched" believer is as likely to assume that God intentionally presented them with this opportunity as they are to believe that God wants them to find the proper owner. Therefore, in situations with ambiguous moral norms or in which there are opportunities for moral re-construal (i.e., from immoral to moral), supernatural monitoring and punishment beliefs are less relevant.

Implications for R/S-Enhanced Moral Self-Image and Identity

Another area of relevance of these findings is the complicated and mixed effect of internalized stereotypes of enhanced morality, as reflected by abstract assessments of oneself as possessing a strong moral identity or high moral self-image (MSI). These trait-like measures are not strong predictors of performing specific moral behaviors (Hertz & Krettenauer, 2016). As mentioned above, some evidence indicates that those with a high MSI (e.g., those with high intrinsic religiosity) are more motivated to engage in compensatory prosocial actions and less likely to cheat under certain conditions. Specifically, Ward and King (2018) suggest that, contrary to moral credentials being impervious to threats "… people with high moral identity will behave especially morally following a threat to moral self-image to reduce the gap between moral goals and one's current (deficient) moral standing" (p. 496). Ward and King base this hypothesis on experimental threat induction procedures (i.e., "write about a time when you recently acted immorally"). However, for MSI to be threatened, one must first construe that one has, in fact, acted immorally (e.g., imagined as a counterfactual). Outside of explicit instruction to do so, those high in MSI are not likely to view themselves as having actually acted immorally and so they are not normally in a state of MSI threat, and thus are less likely to increase compensatory moral behaviors.

As we have seen, those with enhanced views of their own morality based on internalized stereotypes are less likely to think they have acted immorally, mainly because they utilize a plethora of self-protective mechanisms obviating such a construal. In the series of studies by Batson and colleagues pertaining to hypocrisy, self-awareness of immorality was unlikely because of the existence of justificatory "wiggle room" (e.g., "keeping the best task is not immoral"). Consistent with rationalizable gaps between self-perceived values (e.g., humility, forgivingness) and actual behaviors, those with a high MSI are, in naturalistic contexts, more likely to have cognitively accessible examples of their virtue and are less likely to think of themselves as having committed immoral actions. This lack of awareness of immorality can be observed where those high in intrinsic religiosity are unaware of engaging in selective helping (e.g., attributing their actions to "fairness"; Batson et al., 1999a). Also, the potentially threatening self-awareness of not having lived up to moral standards is, by itself, insufficient to induce prosociality when expected norms are ambiguous, allowing for rationalizations. Even in situations where attention is clearly drawn to one's immoral actions, any compensatory response can include options other than prosocial actions, such as dissonance-induced shifting of standards. There are also mechanisms in the compensatory process that mitigate moral reactivity, such as R/S-related behaviors associated with atonement. These can produce a "pseudo-absolution" that reinstates moral credentials (e.g., "My sins have been washed clean"). As stated by Ward and King (2018), "Religions have a variety of ways that individuals might atone for past immoral acts (e.g., praying, seeking forgiveness via confession) and these do not necessarily involve actual behavior to redress a wrongdoing" (p. 506). Indeed, as identified by Zhong and Liljenquist (2006), the superficial cleansing act of "wiping away" sin can decrease guilt and diminish any motivation to engage in tangible atonement.

Implications of Dual Processing for Misattributions of R/S Morality

Interwoven within each of the above patterns of R/S morality are biases in individuals' attributions regarding the overall level, source, and content of their morality. These derive from introspective cognitive processes, in accordance with dual processing theories. Our conscious experience of our morality (e.g., "How moral am I?," "What prosocial actions have I performed?") is affected by what stereotypically "should" be the case or how we "ought" to have behaved. This type of information, as obtained via self-report measures, refers to deliberative behaviors processed by Type two cognition. By contrast, spontaneous behaviors, as reflective of Type one processes, are elicited by features in the environment, lack conscious deliberation, and are less affected by socially desirable responding (Wilson, 2002). To the degree that one has internalized a stereotype of enhanced morality, motivated cognitive processes create moral "blind spots" that make it less likely that one will be aware of counter-stereotypic immoral behaviors. For instance, for a person engaging in parochialism or selective helping based on social identity biases, their self-attributions regarding motives will be dominated by the salience of their helpful intentions, rather than any awareness of parochialism or self-enhancement needs.

In accordance with dual processing models of cognition featuring introspective limitations, R/S beliefs appear to promote explicit stereotypic content (e.g., what a religious person should be), unmoored from implicit effects (e.g., parochialism, moral enhancement). Ward and King (2018) suggest that religious people are more likely to form their sense of moral self-concept by imbuing everyday actions with moral significance and focusing on their intentions or stereotypic traits when constructing their identity. By contrast, the nonreligious more often base their self-concept on actual behavior and are less likely to stereotypically believe that they are more moral. To the extent that the individual is selectively focused on presumed stereotypic influences ("My religion makes me a better person"), they will lack a realistic assessment of their actual morality ("I'm probably about as moral as anyone else") and downplay more basic secular explanations for morality ("I'm conforming to peer norms" or "I was not under time pressure").

This selective focus, however, is not merely the product of introspective limitations or "cold" cognitions, but rather has elements of "hot" or affectively driven motivated cognition, such as defending one's image as a moral person. For example, Burris and Navara (2002) found that those who were high in intrinsic religiosity, following an induced negative self-disclosure, showed a compensatory increase in self-deceptive enhanced responding. This indicates that a portion of religious responding, especially pertaining to morality, consists of artifactually enhanced response distortions. More relevant to the present point, such results also indicate that the religiously based motivation to defend a positive self-image operates largely on an unconscious level. This may explain results from Ward and King (2018) in which a bogus pipeline procedure (to circumvent conscious impression management) did not have an impact on religious participants' inflated moral self-image. Such procedures are ineffective when individuals' motivation is nonconscious and self-deceptive. As Burris and Navara state: "For some—those who self-deceive when threatened—believing that one is morally upright may be paramount, whether or not that belief accurately reflects past or present behavior ... believing that the role that they are enacting on the inner stage of the mind is, in fact, who they are" (p. 74).

Conclusion

A Social-Cognitive Model of Belief

Religious and spiritual (R/S) beliefs are often presumed to be unique in their origin and causal role in psychological functioning. As demonstrated in the preceding chapters, experimental work from fields such as social cognition, interpersonal social psychology, and cognitive psychology indicates that R/S phenomena originate from secular and naturalistic psychological mechanisms. However, the beliefs generated by these inter- and intrapersonal sources are consistently misattributed as originating in R/S agency or as representing R/S processes. Such misattributions are due in part to the structure of mental operations where, in accordance with dual processing theories, the functioning of intuitive and implicit processes is inaccessible to conscious awareness. Both Type one and Type two cognitions are affected by ubiquitous biases and heuristics that also vary as a function of individual differences and contextual conditions. Our lack of awareness of these biases impedes the ability to accurately assign causality for our beliefs, triggering efforts to fill this introspective vacuum by substituting other presumed causal sources producing explanatory rationalizations, confabulations, and self-deceptions. Social stereotypes regarding R/S have an enhancing influence on well-being and morality. These functions are internalized, decreasing individuals' ability to accurately self-evaluate in these domains. Consequently, rather than accurately attributing phenomena such as emotional states or moral behaviors as deriving from their internal dispositions, motivational states, social learning, or contextual influences, R/S believers perceive these as originating in external spiritual agency. In essence, subjective mental states are projected externally so that "I feel and think X" leads to "God feels or thinks X."

This model of R/S beliefs holds several implications for areas of scientific inquiry into the phenomenology of R/S believers, specifically regarding the self-reported content of beliefs, experiences, and attitudes. As demonstrated by empirical findings from multiple disciplines reported throughout the book, the presumption that subjective R/S material is veridical in the sense of representing an accurate attribution of the origins and content of experience is not supported. Without independent verification such as cross-validation from independent sources or the use of blinded randomized placebo-controlled trials, there is no truly objective way to determine whether an experience or belief is based on external spiritual agency or "unique" R/S influences as opposed to representing a misattribution stemming from another causal source.

Further, the assumption of "unique" R/S influence reported in domains such as exceptional experiences, mental health, and moral behaviors is also an erroneous interpretation deriving from the failure to control for more parsimonious secular explanations. These include the strength or coherence of individuals' worldview, the degree of fit between their beliefs and those in the surrounding milieu, and the contaminating effect of internalized stereotypes (see Figure 6.1). Rather than representing something that cannot be satisfied by other psychological mechanisms, R/S beliefs and experiences are products of secular functions, differing only in the subjective attributions formed regarding their origin and content.

Philosophical Implications of Biased Belief Forming Functions

As discussed in the introductory chapter, there is a range of interpretations of phenomena related to the mechanisms of R/S belief formation identified by the Cognitive Sciences of Religion. Some scholars have suggested that religious experiences and perceived interactions with the supernatural may represent evidence of ontologically genuine external agency (Barrett & Church, 2013). This view posits that belief-forming functions may even constitute a type of "*sensus divinitatus*" or "god-faculty" indicative of religious predilections, at least when operating in "optimal environments" (Clark & Barrett, 2010: 188). Barrett (2007) suggests that the existence of naturalistic mechanisms does not rule out the possibility that "... a god or gods put into place the natural order ... such that human brains naturally give rise to religious experiences under particular situations" (p. 61). Such implications of CSR models have also generated interest from the public. New York Times columnist Ross Douthat writes that, given the persistence of experiences such as near-death encounters and spirit possession, the search for reasons people believe in the plausibility of religion makes a "... concession to religion's plausibility — because most of our evolved impulses and appetites correspond directly to something in reality itself" (Douthat, 2021).

A more limited interpretation is that findings from the CSR regarding belief-forming functions cannot undermine the veracity of R/S intuitions (Van Eyghen, 2020). For instance, some philosophers have referred to differences between believers and nonbelievers in the output of putative cognitive mechanisms such as Hyperactive Agency Detection (HADD), by stating that we cannot necessarily say that one group over-detects (i.e., false positives) and the other under-detects (false negatives) without question begging regarding the existence of the putative agent. Launonen (2021) posits "it cannot be argued that intuitions of supernatural agency are instances of HADD misfiring unless we already assume that no supernatural agents exist" (p. 421). Without an objective benchmark or verifiable criterion, it could be that atheists are limited by "epistemic beer goggles" or suffering a malady rendering them oblivious to spiritual realities akin to "not being able to walk" (Barrett, 2012: 203).

This line of argumentation refers to the nonspecific quality of the intuitions generated by the belief forming mechanism, which involve Type one processing. Nonspecific belief output (e.g., general spiritual agency), despite being "coarse-grained," is thought to be further refined or "scaffolded" by rational mental operations (i.e., Type two processes) such as theological teachings, apologetics, and philosophical logic. Therefore, any critiques of the overly broad, inaccurate T1 output are irrelevant to rationally based R/S beliefs. "The only way," Thurow (2013) states, "that findings could challenge the rationality of religious belief is if they could show that our religious argument evaluating processes are unreliable" (2013: 97). Rather, as Vainio (2016) writes, "So far CSR has concentrated almost solely on religion as a product of T1 ... it is obvious that religious believers engage in T2 information processing ... the number of studies that analyze religious T2 cognition is virtually zero" (p. 109). Further, any suggestion that T2 processes themselves could be biased has incurred what are known as "collateral damage" counterarguments. These warn of the epistemological consequences for other areas of knowledge, such as scientific reasoning, if the reliability of Type two cognition is considered compromised. Vainio asks: "If all T2 cognition is just post hoc rationalization, why should we think that there are superior forms of cognition in the first place and that we are not just replacing one set of biases with another set of biases, both of which are equally bad?" (2016: 110).

As can be seen from these arguments, the scholarly debates involving the psychological mechanisms associated with R/S belief often hinge upon the issue of reliability, specifically whether R/S thoughts, intuitions, and experiences accurately reflect the ontological existence of supernatural agency (e.g., indicators of God). Some scholars argue that output from belief-forming functions should be considered "truth-sensitive" as evidenced by their promotion of evolutionary fitness or "flourishing" (Van Eyghen & Bennett, 2022). This is similar to the previously mentioned statement of columnist Ross Douthat in the assumption that, if mental outputs are a product of an evolved mechanism, this must therefore correspond to something in reality itself. Van Eyghen (2022) refers to the evident success of systems such as the human visual sense:

> Cognitive faculties can be judged as reliable if contact with their presumed objects has certain practical effects. These effects can serve as evidence for the existence of those presumed objects. I can regard my beliefs about the physical environment as justified because my beliefs allow me to avoid objects and find resources. Similarly, I can regard my beliefs about God or other supernatural beings as justified because reciprocal engagement allows me to flourish.

One problem with these arguments is the unfalsifiable stance in how the output of belief forming functions should be regarded. On the one hand, the mere existence of R/S intuitions is referred to as representing a reliable indicator of agency, but at the same time, the output is acknowledged to be overly broad ("coarse-grained"), susceptible to biases, and in need of rational refinement. The lack of falsifiability of such an argument is illustrated by the circular quality of the reasoning. In response to a declaration such as "Intuitions are reliable indications of R/S agency," subsequent discussion could resemble the following hypothetical dialogue:

> Q: "How do we know that these intuitions are reliable?"
> A: "Because intuitions are produced by mechanisms that are generally truth-tracking."
> Q: "What is the specific agent then?"
> A: "The intuitions are too broad to indicate that."
> Q: "If they are truth tracking, why do belief functions generate biased intuitions?"
> A: "Those were generated in an environment that is not optimal."

It is noteworthy that these arguments refer to only one body of work—evolutionary-based CSR findings—but they elide how results using an evolutionary framework fit into the broader context of complementary work from other disciplines such as experimental social-psychological and social cognition research. The material presented throughout this book demonstrates the utility of such a complementary, multi-disciplinary approach in addressing criticisms based on putative gaps CSR knowledge.

Viewed from a social-cognitive perspective, it is erroneous to conceptualize belief-forming functions (e.g., HAAD, Theory of Mind, Credibility Enhancing Displays, and others) as producing a fixed output characterized as either reliable or unreliable. Rather, a view more consistent with the operation of other heuristics and biases is that the output of belief-forming mechanisms is malleable as a function of proximal conditions (e.g., threats, ambiguity, or cognitive load). Further, beliefs produced by T1 heuristics may indeed constitute vague, inchoate intuitions that can be modified by T2, but the ability to do so varies as a function of individual cognitive abilities and the motivation and willingness to apply them. Therefore, it is misleading to frame the argument as "Are belief-forming functions identified by CSR reliable?" Instead, the relevant issues are better framed as: "Are some people more prone to greater reliance on belief-forming functions without engaging in critical analysis?" or "Are some conditions more likely to produce erroneous intuitive output?" Apropos to the present issue of R/S beliefs, similar questions should include: "What conditions lead to the misperception of known pseudo-agents?" or "Can externally originating beliefs be distinguished from internally originating (i.e., projective) ones?" or "Is the degree to which a belief is supported by high levels of emotional conviction related to the veracity of the belief-referent?"

Results specifically relevant to these questions have been presented throughout the book, indicating that R/S beliefs are associated with cognitive errors such as perceptual over-detection and apophenia (false positives) rather than accurate pattern recognition. Conditions that attenuate analytic T2 thought are more likely to permit misattribution of agency. However, unreliable output is not inconsistent with the existence of cognitive mechanisms that evolved for specific purposes. The abovementioned argument positing that the output of any mental function (e.g., the human visual system) shaped by evolutionary fitness priorities must be presumed accurate (Van Eyghen, 2022) is based on a misrepresentative analogy. First, evolved features have resulted from selection (by definition) by being "good enough" to promote fitness (e.g., physical navigation, finding resources) but this does not imply that they function optimally in the sense of perfect fidelity, as evidenced by common trade-offs (in the case of vision, the susceptibility to optical illusions, retinal blind-spot fillers, myopia, etc.). This is evident by comparisons with species shaped by different selective pressures who have abilities superior to those of humans (e.g., the visual acuity of birds of prey, the olfaction of canines).

A more apt evolutionary analogue for belief-forming functions and what can be inferred regarding their output are those cognitive heuristics utilizing Type one processes such as the tendency to readily form and endorse social stereotypes indicating group identity (e.g., race) or the tendency toward biased information processing (e.g., negativity bias, loss aversion). Even seemingly maladaptive tendencies such as the susceptibility to phobias of certain stimuli ("prepared fears"; Cook & Mineka, 1989) can perform general fitness-serving functions while failing to produce accurate beliefs. Cognitive heuristics exhibit cross-species universality but also display variation between individuals and are malleable as a function of contextual conditions. Therefore, when conceptualized as akin to heuristics and biases, the R/S output of belief forming functions, despite being a product of an evolved mechanism, cannot be presumed reliable.

Another erroneous assertion made in the abovementioned criticisms of CSR work is that existing methods lack the ability to objectively calibrate belief-forming mechanisms (thereby limiting claims of R/S belief inaccuracy to question-begging). As discussed in the first several chapters of this book, experimental research using objective target criteria allows us to understand how factors associated with R/S beliefs are associated with inaccurate perception, such as over-detection and the inability to distinguish signal from noise. Additionally, in accordance with compensatory models (Chapter 3), these tendencies are malleable such that fluctuations in R/S beliefs occur as a function of manipulating individuals' emotional, epistemic, or existential needs. Therefore, it does not represent question-begging to refer to beliefs resulting from these processes as objectively inaccurate.

The proper contextualization of the implications of CSR work could benefit by expanding discussion beyond the typically narrow set of concepts (i.e., HADD, TOM, CREDs) to include heuristics associated with social cognition (e.g., Just World Belief, System Justification bias, effort justification effect, false consensus, egocentric attitude projection) as well as heuristics featured in research regarding cognitive psychology, all of which are supported by a substantial evidential basis in the literature. This could address the above mischaracterization arguing that studies are limited to intuitive (Type one) processes. The CSR is not the only body of work capable of scrutinizing the accuracy of R/S beliefs shaped by T2 processes. Rather, the social cognition literature is replete with information relevant to biases in T2 processing, including that related to religious content. This is also germane to the assertion regarding T2's ability to "scaffold" biased T1 output. There is no evidence that unreliable T1 intuitions are routinely corrected or refined by T2 reasoning; instead, they are more likely to be rationalized and justified (e.g., by apologetical theology). As seen throughout this book, prior beliefs, particularly those functioning to support emotionally charged worldviews, are heavily defended by biased T2 processes such as motivated reasoning, dissonance reduction, and rationalization.

As seen earlier (Chapter 2) pertaining to the phenomenon of self-attributions, R/S believers do refer to rational arguments in supporting their worldviews. But just as secular T2 cognition is infused with motivated biases in which previous beliefs are justified (i.e., *post hoc* rationalization; Evans & Wason, 1976; Kunda, 1990), R/S beliefs are no exception. Rather than successfully scaffolded in the direction of greater accuracy, believers' cognition regarding the origin and content of their R/S beliefs is affected by common biases such as attributions that beliefs originated with rational reasons and the failure to acknowledge emotional or situational influences (Kenworthy, 2003). Just as challenges to secular worldviews (e.g., social and political attitudes) can trigger a defensive reaction that further entrenches prior beliefs (Lewandowsky et al., 2012), emotional reactions elicited by debunking R/S worldviews also triggers dissonance-based efforts to defend cherished beliefs, rather than resulting in any Bayesian updating (Batson, 1975; Burns, 2006). Information perceived as potentially worldview-threatening elicits a compensatory response, leading to a belief-bolstering "double-down" response. In sum, Type two rationality does not correct R/S beliefs.

Likewise, scientific principles, philosophical logic, and apologetics are enlisted to protect and promote, rather than correct R/S beliefs (Klaczynski & Gordon, 1996; Tobia, 2016). This does not, however indicate that other domains of knowledge are "collaterally damaged" by Type two biases. The suggestion that scientific epistemology is based solely on reasoning elides the crucial component of empirical testing and elimination of hypotheses. This point also relates to the charge of question begging, including the suggestion that scientific evaluation of R/S beliefs relies on metaphysical chauvinism that excludes potential supernatural explanations. Rather, methods of empirical comparison treat R/S cognition similarly to any other form of psychological knowledge. Beliefs represent subjective statements of reality amenable to the requisite cross checking with other measures of the same content. For instance, in the earlier section regarding mental well-being (Chapter 6), the analogy of a randomized double-blind placebo-controlled drug trial illustrates the proper empirical approach to any disjunction between a participant's subjective attribution for their phenomenological state versus a researcher's objective explanation of the same. When describing this type of study, we do not say that the scientist "excludes" the possibility that someone in the placebo group could have been influenced by (what they mistakenly believe to be) the medication. We simply say that the belief of those in that group represents a demonstrable misattribution as evidenced by their placement in the placebo group, regardless of the attribution of the participant. This also illustrates the benefits of the (largely non-CSR) portion of the social cognition literature, where experimental studies allow identification of causality and degrees of accuracy as a function of variable manipulation. As exemplified by research on exceptional experiences and agentic over-attribution (Chapter 5), dispositional characteristics can interact with the use of contextual manipulation. As a result, agentic false positives (i.e., demonstrated by incorrect subjective perceptions of spiritual agency) emerge. Therefore, this type of empirical comparison does not represent an *a priori* exclusion of the transcendent and is not collaterally damaged by failures of rational cognition, yet it is also capable of indicating when subjective perceptions are indeed biased.

Philosophical Implications of Tangible Outcomes

Some scholars have suggested that the ultimate reliability of R/S beliefs can be inferred by using tangible outcome measures as validation, such as those used in social science research (e.g., well-being, prosociality, or flourishing). This approach essentially posits that inferences regarding the ultimate truth referent of beliefs can be gauged by observing the consequences of holding the belief, reminiscent of the pragmatist William James's assertion that a tree must be judged by its fruit. Some social scientists refrain from explicitly suggesting that tangible effects attributed to R/S are necessarily indicative of ontological reality (Wong et al., 2018). However, others have posited that experiences or observable behaviors could be viewed as revelatory of God's existence and intentions. For example, Slife, Reber, and Lefevor (2012) suggest that "God may not be observed but that does not mean that the influence of God cannot be deduced, and its manifestations measured" (p. 224). Prosocial behavior, these authors offer, "could be viewed from a theistic perspective as God prompting a person to altruistic action" (p. 228). In a similar vein, Van Eyghen (2019) argues that the "pragmatic success of supernatural belief lies in the spiritual fruits it delivers. Supernatural beliefs can lead to greater spiritual fulfillment and a life of increased sanctity ... If supernatural beliefs were to lead to a life of lesser sanctity or more evil, people would function less well" (p. 134).

Some aspects of the social cognition model outlined in this book are relevant to such "tangible evidence" arguments. As stated in the preceding chapters pertaining to mental health and morality, the primary counterargument is simply that many "outcomes" presumed to be uniquely causally linked to R/S beliefs instead stem from spurious relationships and are caused by underlying secular influences. Beyond the previously discussed relationships with specific operationalizations of R/S (e.g., specific denominations, belief in God, religious attendance), one way to approach tangible evidence arguments is to broaden the focus and instead evaluate general attributional frameworks associated with these worldviews to identify any evidence of putative positive impact. In this way we can determine whether these broad frameworks underlying R/S beliefs are predictive of tangible outcomes and whether this has any bearing on their ontological referents.

Holding a religious and spiritual worldview requires endorsement (often implicit) of a set of other philosophical beliefs related to epistemology, meta-ethics, and basic causation. For instance, theistic worldviews entail attributing events as being controlled by a personally accessible benevolent deity (i.e., a "difference-making God") in a way that contrasts with atheistic or deistic worldviews. This is, in turn, linked to broader assumptions such as that the universe operates in a predictable and purposeful manner where appropriate outcomes result from prior actions (e.g., Just World Belief, System Justification). Theistic worldviews also typically assert a version of meta-ethics involving objectively determined moral principles (e.g., deontology) established by the deity. Granted, not all R/S believers psychologically emphasize each of these to the same degree. For instance, liberal and conservative Christians differ in their tendency to see outcomes as deserved such as in their differing attributions of personal responsibility for misfortune (Skitka, 1999). However, there is a general alignment in these philosophical stances associated with theism as opposed to atheism (Piazza & Landy, 2013).

Framed as an empirical hypothesis, the tangible outcome argument posits that belief in these philosophical stances and attributional worldviews should bear some identifiable relationship with outcomes indicative of well-being, prosociality, and human flourishing. However, as indicated throughout this book, such outcome evidence is at best, mixed, and dependent upon which variables are chosen to best exemplify optimal outcomes. Beliefs that the universe bends toward justice (i.e., Just World Belief) or that a benevolent deity is in charge (a divine Locus of Control) are associated with a mixture of outcomes such as those associated with morality as a function of R/S beliefs (Chapter 7). For instance, those with a strong JWB have been found to have greater personal well-being and a higher sense of control (Dzuka & Dalbert, 2006). On the other hand, when they are confronted with innocent victims, the dissonance that arises between elements of the JWB worldview (e.g., theodicy) results in victim blaming (Van den Bos & Maas, 2009). By contrast, those with a weak JWB experience the universe as being uncontrolled; however, this also reduces the experience of inconsistency when encountering misfortune, and therefore any need to blame victims ("the rain falls on the just and the unjust"). Likewise, beliefs in religious forms of JWB-based morality (e.g., Big Gods or supernatural monitors who mete out rewards and punishments) also have a mixed track record regarding tangible outcomes. On the one hand, although beliefs in a God capable of retribution (e.g., a literal hell) may deter unethical behavior, these are also associated with aggression and lower happiness among believers (Shariff & Aknin, 2014; Shepperd et al., 2019).

Another example of mixed results associated with broad worldviews involves theistic beliefs amalgamated with attributions of specific loci of control (i.e., internal versus external). Although often treated as representing opposite points of a single dimension, in practice, religious external control (belief that outcomes are determined by forces outside the self) and internal control (personal responsibility) are not mutually exclusive. As mentioned in Chapter 2, belief in God as an external agent is often combined with a sense of internal agency such that relying on God as working through the Self ("God wants me to take charge" or "God helps me cope") improves a sense of control and subsequent outcomes (Pargament & Hahn, 1986). However, there are other instances where people believe that, since their outcomes depend on external factors, they need not take action, leading to passivity and undermining motivation to engage in preventive behaviors. For instance, in the recent Covid-19 pandemic, religiosity was negatively linked with the intention to vaccinate, an association mediated by the belief in an external health locus of control (Olagoke et al., 2021).

One final example of an attributional worldview associated with religious belief and often presumed to produce uniformly positive outcomes involves the domain of meta-ethics. Religious worldviews are associated with an objectivist or deontological meta-ethical stance, viewing morality as derived from fixed principles such as divine commandment or scriptural authority (Piazza & Landy, 2013). It is commonly believed that alternative worldviews lacking in external theistic grounding (e.g., secular humanism) lead to inferior outcomes. Even in the present era, among those with exposure to exemplars of secular ethics, it is still culturally *de rigueur* to cede the ground of objective morality to theism. Columnist David Brooks (2022) warns of the creeping "emotivism" where what is morally right is whatever "feels right to me," which will lead to "creating our own moral criteria based on feelings" and "[grading] ourselves on a forgiving curve." He contrasts this unfavorably in comparison with an objective religious moral order "independent of the knower" where the "ultimate authority is outside the self." This common view implies that meta-ethics based on external religious grounding produces greater moral adherence with less subjective "wiggle room."

As indicated in the preceding chapters, although believers often refer to their moral attitudes as being motivated by external R/S sources, these are largely misattributions. This is not to gainsay that some personal attitudes and behaviors represent attempts to follow religious principles. Numerous examples include Ultra-Orthodox Jews keeping kosher, Christian Mennonites practicing pacifism, or Jains following dietary restrictions in adherence to principles of Ahimsa, or non-harming. However, even in such examples where practitioners attribute their behaviors to a scrupulous literalistic interpretation of religious edicts, there is always the issue of selectivity. Even those who ostensibly share the same nominal religion differ in selecting some moral precepts versus others. For example, White Catholics in the United States are more supportive than Hispanic Catholics of both legal abortion (56 percent vs. 43 percent), as well as the death penalty (47 percent vs. 30 percent; PRRI, 2012). As mentioned in Chapter 8, liberal Christians emphasize Jesus's teachings on social justice whereas conservatives emphasize ascetic personal morals. The sheer diversity of interpretations of identical religious texts or teachings is sufficient to indicate that a selective process is operative, driven by extra-religious sources such as race, class, education, region, age, cohort, and—as is the current theme—psychosocial influences. Individuals who report that their religion is the primary motivating factor for their moral views emphasize only one portion of a causal chain of (in some cases, contradictory) influences.

To return to the issue of evaluating the tangible "outcomes" of various R/S related meta-ethics, as stated in Chapter 8, there is ample evidence that specific moral emphases are associated with factors such as divine attributions and deontology (e.g., the valuation of binding, rather than individualizing moral foundations; Piazza & Landy, 2013). However, there is scant evidence of overall differences in moral virtue versus turpitude such as would be predicted by a theory of R/S morality as representing tangible outcomes. Major moral dimensions such as empathy and prosociality do not observably differ between the religious and nonreligious (Galen, 2012; Rabelo & Pilati, 2021). Indeed, observable differences as a function of meta-ethical beliefs are sufficiently small as to call into question the broader hypothesis that morality substantially derives from such sources at all. As indicated throughout this book regarding psychological theories of dual processing, rationalization, and introspective opacity, it is more likely that references to meta-ethical sources represent confabulated justifications for individuals' attitudes and behaviors shaped by other causal sources. Intuitive impulses and socially derived norms are internalized, producing a justificatory search for supporting reasons when a rational explanation is needed. Therefore, any conclusion based upon tangible outcomes regarding the ultimate ontological existence of a meta-ethical source reveals that such a God thinks very much as we do.

References

Aarnio, K., & Lindeman, M. (2007). Religious people and paranormal believers: Alike or different? *Journal of Individual Differences, 28*(1), 1-9.

Abelson, R. P. (1959). Modes of resolution of belief dilemmas. *Journal of Conflict Resolution, 3*(4), 343-52.

Abeyta, A. A., & Routledge, C. (2018). The need for meaning and religiosity: An individual differences approach to assessing existential needs and the relation with religious commitment, beliefs, and experiences. *Personality and Individual Differences, 123*, 6-13.

Abu-Raiya, H., & Pargament, K. I. (2015). Religious coping among diverse religions: Commonalities and divergences. *Psychology of Religion and Spirituality, 7*(1), 24-33.

Abu-Raiya, H., Sasson, T., & Cohen, R. A. (2021). Is religiousness a unique predictor of self-esteem? An empirical investigation with a diverse Israeli sample. *Psychology of Religion and Spirituality*. Advance online publication. doi: 10.1037/rel0000406

Al-Issa, R. S., Krauss, S. E., Roslan, S., & Abdullah, H. (2021). To Heaven through Hell: Are there cognitive foundations for Purgatory? Evidence from Islamic cultures. *Religions, 12*(11), 1026.

Altemeyer, B. (1988). *Enemies of freedom: Understanding right-wing authoritarianism.* San Francisco: Jossy-Bass.

Altemeyer, B. (2002). Dogmatic behavior among students: Testing a new measure of dogmatism. *The Journal of Social Psychology, 142*(6), 713-21.

Altemeyer, B., & Hunsberger, B. (1992). Authoritarianism, religious fundamentalism, quest, and prejudice. *The International Journal for the Psychology of Religion, 2*(2), 113-33.

Andersen, M., Pfeiffer, T., Müller, S., & Schjoedt, U. (2019). Agency detection in predictive minds: A virtual reality study. *Religion, Brain & Behavior, 9*(1), 52-64.

Andersen, M., Schjoedt, U., Nielbo, K. L., & Sørensen, J. (2014). Mystical experience in the lab. *Method & Theory in the Study of Religion, 26*(3), 217-45.

Armaly, M. T., Buckley, D. T., & Enders, A. M. (2022). Christian nationalism and political violence: Victimhood, racial identity, conspiracy, and support for the capitol attacks. *Political Behavior, 44*(2), 937-60.

Asch, S. E. (1956). Studies of independence and conformity: I. A minority of one against a unanimous majority. *Psychological Monographs: General and Applied, 70*(9), 1-70.

Ashton, M. C., & Lee, K. (2019). Religiousness and the HEXACO personality factors and facets in a large online sample. *Journal of Personality, 87*(6), 1103-18.

Aydin, N., Fischer, P., & Frey, D. (2010). Turning to God in the face of ostracism: Effects of social exclusion on religiousness. *Personality and Social Psychology Bulletin, 36*, 742–53.

Baimel, A., White, C. J., Sarkissian, H., & Norenzayan, A. (2021). How is analytical thinking related to religious belief? A test of three theoretical models. *Religion, Brain & Behavior, 11*(3), 239–60.

Balcetis, E., & Dunning, D. (2006). See what you want to see: Motivational influences on visual perception. *Journal of Personality and Social Psychology, 91*(4), 612–25.

Bandura, A. (1991). Social cognitive theory of moral thought and action. In W. M. Kurtines, & J. L. Gewirtz (Eds.), *Handbook of moral behavior and development*: Vol. 1. Theory (pp. 45–103). Hillsdale, NJ: Erlbaum.

Banerjee, K., & Bloom, P. (2014). Why did this happen to me? Religious believers' and non-believers' teleological reasoning about life events. *Cognition, 133*(1), 277–303.

Bar-Anan, Y., Wilson, T. D., & Hassin, R. R. (2010). Inaccurate self-knowledge formation as a result of automatic behaviour. *Journal of Experimental Social Psychology, 46*, 884–94.

Barber, N. (2011). A cross-national test of the uncertainty hypothesis of religious belief. *Cross-Cultural Research, 45*, 318–33.

Barber, N. (2015). Why is Mississippi more religious than New Hampshire? Material security and ethnicity as factors. *Cross-Cultural Research, 49*(3), 315–25.

Bargh, J. A., & Chartrand, T. L. (1999). The unbearable automaticity of being. *American Psychologist, 54*(7), 462.

Barrett, J. L. (2007). Is the spell really broken? Bio-psychological explanations of religion and theistic belief. *Theology and Science, 5*(1), 57–72.

Barrett, J. L. (2012). *Born Believers: The science of children's religious belief*. Simon and Schuster.

Barrett, J. L., & Church, I. M. (2013). Should CSR give atheists epistemic assurance? On beer-goggles, BFFs, and skepticism regarding religious beliefs. *The Monist, 96*(3), 311–24.

Barrett, J. L., & Keil, F. C. (1996). Conceptualizing a nonnatural entity: Anthropomorphism in God concepts. *Cognitive Psychology, 31*(3), 219–47.

Bartholomew, R. E., Wessely, S., & Rubin, G. J. (2012). Mass psychogenic illness and the social network: Is it changing the pattern of outbreaks? *Journal of the Royal Society of Medicine, 105*(12), 509–12.

Bartz, J. A., Tchalova, K., & Fenerci, C. (2016). Reminders of social connection can attenuate anthropomorphism: A replication and extension of Epley, Akalis, Waytz, and Cacioppo (2008). *Psychological Science, 27*(12), 1644–50.

Batson, C. D. (1975). Rational processing or rationalization? The effect of disconfirming information on a stated religious belief. *Journal of Personality and Social Psychology, 32*(1), 176–184.

Batson, C. D., Floyd, R. B., Meyer, J. M., & Winner, A. L. (1999a). "And who is my neighbor?": Intrinsic religion as a source of universal compassion. *Journal for the Scientific Study of Religion, 38*, 445–57.

Batson, C. D., Thompson, E. R., Seuferling, G., Whitmey, H., & Strongman, J. A. (1999b). Moral hypocrisy: Appearing moral to oneself without being so. *Journal of Personality and Social Psychology, 77*, 525–37.

Batson, C. D., Kobrynowicz, D., Dinnerstein, J. L., Kampf, H. C., & Wilson, A. D. (1997). In a very different voice: Unmasking moral hypocrisy. *Journal of Personality and Social Psychology, 72*, 1335–48.

Batson, C. D., Oleson, K. C., Weeks, J. L., Healy, S. P., Reeves, P. J., Jennings, P., & Brown, T. (1989). Religious prosocial motivation: Is it altruistic or egoistic? *Journal of Personality and Social Psychology, 57*(5), 873–84.

Batson, C. D., Thompson, E. R., & Chen, H. (2002). Moral hypocrisy: Addressing some alternatives. *Journal of Personality and Social Psychology, 83*, 330–9.

Baumard, N., & Boyer, P. (2013a). Explaining moral religions. *Trends in Cognitive Sciences, 17*(6), 272–80.

Baumard, N., & Boyer, P. (2013b). Religious beliefs as reflective elaborations on intuitions: A modified dual-process model. *Current Directions in Psychological Science, 22*(4), 295–300.

Baumard, N., & Chevallier, C. (2012). What goes around comes around: The evolutionary roots of the belief in immanent justice. *Journal of Cognition and Culture, 12*(1–2), 67–80.

Baumeister, R. F., Bratslavsky, E., Finkenauer, C., & Vohs, K. D. (2001). Bad is stronger than good. *Review of General Psychology, 5*(4), 323–70.

Beck, R., & Taylor, S. (2008). The emotional burden of monotheism: Satan, theodicy, and relationship with God. *Journal of Psychology and Theology, 36*(3), 151–60.

Becker, P. E., & Dhingra, P. H. (2001). Religious involvement and volunteering: Implications for civil society. *Sociology of Religion, 62*(3), 315–35.

Bègue, L. (2002). Beliefs in justice and faith in people: Just world, religiosity and interpersonal trust. *Personality and Individual Differences, 32*(3), 375–82.

Bekkers, R., & Schuyt, T. (2008). And who is your neighbor? Explaining denominational differences in charitable giving and volunteering in the Netherlands. *Review of Religious Research, 50*, 74–96.

Belding, J. N., Howard, M. G., McGuire, A. M., Schwartz, A. C., & Wilson, J. H. (2010). Social buffering by God: Prayer and measures of stress. *Journal of Religion and Health, 49*, 179–87.

Bendixen, T., Apicella, C., Atkinson, Q., Cohen, E., Henrich, J., McNamara, R. A., ... & Purzycki, B. G. (2021). Appealing to the minds of gods: Religious beliefs and appeals correspond to features of local social ecologies. https://doi.org/10.31234/osf.io/tjn3e. October, 26.

Benson, J. M., & Herrmann, M. J. (1999, February/March). "... If we live that long in Earthly form: Waiting for the Apocalypse." *The Public Perspective, 10*(2), 33–6.

Bentall, R. P. (1990). The illusion of reality: A review and integration of psychological research on hallucinations. *Psychological Bulletin, 107*(1), 82–95.

Bentzen, J. S. (2019). Acts of God? Religiosity and natural disasters across subnational world districts. *The Economic Journal, 129*(622), 2295–321.

Berggren, N., & Bjørnskov, C. (2011). Is the importance of religion in daily life related to social trust? Cross-country and cross-state comparisons. *Journal of Economic Behavior & Organization, 80*(3), 459–80.

Bergmann, B. A. B., & Todd, N. R. (2019). Religious and spiritual beliefs uniquely predict poverty attributions. *Social Justice Research, 32*(4), 459–85.

Berns, G. S., Chappelow, J., Zink, C. F., Pagnoni, G., Martin-Skurski, M. E., & Richards, J. (2005). Neurobiological correlates of social conformity and independence during mental rotation. *Biological Psychiatry, 58*(3), 245–53.

Birgegard, A., & Granqvist, P. (2004). The correspondence between attachment to parents and God: Three experiments using subliminal separation cues. *Personality and Social Psychology Bulletin, 30*(9), 1122–35.

Black, S. W., Pössel, P., Jeppsen, B. D., Bjerg, A. C., & Wooldridge, D. T. (2015). Disclosure during private prayer as a mediator between prayer type and mental health in an adult Christian sample. *Journal of Religion and Health, 54*, 540–53.

Blakemore, S. J., Oakley, D. A., & Frith, C. D. (2003). Delusions of alien control in the normal brain. *Neuropsychologia, 41*(8), 1058–67.

Blogowska, J., Lambert, C., & Saroglou, V. (2013). Religious prosociality and aggression: It's real. *Journal for the Scientific Study of Religion, 52*(3), 524–36.

Blogowska, J., & Saroglou, V. (2013). For better or worse: Fundamentalists' attitudes toward outgroups as a function of exposure to authoritative religious texts. *International Journal for the Psychology of Religion, 23*(2), 103–25.

Bloom, P. B. N., Arikan, G., & Courtemanche, M. (2015). Religious social identity, religious belief, and anti-immigration sentiment. *American Political Science Review, 109*(2), 203–21.

Borgonovi, F. (2008). Divided we stand, united we fall: Religious pluralism, giving, and volunteering. *American Sociological Review, 73*(1), 105–28.

Botero, C. A., Gardner, B., Kirby, K. R., Bulbulia, J., Gavin, M. C., & Gray, R. D. (2014). The ecology of religious beliefs. *Proceedings of the National Academy of Sciences, 111*(47), 16784–9.

Boudry, M., & De Smedt, J. (2011). In mysterious ways: On petitionary prayer and subtle forms of supernatural causation. *Religion, 41*(3), 449–69.

Bouvet, R., & Bonnefon, J. F. (2015). Non-reflective thinkers are predisposed to attribute supernatural causation to uncanny experiences. *Personality and Social Psychology Bulletin, 41*, 955–61.

Boyer, P. (2001). *Religion explained: The evolutionary origin of religious thought.* New York: Basic Books.

Boyer, P. (2013). Why "belief" is hard work: Implications of Tanya Luhrmann's when God talks back. *HAU: Journal of Ethnographic Theory, 3*(3), 349–57.

Braam, A. W., Mooi, B., Jonker, J. S., Tilburg, W. V., & Deeg, D. J. H. (2008). God image and Five-Factor Model personality characteristics in later life: A study among inhabitants of Sassenheim in The Netherlands. *Mental Health, Religion and Culture, 11*(6), 547–59.

Brahinsky, J. (2020). Crossing the buffer: Ontological anxiety among US evangelicals and an anthropological theory of mind. *Journal of the Royal Anthropological Institute, 26*(S1), 45–60.

Brasil-Neto, J. P., Pascual-Leone, A., Valls-Sole, J., Cohen, L. G., & Hallett, M. (1992). Focal transcranial magnetic stimulation and response bias in a forced-choice task. *Journal of Neurology, Neurosurgery & Psychiatry, 55*(10), 964–6.

Brenner, P. S. (2011). Exceptional behavior or exceptional identity? Overreporting of church attendance in the U.S. *Public Opinion Quarterly, 75*, 19–41.

Brenner, P. S. (2012). Identity as a determinant of the overreporting of church attendance in Canada. *Journal for the Scientific Study of Religion, 51*(2), 377–85.

Brenner, P. S. (2014). Testing the veracity of self-reported religious practice in the Muslim world. *Social Forces, 92*(3), 1009–37.

Brewster, M. E., Velez, B. L., Geiger, E. F., & Sawyer, J. S. (2020). It's like herding cats: Atheist minority stress, group involvement, and psychological outcomes. *Journal of Counseling Psychology, 67*(1), 1–13.

Brimeyer, T. M. (2008). Research note: Religious affiliation and poverty explanations: Individual, structural, and divine causes. *Sociological Focus, 41*(3), 226–37.

Brock, T. C., & Balloun, J. L. (1967). Behavioral receptivity to dissonant information. *Journal of Personality and Social Psychology, 6*(4, Pt.1), 413–28.

Brooks, A. C. (2006). *Who really cares: The surprising truth about compassionate conservatism*. New York, NY: Basic Books.

Brooks, D. (2022, May 19). How Democrats Can Win the Morality Wars. *The New York Times*. https://www.nytimes.com/2022/05/19/opinion/democrats-morality-wars.html.

Brookwell, M. L., Bentall, R. P., & Varese, F. (2013). Externalizing biases and hallucinations in source-monitoring, self-monitoring and signal detection studies: A meta-analytic review. *Psychological Medicine, 43*(12), 2465–75.

Brotherton, R., & French, C. C. (2014). Belief in conspiracy theories and susceptibility to the conjunction fallacy. *Applied Cognitive Psychology, 28*(2), 238–48.

Brown, R. P., Barnes, C. D., & Campbell, N. J. (2007). Fundamentalism and forgiveness. *Personality and Individual Differences, 43*, 1437–47.

Brown, S. L., Nesse, R. M., House, J. S., & Utz, R. L. (2004). Religion and emotional compensation: Results from a prospective study of widowhood. *Personality and Social Psychology Bulletin, 30*(9), 1165–74.

Bulbulia, J., & Sosis, R. (2011). Signaling theory and the evolution of religious cooperation. *Religion, 41*(3), 363–88.

Bulman, R. J., & Wortman, C. B. (1977). Attributions of blame and coping in the real world: Severe accident victims react to their lot. *Journal of Personality and Social Psychology, 35*, 351–63.

Burns, C. P. E. (2006). Cognitive dissonance theory and the induced-compliance paradigm: Concerns for teaching religious studies. *Teaching Theology and Religion, 9*, 3–8.

Burris, C. T., Batson, C. D., Altstaedten, M., & Stephens, K. (1994). "What a friend …": Loneliness as a motivator of intrinsic religion. *Journal for the Scientific Study of Religion, 33*, 326–34.

Burris, C. T., Harmon-Jones, E., & Tarpley, W. R. (1997). "By faith alone": Religious agitation and cognitive dissonance. *Basic and Applied Social Psychology, 19*(1), 17–31.

Burris, C. T., & Jackson, L. M. (2000). Social identity and the true believer: Responses to threatened self-stereotypes among the intrinsically religious. *British Journal of Social Psychology, 39*(2), 257–78.

Burris, C. T., & Navara, G. S. (2002). Morality play or playing morality?: Intrinsic religious orientation and socially desirable responding. *Self and Identity, 1*(1), 67–76.

Burris, C. T., & Rempel, J. K. (2011). "Just look at him": Punitive responses cued by "evil" symbols. *Basic and Applied Social Psychology, 33*(1), 69–80.

Bushman, B. J., Ridge, R. D., Das, E., Key, C. W., & Busath, G. L. (2007). When God sanctions killing: Effect of scriptural violence on aggression. *Psychological Science, 18*(3), 204–7.

Cacioppo, J. T., & Petty, R. E. (1982). The need for cognition. *Journal of Personality and Social Psychology, 42*(1), 116–31.

Callan, M. J., Ellard, J. H., & Nicol, J. E. (2006). The belief in a just world and immanent justice reasoning in adults. *Personality and Social Psychology Bulletin, 32*, 1646–58.

Callan, M. J., Kay, A. C., Davidenko, N., & Ellard, J. H. (2009). The effects of justice motivation on memory for self-and other-relevant events. *Journal of Experimental Social Psychology, 45*(4), 614–23.

Callan, M. J., Sutton, R. M., & Dovale, C. (2010). When deserving translates into causing: The effect of cognitive load on immanent justice reasoning. *Journal of Experimental Social Psychology, 46*(6), 1097–100.

Caluori, N., Jackson, J. C., Gray, K., & Gelfand, M. (2020). Conflict changes how people view God. *Psychological Science, 31*(3), 280–92.

Campbell, D. E., & Yonish, S. J. (2003). Religion and volunteering in America. In C. Smidt (Ed.), *Religion as social capital: Producing the common good* (pp. 87–106). Waco, TX: Baylor University Press.

Cardwell, B. A., & Halberstadt, J. (2019). Religious believers do not distinguish good from poor reasons for God's existence. *The International Journal for the Psychology of Religion, 29*(3), 147–60.

Carlson, K. M., & González-Prendes, A. A. (2016). Cognitive behavioral therapy with religious and spiritual clients: A critical perspective. *Journal of Spirituality in Mental Health, 18*(4), 253–82.

Carlson, S. J., Levine, L. J., Lench, H. C., Flynn, E., Carpenter, Z. K., Perez, K. A., & Bench, S. W. (2022). You shall go forth with joy: Religion and aspirational judgments about emotion. *Psychology of Religion and Spirituality, 14*(4), 548–557.

Carroll, R. T. (2003). *The skeptic's dictionary: A collection of strange beliefs, amusing deceptions, & dangerous delusions.* New York: Wiley.

Chan, S. W. Y., Lau, W. W. F., Hui, C. H., Lau, E. Y. Y., & Cheung, S. f. (2020). Causal relationship between religiosity and value priorities: Cross-sectional and longitudinal investigations. *Psychology of Religion and Spirituality*, *12*(1), 77–87.

Chan, T., Michalak, N. M., & Ybarra, O. (2019). When God is your only friend: Religious beliefs compensate for purpose in life in the socially disconnected. *Journal of Personality*, *87*(3), 455–71.

Charles, S. J., van Mulukom, V., Brown, J. E., Watts, F., Dunbar, R. I., & Farias, M. (2021). United on Sunday: The effects of secular rituals on social bonding and affect. *PloS One*, *16*(1), e0242546.

Choi, J. K., & Bowles, S. (2007). The coevolution of parochial altruism and war. *Science*, *318*(5850), 636–40.

Clark, E. T. (1929). *The psychology of religious awakening*. New York: Macmillan.

Clark, K. J. (2014). *Religion and the sciences of origins: Historical and contemporary discussions*. New York: Palgrave Macmillan.

Clark, K. J., & Barrett, J. L. (2010). Reformed epistemology and the cognitive science of religion. *Faith and Philosophy*, *27*(2), 174–89.

Clarke, P., & James, J. (1967). The effects of situation, attitude intensity and personality on information-seeking. *Sociometry*, *30*, 235–45.

Coleman, S. L., & Beitman, B. D. (2009). Characterizing high-frequency coincidence detectors. *Psychiatric Annals*, *39*(5), 271–9.

Conway III, L. G., & Schaller, M. (2002). On the verifiability of evolutionary psychological theories: An analysis of the psychology of scientific persuasion. *Personality and Social Psychology Review*, *6*(2), 152–66.

Cook, M., & Mineka, S. (1989). Observational conditioning of fear to fear-relevant versus fear-irrelevant stimuli in rhesus monkeys. *Journal of Abnormal Psychology*, *98*(4), 448–59.

Cook, T., & Wimberly, D. (1983). If I should die before I wake: Religious commitment and adjustment to the death of a child. *Journal for the Scientific Study of Religion*, *22*, 222–38.

Corriveau, K. H., Chen, E. E., & Harris, P. L. (2015). Judgments about fact and fiction by children from religious and nonreligious backgrounds. *Cognitive Science*, *39*(2), 353–82.

Cotterill, S., Sidanius, J., Bhardwaj, A., & Kumar, V. (2014). Ideological support for the Indian caste system: Social dominance orientation, right-wing authoritarianism and karma. *Journal of Social and Political Psychology*, *2*(1), 98–116.

Cragun, R. T. (2014). *What you don't know about religion (but should)*. Durham, NC: Pitchstone Publishing.

Cragun, R. T., & Sumerau, J. E. (2015). God may save your life, but you have to find your own keys: Religious attributions, secular attributions, and religious priming. *Archive for the Psychology of Religion*, *37*(3), 321–42.

Crandall, C. S., & Eshleman, A. (2003). A justification-suppression model of the expression and experience of prejudice. *Psychological Bulletin*, *129*(3), 414–46.

Crozier, S., & Joseph, S. (1997). Religiosity and sphere-specific just world beliefs in 16- to 18-year-olds. *The Journal of Social Psychology, 137*(4), 510–13.

Cunha, Jr. M., & Caldieraro, F. (2009). Sunk-cost effects on purely behavioral investments. *Cognitive Science, 33*(1), 105–13.

Cushman, F. A. (2020). Rationalization is rational. *Behavioral and Brain Sciences, 43*, e28.

Cushman, F. A., Young, L., & Hauser, M. D. (2006). The role of conscious reasoning and intuition in moral judgment testing three principles of harm. *Psychological Science, 17*(12), 1082–9.

Dalbert, C. (2001). *The justice motive as a personal resource: Dealing with challenges and critical life events*. New York: Plenum Press.

Darley, J. M., & Batson, C. D. (1973). "From Jerusalem to Jericho": A study of situational and dispositional variables in helping behavior. *Journal of Personality and Social Psychology, 27*, 100–8.

Davies, M. F., Griffin, M., & Vice, S. (2001). Affective reactions to auditory hallucinations in psychotic, evangelical and control groups. *British Journal of Clinical Psychology, 40*(4), 361–70.

Davis, D. E., Hook, J. N., McAnnally-Linz, R., Choe, E., & Placeres, V. (2017). Humility, religion, and spirituality: A review of the literature. *Psychology of Religion and Spirituality, 9*(3), 242–53.

Davis, E. B., Granqvist, P., & Sharp, C. (2021). Theistic relational spirituality: Development, dynamics, health, and transformation. *Psychology of Religion and Spirituality, 13*(4), 401–15.

Daws, R. E., & Hampshire, A. (2017). The negative relationship between reasoning and religiosity is underpinned by a bias for intuitive responses specifically when intuition and logic are in conflict. *Frontiers in Psychology, 8*, 2191.

de Jager Meezenbroek, E., Garssen, B., van den Berg, M., van Dierendonck, D., Visser, A., & Schaufeli, W. B. (2012). Measuring spirituality as a universal human experience: A review of spirituality questionnaires. *Journal of Religion and Health, 51*, 336–54.

De Neys, W. (2021). On dual- and single-process models of thinking. *Perspectives on Psychological Science, 16*(6), 1412–27.

De Roos, S. A., Miedema, S., & Iedema, J. (2001). Attachment, working models of self and others, and God concept in kindergarten. *Journal for the Scientific Study of Religion, 40*(4), 607–18.

DeBono, A., Poepsel, D., & Corley, N. (2020). Thank God for my successes (not my failures): Feeling God's presence explains a God attribution bias. *Psychological Reports, 123*(5), 1663–87.

DeBono, A., Shariff, A. F., Poole, S., & Muraven, M. (2017). Forgive us our trespasses: Priming a forgiving (but not a punishing) God increases unethical behavior. *Psychology of Religion and Spirituality, 9*(S1), S1–S10.

Dein, S., & Pargament, K. (2012). On not praying for the return of an amputated limb: Conserving a relationship with God as the primary function of prayer. *Bulletin of the Menninger Clinic, 76*(3), 235–59.

Delevry, D., & Le, Q. A. (2019). Effect of treatment preference in randomized controlled trials: Systematic review of the literature and meta-analysis. *The Patient-Patient-Centered Outcomes Research, 12*(6), 593–609.

Delhey, J., & Newton, K. (2005). Predicting cross-national levels of social trust: Global pattern or Nordic exceptionalism? *European Sociological Review, 21*(4), 311–27.

Depalma, M. T., Madey, S. F., Tillman, T. C., & Wheeler, J. (1999). Perceived patient responsibility and belief in a just world affect helping. *Basic and Applied Social Psychology, 21*, 131–7.

Diener, E., Tay, L., & Myers, D. G. (2011). The religion paradox: If religion makes people happy, why are so many dropping out? *Journal of Personality and Social Psychology, 101*, 1278–90.

Dijksterhuis, A., Preston, J., Wegner, D. M., & Aarts, H. (2008). Effects of subliminal priming of self and God on self-attribution of authorship for events. *Journal of Experimental Social Psychology, 44*(1), 2–9.

Douthat, R. (2021, August 14). A guide to finding faith. *The New York Times.* https://www.nytimes.com/2021/08/14/opinion/sunday/faith-religion.html.

Du, H., & Chi, P. (2016). War, worries, and religiousness. *Social Psychological and Personality Science, 7*(5), 444–51.

Dunning, D., Perie, M., & Story, A. L. (1991). Self-serving prototypes of social categories. *Journal of Personality and Social Psychology, 61*(6), 957–68.

Dürlinger, F., & Pietschnig, J. (2022). Meta-analyzing intelligence and religiosity associations: Evidence from the multiverse. *PLoS One, 17*(2), e0262699.

Dutton, D. G., & Aron, A. P. (1974). Some evidence for heightened sexual attraction under conditions of high anxiety. *Journal of Personality and Social Psychology, 30*(4), 510–17.

Dutton, E., & Kirkegaard, E. (2022). The negative religiousness-IQ nexus is a Jensen effect on individual-level data: A refutation of Dutton et al.'s "The myth of the stupid believer". *Journal of Religion and Health, 61*(4), 3253–75.

Dzuka, J., & Dalbert, C. (2006). The belief in a just world's impact on subjective well-being in old age. *Aging and Mental Health, 10*, 439–44.

Echeverría Vicente, N. J., Hemmerechts, K., & Kavadias, D. (2022). Armed conflict and religious adherence across countries: A time series analysis. *Sociology of Religion, 83*(3), 371–401.

Egan, P. J. (2020). Identity as dependent variable: How Americans shift their identities to align with their politics. *American Journal of Political Science, 64*(3), 699–716.

Ellemers, N. (2017). *Morality and the regulation of social behavior: Groups as moral anchors.* New York: Psychology Press.

Ellison, C. G., & George, L. K. (1994). Religious involvement, social ties, and social support in a southeastern community. *Journal for the Scientific Study of Religion, 33*, 46–61.

Emmons, R. A., Cheung, C., & Tehrani, K. (1998). Assessing spirituality through personal goals: Implications for research on religion and subjective well-being. *Social Indicators Research, 45*, 391–422.

Engstrom, H. R., & Laurin, K. (2020). Existential uncertainty and religion. In K. E. Vail & C. Routledge (Eds.), *The science of religion, spirituality, and existentialism* (pp. 243–60). San Diego, CA: Elsevier.

Entringer, T. M., Gebauer, J. E., & Kroeger, H. (2022). Big five personality and religiosity: Bidirectional cross-lagged effects and their moderation by culture. *Journal of Personality.* Advance online publication. doi: 10.1111/jopy.12770

Epley, N., Akalis, S., Waytz, A., & Cacioppo, J. T. (2008). Creating social connection through inferential reproduction: Loneliness and perceived agency in gadgets, gods, and greyhounds. *Psychological Science, 19*(2), 114–20.

Epley, N., Converse, B. A., Delbosc, A., Monteleone, G. A., & Cacioppo, J. T. (2009). Believers' estimates of God's beliefs are more egocentric than estimates of other people's beliefs. *Proceedings of the National Academy of Sciences, 106*(51), 21533–8.

Epley, N., & Dunning, D. (2000). Feeling "holier than thou": Are self-serving assessments produced by errors in self- or social prediction. *Journal of Personality & Social Psychology, 79*, 861–75.

Epley, N., Waytz, A., & Cacioppo, J. T. (2007). On seeing human: A three-factor theory of anthropomorphism. *Psychological Review, 114*, 864–86.

Epstein, S., Pacini, R., Denes-Raj, V., & Heier, H. (1996). Individual differences in intuitive-experiential and analytical-rational thinking styles. *Journal of Personality and Social Psychology, 71*, 390–405.

Erdelyi, M. H. (1994). Hypnotic hypermnesia: The empty set of hypermnesia. *International Journal of Clinical and Experimental Hypnosis, 42*(4), 379–90.

Erickson-Davis, C., Luhrmann, T. M., Kurina, L. M., Weisman, K., Cornman, N., Corwin, A., & Bailenson, J. (2021). The sense of presence: Lessons from virtual reality. *Religion, Brain & Behavior, 11*(3), 335–51.

Erikson, E. (1958). *Young man Luther: A study in psychoanalysis and history.* New York: W. W. Norton.

Eriksson, K., & Funcke, A. (2014). Humble self-enhancement: Religiosity and the better-than-average effect. *Social Psychological and Personality Science, 5*, 76–83.

Erlandsson, A., Nilsson, A., Tinghög, G., & Västfjäll, D. (2018). Bullshit-sensitivity predicts prosocial behavior. *PloS One, 13*(7), e0201474.

Eurelings-Bontekoe, E. H. M., Hekman-Van Steeg, J., & Verschuur, M. (2005). The association between personality, attachment, psychological distress, church denomination and the God concept among a non-clinical sample. *Mental Health, Religion and Culture, 8*, 141–54.

Evans, J. S. B. (2008). Dual-processing accounts of reasoning, judgment, and social cognition. *Annual Review of Psychology*, 59, 255–78.

Evans, J. S. B., & Wason, P. C. (1976). Rationalization in a reasoning task. *British Journal of Psychology*, 67(4), 479–86.

Exline, J. J., & Pait, K. C. (2021). Perceiving messages from the divine and departed: An attributional perspective. In T. G. Plante, & G. Schwartz (Eds.), *Human interaction with the divine, the sacred, and the deceased: Psychological, scientific, and theological perspectives* (pp. 245–59). New York: Routledge.

Eysenck, H. J. (1952). The effects of psychotherapy: An evaluation. *Journal of Consulting Psychology*, 16(5), 319–24.

Farias, M., Newheiser, A. K., Kahane, G., & de Toledo, Z. (2013). Scientific faith: Belief in science increases in the face of stress and existential anxiety. *Journal of Experimental Social Psychology*, 49(6), 1210–13.

Ferrero, M. (2014). From Jesus to Christianity: The economics of sacrifice. *Rationality and Society*, 26, 397–424.

Festinger, L. (1954). A theory of social comparison processes. *Human Relations*, 7(2), 117–40.

Festinger, L. (1957). *A theory of cognitive dissonance*. Evanston, IL: Row, Peterson, & Co.

Festinger, L., Riecken, H. W., & Schachter, S (1956). *When prophecy fails: A social and psychological study of a modern group that predicted the end of the world*. Minneapolis: University of Minnesota Press.

Feuerbach, L. (2004). *The essence of Christianity*. New York: Barnes & Noble books.

Feuille, M., & Pargament, K. (2015). Pain, mindfulness, and spirituality: A randomized controlled trial comparing effects of mindfulness and relaxation on pain-related outcomes in migraineurs. *Journal of Health Psychology*, 20, 1090–106.

Fincher, C. L., & Thornhill, R. (2012). Parasite-stress promotes in-group assortative sociality: The cases of strong family ties and heightened religiosity. *Behavioral and Brain Sciences*, 35(2), 61–79.

FioRito, T. A., Abeyta, A. A., & Routledge, C. (2021). Religion, paranormal beliefs, and meaning in life. *Religion, Brain & Behavior*, 11(2), 139–46.

Fitouchi, L., & Singh, M. (2022). Supernatural punishment beliefs as cognitively compelling tools of social control. *Current Opinion in Psychology*, 44, 252–7.

Frederick, S. (2005). Cognitive reflection and decision making. *Journal of Economic Perspectives*, 19(4), 25–42.

Frenda, S. J., Knowles, E. D., Saletan, W., & Loftus, E. F. (2013). False memories of fabricated political events. *Journal of Experimental Social Psychology*, 49(2), 280–6.

Friedman, J. P., & Jack, A. I. (2018). What makes you so sure? Dogmatism, fundamentalism, analytic thinking, perspective taking and moral concern in the religious and nonreligious. *Journal of Religion and Health*, 57(1), 157–90.

Friedman, M., & Rholes, W. S. (2007). Successfully challenging fundamentalist beliefs results in increased death awareness. *Journal of Experimental Social Psychology*, 43(5), 794–801.

Friesen, J. P., Campbell, T. H., & Kay, A. C. (2015). The psychological advantage of unfalsifiability: The appeal of untestable religious and political ideologies. *Journal of Personality and Social Psychology, 108*(3), 515–29.

Fritsche, I. (2022). Agency through the we: Group-based control theory. *Current Directions in Psychological Science.*

Froese, P., & Bader, C. D. (2007). God in America: Why theology is not simply the concern of philosophers. *Journal for the Scientific Study of Religion, 46*(4), 465–81.

Froese, P., & Bader, C. D. (2010). *America's four gods: What we say about God–and what that says about us.* New York: Oxford University Press.

Furnham, A. F. (1997). Knowing and faking one's five-factor personality score. *Journal of Personality Assessment, 69,* 229–43.

Furnham, A. F. (2003). Belief in a just world: Research progress over the past decade. *Personality and Individual Differences, 34*(5), 795–817.

Furnham, A. F., & Brown, L. B. (1992). Theodicy: A neglected aspect of the psychology of religion. *The International Journal for the Psychology of Religion, 2*(1), 37–45.

Gal, D., & Rucker, D. D. (2010). When in doubt, shout! Paradoxical influences of doubt on proselytizing. *Psychological Science, 21*(11), 1701–7.

Galen, L. W. (2012). Does religious belief promote prosociality? A critical examination. *Psychological Bulletin, 138*(5), 876–906.

Galen, L. W. (2017). Overlapping mental magisteria: Implications of experimental psychology for a theory of religious belief as misattribution. *Method & Theory in the Study of Religion, 29*(3), 221–67.

Galen, L. W., Gore, R., & Shults, F. L. (2021). Modeling the effects of religious belief and affiliation on prosociality. *Secularism and Nonreligion, 10*(1), 6.

Galen, L. W., & Kloet, J. (2011a). Mental well-being in the religious and the non-religious: Evidence for a curvilinear relationship. *Mental Health, Religion & Culture, 14,* 673–89.

Galen, L. W., & Kloet, J. (2011b). Personality and social integration factors distinguishing non-religious from religious groups: The importance of controlling for attendance and demographics. *Archive for the Psychology of Religion, 33,* 205–28.

Galen, L. W., Smith, C. M., Knapp, N., & Wyngarden, N. (2011). Perceptions of religious and nonreligious targets: Exploring the effects of perceivers' religious fundamentalism. *Journal of Applied Social Psychology, 41*(9), 2123–43.

Galen, L. W., Kurby, C. A., & Fles, E. H. (2022). Religiosity, shared identity, trust, and punishment of norm violations: No evidence of generalized prosociality. *Psychology of Religion and Spirituality, 14*(2), 260–72.

Galen, L. W., & Miller, T. R. (2011). Perceived deservingness of outcomes as a function of religious fundamentalism and target responsibility. *Journal of Applied Social Psychology, 41,* 2144–64.

Galen, L. W., Sharp, M., & McNulty, A. (2015). Nonreligious group factors versus religious belief in the prediction of prosociality. *Social Indicators Research, 122*(2), 411–32.

Galen, L. W., Williams, T. J., & Ver Wey, A. L. (2014). Personality ratings are influenced by religious stereotype and ingroup bias. *The International Journal for the Psychology of Religion, 24*(4), 282–97.

Galen, L. W., Wolfe, M. B., Deleeuw, J., & Wyngarden, N. (2009). Religious fundamentalism as schema: Influences on memory for religious information. *Journal of Applied Social Psychology, 39*(5), 1163–90.

Gantman, A. P., Adriaanse, M. A., Gollwitzer, P. M., & Oettingen, G. (2017). Why did I do that? Explaining actions activated outside of awareness. *Psychonomic Bulletin & Review, 24*(5), 1563–72.

Ganzach, Y., Ellis, S., & Gotlibovski, C. (2013). On intelligence education and religious beliefs. *Intelligence, 41*(2), 121–8.

Garrett, R. K., & Weeks, B. E. (2013, February). The promise and peril of real-time corrections to political misperceptions. In *Proceedings of the 2013 conference on computer supported cooperative work* (pp. 1047–58). New York: ACM Press.

Garssen, B., Visser, A., & de Jager Meezenbroek, E. (2016). Examining whether spirituality predicts subjective well-being: How to avoid tautology. *Psychology of Religion and Spirituality, 8*, 141–8.

Garssen, B., Visser, A., & Pool, G. (2021). Does spirituality or religion positively affect mental health? Meta-analysis of longitudinal studies. *The International Journal for the Psychology of Religion, 31*(1), 4–20.

Gawronski, B., & Brannon, S. M. (2019). What is cognitive consistency, and why does it matter? In E. Harmon-Jones (Ed.), *Cognitive dissonance: Reexamining a pivotal theory in psychology* (2nd ed.) (pp. 91–116). Washington, DC: American Psychological Association.

Gawronski, B., & Strack, F. (2004). On the propositional nature of cognitive consistency: Dissonance changes explicit, but not implicit attitudes. *Journal of Experimental Social Psychology, 40*(4), 535–42.

Gebauer, J. E., & Maio, G. R. (2012). The need to belong can motivate belief in God. *Journal of Personality, 80*(2), 465–501.

Gebauer, J. E., Nehrlich, A. D., Stahlberg, D., Sedikides, C., Hackenschmidt, A., Schick, D., ... & Mander, J. (2018). Mind-body practices and the self: Yoga and meditation do not quiet the ego but instead boost self-enhancement. *Psychological Science, 29*(8), 1299–308.

Gebauer, J. E., Paulhus, D. L., & Neberich, W. (2013). Big Two personality and religiosity across cultures: Communals as religious conformists and agentics as religious contrarians. *Social Psychological and Personality Science, 4*(1), 21–30.

Gebauer, J. E., Sedikides, C., Schönbrodt, F. D., Bleidorn, W., Rentfrow, P. J., Potter, J., & Gosling, S. D. (2017a). The religiosity as social value hypothesis: A multi-method replication and extension across 65 countries and three levels of spatial aggregation. *Journal of Personality and Social Psychology, 113*(3), e18–e39.

Gebauer, J. E., Sedikides, C., & Schrade, A. (2017b). Christian self-enhancement. *Journal of Personality and Social Psychology, 113*(5), 786–809.

Gerard, H. B., & Mathewson, G. C. (1966). The effects of severity of initiation on liking for a group: A replication. *Journal of Experimental Social Psychology, 2*(3), 278–87.

Gervais, W. M. (2014). Everything is permitted? People intuitively judge immorality as representative of atheists. *PloS One, 9*(4), e92302.

Gervais, W. M., & Najle, M. B. (2015). Learned faith: The influences of evolved cultural learning mechanisms on belief in Gods. *Psychology of Religion and Spirituality, 7*(4), 327–35.

Gervais, W. M., Najle, M. B., & Caluori, N. (2021). The origins of religious disbelief: A dual inheritance approach. *Social Psychological and Personality Science, 12*(7), 1369–79.

Gervais, W. M., & Norenzayan, A. (2012). Analytic thinking promotes religious disbelief. *Science, 336*(6080), 493–6.

Gervais, W. M., Shariff, A. F., & Norenzayan, A. (2011). Do you believe in atheists? Distrust is central to anti-atheist prejudice. *Journal of Personality and Social Psychology, 101*(6), 1189–206.

Gervais, W. M., van Elk, M., Xygalatas, D., McKay, R. T., Aveyard, M., Buchtel, E. E., … & Bulbulia, J. (2018). Analytic atheism: A cross-culturally weak and fickle phenomenon? *Judgment and Decision Making, 13*, 268–74.

Gervais, W. M., Xygalatas, D., McKay, R. T., van Elk, M., Buchtel, E. E., Aveyard, M., Schiavone, S. R., Dar-Nimrod, I., Svedholm-Hakkinen, A. M., Riekki, T., Klocova, E. K., Ramsay, J. E., & Bulbulia, J. A. (2017). Global evidence of extreme intuitive moral prejudice against atheists. *Nature Human Behaviour, 1*(8), Article 0151.

Gibbons, D., & De Jarnette, J. (1972). Hypnotic susceptibility and religious experience. *Journal for the Scientific Study of Religion, 11*, 152–6.

Gillum, R. F., & Masters, K. S. (2010). Religiousness and blood donation: Findings from a national survey. *Journal of Health Psychology, 15*, 163–72.

Glicksohn, J., & Barrett, T. R. (2003). Absorption and hallucinatory experience. *Applied Cognitive Psychology, 17*(7), 833–49.

Global Market Insite, Inc. (2005). *One in four Americans believe the South Asian tsunami was an act of God.* http://www.gmi-mr.com/gmipoll/release.php?p=20050119.

Goplen, J., & Plant, E. A. (2015). A religious worldview: Protecting one's meaning system through religious prejudice. *Personality and Social Psychology Bulletin, 41*(11), 1474–87.

Gorsuch, R. L., & McPherson, S. E. (1989). Intrinsic/extrinsic measurement: I/E-revised and single-item scales. *Journal for the Scientific Study of Religion, 28*, 348–54.

Gorsuch, R. L., & Smith, C. S. (1983). Attributions of responsibility to God: An interaction of religious beliefs and outcomes. *Journal for the Scientific Study of Religion, 22*, 340–52.

Gosling, P., Denizeau, M., & Oberle, D. (2006). Denial of responsibility: A new mode of dissonance reduction. *Journal of Personality and Social Psychology, 90*, 722–33.

Grady, B., & Loewenthal, K. M. (1997). Features associated with speaking in tongues (glossolalia). *British Journal of Medical Psychology, 70*(Pt. 2), 185–91.

Graham, J., & Haidt, J. (2010). Beyond beliefs: Religions bind individuals into moral communities. *Personality and Social Psychology Review, 14,* 140–50.

Granqvist, P. (2020). *Attachment in religion and spirituality: A wider view.* New York: The Guilford Press.

Granqvist, P., Fredrikson, M., Unge, P., Hagenfeldt, A., Valind, S., Larhammar, D., & Larsson, M. (2005). Sensed presence and mystical experiences are predicted by suggestibility, not by the application of transcranial weak complex magnetic fields. *Neuroscience Letters, 379*(1), 1–6.

Granqvist, P., & Hagekull, B. (2000). Religiosity, adult attachment, and why "singles" are more religious. *International Journal for the Psychology of Religion, 10,* 111–23.

Granqvist, P., & Hagekull, B. (2003). Longitudinal predictions of religious change in adolescence: Contributions from the interaction of attachment and relationship status. *Journal of Social and Personal Relationships, 20*(6), 793–817.

Granqvist, P., Ivarsson, T., Broberg, A. G., & Hagekull, B. (2007). Examining relations among attachment, religiosity, and new age spirituality using the Adult Attachment Interview. *Developmental Psychology, 43*(3), 590–601.

Granqvist, P., & Kirkpatrick, L. A. (2004). Religious conversion and perceived childhood attachment: A meta-analysis. *The International Journal for the Psychology of Religion, 14*(4), 223–50.

Granqvist, P., Mikulincer, M., Gewirtz, V., & Shaver, P. R. (2012). Experimental findings on God as an attachment figure: Normative processes and moderating effects of internal working models. *Journal of Personality and Social Psychology, 103*(5), 804–18.

Grasmick, H. G., & McGill, A. L. (1994). Religion, attribution style, and punitiveness toward juvenile offenders. *Criminology, 32,* 23–42.

Gray, K., Jenkins, A. C., Heberlein, A. S., & Wegner, D. M. (2011). Distortions of mind perception in psychopathology. *Proceedings of the National Academy of Sciences, 108*(2), 477–9.

Gray, K., & Wegner, D. M. (2009). Moral typecasting: Divergent perceptions of moral agents and moral patients. *Journal of Personality and Social Psychology, 96*(3), 505–20.

Green, M., & Elliott, M. (2010). Religion, health, and psychological well-being. *Journal of Religion and Health, 49*(2), 149–63.

Greenberg, J., Pyszczynski, T., Solomon, S., Rosenblatt, A., Veeder, M., Kirkland, S., & Lyon, D. (1990). Evidence for terror management theory II: The effects of mortality salience on reactions to those who threaten or bolster the cultural worldview. *Journal of Personality and Social Psychology, 58,* 308–18.

Greenberg, J., Solomon, S., & Pyszczynski, T. (1997). Terror management theory of self-esteem and cultural worldviews: Empirical assessments and conceptual refinements. In M. P. Zanna (Ed.), *Advances in experimental social psychology* (pp. 61–139). New York: Academic Press.

Greenfield, E. A., & Marks, N. F. (2007). Religious social identity as an explanatory factor for associations between more frequent formal religious participation and psychological well-being. *The International Journal for the Psychology of Religion*, *17*(3), 245–59.

Greenway, A. P., Milne, L. C., & Clarke, V. (2003). Personality variables, self-esteem and depression and an individual's perception of God. *Mental Health, Religion & Culture*, *6*(1), 45–58.

Greer, C. L., Worthington, E. L., Jr., Van Tongeren, D. R., Gartner, A. L., Jennings, D. J. II, Lin, Y., Lavelock, C., Greer, T. W., & Ho, M. Y. (2014). Forgiveness of in-group offenders in Christian congregations. *Psychology of Religion and Spirituality*, *6*(2), 150–61.

Greer, T., Berman, M., Varan, V., Bobrycki, L., & Watson, S. (2005). We are a religious people; we are a vengeful people. *Journal for the Scientific Study of Religion*, *44*, 45–57.

Grossman, P. J., & Parrett, M. B. (2011). Religion and prosocial behaviour: A field test. *Applied Economics Letters*, *18*, 523–6.

Gunnoe, M. L., & Moore, K. A. (2002). Predictors of religiosity among youth aged 17–22: A longitudinal study of the national survey of children. *Journal for the Scientific Study of Religion*, *41*(1), 613–22.

Hafer, C. L. (2000). Do innocent victims threaten the belief in a just world? Evidence from a modified Stroop task. *Journal of Personality and Social Psychology*, *79*(2), 165–73.

Hafer, C. L., & Begue, L. (2005). Experimental research on just-world theory: Problems, developments, and future challenges. *Psychological Bulletin*, *131*, 128–67.

Hafer, C. L., & Choma, B. L. (2009). Belief in a just world, perceived fairness, and justification of the status quo. In J. T. Jost, A. C. Kay, & H. Thorisdottir (Eds.), *Social and psychological bases of ideology and system justification* (pp. 107–25). New York: Oxford University Press.

Hagerty, B. B. (2011). "*Army's 'spiritual fitness' rests angers some soldiers.*" https://www.npr.org/2011/01/13/132904866/armys-spiritual-fitness-test-angers-some-soldiers.

Haidt, J. (2001). The emotional dog and its rational tail: A social intuitionist approach to moral judgment. *Psychological Bulletin*, *108*, 814–34.

Haidt, J., Bjorklund, F., & Murphy, S. (2000). Moral dumbfounding: When intuition finds no reason. Unpublished manuscript, University of Virginia, 191–221.

Halama, P. (2015). Empirical approach to typology of religious conversion. *Pastoral Psychology*, *64*(2), 185–94.

Hall, D. L., Matz, D. C., & Wood, W. (2010). Why don't we practice what we preach? A meta-analytic review of religious racism. *Personality and Social Psychology Review*, *14*(1), 126–39.

Hall, L., Johansson, P., & Strandberg, T. (2012). Lifting the veil of morality: Choice blindness and attitude reversals on a self-transforming survey. *PloS One*, *7*(9), e45457.

Hammer, J. H., & Cragun, R. T. (2019). Daily spiritual experiences and well-being among the nonreligious, spiritual, and religious: A bifactor analysis. *Psychology of Religion and Spirituality, 11*(4), 463–73.

Hampton A. J., & Sprecher S. (2017) Consensual Validation. In V. Zeigler-Hill, & T. K. Shackelford (Eds.) (2020). *Encyclopedia of personality and individual differences* (pp. 864–71). Cham: Springer International Publishing.

Harmon-Jones, E., & Mills, J. (Eds.). (1999). *Cognitive dissonance: Reexamining a pivotal theory in psychology* (2nd ed.). Washington, DC: American Psychological Association.

Harris, M. (1977). *Cannibals and kings: The origins of cultures*. New York: Vintage.

Harvey, A. J., & Callan, M. J. (2014). The role of religiosity in ultimate and immanent justice reasoning. *Personality and Individual Differences, 56*, 193–6.

Heaven, P. C., & Ciarrochi, J. (2007). Personality and religious values among adolescents: A three-wave longitudinal analysis. *British Journal of Psychology, 98*(4), 681–94.

Hecker, T., Braitmayer, L., & Van Duijl, M. (2015). Global mental health and trauma exposure: The current evidence for the relationship between traumatic experiences and spirit possession. *European Journal of Psychotraumatology, 6*(1), 29126.

Heiphetz, L., Spelke, E. S., & Banaji, M. R. (2013). Patterns of implicit and explicit attitudes in children and adults: Tests in the domain of religion. *Journal of Experimental Psychology: General, 142*, 864–79.

Henrich, J. (2009). The evolution of costly displays, cooperation and religion: Credibility enhancing displays and their implications for cultural evolution. *Evolution and Human Behavior 30*(4), 244–60.

Henrich, J., Bauer, M., Cassar, A., Chytilová, J., & Purzycki, B. G. (2019). War increases religiosity. *Nature Human Behaviour, 3*(2), 129–35.

Henrich, J., & Boyd, R. (1998). The evolution of conformist transmission and the emergence of between-group differences. *Evolution and Human Behavior, 19*(4), 215–41.

Henrich, J., & Gil-White, F. J. (2001). The evolution of prestige: Freely conferred deference as a mechanism for enhancing the benefits of cultural transmission. *Evolution and Human Behavior, 22*(3), 165–96.

Hepper, E. G., Gramzow, R. H., & Sedikides, C. (2010). Individual differences in self-enhancement and self-protection strategies: An integrative analysis. *Journal of Personality, 78*(2), 781–814.

Hertel, B. R., & Donahue, M. J. (1995). Parental influences on God images among children: Testing Durkheim's metaphoric parallelism. *Journal for the Scientific Study of Religion, 34*, 186–99.

Hertz, S. G., & Krettenauer, T. (2016). Does moral identity effectively predict moral behavior?: A meta-analysis. *Review of General Psychology, 20*(2), 129–40.

Hildebrandt, A., & Jäckle, S. (2020). Pervasive polarization or partial convergence? Moral attitudes of religious and secular people at various levels of development. *International Journal of Public Opinion Research, 32*, 306–17.

Hill, P. C., & Gibson, N. J. (2008). Whither the roots? Achieving conceptual depth in psychology of religion. *Archive for the Psychology of Religion*, *30*(1), 19–36.

Hine, V. H. (1969). Pentecostal glossolalia toward a functional interpretation. *Journal for the Scientific Study of Religion*, *8*, 211–26.

Hodges, S. D., Sharp, C. A., Gibson, N. J., & Tipsord, J. M. (2013). Nearer my God to thee: Self–God overlap and believers' relationships with God. *Self and Identity*, *12*(3), 337–56.

Hoffarth, M. R., Hodson, G., & Molnar, D. S. (2018). When and why is religious attendance associated with antigay bias and gay rights opposition? A justification-suppression model approach. *Journal of Personality and Social Psychology*, *115*(3), 526–63.

Hofmann, W., Wisneski, D. C., Brandt, M. J., & Skitka, L. J. (2014). Morality in everyday life. *Science*, *345*(6202), 1340–3.

Hogg, M. A. (2014). From uncertainty to extremism: Social categorization and identity processes. *Current Directions in Psychological Science*, *23*(5), 338–42.

Hogg, M. A., & Adelman, J. (2013). Uncertainty identity theory: Extreme groups, radical behavior, and authoritarian leadership. *Journal of Social Issues*, *69*(3), 436–54.

Hogg, M. A., Adelman, J. R., & Blagg, R. D. (2010). Religion in the face of uncertainty: An uncertainty-identity theory account of religiousness. *Personality and Social Psychology Review*, *14*(1), 72–83.

Hogg, M. A., Meehan, C., & Farquharson, J. (2010). The solace of radicalism: Self-uncertainty and group identification in the face of threat. *Journal of Experimental Social Psychology*, *46*, 1061–6.

Holm, N. G. (1987). Sundén's role theory and glossolalia. *Journal for the Scientific Study of Religion*, *26*, 383–9.

Hood, R. W., Jr. (2001). *Dimensions of mystical experiences: Empirical studies and psychological links*. Amsterdam - New York, NY: Rodopi.

Hoogeveen, S., Wagenmakers, E. J., Kay, A. C., & Van Elk, M. (2018). Compensatory control and religious beliefs: A registered replication report across two countries. *Comprehensive Results in Social Psychology*, *3*(3), 240–65.

Hovey, J. D., Hurtado, G., Morales, L. R. A., & Seligman, L. D. (2014). Religion-based emotional social support mediates the relationship between intrinsic religiosity and mental health. *Archives of Suicide Research*, *18*, 376–91.

Hubble, M. A., Duncan, B. L., & Miller, S. D. (1999). *The heart and soul of change: What works in therapy*. Washington, DC: American Psychological Association.

Iannaccone, L. (1994). Why strict churches are strong. *American Journal of Sociology*, *99*, 1180–211.

Immerzeel, T., & Van Tubergen, F. (2013). Religion as reassurance? Testing the insecurity theory in 26 European countries. *European Sociological Review*, *29*(2), 359–72.

Innes, J. M. (1978). Selective exposure as a function of dogmatism and incentive. *Journal of Social Psychology*, *106*, 261–5.

International Theological Commission (2007). *The hope of salvation for infants who die without being baptized.* http://www.vatican.va/roman_curia/congregations/cfaith/cti_documents/rc_con_cfaith_doc_20070419_un-baptised-infants_en.html.
Jackson, J. C., Caluori, N., Abrams, S., Beckman, E., Gelfand, M., & Gray, K. (2021a). Tight cultures and vengeful gods: How culture shapes religious belief. *Journal of Experimental Psychology: General, 150*(10), 2057–77.
Jackson, J. C., Caluori, N., Gray, K., & Gelfand, M. (2021b). The new science of religious change. *American Psychologist, 76*(6), 838–50.
Jackson, J. C., & Gray, K. (2019). When a good god makes bad people: Testing a theory of religion and immorality. *Journal of Personality and Social Psychology, 117*(6), 1203–30.
Jackson, J. C., Hester, N., & Gray, K. (2018). The faces of God in America: Revealing religious diversity across people and politics. *PLoS One, 13*, e0198745.
Jackson, L. M., & Hunsberger, B. (1999). An intergroup perspective on religion and prejudice. *Journal for the Scientific Study of Religion, 38*, 509–23.
Jacobs, R. C., & Campbell, D. T. (1961). The perpetuation of an arbitrary tradition through several generations of a laboratory microculture. *Journal of Abnormal and Social Psychology, 62*, 649–58.
James, W. (2003). *The varieties of religious experience: A study in human nature.* London: Routledge.
Janis, I. L. (1972). *Victims of groupthink.* Boston: Houghton Mifflin.
Järnefelt, E., Canfield, C. F., & Kelemen, D. (2015). The divided mind of a disbeliever: Intuitive beliefs about nature as purposefully created among different groups of non-religious adults. *Cognition, 140*, 72–88.
Jasinskaja-Lahti, I., & Jetten, J. (2019). Unpacking the relationship between religiosity and conspiracy beliefs in Australia. *British Journal of Social Psychology, 58*(4), 938–54.
Jegindø, E. M., Vase, L., Skewes, J. C., Terkelsen, A. J., Hansen, J., Geertz, A. W., ... & Jensen, T. S. (2013). Expectations contribute to reduced pain levels during prayer in highly religious participants. *Journal of Behavioral Medicine, 36*, 413–26.
Ji, C. C., Pendergraft, L., & Perry, M. (2006). Religiosity, altruism, and altruistic hypocrisy. *Review of Religious Research, 48*, 156–78.
Johnson, D. (2016). *God is watching you: How the fear of God makes us human.* USA: Oxford University Press.
Johnson, M. K., Rowatt, W. C., & LaBouff, J. (2010). Priming Christian religious concepts increases racial prejudice. *Social Psychological and Personality Science, 1*(2), 119–26.
Johnson, M. K., Rowatt, W. C., & LaBouff, J. P. (2012). Religiosity and prejudice revisited: In-group favoritism, out-group derogation, or both? *Psychology of Religion and Spirituality, 4*(2), 154–68.
Jones, A. E., & Elliott, M. (2017). Examining social desirability in measures of religion and spirituality using the bogus pipeline. *Review of Religious Research, 59*(1), 47–64.

Jong, J. (2021). Death anxiety and religion. *Current Opinion in Psychology*, *40*, 40–4.

Jong, J., & Halberstadt, J. (2018). *Death anxiety and religious belief: An existential psychology of religion*. London: Bloomsbury Publishing.

Jong, J., Halberstadt, J., & Bluemke, M. (2012). Foxhole atheism, revisited: The effects of mortality salience on explicit and implicit religious belief. *Journal of Experimental Social Psychology*, *48*(5), 983–9.

Jong, J., Kavanagh, C., & Visala, A. (2015). Born idolaters: The limits of the philosophical implications of the cognitive science of religion. *Neue Zeitschrift für Systematische Theologie und Religionsphilosophie*, *57*(2), 244–66.

Jordan, J. J., & Kouchaki, M. (2021). Virtuous victims. *Science Advances*, *7*(42), eabg5902.

Joshanloo, M., Weijers, D., & Bond, M. H. (2021). Cultural religiosity moderates the relationship between perceived societal injustice and satisfaction with one's life. *Personality and Individual Differences*, *179*, 110891.

Jost, J. T., Hawkins, C. B., Nosek, B. A., Hennes, E. P., Stern, C., Gosling, S. D., & Graham, J. (2014). Belief in a just God (and a just society): A system justification perspective on religious ideology. *Journal of Theoretical and Philosophical Psychology*, *34*(1), 56–81.

Jugel, M., & Lecigne, A. (2015). Beliefs in the end of the world, justice, religiosity and system preservation: A psychological study of how the "end of the world" could match common belief systems. *Journal of Beliefs & Values*, *36*(2), 175–89.

Kagan, J., & Snidman, N. (2005). Temperament and a religious perspective. *APS Observer*, *18*(10).

Kahneman, D. (2011). *Thinking, fast and slow*. New York: Farrar, Straus and Giroux.

Kalckert, A., & Ehrsson, H. H. (2012). Moving a rubber hand that feels like your own: A dissociation of ownership and agency. *Frontiers in Human Neuroscience*, *6*, 40.

Kay, A. C., Gaucher, D., Napier, J. L., Callan, M. J., & Laurin, K. (2008). God and the government: Testing a compensatory control mechanism for the support of external systems. *Journal of Personality and Social Psychology*, *95*, 18–35.

Kay, A. C., Gaucher, D., McGregor, I., & Nash, K. (2010a). Religious belief as compensatory control. *Personality and Social Psychology Review*, *14*, 37–48.

Kay, A. C., Shepherd, S., Blatz, C. W., Chua, S. N., & Galinsky, A. D. (2010b). For God (or) country: The hydraulic relation between government instability and belief in religious sources of control. *Journal of Personality and Social Psychology*, *99*(5), 725–39.

Kelemen, D. (1999). *Beliefs about purpose: On the origins of teleological thought*. Oxford: Oxford University Press.

Kelley, J., & De Graaf, N. D. (1997). National context, parental socialization, and religious belief: Results from 15 nations. *American Sociological Review*, *62*, 639–59.

Kelly, J. F. (2017). Is Alcoholics Anonymous religious, spiritual, neither? Findings from 25 years of mechanisms of behavior change research. *Addiction*, *112*, 929–36.

Kelly, J. F., Hoeppner, B., Stout, R. L., & Pagano, M. (2012). Determining the relative importance of the mechanisms of behavior change within Alcoholics Anonymous: A multiple mediator analysis. *Addiction, 107*(2), 289–99.

Kenworthy, J. B. (2003). Explaining the belief in God for self, in-group, and out-group targets. *Journal for the Scientific Study of Religion, 42*(1), 137–46.

Khan, U., & Dhar, R. (2006). Licensing effect in consumer choice. *Journal of Marketing Research, 43*(2), 259–66.

Kim-Prieto, C., & Diener, E. (2009). Religion as a source of variation in the experience of positive and negative emotions. *The Journal of Positive Psychology, 4*(6), 447–60.

King, M., Marston, L., McManus, S., Brugha, T., Meltzer, H., & Bebbington, P. (2013). Religion, spirituality and mental health: Results from a national study of English households. *The British Journal of Psychiatry, 202*, 68–73.

Kirkpatrick, L. A. (1997). A longitudinal study of changes in religious belief and behavior as a function of individual differences in adult attachment style. *Journal for the Scientific Study of Religion, 36*, 207–17.

Kirkpatrick, L. A. (1998). God as a substitute attachment figure: A longitudinal study of adult attachment style and religious change in college students. *Personality and Social Psychology Bulletin, 24*, 961–73.

Klaczynski, P. A., & Gordon, D. H. (1996). Self-serving influences on adolescents' evaluations of belief-relevant evidence. *Journal of Experimental Child Psychology, 62*(3), 317–39.

Kleck, R., & Wheaton, J. (1967). Dogmatism and responses to opinion-consistent and opinion inconsistent information. *Journal of Personality and Social Psychology, 5*, 249–52.

Klein, R. A., Cook, C. L., Ebersole, C. R., Vitiello, C., Nosek, B. A., Hilgard, J., ... & Ratliff, K. A. (2022). Many Labs 4: Failure to replicate mortality salience effect with and without original author involvement. *Collabra: Psychology, 8*(1), 35271.

Knobe, J. (2003). Intentional action in folk psychology: An experimental investigation. *Philosophical Psychology, 16*(2), 309–24.

Kober, S. E., & Neuper, C. (2013). Personality and presence in virtual reality: Does their relationship depend on the used presence measure? *International Journal of Human-Computer Interaction, 29*(1), 13–25.

Koenig, H. G. (2008). Concerns about measuring "spirituality" in research. *Journal of Nervous and Mental Disease, 196*, 349–55.

Koenig, H. G. (2018). *Religion and mental health: Research and clinical applications*. London: Academic Press.

Koenig, H. G., Pearce, M. J., Nelson, B., & Erkanli, A. (2016). Effects on daily spiritual experiences of religious versus conventional cognitive behavioral therapy for depression. *Journal of Religion and Health, 55*, 1763–77.

Koenig, H. G., Pearce, M. J., Nelson, B., Shaw, S. F., Robins, C. J., Daher, N. S., ... & King, M. B. (2015). Religious vs. conventional cognitive behavioral therapy for major depression in persons with chronic medical illness: A pilot randomized trial. *Journal of Nervous and Mental Disease, 203*, 243–51.

Koenig, L. B., & Schneider, M. (2019, February). *Does my life have purpose? How threatening meaning affects meaning in life, religiousness, and spirituality*. [Poster presentation]. Portland, OR: Society for Personality and Social Psychology.

Kogan, A., Sasaki, J., Zou, C., Kim, H., & Cheng, C. (2013). Uncertainty avoidance moderates the link between faith and subjective well-being around the world. *The Journal of Positive Psychology, 8*(3), 242–8.

Kohlberg, L. (1976). Moral stages and moralization: The cognitive developmental approach. In T. Lickona (Ed.), Moral development and behavior: Theory, research, and social issues (pp. 31–53). New York: Holt, Rinehart, & Winston.

Kokis, J. V., Macpherson, R., Toplak, M. E., West, R. F., & Stanovich, K. E. (2002). Heuristic and analytic processing: Age trends and associations with cognitive ability and cognitive styles. *Journal of Experimental Child Psychology, 83*(1), 26–52.

Koleva, S. P., Graham, J., Iyer, R., Ditto, P. H., & Haidt, J. (2012). Tracing the threads: How five moral concerns (especially Purity) help explain culture war attitudes. *Journal of Research in Personality, 46*(2), 184–94.

Koopmans, R., Kanol, E., & Stolle, D. (2021). Scriptural legitimation and the mobilization of support for religious violence: experimental evidence across three religions and seven countries. *Journal of Ethnic and Migration Studies, 47*(7), 1498–516.

Kossowska, M., Czernatowicz-Kukuczka, A., & Sekerdej, M. (2017). Many faces of dogmatism: Prejudice as a way of protecting certainty against value violators among dogmatic believers and atheists. *British Journal of Psychology, 108*(1), 127–47.

Kouchaki, M. (2011). Vicarious moral licensing: The influence of others' past moral actions on moral behavior. *Journal of Personality and Social Psychology, 101*(4), 702–15.

Kraft, C. H. (2016). *Defeating dark angels: Breaking demonic oppression in the believer's life*. Grand Rapids, MI: Baker Books.

Kruger, J., & Gilovich, T. (2004). Actions, intentions, and self-assessment: The road to self-enhancement is paved with good intentions. *Personality and Social Psychology Bulletin, 30*(3), 328–39.

Krull, D. S. (2022). On nudges from the unseen: Attributions to God and Satan for major historical events. *Psychology of Religion and Spirituality, 14*(1), 51–8.

Kugelmass, H., & Garcia, A. (2015). Mental disorder among nonreligious adolescents. *Mental Health, Religion & Culture, 18*(5), 368–79.

Kunda, Z. (1990). The case for motivated reasoning. *Psychological Bulletin, 108*(3), 480–98.

Lam, P. Y. (2002). As the flocks gather: How religion affects voluntary association participation. *Journal for the Scientific Study of Religion, 41*(3), 405–22.

Lambert, W. W., Triandis, L. M., & Wolf, M. (1959). Some correlates of beliefs in the malevolence and benevolence of supernatural beings: A cross-societal study. *The Journal of Abnormal and Social Psychology, 58*(2), 162–9.

Lanman, J. A., & Buhrmester, M. D. (2017). Religious actions speak louder than words: Exposure to credibility-enhancing displays predicts theism. *Religion, Brain & Behavior, 7*(1), 3–16.

Lanz, L., Thielmann, I., & Gerpott, F. H. (2022). Are social desirability scales desirable? A meta-analytic test of the validity of social desirability scales in the context of prosocial behavior. *Journal of Personality, 90*(2), 203–21.

Latane, B., & Darley, J. M. (1970). *The unresponsive bystander: Why doesn't he help.* London: Appleton, Century-Crofts.

Lattin, D. (1997, April 13). Sunday Interview—Musings of the Main Mormon/Gordon B. Hinckley, "president, prophet, seer and revelator" of the Church of Jesus Christ of Latter-day Saints, sits at the top of one of the world's fastest-growing religions. SFGATE. https://www.sfgate.com/news/article/SUNDAY-INTERVIEW-Musings-of-the-Main-Mormon-2846138.php.

Launay, G., & Slade, P. (1981). The measurement of hallucinatory predisposition in male and female prisoners. *Personality and Individual Differences, 2*(3), 221–34.

Launonen, L. (2021). Debunking arguments gain little from cognitive science of religion. *Zygon, 56*(2), 416–33.

Laurin, K., & Kay, A. C. (2017). The motivational underpinnings of belief in God. In J. M. Olson (Ed.), *Advances in experimental social psychology* (Vol. 56, pp. 201–57). Cambridge, MA: Academic Press.

Laurin, K., Schumann, K., & Holmes, J. G. (2014). A relationship with God? Connecting with the divine to assuage fears of interpersonal rejection. *Social Psychological and Personality Science, 5*(7), 777–85.

Lavine, H., Lodge, M., & Freitas, K. (2005). Threat, authoritarianism, and selective exposure to information. *Political Psychology, 26*(2), 219–44.

Laythe, B., Finkel, D., & Kirkpatrick, L. A. (2001). Predicting prejudice from religious fundamentalism and right-wing authoritarianism: A multiple-regression approach. *Journal for the Scientific Study of Religion, 40*(1), 1–10.

Lea, J. A., & Hunsberger, B. E. (1990). Christian orthodoxy and victim derogation: The impact of the salience of religion. *Journal for the Scientific Study of Religion, 29*, 512–18.

Leach, M. M., Berman, M. E., & Eubanks, L. (2008). Religious activities, religious orientation, and aggressive behavior. *Journal for the Scientific Study of Religion, 47*, 311–19.

Leak, G. K., & Fish, S. (1989). Religious orientation, impression management, and self-deception: Toward a clarification of the link between religiosity and social desirability. *Journal for the Scientific Study of Religion, 28*, 355–9.

Legare, C. H., & Gelman, S. A. (2008). Bewitchment, biology, or both: The co-existence of natural and supernatural explanatory frameworks across development. *Cognitive Science, 32*(4), 607–42.

Legare, C. H., & Wen, N. (2014). The effects of ritual on the development of social group cognition. *International Society for the Study of Behavioral Development, 2*(66), 9–12.

Legare, C. H., Evans, E. M., Rosengren, K. S., & Harris, P. L. (2012). The coexistence of natural and supernatural explanations across cultures and development. *Child Development*, *83*(3), 779–93.

Lerner, M. J. (1965). Evaluation of performance as a function of performer's reward and attractiveness. *Journal of Personality and Social Psychology*, *1*, 335–60.

Lerner, M. J., & Simmons, C. H. (1966). Observer's reaction to the "innocent victim": Compassion or rejection? *Journal of Personality and Social Psychology*, *4*, 203–10.

Levin, J. S., Wickramasekera, I. E., & Hirshberg, C. (1998). Is religiousness a correlate of absorption? Implications for psychophysiology, coping, and morbidity. *Alternative Therapies in Health and Medicine*, *4*(6), 72.

Levy, I., & Reuven, Y. (2017). Predicting punitive disciplinary techniques among juvenile care workers based on ethnicity, nationality, religiosity and belief in a just world. *Child & Youth Care Forum*, *46*, 519–37.

Lewandowsky, S., Ecker, U. K., Seifert, C. M., Schwarz, N., & Cook, J. (2012). Misinformation and its correction: Continued influence and successful debiasing. *Psychological Science in the Public Interest*, *13*(3), 106–31.

Libby, L. K., & Eibach, R. P. (2002). Looking back in time: Self-Concept change affects visual perspective in autobiographical memory. *Journal of Personality and Social Psychology*, *82*, 167–79.

Lieberman, M. D., Ochsner, K. N., Gilbert, D. T., & Schacter, D. L. (2001). Do amnesics exhibit cognitive dissonance reduction? The role of explicit memory and attention in attitude change. *Psychological Science*, *12*, 135–40.

Lifshitz, M., van Elk, M., & Luhrmann, T. M. (2019). Absorption and spiritual experience: A review of evidence and potential mechanisms. *Consciousness and Cognition*, *73*, 102760.

Lilienfeld, S. O., Ritschel, L. A., Lynn, S. J., Cautin, R. L., & Latzman, R. D. (2014). Why ineffective psychotherapies appear to work: A taxonomy of causes of spurious therapeutic effectiveness. *Perspectives on Psychological Science*, *9*(4), 355–87.

Lim, C., & Putnam, R. D. (2010). Religion, social networks, and life satisfaction. *American Sociological Review*, *75*(6), 914–33.

Lindeman, M., & Aarnio, K. (2006). Paranormal beliefs: Their dimensionality and correlates. *European Journal of Personality*, *20*, 585–602.

Lindeman, M., & Aarnio, K. (2007). Superstitious, magical, and paranormal beliefs: An integrative model. *Journal of Research in Personality*, *41*, 731–44.

Lindeman, M., & Lipsanen, J. (2016). Diverse cognitive profiles of religious believers and nonbelievers. *The International Journal for the Psychology of Religion*, *26*(3), 185–92.

Lindeman, M., & Svedholm-Häkkinen, A. M. (2016). Does poor understanding of physical world predict religious and paranormal beliefs? *Applied Cognitive Psychology*, *30*(5), 736–42.

Lindeman, M., Svedholm-Häkkinen, A. M., & Lipsanen, J. (2015). Ontological confusions but not mentalizing abilities predict religious belief, paranormal belief, and belief in supernatural purpose. *Cognition*, *134*, 63–76.

Liquin, E. G., Metz, S. E., & Lombrozo, T. (2020). Science demands explanation, religion tolerates mystery. *Cognition*, *204*, 104398.

Lobato, E. J., Tabatabaeian, S., Fleming, M., Sulzmann, S., & Holbrook, C. (2020). Religiosity predicts evidentiary standards. *Social Psychological and Personality Science*, *11*(4), 546–51.

Lobato, E., Mendoza, J., Sims, V., & Chin, M. (2014). Examining the relationship between conspiracy theories, paranormal beliefs, and pseudoscience acceptance among a university population. *Applied Cognitive Psychology*, *28*(5), 617–25.

Lockhart, C., Sibley, C. G., & Osborne, D. (2022). The authoritarian incubator: Examining the effect of conversion to Christianity on right-wing authoritarianism and social dominance orientation. *Group Processes & Intergroup Relations*.

Loveland, M. T., Capella, A. G., & Maisonet, I. (2017). Prosocial skeptics: Skepticism and generalized trust. *Critical Research on Religion*, *5*(3), 251–65.

Low, N., Butt, S., Ellis, P., & Davis Smith, J. (2007). *Helping out: A national survey of volunteering and charitable giving.* London: Cabinet Office.

Ludeke, S. G., & Carey, B. (2015). Two mechanisms of biased responding account for the association between religiousness and misrepresentation in Big Five self-reports. *Journal of Research in Personality*, *57*, 43–7.

Ludeke, S., Johnson, W., & Bouchard Jr., T. J. (2013). "Obedience to traditional authority": A heritable factor underlying authoritarianism, conservatism and religiousness. *Personality and Individual Differences*, *55*(4), 375–80.

Luhrmann, T. M. (2012). *When God talks back: Understanding the American evangelical relationship with God.* New York: Knopf.

Luhrmann, T. M. (2020). *How God becomes real: Kindling the presence of invisible others.* Princeton, NJ: Princeton University Press.

Luhrmann, T. M., Nusbaum, H., & Thisted, R. (2010). The absorption hypothesis: Learning to hear God in evangelical Christianity. *American Anthropologist*, *112*(1), 66–78.

Luhrmann, T. M., & Weisman, K. (2022). Porosity is the heart of religion. *Current Directions in Psychological Science*, *31*(3), 247–53.

Luhrmann, T. M., Weisman, K., Aulino, F., Brahinsky, J. D., Dulin, J. C., Dzokoto, V. A., … & Smith, R. E. (2021). Sensing the presence of gods and spirits across cultures and faiths. *Proceedings of the National Academy of Sciences*, *118*(5), e2016649118.

Lupfer, M. B., Brock, K. F., & DePaola, S. J. (1992). The use of secular and religious attributions to explain everyday behavior. *Journal for the Scientific Study of Religion*, *31*(4), 486–503.

Lupfer, M. B., de Paola, S. J., Brock, K. F., & Clement, L. (1994). Making secular and religious attributions: The availability hypothesis revisited. *Journal for the Scientific Study of Religion*, *33*(2), 162–71.

Lupfer, M. B., & Layman, E. (1996). Invoking naturalistic and religious attributions: A case of applying the availability heuristic? The representativeness heuristic? *Social Cognition*, *14*(1), 55–76.

Lupfer, M. B., Tolliver, D., & Jackson, M. (1996). Explaining life-altering occurrences: A test of the "God-of-the-gaps" hypothesis. *Journal for the Scientific Study of Religion*, *35*, 379–91.

MacInnis, C. C., & Hodson, G. (2016). Surfing for sexual sin: Relations between religiousness and viewing sexual content online. *Sexual Addiction & Compulsivity*, *23*(2–3), 196–210.

Maes, J. (1998). Immanent justice and ultimate justice. In L. Montada, M. Lerner (Eds.), *Responses to victimizations and belief in a just world* (pp. 9–40). Boston, MA: Springer.

Mahoney, A. (2021). *The science of children's religious and spiritual development*. Cambridge, UK: Cambridge University Press.

Maij, D. L., & van Elk, M. (2018). Getting absorbed in experimentally induced extraordinary experiences: Effects of placebo brain stimulation on agency detection. *Consciousness and Cognition*, *66*, 1–16.

Maij, D. L., van Elk, M., & Schjoedt, U. (2019). The role of alcohol in expectancy-driven mystical experiences: A pre-registered field study using placebo brain stimulation. *Religion, Brain & Behavior*, *9*(2), 108–25.

Maij, D. L., van Harreveld, F., Gervais, W., Schrag, Y., Mohr, C., & van Elk, M. (2017). Mentalizing skills do not differentiate believers from non-believers, but credibility enhancing displays do. *PloS One*, *12*(8), e0182764.

Maij, D. L., Van Schie, H. T., & Van Elk, M. (2019). The boundary conditions of the hypersensitive agency detection device: An empirical investigation of agency detection in threatening situations. *Religion, Brain & Behavior*, *9*(1), 23–51.

Mallery, P., Mallery, S., & Gorsuch, R. (2000). A preliminary taxonomy of attributions to God. *International Journal for the Psychology of Religion*, *10*(3), 135–56.

Mallinas, S. R., & Conway, P. (2022). If you don't believe in God, do you at least believe in Aristotle? Evaluations of religious outgroup members hinge upon moral perceptions. *The International Journal for the Psychology of Religion*, *32*(2), 127–49.

Marcus, Z. J., & McCullough, M. E. (2021). Does religion make people more self-controlled? A review of research from the lab and life. *Current Opinion in Psychology*, *40*, 167–70.

Margolis, M. F. (2018). How politics affects religion: Partisanship, socialization, and religiosity in America. *The Journal of Politics*, *80*(1), 30–43.

Markus, H. R., & Kitayama, S. (1991). Culture and the self: Implications for cognition, emotion, and motivation. *Psychological Review*, *98*(2), 224–53.

Marques, A., Ihle, A., Souza, A., Peralta, M., & de Matos, M. G. (2022). Religious-based interventions for depression: A systematic review and meta-analysis of experimental studies. *Journal of Affective Disorders*, *309*, 289–96.

Marshall, D. A. (2002). Behavior, belonging, and belief: A theory of ritual practice. *Sociological Theory*, *20*(3), 360–80.

Martin, T. F., White, J. M., & Perlman, D. (2003). Religious socialization: A test of the channeling hypothesis of parental influence on adolescent faith maturity. *Journal of Adolescent Research*, *18*(2), 169–87.

Matz, D. C., & Wood, W. (2005). Cognitive dissonance in groups: The consequences of disagreement. *Journal of Personality and Social Psychology, 88*, 22–37.

Mazar, N., Amir, O., & Ariely, D. (2008). The dishonesty of honest people: A theory of self-concept maintenance. *Journal of Marketing Research, 45*, 633–44.

Mazzoni, G. A. L., Loftus, E. F., Seitz, A., & Lynn, S. J. (1999). Changing beliefs and memories through dream interpretation. *Applied Cognitive Psychology, 13*, 125–44.

Mazzoni, G. A. L., & Memon, A. (2003). Imagination can create false autobiographical memories. *Psychological Science, 14*, 186–8.

McCann, S. J. (1999). Threatening times and fluctuations in American church memberships. *Personality and Social Psychology Bulletin, 25*(3), 325–36.

McCauley, R. N. (2017). *Philosophical foundations of the cognitive science of religion: A head start*. London, UK: Bloomsbury Publishing.

McCloud, S. (2015). *American possessions: Fighting demons in the contemporary United States*. USA: Oxford University Press.

McCullough, M. E., Tsang, J. A., & Brion, S. (2003). Personality traits in adolescence as predictors of religiousness in early adulthood: Findings from the Terman Longitudinal Study. *Personality and Social Psychology Bulletin, 29*(8), 980–91.

McCullough, M. E., & Worthington, E. L., Jr. (1999). Religion and the forgiving personality. *Journal of Personality, 67*, 1141–64.

McCutcheon, R. T. (Ed.). (1999). *The insider/outsider problem in the study of religion: A reader*. London, UK: Cassell.

McFarland, C., & Alvaro, C. (2000). The impact of motivation on temporal comparisons: Coping with traumatic events by perceiving personal growth. *Journal of Personality and Social Psychology, 79*(3), 327–43.

McGregor, I., & Marigold, D. C. (2003). Defensive zeal and the uncertain self: What makes you so sure? *Journal of Personality and Social Psychology, 85*, 838–52.

McGregor, I., Haji, R., Nash, K. A., & Teper, R. (2008). Religious zeal and the uncertain self. *Basic and Applied Social Psychology, 30*, 183–8.

McGregor, I., Nash, K., & Prentice, M. (2010). Reactive approach motivation (RAM) for religion. *Journal of Personality and Social Psychology, 99*(1), 148.

McGregor, I., Zanna, M. P., Holmes, J. G., & Spencer, S. J. (2001). Compensatory conviction in the face of personal uncertainty: Going to extremes and being oneself. *Journal of Personality and Social Psychology, 80*, 472–88.

McIntosh, D. N., Silver, R. C., & Wortman, C. B. (1993). Religion's role in adjustment to a negative life event: Coping with the loss of a child. *Journal of Personality and Social Psychology, 65*, 812–21.

McIntosh, J., & McKeganey, N. (2000). Addicts' narratives of recovery from drug use: Constructing a non-addict identity. *Social Science & Medicine, 50*, 1501–10.

McKay, R., & Whitehouse, H. (2015). Religion and morality. *Psychological Bulletin, 141*(2), 447–73.

McNally, R. J. (2005). Debunking myths about trauma and memory. *Canadian Journal of Psychiatry, 50*, 817–22.

McPhetres, J., & Zuckerman, M. (2017). Religious people endorse different standards of evidence when evaluating religious versus scientific claims. *Social Psychological and Personality Science*, 8, 836–42.

Melton, J. G. (1985). Spiritualization and reaffirmation: What really happens when prophecy fails. *American Studies*, 26, 17–29.

Mencken, F. C., Bader, C., & Embry, E. (2009). In God we trust: Images of God and trust in the United States among the highly religious. *Sociological Perspectives*, 52(1), 23–38.

Merino, S. M. (2013). Religious social networks and volunteering: Examining recruitment via close ties. *Review of Religious Research*, 55(3), 509–27.

Merritt, A. C., Effron, D. A., Fein, S., Savitsky, K. K., Tuller, D. M., & Monin, B. (2012). The strategic pursuit of moral credentials. *Journal of Experimental Social Psychology*, 48(3), 774–7.

Merritt, A. C., Effron, D. A., & Monin, B. (2010). Moral self-licensing: When being good frees us to be bad. *Social and Personality Psychology Compass*, 4, 344–57.

Miller, D. T., & Ross, M. (1975). Self-serving biases in the attribution of causality: Fact or fiction? *Psychological Bulletin*, 82(2), 213–25.

Monroe, A. E., & Plant, E. A. (2019). The dark side of morality: Prioritizing sanctity over care motivates denial of mind and prejudice toward sexual outgroups. *Journal of Experimental Psychology: General*, 148(2), 342–60.

Monsma, S. V. (2007). Religion and philanthropic giving and volunteering: Building blocks for civic responsibility. *Interdisciplinary Journal of Research on Religion*, 3, 2–28. Article 3.

Moon, J. W., Krems, J. A., Cohen, A. B., & Kenrick, D. T. (2019). Is nothing sacred? Religion, sex, and reproductive strategies. *Current Directions in Psychological Science*, 28(4), 361–5.

Morgan, J. (2016). Religion and dual-process cognition: A continuum of styles or distinct types? *Religion, Brain & Behavior*, 6(2), 112–29.

Morgan, J., Wood, C., & Caldwell-Harris, C. (2018). Reflective thought, religious belief, and the social foundations hypothesis. In G. Pennycook (Ed.), *The new reflectionism in cognitive psychology: Why reason matters* (pp. 9–30). New York, NY: Routledge.

Morris Trainor, Z., Jong, J., Bluemke, M., & Halberstadt, J. (2019). Death salience moderates the effect of trauma on religiosity. *Psychological Trauma: Theory, Research, Practice, and Policy*, 11(6), 639–46.

Mulder, L. B., & Aquino, K. (2013). The role of moral identity in the aftermath of dishonesty. *Organizational Behavior and Human Decision Processes*, 121, 219–30.

Musch, J., & Ehrenberg, K. (2002). Probability misjudgment, cognitive ability, and belief in the paranormal. *British Journal of Psychology*, 93(2), 169–77.

Muturi, N., & An, S. (2010). HIV/AIDS stigma and religiosity among African American women. *Journal of Health Communication*, 15(4), 388–401.

Myers, D. G. (2012). Reflections on religious belief and prosociality: Comment on Galen (2012). *Psychological Bulletin*, 138, 913–17.

Nehrlich, A. D., Gebauer, J. E., Sedikides, C., & Schoel, C. (2019). Agentic narcissism, communal narcissism, and prosociality. *Journal of Personality and Social Psychology*, *117*(1), 142–65.

Nelson, T. A., Abeyta, A. A., & Routledge, C. (2020). Does meaning motivate magical thinking among theists and atheists? *Social Psychological and Personality Science*, *11*(2), 176–84.

Neuberg, S. L., Warner, C. M., Mistler, S. A., Berlin, A., Hill, E. D., Johnson, J. D., ... & Schober, J. (2014). Religion and intergroup conflict: Findings from the global group relations project. *Psychological Science*, *25*(1), 198–206.

Newberg, A. B., Wintering, N. A., Morgan, D., & Waldman, M. R. (2006). The measurement of regional cerebral blood flow during glossolalia: A preliminary SPECT study. *Psychiatry Research: Neuroimaging*, *148*(1), 67–71.

Nezlek, J. B. (2022). Relationships among belief in God, well-being, and social capital in the 2020 European and World Values Surveys: Distinguishing interpersonal and ideological prosociality. *Journal of Religion and Health*, *61*(3), 2569–88.

Nie, F., & Olson, D. V. (2016). Demonic influence: The negative mental health effects of belief in demons. *Journal for the Scientific Study of Religion*, *55*(3), 498–515.

Niemyjska, A., & Drat-Ruszczak, K. (2013). When there is nobody, angels begin to fly: Supernatural imagery elicited by a loss of social connection. *Social Cognition*, *31*(1), 57–71.

Nieuwboer, W., Van Schie, H. T., & Wigboldus, D. (2014). Priming with religion and supernatural agency enhances the attribution of intentionality to natural phenomena. *Journal for the Cognitive Science of Religion*, *2*(2), 97–120.

Nilsson, A., Erlandsson, A., & Västfjäll, D. (2019). The complex relation between receptivity to pseudo-profound bullshit and political ideology. *Personality and Social Psychology Bulletin*, *45*(10), 1440–54.

Nisbett, R. E., & Wilson, T. D. (1977). Telling more than we can know: Verbal reports on mental processes. *Psychological Review*, *84*(3), 231–59.

Noordewier, M. K., & Rutjens, B. T. (2021). Personal need for structure shapes the perceived impact of reduced personal control. *Personality and Individual Differences*, *170*, 110478.

Norenzayan, A. (2013). *Big gods: How religion transformed cooperation and conflict*. Princeton, NJ: Princeton University Press.

Norenzayan, A., & Hansen, I. G. (2006). Belief in supernatural agents in the face of death. *Personality and Social Psychology Bulletin*, *32*(2), 174–87.

Norenzayan, A., Shariff, A. F., Gervais, W. M., Willard, A. K., McNamara, R. A., Slingerland, E., & Henrich, J. (2016). The cultural evolution of prosocial religions. *Behavioral and Brain Sciences*, *39*, 1–19.

Norris, P., & Inglehart, R. (2011). *Sacred and secular: Religion and politics worldwide*. New York: Cambridge University Press.

Norton, M. I., Vandello, J. A., & Darley, J. M. (2004). Casuistry and social category bias. *Journal of Personality and Social Psychology*, *87*(6), 817.

Obaidi, M., Kunst, J. R., Kteily, N., Thomsen, L., & Sidanius, J. (2018). Living under threat: Mutual threat perception drives anti-Muslim and anti-Western hostility in the age of terrorism. *European Journal of Social Psychology, 48*(5), 567–84.

O'Grady, K. A., & Richards, P. S. (2007). God image and theistic psychotherapy. *Journal of Spirituality and Mental Health, 9*, 183–209.

Oishi, S., Seol, K. O., Koo, M., & Miao, F. F. (2011). Was he happy? Cultural difference in conceptions of Jesus. *Journal of Research in Personality, 45*(1), 84–91.

Olagoke, A. A., Olagoke, O. O., & Hughes, A. M. (2021). Intention to vaccinate against the novel 2019 coronavirus disease: The role of health locus of control and religiosity. *Journal of Religion and Health, 60*(1), 65–80.

Olson, J. A., Landry, M., Appourchaux, K., & Raz, A. (2016). Simulated thought insertion: Influencing the sense of agency using deception and magic. *Consciousness and Cognition, 43*, 11–26.

Osborne, D., & Sibley, C. G. (2014). Endorsement of system-justifying beliefs strengthens the relationship between church attendance and right-wing authoritarianism. *Group Processes & Intergroup Relations, 17*(4), 542–51.

Oviedo, L. (2015). Religious cognition as a dual-process: Developing the model. *Method & Theory in the Study of Religion, 27*(1), 31–58.

Pagels, E. H. (1996). *The origin of Satan*. New York: Vintage.

Palasinski, M., & Seol, K. O. (2015). Examination of religious identity meta-stereotypes when defying its relevant source through out-group helping. *Psychology of Religion and Spirituality, 7*(1), 80–9.

Paloutzian, R. F., Richardson, J. T., & Rambo, L. R. (1999). Religious conversion and personality change. *Journal of Personality, 67*(6), 1047–79.

Pargament, K. I. (2002). Is religion nothing but …? Explaining religion versus explaining religion away. *Psychological Inquiry, 13*, 239–44.

Pargament, K. I., & Hahn, J. (1986). God and the just world: Causal and coping attributions to God in health situations. *Journal for the Scientific Study of Religion, 25*, 193–207.

Pargament, K. I., Magyar-Russell, G. M., & Murray-Swank, N. A. (2005). The sacred and the search for significance: Religion as a unique process. *Journal of Social Issues, 61*, 665–87.

Pargament, K. I., & Sweeney, P. J. (2011). Building spiritual fitness in the Army: An innovative approach to a vital aspect of human development. *American Psychologist, 66*(1), 58–64.

Parsons, S. (2022). Fear of punishment in another world: A follow-up examination of the religious beliefs about HIV/AIDS—A decade of progress? *Journal of Religion and Health, 61*, 3350–62.

Partos, T. R., Cropper, S. J., & Rawlings, D. (2016). You don't see what I see: Individual differences in the perception of meaning from visual stimuli. *PloS One, 11*(3), e0150615.

Paulhus, D. L., & John, O. P. (1998). Egoistic and moralistic biases in self-perception: The interplay of self-deceptive styles with basic traits and motives. *Journal of Personality, 66*(6), 1025–60.

Paunonen, S. V., & LeBel, E. P. (2012). Socially desirable responding and its elusive effects on the validity of personality assessments. *Journal of Personality and Social Psychology, 103*(1), 158–75.

Pearce, M. J., & Koenig, H. G. (2016). Spiritual struggles and religious cognitive behavioral therapy: A randomized clinical trial in those with depression and chronic medical illness. *Journal of Psychology and Theology, 44*, 3–15.

Pearce, M. J., Koenig, H. G., Robins, C. J., Daher, N., Shaw, S. F., Nelson, B., … & King, M. B. (2015). Effects of religious versus conventional cognitive-behavioral therapy on generosity in major depression and chronic medical illness: A randomized clinical trial. *Spirituality in Clinical Practice, 2*, 202–15.

Pelham, B. W., Shimizu, M., Arndt, J., Carvallo, M., Solomon, S., & Greenberg, J. (2018). Searching for god: Illness-related mortality threats and religious search volume in Google in 16 nations. *Personality and Social Psychology Bulletin, 44*(3), 290–303.

Pennycook, G., Bago, B., & McPhetres, J. (2023). Science beliefs, political ideology, and cognitive sophistication. *Journal of Experimental Psychology: General*, (152)1, 80–97. Advance online publication. doi: 10.1037/xge0001267

Pennycook, G., Cheyne, J. A., Barr, N., Koehler, D. J., & Fugelsang, J. A. (2014). Cognitive style and religiosity: The role of conflict detection. *Memory & Cognition, 42*(1), 1–10.

Pennycook, G., Cheyne, J. A., Barr, N., Koehler, D. J., & Fugelsang, J. A. (2015). On the reception and detection of pseudo-profound bullshit. *Judgment and Decision Making, 10*(6), 549–63.

Pennycook, G., Cheyne, J. A., Koehler, D. J., & Fugelsang, J. A. (2013). Belief bias during reasoning among religious believers and skeptics. *Psychonomic Bulletin and Review, 20*, 806–11.

Pennycook, G., Cheyne, J. A., Koehler, D. J., & Fugelsang, J. A. (2020). On the belief that beliefs should change according to evidence: Implications for conspiratorial, moral, paranormal, political, religious, and science beliefs. *Judgment and Decision Making, 15*(4), 476.

Pennycook, G., Ross, R. M., Koehler, D. J., & Fugelsang, J. A. (2016). Atheists and agnostics are more reflective than religious believers: Four empirical studies and a meta-analysis. *PloS One, 11*(4), e0153039.

Perry, S. L. (2018). Not practicing what you preach: Religion and incongruence between pornography beliefs and usage. *The Journal of Sex Research, 55*(3), 369–80.

Perry, S. L., & McElroy, E. E. (2020). Does the Bible tell me so? Weighing the influence of content versus bias on Bible interpretation using survey experiments. *Journal for the Scientific Study of Religion, 59*(4), 569–85.

Perry, S. L., & Whitehead, A. L. (2021). Racialized religion and judicial injustice: how whiteness and Biblicist Christianity intersect to promote a preference for (unjust) punishment. *Journal for the Scientific Study of Religion, 60*(1), 46–63.

Pew Research Center (2006). *Spirit and Power—A 10-Country Survey of Pentecostals*. https://www.pewresearch.org/religion/2006/10/05/spirit-and-power/.

Pew Research Center (2008). *U.S. Religious Landscape Survey*. http://religions.pewforum.org/pdf/report-religious-landscape-study-full.pdf.

Pew Research Center (October 9, 2012). *Nones on the rise.* https://www.pewresearch.org/religion/2012/10/09/nones-on-the-rise/.

Pew Research Center (2017). *A growing share of Americans say it's not necessary to believe in God to be moral.* https://www.pewresearch.org/fact-tank/2017/10/16/a-growing-share-of-americans-say-its-not-necessary-to-believe-in-god-to-be-moral/.

Pew Research Center (November 3, 2021). *Few Americans blame God or say faith has been shaken amid pandemic, other tragedies.* https://www.pewforum.org/2021/11/23/few-americans-blame-god-or-say-faith-has-been-shaken-amid-pandemic-other-tragedies/.

Piazza, J., & Landy, J. (2013). "Lean not on your own understanding": Belief that morality is founded on divine authority and non-utilitarian moral thinking. *Judgment and Decision Making, 8*(6), 639–61.

Pichon, I., & Saroglou, V. (2009). Religion and helping: Impact of target, thinking styles and just-world beliefs. *Archive for the Psychology of Religion, 31*, 215–36.

Piedmont, R. L. (2004). Spiritual transcendence as a predictor of psychosocial outcome from an outpatient substance abuse program. *Psychology of Addictive Behaviors, 18*, 213–22.

Pietkiewicz, I. J., Kłosińska, U., Tomalski, R., & van der Hart, O. (2021). Beyond dissociative disorders: A qualitative study of Polish Catholic women reporting demonic possession. *European Journal of Trauma & Dissociation, 5*(4), 100204.

Piff, P. K., Dietze, P., Feinberg, M., Stancato, D. M., & Keltner, D. (2015). Awe, the small self, and prosocial behavior. *Journal of Personality and Social Psychology, 108*, 883–99.

Pöhls, K., Schlösser, T., & Fetchenhauer, D. (2020). Non-religious identities and life satisfaction: Questioning the universality of a linear link between religiosity and well-being. *Journal of Happiness Studies, 21*(7), 2327–53.

Poloma, M. M., & Green, J. C. (2010). *The assemblies of god: Godly love and the revitalization of American Pentecostalism.* New York, NY: New York University Press.

Portmann, J. (2000). *When bad things happen to other people.* New York, NY: Routledge.

Powers, M. B., Halpern, J. M., Ferenschak, M. P., Gillihan, S. J., & Foa, E. B. (2010). A meta-analytic review of prolonged exposure for posttraumatic stress disorder. *Clinical Psychology Review, 30*, 635–41.

Prade, C., & Saroglou, V. (2016). Awe's effects on generosity and helping. *The Journal of Positive Psychology, 11*, 522–30.

Prasad, M., Perrin, A. J., Bezila, K., Hoffman, S. G., Kindleberger, K., Manturuk, K., & Powers, A. S. (2009). "There must be a reason": Osama, Saddam, and inferred justification. *Sociological Inquiry, 79*(2), 142–62.

Pratt, J. B. (1920). *The religious consciousness: A psychological study.* New York: Macmillan.

Preston, J. L., & Ritter, R. S. (2013). Different effects of religion and God on prosociality with the ingroup and outgroup. *Personality and Social Psychology Bulletin, 39*(11), 1471–83.

Price, M. E., & Launay, J. (2018). Increased wellbeing from social interaction in a secular congregation. *Secularism and Nonreligion, 7*(1), 6.

Pronin, E. (2008). How we see ourselves and how we see others. *Science, 320*(5880), 1177–80.

Pruckner, G. J., & Sausgruber, R. (2008). *Honesty on the streets-A natural field experiment on newspaper purchasing.* Available at SSRN 1277208.

Public Religion Research Institute (2012), *The 2012 American Values survey: How Catholics and the religiously unaffiliated will shape the 2012 election and beyond.* http://publicreligion.org/site/wp-content/uploads/2012/10/AVS-2012-Pre-election-Report-for-Web.pdf.

Public Religion Research Institute (2015). *Nearly one in three support lifetime ban for football players who commit domestic violence.* http://publicreligion.org/research/2015/01/prri-rns-ahead-of-super-bowl-nearly-three-in-ten-americans-support-lifetime-ban-for-football-players-who-commit-domestic-violence/.

Purzycki, B. G. (2016). The evolution of gods' minds in the Tyva Republic. *Current Anthropology, 57*(S13), S88–S104.

Purzycki, B. G., Apicella, C., Atkinson, Q. D., Cohen, E., McNamara, R. A., Willard, A. K., ... & Henrich, J. (2016). Moralistic gods, supernatural punishment and the expansion of human sociality. *Nature, 530*(7590), 327–30.

Purzycki, B. G., Stagnaro, M. N., & Sasaki, J. (2020). Breaches of trust change the content and structure of religious appeals. *Journal for the Study of Religion, Nature and Culture, 14*(1), 71–94.

Putnam, R. D. (2000). *Bowling alone: The collapse and revival of American community.* New York, NY: Touchstone.

Putnam, R. D., & Campbell, D. E. (2010). *American grace: How religion divides and unites us.* New York, NY: Simon & Schuster.

Pyszczynski, T., Greenberg, J., & Solomon, S. (1999). A dual-process model of defense against conscious and unconscious death-related thoughts: An extension of terror management theory. *Psychological Review, 106,* 835–45.

Rabelo, A. L., & Pilati, R. (2021). Are religious and nonreligious people different in terms of moral judgment and empathy? *Psychology of Religion and Spirituality, 13*(1), 101–10.

Raine, A. (1991). The SPQ: A scale for the assessment of schizotypal personality based on DSM-III-R criteria. *Schizophrenia Bulletin, 17*(4), 555–64.

Randles, D., Inzlicht, M., Proulx, T., Tullett, A. M., & Heine, S. J. (2015). Is dissonance reduction a special case of fluid compensation? Evidence that dissonant cognitions cause compensatory affirmation and abstraction. *Journal of Personality and Social Psychology, 108*(5), 697–710.

Ray, S. D., Lockman, J. D., Jones, E. J., & Kelly, M. H. (2015). Attributions to God and Satan about life-altering events. *Psychology of Religion and Spirituality, 7*(1), 60–9.

Razmyar, S., & Reeve, C. L. (2013). Individual differences in religiosity as a function of cognitive ability and cognitive style. *Intelligence, 41,* 667–73.

Reddish, P., & Tong, E. M. W. (2021, September 2). A longitudinal investigation of religious prosociality: What predicts it and who benefits? *Psychology of Religion and Spirituality*. Advance online publication. doi: 10.1037/rel0000442

Reeder, G. D. (2013). Attribution as a gateway to social cognition. In D. E. Carlston (Ed.), *The Oxford handbook of social cognition* (pp. 95–117). New York: Oxford University Press.

Rest, J. R., Narvaez, D., Thoma, S. J., & Bebeau, M. J. (1999). DIT2: Devising and testing a revised instrument of moral judgment. *Journal of Educational Psychology*, 91(4), 644–59.

Riekki, T., Lindeman, M., Aleneff, M., Halme, A., & Nuortimo, A. (2013). Paranormal and religious believers are more prone to illusory face perception than skeptics and non-believers. *Applied Cognitive Psychology*, 27, 150–5.

Riekki, T., Lindeman, M., & Raij, T. T. (2014). Supernatural believers attribute more intentions to random movement than skeptics: An fMRI study. *Social Neuroscience*, 9, 400–11.

Riggio, H. R., Uhalt, J., & Matthies, B. K. (2014). Unanswered prayers: Religiosity and the God-serving bias. *The Journal of Social Psychology*, 154, 491–514.

Riggio, H. R., Uhalt, J., Matthies, B. K., Harvey, T., Lowden, N., & Umana, V. (2018). Explaining death by tornado: Religiosity and the God-serving bias. *Archive for the Psychology of Religion*, 40(1), 32–59.

Risen, J. L. (2016). Believing what we do not believe: Acquiescence to superstitious beliefs and other powerful intuitions. *Psychological Review*, 123, 182–207.

Ritter, C., Benson, D. E., & Synder, C. (1990). Belief in a just world and depression. *Sociological Perspectives*, 33, 235–52.

Rizeq, J., Flora, D. B., & Toplak, M. E. (2021). An examination of the underlying dimensional structure of three domains of contaminated mindware: Paranormal beliefs, conspiracy beliefs, and anti-science attitudes. *Thinking & Reasoning*, 27(2), 187–211.

Roberts, A. J., Handley, S. J., & Polito, V. (2021). The design stance, intentional stance, and teleological beliefs about biological and nonbiological natural entities. *Journal of Personality and Social Psychology*, 120(6), 1720–48.

Roberts, A. J., Wastell, C. A., & Polito, V. (2020). Teleology and the intentions of supernatural agents. *Consciousness and Cognition*, 80, 102905.

Roberts, C. W. (1989). Imagining God: Who is created in whose image? *Review of Religious Research*, 30, 375–86.

Robinson, E. A. R., Krentzman, A. R., Webb, J. R., & Brower, K. J. (2011). Six-month changes in spirituality and religiousness in alcoholics predict drinking outcomes at nine months. *Journal of Studies on Alcohol and Drugs*, 72, 660–8.

Rogers, P., Fisk, J. E., & Lowrie, E. (2018). Paranormal belief, thinking style preference and susceptibility to confirmatory conjunction errors. *Consciousness and Cognition*, 65, 182–96.

Rokeach, M. (1969). Religious values and social compassion. *Review of Religious Research*, 11, 24–39.

Rosenblatt, P. C., Meyer, C. J., & Karis, T. A. (1991). Internal interactions with God. *Imagination, Cognition and Personality, 11*, 85–97.

Ross, L. D., Lelkes, Y., & Russell, A. G. (2012). How Christians reconcile their personal political views and the teachings of their faith: Projection as a means of dissonance reduction. *Proceedings of the National Academy of Sciences, 109*(10), 3616–22.

Ross, M. (1989). Relation of implicit theories to the construction of personal histories. *Psychological Review, 96*, 341–57.

Ross, R. M., Pennycook, G., McKay, R., Gervais, W. M., Langdon, R., & Coltheart, M. (2016). Analytic cognitive style, not delusional ideation, predicts data gathering in a large beads task study. *Cognitive Neuropsychiatry, 21*(4), 300–14.

Rosset, E. (2008). It's no accident: Our bias for intentional explanations. *Cognition, 108*(3), 771–80.

Routledge, C., Abeyta, A. A., & Roylance, C. (2016). An existential function of evil: The effects of religiosity and compromised meaning on belief in magical evil forces. *Motivation and Emotion, 40*(5), 681–8.

Routledge, C., Abeyta, A. A., & Roylance, C. (2018). Death and end times: The effects of religious fundamentalism and mortality salience on apocalyptic beliefs. *Religion, Brain & Behavior, 8*(1), 21–30.

Routledge, C., Roylance, C., & Abeyta, A. A. (2017). Miraculous meaning: Threatened meaning increases belief in miracles. *Journal of Religion and Health, 56*(3), 776–83.

Rowatt, W. C., Kang, L. L., Haggard, M. C., & LaBoufff, J. P. (2014). A social-personality perspective on humility, religiousness, and spirituality. *Journal of Psychology and Theology, 42*(1), 31–40.

Rowatt, W. C., Ottenbreit, A., Nesselroade, K. P., Jr., & Cunningham, P. A. (2002). On being holier-than-thou or humbler-than-thee: A social-psychological perspective on religiousness and humility. *Journal for the Scientific Study of Religion, 41*, 227–37.

Rubin, Z., & Peplau, L. A. (1975). Who believes in a just world? *Journal of Social Issues, 31*(3), 65–89.

Rufi, S., Wlodarczyk, A., Páez, D., & Javaloy, F. (2016). Flow and emotional experience in spirituality: Differences in interactive and coactive collective rituals. *Journal of Humanistic Psychology, 56*, 373–93.

Rutjens, B. T., van der Pligt, J., & van Harreveld, F. (2010). Deus or Darwin: Randomness and belief in theories about the origin of life. *Journal of Experimental Social Psychology, 46*, 1078–80.

Rutjens, B. T., van Harreveld, F., & van der Pligt, J. (2010). Yes we can: Belief in progress as compensatory control. *Social Psychological and Personality Science, 1*, 246–52.

Rutjens, B. T., van Harreveld, F., van Der Pligt, J., van Elk, M., & Pyszczynski, T. (2016). A march to a better world? Religiosity and the existential function of belief in social-moral progress. *The International Journal for the Psychology of Religion, 26*(1), 1–18.

Salsman, J. M., Brown, T. L., Brechting, E. H., & Carlson, C. R. (2005). The link between religion and spirituality and psychological adjustment: The mediating role of optimism and social support. *Personality and Social Psychology Bulletin, 31*, 522–35.

Samarin, W. J. (1972). *Tongues of men and angels: The religious language of Pentecostalism*. New York: Macmillan.

Sanchez, C., Sundermeier, B., Gray, K., & Calin-Jageman, R. J. (2017). Direct replication of Gervais & Norenzayan (2012): No evidence that analytic thinking decreases religious belief. *PLoS One, 12*(2), e0172636.

Sarıbay, S. A., Yılmaz, O., & Körpe, G. G. (2020). Does intuitive mindset influence belief in God? A registered replication of Shenhav, Rand and Greene (2012). *Judgment and Decision Making, 15*, 193–202.

Saroglou, V. (2002). Religion and the five factors of personality: A meta-analytic review. *Personality and Individual Differences, 32*, 15–25.

Saroglou, V. (2006, Spring). Religion's role in prosocial behavior: Myth or reality? *Psychology of Religion Newsletter, 31*, 1–8.

Saroglou, V. (2010). Religiousness as a cultural adaptation of basic traits: A five-factor model perspective. *Personality and Social Psychology Review, 14*(1), 108–25.

Saroglou, V., Corneille, O., & Van Cappellen, P. (2009). "Speak, Lord, your servant is listening": Religious priming activates submissive thoughts and behaviors. *The International Journal for the Psychology of Religion, 19*(3), 143–54.

Saroglou, V., Delpierre, V., & Dernelle, R. (2004). Values and religiosity: A meta-analysis of studies using Schwartz's model. *Personality and Individual Differences, 37*(4), 721–34.

Saroglou, V., Yzerbyt, V., & Kaschten, C. (2011). Meta-stereotypes of groups with opposite religious views: Believers and non-believers. *Journal of Community & Applied Social Psychology, 21*(6), 484–98.

Schaafsma, J., & Williams, K. D. (2012). Exclusion, intergroup hostility, and religious fundamentalism. *Journal of Experimental Social Psychology, 48*(4), 829–37.

Schachter, S., & Singer, J. (1962). Cognitive, social, and physiological determinants of emotional state. *Psychological Review, 69*(5), 379–99.

Schienle, A., Gremsl, A., & Wabnegger, A. (2021). Placebo effects in the context of religious beliefs and practices: A resting-state functional connectivity study. *Frontiers in Behavioral Neuroscience, 15*, 653359.

Schimel, J., Hayes, J., Williams, T., & Jahrig, J. (2007). Is death really the worm at the core? Converging evidence that worldview threat increases death-thought accessibility. *Journal of Personality and Social Psychology, 92*(5), 789–803.

Schindler, S., Reinhardt, N., & Reinhard, M. (2021). Defending one's worldview under morality salience: Testing the validity of an established idea. *Journal of Experimental Social Psychology, 93*, 104087.

Schmitt, M., Gollwitzer, M., Maes, J., & Arbach, D. (2005). Justice sensitivity. *European Journal of Psychological Assessment, 21*(3), 202–11.

Schnall, S., Haidt, J., Clore, G. L., & Jordan, A. H. (2008). Disgust as embodied moral judgment. *Personality and Social Psychology Bulletin, 34*(8), 1096–109.

Schnell, T., & Keenan, W. J. (2011). Meaning-making in an atheist world. *Archive for the Psychology of Religion, 33*(1), 55–78.

Schofield, M. B., Roberts, B. L., Harvey, C. A., Baker, I. S., & Crouch, G. (2022). Tales from the dark side: The dark tetrad of personality, supernatural, and scientific belief. *Journal of Humanistic Psychology, 62*(2), 298–315.

Schuurmans-Stekhoven, J. B. (2013b). "As a shepherd divideth his sheep from the goats": Does the daily spiritual experiences scale encapsulate separable theistic and civility components? *Social Indicators Research, 110*, 131–46.

Schuurmans-Stekhoven, J. B. (2013a). Is God's call more than audible? A preliminary exploration using a two-dimensional model of theistic/spiritual beliefs and experiences. *Australian Journal of Psychology, 65*(3), 146–55.

Schuurmans-Stekhoven, J. B. (2021). Just world beliefs mediate the well-being effects of spiritual/afterlife beliefs among older Australians. *Journal of Religion, Spirituality & Aging, 33*(3), 332–49.

Scott, M. J. (2022). Reasons things happen for a reason: An integrative theory of teleology. *Perspectives on Psychological Science, 17*(2), 452–64.

Sedikides, C., & Gebauer, J. E. (2010). Religiosity as self-enhancement: A meta-analysis of the relation between socially desirable responding and religiosity. *Personality and Social Psychology Review, 14*(1), 17–36.

Shaffer, B. A., & Hastings, B. M. (2007). Authoritarianism and religious identification: Response to threats on religious beliefs. *Mental Health, Religion & Culture, 10*(2), 151–8.

Shai, O. (2022). Does armed conflict increase individuals' religiosity as a means for coping with the adverse psychological effects of wars? *Social Science & Medicine, 296*, 114769.

Shapiro, F. (1989). Efficacy of the eye movement desensitization procedure in the treatment of traumatic memories. *Journal of Traumatic Stress, 2*(2), 199–223.

Shariff, A. F. (2009, October). *Religious prosociality: How Gods make us good.* Paper presented at the Society for the Scientific Study of Religion, Denver, CO.

Shariff, A. F., & Aknin, L. B. (2014). The emotional toll of hell: Cross-national and experimental evidence for the negative well-being effects of hell beliefs. *PLoS One, 9*(1), e85251.

Sharp, S. (2013). When prayers go unanswered. *Journal for the Scientific Study of Religion, 52*(1), 1–16.

Shaver, J. H., White, T. A., Vakaoti, P., & Lang, M. (2021). A comparison of self-report, systematic observation and third-party judgments of church attendance in a rural Fijian Village. *PloS One, 16*(10), e0257160.

Shaw, J., & Porter, S. (2015). Constructing rich false memories of committing crime. *Psychological Science, 26*, 291–301.

Shaw, M., Quezada, S. A., & Zárate, M. A. (2011). Violence with a conscience: Religiosity and moral certainty as predictors of support for violent warfare. *Psychology of Violence, 1*(4), 275–86.

Shepherd, S., & Kay, A. C. (2012). On the perpetuation of ignorance: System dependence, system justification, and the motivated avoidance of sociopolitical information. *Journal of Personality and Social Psychology, 102*(2), 264–80.

Shepperd, J. A., Pogge, G., Lipsey, N. P., Miller, W. A., & Webster, G. D. (2019). Belief in a loving versus punitive God and behavior. *Journal of Research on Adolescence, 29*(2), 390–401.

Sherif, M. (1935). A study of some social factors in perception. *Archives of Psychology, 27*(187), 17–22.

Sherman, A. C., Park, C. L., Salsman, J. M., Williams, M. L., Amick, B. C., Hudson, T. J., … & Simonton-Atchley, S. (2021). Anxiety, depressive, and trauma symptoms during the COVID-19 pandemic: Evaluating the role of disappointment with God. *Journal of Affective Disorders, 293*, 245–53.

Shermer, M. (2000). *How we believe: The search for God in an age of science*. New York: W. H. Freeman.

Shidlovski, D., Schul, Y., & Mayo, R. (2014). If I imagine it, then it happened: The implicit truth value of imaginary representations. *Cognition, 133*(3), 517–29.

Shor, E., & Roelfs, D. J. (2013). The longevity effects of religious and nonreligious participation: A meta-analysis and meta-regression. *Journal for the Scientific Study of Religion, 52*(1), 120–45.

Shtulman, A., & Valcarcel, J. (2012). Scientific knowledge suppresses but does not supplant earlier intuitions. *Cognition, 124*(2), 209–15.

Shu, L. L., & Gino, F. (2012). Sweeping dishonesty under the rug: How unethical actions lead to forgetting of moral rules. *Journal of Personality and Social Psychology, 102*(6), 1164–77.

Shu, L. L., Gino, F., & Bazerman, M. H. (2011). Dishonest deed, clear conscience: When cheating leads to moral disengagement and motivated forgetting. *Personality and Social Psychology Bulletin, 37*(3), 330–49.

Shults, F. L. (2016). Can theism be defeated? CSR and the debunking of supernatural agent abductions. *Religion, Brain & Behavior, 6*(4), 349–55.

Sibley, C. G., & Bulbulia, J. (2012). Faith after an earthquake: A longitudinal study of religion and perceived health before and after the 2011 Christchurch New Zealand earthquake. *PloS One, 7*(12), e49648.

Skitka, L. J. (1999). Ideological and attributional boundaries on public compassion: Reactions to individuals and communities affected by a natural disaster. *Personality and Social Psychology Bulletin, 25*, 793–808.

Skoggard, I., Ember, C. R., Pitek, E., Jackson, J. C., & Carolus, C. (2020). Resource stress predicts changes in religious belief and increases in sharing behavior. *Human Nature, 31*(3), 249–71.

Slife, B. D., Reber, J. S., & Lefevor, G. T. (2012). When God truly matters: A theistic approach to psychology. *Research in the Social Scientific Study of Religion, 23*, 213–37.

Slingerland, E. (2008). Who's afraid of reductionism? The study of religion in the age of cognitive science. *Journal of the American Academy of Religion, 76*(2), 375–411.

Slone, D. J., & McCorkle Jr, W. W. (Eds.). (2019). *The cognitive science of religion: A methodological introduction to key empirical studies*. London: Bloomsbury Publishing.

Slone, J. (2007). *Theological incorrectness: Why religious people believe what they shouldn't*. New York: Oxford University Press.

Smidt, C., Kellstedt, L., & Guth, J. L. (Eds.). (2017). *The Oxford handbook of religion and American politics*. New York: Oxford University Press.

Smith, J. M., Pasek, M. H., Vishkin, A., Johnson, K. A., Shackleford, C., & Ginges, J. (2022). Thinking about God discourages dehumanization of religious outgroups. *Journal of Experimental Psychology: General, 151*(10), 2586–603.

Snarey, J. (1996). The natural environment's impact upon religious ethics: A cross-cultural study. *Journal for the Scientific Study of Religion, 35,* 85–96.

Snow, D., & Philips, C. L. (1980). The Lofland-Stark conversion model. A critical reassessment. *Social Problems, 27,* 430–7.

Sorrentino, R. M., & Roney, C. J. (2013). *The uncertain mind: Individual differences in facing the unknown*. New York: Psychology Press.

Spanos, N. P. (1994). Multiple identity enactments and multiple personality disorder: A sociocognitive perspective. *Psychological Bulletin, 116,* 143–65.

Spanos, N. P., Cross, W. P., Lepage, M., & Coristine, M. (1986). Glossolalia as learned behavior: An experimental demonstration. *Journal of Abnormal Psychology, 95,* 21–3.

Spanos, N. P., & Gottlieb, J. (1979). Demonic possession, mesmerism, and hysteria: A social psychological perspective on their historical interrelations. *Journal of Abnormal Psychology, 88*(5), 527–46.

Spanos, N. P., & Moretti, P. (1988). Correlates of mystical and diabolical experiences in a sample of female university students. *Journal for the Scientific Study of Religion, 27,* 105–16.

Spanos, N. P., Weekes, J. R., & Bertrand, L. D. (1985). Multiple personality: A social psychological perspective. *Journal of Abnormal Psychology, 94,* 362–76.

Speed, D., & Fowler, K. (2017). Good for all? Hardly! Attending church does not benefit religiously unaffiliated. *Journal of Religion and Health, 56*(3), 986–1002.

Speed, D., & Fowler, K. (2021). One size doesn't fit all: Religious/spiritual identities moderate salutary effects of religion. *Mental Health, Religion & Culture, 24*(2), 111–27.

Spilka, B., & Schmidt, G. (1983). General attribution theory for the psychology of religion: The influence of event-character on attributions to God. *Journal for the Scientific Study of Religion, 22,* 326–339.

Spilka, B., Shaver, P., & Kirkpatrick, L. A. (1985). A general attribution theory for the psychology of religion. *Journal for the Scientific Study of Religion, 24*(1), 1–20.

Stagnaro, M. N., Ross, R. M., Pennycook, G., & Rand, D. G. (2019). Cross-cultural support for a link between analytic thinking and disbelief in God: Evidence from India and the United Kingdom. *Judgment and Decision Making, 14*(2), 179–86.

Ståhl, T. (2021). The amoral atheist? A cross-national examination of cultural, motivational, and cognitive antecedents of disbelief, and their implications for morality. *PloS One, 16*(2), e0246593.

Ståhl, T., & Van Prooijen, J. W. (2018). Epistemic rationality: Skepticism toward unfounded beliefs requires sufficient cognitive ability and motivation to be rational. *Personality and Individual Differences, 122*, 155–63.

Ståhl, T., & van Prooijen, J. W. (2021). Analytic atheism: Valuing epistemic rationality strengthens the association between analytic thinking and religious disbelief. *Personality and Individual Differences, 179*, 110914.

Stankov, L., & Lee, J. (2018). Conservative syndrome and the understanding of negative correlations between religiosity and cognitive abilities. *Personality and Individual Differences, 131*, 21–5.

Stanley, M. L., & Kay, A. C. (2022). Belief in divine moral authority satisfies the psychological need for structure and increases in the face of perceived injustice. *Journal of Experimental Social Psychology, 101*, 104302.

Stanovich, K. E., Toplak, M. E., & West, R. F. (2008). The development of rational thought: A taxonomy of heuristics and biases. *Advances in child development and behavior, 36*, 251–85.

Stanovich, K. E., West, R. F., & Toplak, M. E. (2011). Individual differences as essential components of heuristics and biases research. In K. Manktelow, D. Over, & S. Elqayam (Eds.), *The science of reason: A festschrift for Jonathan St B. T. Evans* (pp. 355–96). New York, NY: Psychology Press.

Starbuck, E. D. (1899). *The psychology of religion*. New York: Scribner.

Stavrova, O., Fetchenhauer, D., & Schlösser, T. (2013). Why are religious people happy? The effect of the social norm of religiosity across countries. *Social Science Research, 42*(1), 90–105.

Stavrova, O., & Siegers, P. (2014). Religious prosociality and morality across cultures: How social enforcement of religion shapes the effects of personal religiosity on prosocial and moral attitudes and behaviors. *Personality and Social Psychology Bulletin, 40*(3), 315–33.

Steele, C. M. (1988). The psychology of self-affirmation: Sustaining the integrity of the self. In L. Berkowitz (Ed.), *Advances in experimental social psychology* (Vol. 21, pp. 261–302). New York: Academic Press.

Steger, M. F., & Frazier, P. (2005). Meaning in life: One link in the chain from religiousness to well-being. *Journal of Counseling Psychology, 52*(4), 574–82.

Stein, R. (2013). The pull of the group: Conscious conflict and the involuntary tendency towards conformity. *Consciousness and Cognition, 22*(3), 788–94.

Stephens, N. M., Fryberg, S. A., Markus, H. R., & Hamedani, M. G. (2013). Who explains Hurricane Katrina and the Chilean earthquake as an act of God? The experience of extreme hardship predicts religious meaning-making. *Journal of Cross-Cultural Psychology, 44*(4), 606–19.

Stone, J. R. (2000). *Expecting armageddon: Essential readings in failed prophecy*. New York: Routledge.

Storm, I. (2015). Civic engagement in Britain: The role of religion and inclusive values. *European Sociological Review, 31*(1), 14–29.

Strupp, H. H., & Hadley, S. W. (1979). Specific vs nonspecific factors in psychotherapy: A controlled study of outcome. *Archives of General Psychiatry*, *36*(10), 1125–36.

Svedholm, A. M., Lindeman, M., & Lipsanen, J. (2010). Believing in the purpose of events—why does it occur, and is it supernatural? *Applied Cognitive Psychology*, *24*(2), 252–65.

Swami, V., Voracek, M., Stieger, S., Tran, U. S., & Furnham, A. (2014). Analytic thinking reduces belief in conspiracy theories. *Cognition*, *133*(3), 572–85.

Swiney, L., & Sousa, P. (2013). When our thoughts are not our own: Investigating agency misattributions using the Mind-to-Mind paradigm. *Consciousness and Cognition*, *22*(2), 589–602.

Tajfel, H., & Turner, J. C. (1979). An integrative theory of intergroup conflict. In W. G. Austin, & S. Worchel (Eds.), *The social psychology of intergroup relations* (pp. 33–7). Monterey, CA: Brooks/Cole.

Tamarin, G. R. (1966). The influence of ethnic and religious prejudice on moral judgment. *New Outlook*, *9*, 49–58.

Tan, J. H., & Vogel, C. (2008). Religion and trust: An experimental study. *Journal of Economic Psychology*, *29*(6), 832–48.

Tappin, B. M., & McKay, R. T. (2017). The illusion of moral superiority. *Social Psychological and Personality Science*, *8*(6), 623–31.

Taves, A. (2009). *Religious experience reconsidered: A building-block approach to the study of religion and other special Things*. Princeton, NJ: Princeton University Press.

Taylor, E. C., Clutterbuck, R. A., Player, L., Shah, P., & Callan, M. J. (2022). The role of karmic beliefs in immanent justice reasoning. *Psychology of Religion and Spirituality*, *14*(2), 278–82.

Tellegen, A., & Atkinson, G. (1974). Openness to absorbing and self-altering experiences ("absorption"), a trait related to hypnotic susceptibility. *Journal of Abnormal Psychology*, *83*(3), 268–77.

Tenbrunsel, A. E., Diekmann, K. A., Wade-Benzoni, K. A., & Bazerman, M. H. (2010). The ethical mirage: A temporal explanation as to why we are not as ethical as we think we are. *Research in Organizational Behavior*, *30*, 153–73.

Thauvoye, E., Granqvist, P., Golovchanova, N., & Dezutter, J. (2018). Attachment to God, depression and loss in late life: A longitudinal study. *Mental Health, Religion & Culture*, *21*(8), 825–37.

Thibodeau, R. B., Brown, M. M., Nancarrow, A. F., Elpers, K. E., & Gilpin, A. T. (2018). Conceptual similarities among fantasy and religious orientations: A developmental perspective. *Journal of Cognition and Culture*, *18*(1–2), 31–46.

Thiruchselvam, R., Gopi, Y., Kilekwang, L., Harper, J., & Gross, J. J. (2017). In God we trust? Neural measures reveal lower social conformity among non-religious individuals. *Social Cognitive and Affective Neuroscience*, *12*(6), 956–64.

Thomas, A. K., Bulevich, J. B., & Loftus, E. F. (2003). Exploring the role of repetition and sensory elaboration in the imagination inflation effect. *Memory & Cognition*, *31*, 630–40.

Thunström, L., Jones Ritten, C., Bastian, C., Minton, E., & Zhappassova, D. (2021). Trust and trustworthiness of Christians, Muslims, and atheists/agnostics in the United States. *Journal for the Scientific Study of Religion*, 60(1), 147–79.

Thurow, J. C. (2013). Does cognitive science show belief in god to be irrational? The epistemic consequences of the cognitive science of religion. *International Journal for Philosophy of Religion*, 74(1), 77–98.

Tinbergen, N. (1963). On aims and methods of ethology. *Zeitschrift für tierpsychologie*, 20(4), 410–33.

Tix, A. P., & Frazier, P. A. (1998). The use of religious coping during stressful life events: Main effects, moderation, and mediation. *Journal of Consulting and Clinical Psychology*, 66, 411–22.

Tobia, K. P. (2016). Does religious belief infect philosophical analysis? *Religion, Brain & Behavior*, 6(1), 56–66.

Tolin, D. F., McKay, D., Forman, E. M., Klonsky, E. D., & Thombs, B. D. (2015). Empirically supported treatment: Recommendations for a new model. *Clinical Psychology: Science and Practice*, 22(4), 317–38.

Tonigan, J. S. (2007). Spirituality and alcoholics anonymous. *Southern Medical Journal*, 100(4), 437–41.

Tonigan, J. S., Miller, W. R., & Schermer, C. (2002). Atheists, agnostics and alcoholics anonymous. *Journal of Studies on Alcohol*, 63(5), 534–41.

Toplak, M. E., West, R. F., & Stanovich, K. E. (2011). The cognitive reflection test as a predictor of performance on heuristics-and-biases tasks. *Memory & Cognition*, 39(7), 1275–89.

Tracy, J. L., Hart, J., & Martens, J. P. (2011). Death and science: The existential underpinnings of belief in intelligent design and discomfort with evolution. *PLoS One*, 6, e17349.

Tratner, A. E., Shackelford, T. K., Zeigler-Hill, V., Vonk, J., & McDonald, M. M. (2020). Fear the unseen: Supernatural belief and agency detection in virtual reality. *Religion, Brain & Behavior*, 10(2), 118–31.

Tremlin, T. (2006). *Minds and gods: The cognitive foundations of religion*. New York: Oxford University Press.

Trimble, D. E. (1997). The religious orientation scale: Review and meta-analysis of social desirability effects. *Educational and Psychological Measurement*, 57(6), 970–86.

Tsang, J. A. (2002). Moral rationalization and the integration of situational factors and psychological processes in immoral behavior. *Review of General Psychology*, 6(1), 25–50.

Tsang, J. A., McCullough, M. E., & Hoyt, W. T. (2005). Psychometric and rationalization accounts of the religion–forgiveness discrepancy. *Journal of Social Issues*, 61, 785–805.

Tsang, J. A., & Rowatt, W. C. (2007). The relationship between religious orientation, right-wing authoritarianism, and implicit sexual prejudice. *The International Journal for the Psychology of Religion*, 17(2), 99–120.

Tversky, A., & Kahneman, D. (1973). Availability: A heuristic for judging frequency and probability. *Cognitive Psychology, 5*(2), 207–32.

Tversky, A., & Kahneman, D. (1982). Evidential impact of base rates. In D. Kahneman, P. Slovic, & A. Tversky (Eds.), *Judgment under uncertainty: Heuristics and biases* (pp. 153–60). Cambridge, UK: Cambridge University Press.

Vail III, K. E., Arndt, J., & Abdollahi, A. (2012). Exploring the existential function of religion and supernatural agent beliefs among Christians, Muslims, Atheists, and Agnostics. *Personality and Social Psychology Bulletin, 38*(10), 1288–300.

Vainio, O. P. (2016). What does theology have to do with religion? Dual-process accounts, Cognitive science of religion and a curious blind spot in contemporary theorizing. *Open Theology, 2*(1), 106–12.

Valdesolo, P., & DeSteno, D. (2007). Moral hypocrisy: Social groups and the flexibility of virtue. *Psychological Science, 18*(8), 689–90.

Valente, R. R., & Okulicz-Kozaryn, A. (2021). Religiosity and trust: Evidence from the United States. *Review of Religious Research, 63*(3), 343–79.

Van Cappellen, P., Corneille, O., Cols, S., & Saroglou, V. (2011). Beyond mere compliance to authoritative figures: Religious priming increases conformity to informational influence among submissive people. *The International Journal for the Psychology of Religion, 21*(2), 97–105.

Van Cappellen, P., Toth-Gauthier, M., Saroglou, V., & Fredrickson, B. A. (2016). Religion and well-being: The mediating role of positive emotions. *Journal of Happiness Studies, 17*, 485–505.

Van den Bos, K, & Maas, M (2009). On the psychology of the belief in a just World: Exploring experiential and rationalistic paths to victim blaming. *Personality and Social Psychology Bulletin, 35*(12), 1567–78.

Van den Bos, K., Van Ameijde, J., & Van Gorp, H. (2006). On the psychology of religion: The role of personal uncertainty in religious worldview defense. *Basic and Applied Social Psychology, 28*(4), 333–41.

Van der Kolk, B. (2014). *The body keeps the score: Mind, brain and body in the transformation of trauma*. New York, NY: Penguin Random House.

Van Elk, M., & Lodder, P. (2018). Experimental manipulations of personal control do not increase illusory pattern perception. *Collabra: Psychology, 4*(1), 19.

Van Elk, M., Rutjens, B. T., van der Pligt, J., & Van Harreveld, F. (2016). Priming of supernatural agent concepts and agency detection. *Religion, Brain & Behavior, 6*(1), 4–33.

Van Eyghen, H. (2019). Is supernatural belief unreliably formed? *International Journal for Philosophy of Religion, 85*(2), 125–48.

Van Eyghen, H. (2020). *Arguing from cognitive science of religion: Is religious belief debunked?* London: Bloomsbury Academic.

Van Eyghen, H. (2022). Responding to debunking arguments: A reply to Lari Launonen's critique. *Philosophia Reformata, 1*(aop), 1–13.

Van Eyghen, H., & Bennett, C. T. (2022). Did natural selection select for true religious beliefs? *Religious Studies, 58*(1), 113–37.

van Prooijen, J. W., Douglas, K. M., & De Inocencio, C. (2018). Connecting the dots: Illusory pattern perception predicts belief in conspiracies and the supernatural. *European Journal of Social Psychology, 48*(3), 320–35.

van Prooijen, J.-W., Klein, O., & Milošević Đorđević, J. (2020). Social-cognitive processes underlying belief in conspiracy theories. In M. Butter & P. Knight (Eds.), *Handbook of conspiracy theories* (pp. 168–80). London: Routledge.

Van Tongeren, D. R., & Green, J. D. (2010). Combating meaningless: On the automatic defense of meaning. *Personality and Social Psychology Bulletin, 36*, 1372–84.

Van Tongeren, D. R., Davis, D. E., Hook, J. N., Rowatt, W., & Worthington, E. L., Jr. (2018). Religious differences in reporting and expressing humility. *Psychology of Religion and Spirituality, 10*(2), 174–84.

Van Tongeren, D. R., Davis, E. B., Hook, J. N., Davis, D. E., & Aten, J. D. (2021). Existentially threatening stimuli increase religious cognitive dissonance among the less intrinsically religious. *Psychology of Religion and Spirituality, 13*(3), 298–303.

Van Tongeren, D. R., Pennington, A., McIntosh, D. N., Newton, A. T., Green, J. D., Davis, D. E., & Hook, J. N. (2017). Where, o death, is thy sting?: The meaning-providing function of beliefs in literal immortality. *Mental Health, Religion & Culture, 20*, 413–27.

Van Tongeren, D. R., Sanders, M., Edwards, M., Davis, E. B., Aten, J. D., Ranter, J. M., Tsarouhis, A., Short, A., Cuthbert, A., Hook, J. N., & Davis, D. E. (2019). Religious and spiritual struggles alter God representations. *Psychology of Religion and Spirituality, 11*(3), 225–32.

van Veelen, R., Otten, S., Cadinu, M., & Hansen, N. (2016). An integrative model of social identification: Self-stereotyping and self-anchoring as two cognitive pathways. *Personality and Social Psychology Review, 20*(1), 3–26.

VanderWeele, T. J. (2017). Religious communities and human flourishing. *Current Directions in Psychological Science, 26*(5), 476–81.

VanDeursen, M. J., Pope, A. R., & Warner, R. H. (2012). Just world maintenance patterns among intrinsically and extrinsically religious individuals. *Personality and Individual Differences, 52*(6), 755–8.

Vøllestad, J., Nielsen, M. B., & Nielsen, G. H. (2012). Mindfulness- and acceptance-based interventions for anxiety disorders: A systematic review and meta-analysis. *British Journal of Clinical Psychology, 51*, 239–60.

Von Hippel, W., Lakin, J. L., & Shakarchi, R. L. (2005). Individual differences in motivated social cognition: The case of self-serving information processing. *Personality and Social Psychology Bulletin, 31*, 1347–57.

Vonk, J., & Pitzen, J. (2016). Religiosity and the formulation of causal attributions. *Thinking & Reasoning, 22*(2), 119–49.

Vonk, J., Brothers, B., & Zeigler-Hill, V. (2021). Ours is not to reason why: Information seeking across domains. *Psychology of Religion and Spirituality, 13*(3), 314–23.

Vonk, R., & Visser, A. (2021). An exploration of spiritual superiority: The paradox of self-enhancement. *European Journal of Social Psychology, 51*(1), 152–65.

Wachholtz, A. B., & Pargament, K. I. (2005). Is spirituality a critical ingredient of meditation? Comparing the effects of spiritual meditation, secular meditation, and relaxation on spiritual, psychological, cardiac, and pain outcomes. *Journal of Behavioral Medicine, 28*(4), 369–84.

Wachholtz, A. B., & Pargament, K. I. (2008). Migraines and meditation: Does spirituality matter? *Journal of Behavioral Medicine, 31*, 351–66.

Walsh, E., Mehta, M. A., Oakley, D. A., Guilmette, D. N., Gabay, A., Halligan, P. W., & Deeley, Q. (2014). Using suggestion to model different types of automatic writing. *Consciousness and Cognition, 26*, 24–36.

Wang, L., & Graddy, E. (2008). Social capital, volunteering, and charitable giving. *Voluntas: International Journal of Voluntary and Nonprofit Organizations, 19*(1), 23–42.

Ward, C. (1980). Spirit possession and mental health: A psycho-anthropological perspective. *Human Relations, 33*(2), 149–63.

Ward, S. J., & King, L. A. (2018). Moral self-regulation, moral identity, and religiosity. *Journal of Personality and Social Psychology, 115*(3), 495–525.

Ward, S. J., & King, L. A. (2021). Moral stereotypes, moral self-image, and religiosity. *Psychology of Religion and Spirituality, 13*(2), 160–74.

Watanabe, S., & Laurent, S. M. (2021). Past its prime? A methodological overview and critique of religious priming research in social psychology. *Journal for the Cognitive Science of Religion, 6*(1–2), 31–55.

Waytz, A., Cacioppo, J., & Epley, N. (2010). Who sees human? The stability and importance of individual differences in anthropomorphism. *Perspectives on Psychological Science, 5*(3), 219–32.

Weber, S. R., Pargament, K. I., Kunik, M. E., Lomax, J. W., II, & Stanley, M. A. (2012). Psychological distress among religious nonbelievers: A systematic review. *Journal of Religion and Health, 51*, 72–86.

Weeden, J., & Kurzban, R. (2013). What predicts religiosity? A multinational analysis of reproductive and cooperative morals. *Evolution and Human Behavior, 34*(6), 440–5.

Weeks, M., & Lupfer, M. B. (2000). Religious attributions and proximity of influence: An investigation of direct interventions and distal explanations. *Journal for the Scientific Study of Religion, 39*(3), 348–62.

Wegner, D. M. (2017). *The illusion of conscious will (new edition)*. Cambridge, MA: The MIT Press.

Wegner, D. M., Fuller, V. A., & Sparrow, B. (2003). Clever hands: Uncontrolled intelligence in facilitated communication. *Journal of Personality and Social Psychology, 85*(1), 5–19.

Weiss, A., Dorrough, A. R., & Schmitz, L. (2021). Analytic atheism in a low-religiosity culture: Examining the relationship between analytic thinking and religious belief in Germany. *Personality and Individual Differences, 178*, 110854.

Welch, M. R., Sikkink, D., & Loveland, M. T. (2007). The radius of trust: Religion, social embeddedness and trust in strangers. *Social Forces, 86*(1), 23–46.

White, C. J., & Norenzayan, A. (2019). Belief in karma: How cultural evolution, cognition, and motivations shape belief in supernatural justice. In J. M. Olson (Eds.), *Advances in experimental social psychology* (Vol. 60, pp. 1–63). Cambridge, MA: Academic Press.

White, C. J., & Norenzayan, A. (2022). Karma and God: Convergent and divergent mental representations of supernatural norm enforcement. *Psychology of Religion and Spirituality, 14*(1), 70–85.

Whitehead, A. L., & Scheitle, C. P. (2018). We the (Christian) people: Christianity and American identity from 1996 to 2014. *Social Currents, 5*(2), 157–72.

Whitehouse, H., & Lanman, J. A. (2014). The ties that bind us: Ritual, fusion, and identification. *Current Anthropology, 55*(6), 674–95.

Whitney, H., & Barnes, J. (2007). *The Mormons. The American experience.* New York, NY and Washington, DC: PBS.

Whitson, J. A., & Galinsky, A. D. (2008). Lacking control increases illusory pattern perception. *Science, 322*(5898), 115–7.

Wichman, A. L. (2010). Uncertainty and religious reactivity: Uncertainty compensation, repair, and inoculation. *European Journal of Social Psychology, 40*(1), 35–42.

Wikstrom, O. (1987). Attribution, roles and religion: A theoretical analysis of Sunden's role theory of religion and the attributional approach to religious experience. *Journal for the Scientific Study of Religion, 26*, 390–400.

Wilkins, A. C. (2008). "Happier than non-Christians": Collective emotions and symbolic boundaries among evangelical Christians. *Social Psychology Quarterly, 71*(3), 281–301.

Willard, A. K. (2019). Agency detection is unnecessary in the explanation of religious belief. *Religion, Brain & Behavior, 9*(1), 96–8.

Willard, A. K., & Norenzayan, A. (2017). Spiritual but not religious: Cognition, schizotypy, and conversion in alternative beliefs. *Cognition, 165*, 137–46.

Williams, S. (1984). Left-right ideological differences in blaming victims. *Political Psychology, 5*, 573–81.

Williamson, W. P., & Assadi, A. (2005). Religious orientation, incentive, self-esteem, and gender as predictors of academic dishonesty: An experimental approach. *Archive for the Psychology of Religion, 27*, 137–58.

Wilson, A. E., & Ross, M. (2001). From chump to champ: People's appraisals of their earlier and present selves. *Journal of Personality and Social Psychology, 80*, 572–84.

Wilson, T. D. (2002). *Strangers to ourselves: Discovering the adaptive unconscious.* Cambridge, MA: Belknap Press/Harvard University Press.

Wilt, J. A., Stauner, N., & Exline, J. J. (2022a). Beliefs and experiences involving God, the devil, spirits, and fate: Social, motivational, and cognitive predictors. *The International Journal for the Psychology of Religion*, 1–17.

Wilt, J. A., Stauner, N., May, R. W., Fincham, F. D., Pargament, K. I., & Exline, J. J. (2022b). Who engages with supernatural entities? An investigation of personality and cognitive style predictors. *Imagination, Cognition and Personality, 41*(4), 373–414.

Wimer, S., & Kelley, H. H. (1982). An investigation of the dimensions of causal attribution. *Journal of Personality and Social Psychology*, *43*(6), 1142–62.

Winter, J. A. (1973). The metaphoric parallelist approach to the sociology of theistic beliefs: Theme, variations and implications. *Sociological Analysis*, *34*, 212–29.

Wlodarczyk, A., Zumeta, L., Basabe, N., Rimé, B., & Páez, D. (2021). Religious and secular collective gatherings, perceived emotional synchrony and self-transcendent emotions: Two longitudinal studies. *Current Psychology*, 1–18. Advance online publication. doi: 10.1007/s12144-021-01826-0

Wlodarski, R., & Pearce, E. (2016). The God allusion: Individual variation in agency detection, mentalizing and schizotypy and their association with religious beliefs and behaviors. *Human Nature*, *27*(2), 160–72.

Wong, S., Pargament, K. I., & Faigin, C. A. (2018). Sustained by the Sacred: Religious and spiritual factors for resilience in adulthood and aging. In B. Resnick, L. P. Gwyther, & K. A. Roberto (Eds.), *Resilience in aging: Concepts, research, and outcomes* (pp. 191–214). New York, NY: Springer.

Worthington, E. L., Jr., Hook, J. N., Davis, D. E., & McDaniel, M. A. (2011). Religion and spirituality. *Journal of Clinical Psychology*, *67*, 204–14.

Wulff, D. M. (1991). *Psychology of religion: Classic and contemporary views*. New York: Wiley.

Xygalatas, D., Khan, S., Lang, M., Kundt, R., Kundtová-Klocová, E., Krátký, J., & Shaver, J. (2019). Effects of extreme ritual practices on psychophysiological well-being. *Current Anthropology*, *60*(5), 699–707.

Yavuz, H., & Van den Bos, K. (2009). Effects of uncertainty and mortality salience on worldview defense reactions in Turkey. *Social Justice Research*, *22*(4), 384–98.

Yilmaz, O. (2021). Cognitive styles and religion. *Current Opinion in Psychology*, *40*, 150–4.

Yilmaz, O., & Isler, O. (2019). Reflection increases belief in God through self-questioning among non-believers. *Judgment and Decision Making*, *14*(6), 649–57.

Yonker, J. E., Edman, L. R. O., Cresswell, J., & Barrett, J. L. (2016). Primed analytic thought and religiosity: The importance of individual characteristics. *Psychology of Religion and Spirituality*, *8*, 298–308.

Ysseldyk, R., Matheson, K., & Anisman, H. (2010). Religiosity as identity: Toward an understanding of religion from a social identity perspective. *Personality and Social Psychology Review*, *14*(1), 60–71.

Zemla, J. C., Steiner, S. M., & Sloman, S. (2016). Analytical thinking predicts less teleological reasoning and religious belief. In A. Papafragou, D. Grodner, D. Mirman, & J. C. Trueswell (Eds.), *Proceedings of the 38th annual meeting of the cognitive science society* (pp. 1217–22). Cognitive Science Society.

Zhong, C. B., & Liljenquist, K. (2006). Washing away your sins: Threatened morality and physical cleansing. *Science*, *313*(5792), 1451–2.

Zhong, W., Cristofori, I., Bulbulia, J., Krueger, F., & Grafman, J. (2017). Biological and cognitive underpinnings of religious fundamentalism. *Neuropsychologia*, *100*, 18–25.

Zmigrod, L., Eisenberg, I. W., Bissett, P. G., Robbins, T. W., & Poldrack, R. A. (2021). The cognitive and perceptual correlates of ideological attitudes: A data-driven approach. *Philosophical Transactions of the Royal Society B*, *376*(1822), 20200424.

Zmigrod, L., Rentfrow, P. J., Zmigrod, S., & Robbins, T. W. (2019). Cognitive flexibility and religious disbelief. *Psychological Research*, *83*(8), 1749–59.

Zou, J., Yamanaka, Y., John, M., Watt, M., Ostermann, J., & Thielman, N. (2009). Religion and HIV in Tanzania: Influence of religious beliefs on HIV stigma, disclosure, and treatment attitudes. *BMC Public Health*, *9*(1), 1–12.

Zuckerman, M., Li, C., & Diener, E. (2018). Religion as an exchange system: The interchangeability of God and government in a provider role. *Personality and Social Psychology Bulletin*, *44*(8), 1201–13.

Zuckerman, M., Li, C., Lin, S., & Hall, J. A. (2020). The negative intelligence–religiosity relation: New and confirming evidence. *Personality and Social Psychology Bulletin*, *46*(6), 856–68.

Zweigenhaft, R. L., Philips, B. K. G., Adams, K. A., Morse, C. K., & Horan, A. E. (1985). Religious preference and belief in a just world. *Genetic, Social, and General Psychology Monographs*, *3*, 333–48.

Zygmunt, J. F. (1972). When prophecies fail: A theoretical perspective on the comparative evidence. *American Behavioral Scientist*, *16*(2), 245–68.

Index

Aarnio, K. 30, 135
Abelson, R. P., transcendence 82
Abeyta, A. A. 90
Abrahamic faiths 113
absorption 21–2, 47, 129, 132–6, 146, 150
Abu-Raiya, H. 172, 175
academic discipline 3–4
Adaptive Unconscious (AU) 31–3
ad hoc immunization 77, 81
agency detection 4, 12, 21, 37, 46, 67, 100, 134, 136
agentic attributions 41, 67. *See also* attributions/attribution theory
agnostics 168, 176
agreeableness 64, 186, 192, 195, 197, 201, 203–4
Alcoholics Anonymous 152, 159, 174
Al-Issa, R. S. 62, 83
altruism 185–7, 190
analytic cognition 19, 22–5, 27–9, 31, 35–6, 43, 157
  general cognitive ability and 30
  intelligence *vs.* 26
  lower religiosity and higher 29
Anthony, S. B. 39
anthropomorphism 21, 35, 41, 43, 47, 64, 67, 77, 93–4, 100
Anti-Christ 49–50
apophenic over-detection/apophenia 21–2, 30–1, 136, 156, 231
Arikan, G. 118
Aron, A. P., "Love on the Bridge" study 107
Asch, S. 106
  Asch paradigm 106, 111
atheists 12, 70, 90, 116–18, 134, 168, 172, 176–7, 188, 193, 197, 221, 229, 235
attachment theory 65–6, 93–5, 151
attributional ambiguity 140
attributions/attribution theory 5, 7, 39–41, 82, 100, 101, 127, 137, 148, 183, 220
  availability hypothesis 44, 148

biases and misattribution 47–8, 53, 164, 211 (*see also* misattributions)
  causal 37, 39–40, 43, 48, 67, 81, 131, 160–1, 163, 211, 219
  dichotomous 137
  disaster 44–5
  dispositional 42–3, 50, 58–9
  dissonance reduction via alteration 80–3
  divine 58, 219, 222, 237
  emotional 107, 133, 142
  expectancy, role of 45–7, 129, 133
  external volition, compensatory functions 143, 145–7
  face saving 82
  of intentionality 47, 55–6, 71, 93, 223
  malleability of 41, 47, 50, 52, 54, 56, 59, 62–3, 71–2, 107
  of mental illness 146
  natural and supernatural 35, 42, 52
  person by situation interaction 45–7
  predict making, factors 42–3
  religious and spiritual, dimensions of 41–2
  responsibility and deservingness 52–60, 63, 82
  situational and contextual influences 44–5, 59, 132, 136
  social psychological and cognitive influences on 131–7
  supernatural punishment 55–6, 67–8
authoritarianism 54, 57–9, 78, 89, 110, 117, 215
automatic writing 80, 139, 142–3

Bader, C. 64
Balloun, J. L. 75
Bandura, A. 217
Banerjee, K. 55
Barrett, J. L. 8, 12–13, 23, 35, 37, 77, 134, 228–9
Batson, C. D. 86, 196, 207–8, 216, 224, 233

Baumard, N. 33, 55, 61, 71, 157
Becker, E. 96
belief accuracy 13, 15–16, 27, 33, 37, 68–9, 75, 232, 234
belief acquisition 11, 104, 108, 110, 205
belief-as-benefit theory 160–1, 165, 178, 180, 187–8, 192, 197
belief-bolstering mechanism 73, 86, 100, 145, 233
belief-challenge paradigm 86, 89, 96, 233
belief-forming functions 13, 134, 228–34
belief immunization 77–9, 81
belief in a just world. *See* just world belief (JWB)
belief-intensifying effect 86
believers and nonbelievers 10, 12–13, 15, 20–1, 23–5, 27–30, 37, 40, 64, 66, 68–71, 110, 133, 148, 154, 175, 201, 214, 220, 227, 229, 233, 236–7
    and atheists 116, 134
    attributions 68, 70, 90, 93, 137, 211
    morality 187, 197
    rationalizations 81
    specific religious identity 166
benevolent deity 7–8, 49–50, 58, 63, 65, 67, 81–2, 220, 235
better than average effect 51, 197, 200, 205, 223
Bhardwaj, A. 57
Bible 11, 35, 76, 89, 118, 122, 147, 149, 218
Biblical book of Acts 133, 141
bi-directional process 114
"Big Five" personality trait (agreeableness) 192, 204
"Big Gods" beliefs 113, 187, 236
Birgegard, A. 65–6, 151
Bjorklund, F. 212–13
Blind Spot Bias 9, 68–9, 206
Bonnefon, J. F. 35
born-again experience 150–1
Bouvet, R. 35
Boyer, P. 19, 33, 77, 83, 138, 157
    intuitions 71
    moralizing religions 61
    Religion Explained 7, 41
Brahinsky, J. 139–40, 145, 147
Brock, T. C. 75
Brooks, A., *Who Really Cares: The Surprising Truth About Compassionate Conservatism* 186

Brooks, D. 237
Burris, C. T. 50, 82, 86, 93, 202, 226
Bushman, B. J. 122, 218

Cacioppo, J. T. 43, 78
Caluori, N. 28, 113, 222
Campbell, D., *American Grace: How Religion Divides and Unites Us* 186
Campbell, D. E. 189, 192–3
Campbell, T. H. 78
Canfield, C. F. 70
Carey, B. 204
Carlson, S. J. 166
case example 1–2
casuistry 213
Catholic Christians 89, 140, 151, 202, 237
causal attributions 37, 39–40, 43, 48, 67, 81, 131, 160–1, 163, 211, 219
causal direction 10, 36, 47, 52, 64, 95–6, 101, 112, 189, 201, 219, 221
causal priority 95
causal relationship 41, 55, 113, 190
causes of spurious therapeutic effectiveness (CSTEs) 164
charitable giving and volunteering 186, 189, 191–3, 195–6, 209
Charles, S. J. 14, 181
Cheung, C. 168
Chevallier, C. 55
Christians/Christians' beliefs 48–9, 61–2, 76, 80, 96, 113, 118, 130, 140, 144, 166, 194, 205–6, 220, 235. *See also* Jesus
    Biblical Saul/Paul conversion 152
    as discernment 147
    divinity 86
    identity 119
    Pentecostal traditions 130, 133
Church, I. M. 134
Church of Jesus Christ of Latter-Day Saints 85, 148, 131
Cognitive Behavioral Therapy (CBT) 173
cognitive dissonance 7–8, 84, 87, 153, 216
    failed prophesy 81
    inconsistency and 79–80
    reduction (*see* dissonance reduction/ resolution)
    self-perception and 208
cognitive psychology 16, 19, 36, 39, 227, 232

Cognitive Reflection Test (CRT) 23–4, 26
Cognitive Sciences of Religion (CSR) 3–6, 12–13, 19, 21, 23–4, 34, 40, 55–6, 67, 70–1, 77, 83, 100, 115, 187, 228, 232
    anthropological and 84, 214
    group influences and 104–5
    implications 71–2
cognitive styles 6, 20, 27, 29, 36, 43, 47, 89, 132
cognitive traits and R/S 19–22, 89, 105
collateral damage 229, 233
color naming latency 20, 70
Cols, S. 110
common conceptual areas (study) 4
communal narcissism 51, 205, 223
compensatory control theory 96
compensatory conviction 88–9, 97, 100
    and individual difference traits 89
compensatory functions of religion 74
    to external volition 145–7
    social connection and attachment 93–5
complementary approach 4–5
Comprehensive Soldier Fitness program 168
conceptual blending/blurring 167–8, 171, 174–5
confabulation 9–11, 33–4, 36–7, 129, 138, 155, 213, 227
conformist transmission 105
conformity 8, 140, 144, 149
    and emotional contagion 133
    religion and 110–12
    and social influence 105–10
conocer 11
conservative Christianity 49, 59, 120, 123, 218, 220, 235, 237
consistency, need for 74–5, 87. *See also* inconsistency
conspiracy theories 30–1, 90
control-religiosity relationship 91
Conway III, L. G. 5
Corley, N. 51
Corneille, O. 110
Costly Signaling 4, 28, 83–4, 104, 105
Cotterill, S. 57
Courtemanche, M. 118
Covid-19 pandemic 236
Credibility Enhancing Display (CRED) 28, 34, 36, 45, 63, 84, 104, 231

cross-cultural/anthropological comparisons 6
cultivation techniques 140, 149, 154–6
cultural anthropology 5, 15, 193
cultural differences 114
culture-fit model 166, 178, 189–90, 202–3

Daily Spiritual Experiences scale 168, 171, 173
Dante, A., *Inferno* 61
Darley, J. M. 32, 196
Davis, D. E. 103, 173, 199
Daws, R. E. 20, 26
death anxiety 96
    religiosity and 97
DeBono, A. 51, 220
Defining Issues Test 212
Dein, S. 78
deliberative processes 10, 22–4, 35, 79, 138–40, 143, 225
Dhar, R. 209
Diener, E. 92, 98, 166, 178, 190
Dijksterhuis, A., personal (*vs.* external) volition 46–7
discouraging effortful processing 29
dismantling study design 162, 164, 169–70, 173–4, 179, 181, 183
Dissociation 43, 139, 142–3, 146
dissonance reduction/resolution 79, 88, 233
    belief acquisition and internalization 108
    effort justification and 83–5, 164
    via alteration of R/S attributions 80–3
    via consensual validation 109
    via EJ theory 83–5
    via proselytization and increased conviction 86–7
doctrinal rigidity 116
doctrines 7, 49, 62, 83, 147, 218
Donahue, M. J. 65
double blind design 163
Douthat, R. 228–30
Drat-Ruszczak, K. 94
dreams 148, 154, 156
Dual Process (DP) models 22–3, 34, 55, 79, 83, 90, 100, 111, 138, 153–4, 156–7, 167, 183, 197, 213, 227, 238
    of cognition 103, 225
    implications 9, 36–7

intuitions 34–5
intuitive and analytic cognition 8–9, 23–5
and misattributions 69–71, 225–6
mortality salience 97–9
nuances and qualifications 23
theologically incorrect vs. correct 35, 57, 70
Dunning-Kruger effect 199
Dutton, D. G., "Love on the Bridge" study 107

ecological threat 113
Effort Justification theory (EJ) 75, 83–5, 164, 232
egocentrism 10, 16, 35, 66, 121, 209, 220
Elliott, M. 176, 203
Ellis, S. 26
Embry, E. 64
emic and etic perspective 15, 128, 134
Emmons, R. A. 168
emotional attribution theory 107, 133, 142
Empirically Supported Treatment approaches 183
entitativity 109
epistemic functions 75
　certainty, need for 87–9
　consistency, need for 74–5 (*see also* inconsistency)
　needs for meaning and control 90–1
　nonreligious sources of 97–100
　religion 73
Epley, N. 10, 16, 43, 66, 93, 197, 207, 220–1
equanimity 54, 73, 87, 91, 97, 100
Eriksson, K. 51, 197, 200–1, 203, 205
Erkanli, A. 173
evangelical Christians 43, 61, 131–3, 147, 151, 176, 178
evolution theory 6, 55, 61, 99, 190, 212, 230–2
exceptional experiences 14–16, 51, 127–8, 130–7, 140–1, 146, 156–7, 165, 185, 228, 234
　belief-bolstering mechanism 145
　testing and discernment 147–50
existential security theory (EST) 113
　Existential Insecurity Theory 112–13
　existential needs 96–7

living conditions and 92–3
nonreligious sources of 97–100
Exline, J. J. 45–6, 52, 134
experiential self-reports 129, 149
experimental manipulation 6, 16, 33, 93, 112, 129, 150
Eye Movement Desensitization and Reprocessing (EMDR) therapy 169, 173

facilitated communication technique 139
failed prophesy 75, 80–1, 85–6, 108–9
false memories 154–6
False Tagging Theory 28
Festinger, L. 75, 81, 86, 88, 108
　belief-bolstering effect 86
　disconfirmation and inconsistency 79, 88
　When Prophecy Fails 80, 76
Feuerbach, L., *The Essence of Christianity* 36
Fles, E. H. 59
Flora, D. B. 30
fluid compensation 73, 87, 90
Fowler, K. 172
Frazier, P. A. 172
Friesen, J. P. 78
Fugelsang, J. A. 24
Funcke, A. 51, 197, 200–1, 203, 205
Fundamental Attribution Error 7

Galen, L. W. 13, 59, 177, 180, 189, 192, 194–5, 197–8, 201, 218, 237
Ganzach, Y. 26
Gebauer, J. E. 51, 94, 166, 178, 189–90, 203, 205–6
Gelfand, M. 113
Gelman, S. A. 42, 49
general cognitive ability
　and analytic cognition 30
　intelligence and 25–9
Gervais, W. M. 24, 28, 45, 70, 104, 193, 197
Gibson, N. J. 40
glossolalia 128, 130, 137–40, 143–5, 147, 150
　and possession 137–40, 145
　social learning, contagion, and role theory 140–2

God/God image 1, 10, 16, 41, 45, 51, 54, 72, 78, 82, 87, 90, 93–4, 99–101, 113–15, 120–1, 129, 134, 147–8, 171, 181, 185–8, 209, 219–23, 235–6, 238
    anthropomorphic 35, 43, 64, 77, 94
    child development perspective 64–5
    God of the gaps heuristic 42
    as idealized attachment figure 95
    intervention 2–3, 52, 113, 160, 219
    intuitive tendencies 66
    misattribution 63–8, 121
    supernatural agency 129
    and well-being 179–80
    working model 65–6
"God helmet" paradigm 46, 135–6, 165
God-serving biases 48–52, 63, 82
Gotlibovski, C. 26
Gould, S. J., non-overlapping magisteria 76, 101
Granqvist, P. 21, 46, 65–6, 93–5, 135–6, 151
Gray, K. 22, 67–8, 113, 121, 136, 219, 222
Gremsl, A. 165
group influences and CSR 104–5, 112

Hagekull, B. 93, 95
Haidt, J. 111, 187, 190–1, 212–13
Halberstadt, J., *Death anxiety and religious belief: An existential psychology of religion* 48, 77, 96
Hall, D. L. 117, 121
Hall, J. A. 25
Hall, L. 34
hallucination proneness 133, 135
Hampshire, A. 20, 26
harmonization process 7–8, 33, 42, 62, 82, 152–3
Hart, J. 99
Hastings, B. M. 89
Hertel, B. R. 65
Hester, N. 121
heuristics and biases 6–7, 22, 27, 32, 42, 44, 52, 66, 69, 148, 203, 214, 227, 231–2
Hill, P. C. 40
Hinckley, G. B. 148
Hodson, G. 216
Hofmann, W. 204

holier-than-thou effect 187, 197, 207, 211
Holmes, J. G. 95
Holy Spirit 15, 41, 131–3, 137, 139, 141, 147, 149, 154, 157
homophilizing effect 194
Hoogeveen, S. 90–1
Hook, J. N. 173
Hoyt, W. T. 198
humility 51, 199–200, 205–6, 210, 224
Hunsberger, B. 60, 110, 116, 211
hyperactive agency detection (HAAD) 5–6, 13, 19, 24, 34–5, 40, 229, 231
hypnosis 21, 31, 138–9, 142, 144, 150, 156
hypocrisy phenomenon 2, 207, 209, 224

ideomotor effect 139
imagination, encouragement 155
immanent justice beliefs 52–3, 55–7, 63, 83
imprecatory prayer 61
inconsistency, 7, 81–2, 86–7, 216, 236
    ad hoc protection against 77
    avoidance of 75–9
    and cognitive dissonance 79–80
    and disconfirmation 78, 88
    and mutual incoherence 79
    perception of 76
    reduction 75
ingroup assortative sociality 113
intelligence and general cognitive ability 25–9
interactive prayers 15, 130, 132, 134, 137, 140, 142, 144, 147, 149–51, 157
internalization 68, 103, 106, 108–10, 112, 119
    and externalization 116
    and phenomenology 105
    stereotype 200–2, 206, 217
internalizing social norms 8
International Theological Commission, "The Hope of Salvation for Infants Who Die Without Being Baptized" 62
interpersonal modeling 28
interpersonal relationships 95
interpersonal social-psychological processes 8, 16, 105, 108, 227
interpretive creep 182
intra-individual intuitive processes 28, 32

intrapsychic processes 50
intrinsic religiosity (IR) 25, 88, 93, 188, 195–6, 203, 215–16, 224, 226
introspective opacity/introspection 9–10, 15, 31–5, 37, 69, 107, 148, 167, 198, 207, 238
intuitions 7, 10–11, 20, 22, 26–8, 32–6, 40–1, 43–4, 55, 57, 60–2, 67–8, 70–1, 83, 104, 130, 150, 157, 187, 213–14, 229–32
intuitive cognition 23–5, 28–30
Isler, O. 24–5
Israeli schoolchildren 121–2

Jackson, J. C. 112–13, 121, 219, 222
Jackson, L. M. 116, 202
James, W. 150, 234
Järnefelt, E. 70
Jegindø, E. M. 164–5, 171
Jehovah's Witnesses 81, 85
Jesus 11, 41, 61, 64, 85–6, 114, 118, 120–1, 132, 205, 215, 218, 220–1, 237
Johansson, P. 34
Johnson, D. 55–6, 60
Johnson, M. K. 117–18
Jones, A. E. 203
Jong, J., *Death anxiety and religious belief: An existential psychology of religion* 12, 96
Joshua 121–2
Jungian depth psychology 50
justification-suppression model of prejudice 215–16
just world belief (JWB) 7, 52–5, 58, 60, 67–8, 71, 211, 232, 235–6
  cognitive default 55
  and karma 52–3, 57
  malleability of attributions 62–3
  religion and 53–5, 59
  self-defense mechanisms 53
  and System Justifying beliefs 220

Kahneman, D. 8, 22, 44, 157, 207
Kanol, E. 122
karma/karmic beliefs 41, 52–3, 56–8, 63
Kaschten, C. 201
Kataria, M. 141
Kay, A. C. 54, 63, 75, 78, 91, 98–9
Kelemen, D. 56, 70
Kelly, J. F. 174

Khan, U. 209
Kim-Prieto, C. 166
King, L. A. 188, 196–7, 200–1, 205, 224–6
Kirkpatrick, L. A. 46, 94–5
Koehler, D. J. 24
Koenig, H. G. 159, 167, 173
Kohlberg, L. 212
Koleva, S. P. 213
Koopmans, R. 122, 218
Kumar, V. 57
Kurby, C. A. 59

LaBouff, J. P. 118
Lady MacBeth effect 210
LaHaye, T., *Left Behind* 80–1
Lakin, J. L. 219
Latane, B. 32
Late Positive Potential 111
Launay, J. 181
Launonen, L. 229
Laurin, K. 95, 99, 108
Layman, E. 42, 44
Lea, J. A. 60, 211
Lefevor, G. T. 234
Legare, C. H. 42, 49, 109
Lelkes, Y. 64, 120
Lerner, M. J. 52–3, 57, 62
Levy, I. 59
liberals 64, 120, 191, 213, 220–1, 235, 237
Li, C. 25, 98
Lilienfeld, S. O. 164
Liljenquist, K. 210, 225
limbo 61–2, 82–3
Lindeman, M. 21–2, 30, 135
Lindsey, H.
  The Late Great Planet Earth 80
  The 1980's: Countdown to Armageddon 80
linguistic analogy 11
Lin, S. 25
Ludeke, S. G. 59, 204
Luhrmann, T. M. 15, 21, 130, 137, 144, 147–9, 151
  How God Becomes Real 130
  interactive prayers 132, 134, 147, 157
  measure of porosity 135
  Renewalist prayer 137, 147, 149, 154
  When God Talks Back 130
Lupfer, M. B. 42–5, 48–9
Luther, M. 3

Index

MacInnis, C. C. 216
magical thinking 22, 28, 135
Mahoney, A. 15
    risk of reductionism 15–16
Maio, G. R. 94
Marques, A. 171
Martens, J. P. 99
McCauley, R. N., *Philosophical Foundations of the Cognitive Science of Religion: A Head Start* 3
McCorkle, W. W., Jr., *The Cognitive Science of Religion: A Methodological Introduction to Key Empirical Studies* 3
McCullough, M. E. 187, 189, 198
McDaniel, M. A. 173
McGregor, I. 87–9, 97, 100
Mencken, F. C. 64
mental health and well-being 15–16, 66, 147, 159, 165–6, 185, 228, 235–6
    cultural normativity 178
    curvilinear relationship 177–8
    directly causal 182
    dose-response relationship 178
    indirectly causal 182
    and life satisfaction 176
    parallel 182
    parochial 182
    superior 183
    unique 182
meta-analyses 24–6, 64, 94, 117, 173, 177, 204
meta-ethics 235–8
metaphoric parallelism 114
meta-stereotypes 201
millenarist beliefs 61
Miller, W. 81
misattributions 5, 39, 72, 80, 108, 128–9, 134, 136, 156–7, 231, 234, 237
    of agency/presence 130–1, 136
    attributional biases and 47–8
    and belief-as-benefit theory 160–1
    blind spot bias 68–9
    confabulations 33–4, 36
    conformity and social influence on 112
    of conversion experience 150–4
    cultivation techniques 154–6
    of deservingness for misfortune 52–3
    discrepancies 129
    of divine responsibility and blame 48–52
    DP and 69–71
    false-positives 21
    of god's character 63–8
    illusion of conscious will 137–40
    implications 36–7
    introspective opacity 31–2
    justifications 34–5, 37
    manifestations of 33–6
    of morality 187, 200, 206–17
    perceptual 135
    rationalizations 34–5, 37
    for self-reports, implications 15–16
    sources of well-being 161–4
    spiritual 32
    of study effects 13–14
    of supernatural agency 19, 128
    systematic 41, 48, 72
    transitive fallacy of composition 160
    volitional 137–40
misfortune 41, 49, 52, 55–6, 59, 67–8, 81–2, 211, 235–6
    misattribution of deservingness for 52–3
    secular 62
    and victim blaming 7–8, 10, 50, 57–8
moral behaviors 55, 185, 187, 198, 209, 224, 227–8
moral community 187
moral development model, stages 212
Moral Foundations Theory (MFT) 190–1
    care 190–1
    fairness 190–1
    loyalty to ingroup 190–1
    purity/sanctity 190–1, 218
    respect for authority 190
moral incongruence 216
morality and prosociality 14, 16, 32–3, 51–2, 54–6, 60, 185–6, 235
    altruism 185–6
    chronological relationship 189
    complexities and qualifications 222–3
    culture-fit model 189–90
    dispositional traits 189
    MFT and 190–1
    misattribution 187, 200, 206–17, 225–6
    moral enhancement 186–7
    parochialism and trust 192–6
    rationalization of immorality and divine projection 217–22

Religious Self-Enhancement (RSE) theory 202–5, 223–5
  self-enhancement and religious moral stereotyping 206
  spurious influences 188–90
  stereotypes/stereotype internalization 185, 197–202
  supernatural monitoring and punishment 223
  World Values Survey 189, 194
moral self-image (MSI) 200, 205–10, 217, 223–5
Moral Typecasting Theory (MTT) 66–8
mortality salience 96–9, 119
moveable hand model 142
Muraven, M. 220
Murphy, S. 212–13

naïve realism 9, 69, 103, 106, 164
Najle, M. B. 28, 104
Narcotics Anonymous 174
nationalism 97, 119
naturalistic mechanisms 11, 13–14, 228
Navara, G. S. 226
Nelson, B. 173
Nelson, T. A. 90, 100
neutrality 15–16
Newberg, A. B. 143
new science of religious change approach 112
Niemyjska, A. 94
Nisbett, R. E. 34, 129, 138, 214
nonbelievers. *See* believers and nonbelievers
nonreligious equivalents 30–1
nontheistic spirituality 167
Norenzayan, A. 22, 24, 56–7, 96, 187, 193, 195, 201

O'Grady, K. A. 101
Oishi, S. 114
Olson, J. A. 142
ontological confusion 30, 43, 135
organization 16, 189, 192, 194
over-attributions 43–4, 134, 234
over-pathologizing effect 146

Pagels, E., *The Origin of Satan* 49
Pait, K. C. 45–6, 52, 134

Palasinski, M. 202
Paloutzian, R. F. 153
paranormal superstitious beliefs 21, 30–1, 35, 46, 90, 98–100, 132, 205
parental attachment/relationships 65–6, 94–5, 151
Pargament, K. 14, 58, 78, 100, 159, 168, 170–2, 174, 178, 180, 236
partial beliefs 28
Pearce, M. J. 21, 22, 135, 136, 173
Pennycook, G. 20, 24, 26, 30
Pentecostal Christianity 130–1, 133, 140–2, 144, 146, 154
perceived emotional synchrony 180
perceptual over-detection 22, 30, 136, 146, 156, 231
perceptual styles of absorption. *See* absorption
personality psychology approach 3, 5
personality trait of absorption 21–2, 47, 136, 150. *See also* absorption
petitionary prayer 77–8
Philips, C. L. 152–3
philosophical implications, 100
  biased belief forming functions 228–34
  of tangible outcomes 234–8
placebo effect 14, 16, 46, 107, 135–6, 162–5, 170, 228, 233–4
plausibility 1, 60, 229
Poepsel, D. 51
political orientation 53–4, 58–9, 63–4, 117, 119–20, 123, 191, 220–1
Poole, S. 220
Pope, A. R. 59–60
porosity 132, 134–5, 146
Porter, S. 155
possession/trance phenomena 51, 130, 137–40, 143–8, 150
post hoc ergo propter hoc 164, 169
post hoc rationalizations 10, 81, 213, 229, 233
Post-Traumatic Stress Disorder 169
potentiating effect 133
Pratt, J. B. 152
pre-conversion problems 150
Price, M. E. 181
priming techniques 8, 25, 46–7, 66, 71, 91, 95, 99, 110, 113, 118–20, 122, 129, 138, 151, 196, 199, 218, 222

projection 9–11, 33, 35–6, 50, 61, 66, 68, 93–4, 104, 112–14, 121, 134, 149, 187, 211, 217–22, 231–2
prosociality. *See* morality and prosociality
Protestant Christians 43, 58, 131, 140, 151, 176
pseudo-absolution 224
psychological mechanism 12, 128, 137, 148, 161, 227–9
psychological perspectives 3–6
psychotherapy 159, 162–3, 173
purgatory 8, 61–3, 82–3
Purzycki, B. G. 114, 221
Putnam, R. D. 179, 186, 189, 192–4
    American Grace: How Religion Divides and Unites Us 186

quasi-spiritual phenomena 90–1, 173

Rambo, L. R. 153
Rapture 61
rational cognition 28, 31, 212, 234
rationalization 9–11, 33–4, 36–7, 78–81, 208–9, 211, 213, 215, 224, 227, 233, 235, 238
    of immorality 211, 217–22
    post-hoc 81, 213, 229, 233
    self-enhancement and 210
real-world fluctuations 93, 132
re-attributions of theodicy 82
Reber, J. S. 234
reflective religious belief 25, 157
reincarnation 56
re-iterative process 46–7, 134
religion-forgiveness discrepancy 198
religion/religiosity 110–12, 186–7, 214, 237. *See also* religious and spiritual (R/S) beliefs
    and death anxiety 97
    epistemic functions of 73
    and narcissism 205
    and pornography 216
    and social conformity 110–12
    as social identity 115–20
    and transgression-specific forgiveness 198
    warfare and 113
religious and nonreligious cognitions 6, 27, 191, 201, 237

religious and spiritual (R/S) beliefs 6, 12–13, 15, 19, 39, 63, 68, 71–2, 75, 100, 159, 185, 188–9, 192, 196, 211, 222, 227–9, 231–6
    bullshit-sensitivity/receptivity 20, 30–1
    causal role for 167
    cognitive traits and 19–22
    components 14
    conceptualization and measurement 169
    dismantling spiritual *vs.* secular interventions 169–74
    efficacy 173
    epistemic bases for 12
    illusions 12
    implications 11–13
    individual traits, worldview conviction, and cultural fit 175–7
    intelligence and general cognitive ability 25–6
    interpretation 176, 182
    introjected and ego-syntonic 11
    and moral enhancement 186–7
    origins 1–3
    placebos, and aspirational self-presentation 164–7
    religious continuum 177
    and self-esteem 175
    uniqueness 14–15
    and well-being 167–9
religious attendance 14, 172, 181, 188, 192–3, 216, 235
religious concepts 6–8, 28, 70, 75, 77, 81, 104, 110, 118, 133
    explicit 8
    internalized/introjected 11, 112
    vicarious punishment and victim blaming 60–2
religious engagement 179–80, 182, 203
religious fundamentalism 28, 54, 59, 89, 110, 115–17, 193, 196, 218
religious identity 48, 115, 117–20, 122–3, 166, 176, 186, 197, 200, 202
Religious Self-Enhancement (RSE) theory 202–6, 223–5
religious self-identification. *See* religious identity
religious traditions 7, 131, 133

Renewalist prayers 15, 130, 137, 144, 147, 149, 151, 154
Reuven, Y. 59
Richardson, J. T. 153
Richards, P. S. 101
Riggio, H. R. 48, 50, 52, 70
Riecken, H. W., *When Prophecy Fails* 80
Rizeq, J. 30
Rock, C. 220
Rokeach, M. 215
role theory 133, 140–4, 152
Rosenblatt, P. C. 51
Ross, L. D. 64, 120, 149, 220–1
Ross, R. M. 20, 24, 26
Routledge, C. 90, 119
Rowatt, W. C. 118, 197, 199, 205, 215
Roylance, C. 90
Russell, A. G. 64, 120
Rutjens, B. T. 91, 99

saber 11
sacralization/sanctification 121–3, 187
Saint Augustine 152
sanctity/sacredness 14–15, 190–1, 218, 234
Saroglou, V. 54, 59, 64, 110–11, 175, 180–1, 186, 189, 192, 201
Schachter, S. 107, 133, 142
  When Prophecy Fails 80
Schaller, M. 5
Schienle, A. 165
Schizotypic Personality Questionnaire 135
schizotypy 22, 43, 135
Schnall, S. 212
Schrade, A. 205
Schumann, K. 95
science *vs.* religion 76, 99, 101
scriptural fidelity 149
scriptures 2–3, 7, 10, 23, 49, 62, 76, 81, 86, 89, 99, 103, 120, 122, 142, 147–9, 152, 218
secular social cognition 129, 180
Sedikides, C. 166, 205
self-affirmation theory 88, 209
self-anchoring theory 201
self-categorization theory 200–1, 203
self-esteem/-enhancement 48, 51–2, 88, 96, 115, 153, 166–7, 175, 187, 202–3, 209–10, 223, 225
  of morality 203–5
  and religious moral stereotyping 206
  tendency 166
Self-God correlation 220–1
Self-God parallelism 64
self-serving bias 48, 51, 53, 203, 207, 209–10, 213, 217, 219–20, 222
self-stereotyping effect 115, 200–2, 206–7, 219, 222
sensus divinitatus 12, 228
Seol, K. O. 202
Shaffer, B. A. 89
Shakarchi, R. L. 219
shared secularism 111
Shariff, A. F. 118, 220, 236
Sharp, S. 82
Shaver, J. H., accuracy report 33
Shaver, P. 46
Shaw, J. 155
Shepperd, J. A. 65, 222, 235
Sherif, M., autokinetic effect 105–6
Sidanius, J. 57
Siegers, P. 190
Simmons, C. H. 52, 57
Singer, J. 107, 133, 142
sinner-sin religious justification 216
Skoggard, I. 93, 114
Slife, B. D. 14, 187, 234
Slingerland, E., productive/explanatory *vs.* crudely eliminative reductionism 16
Slone, D. J., *The Cognitive Science of Religion: A Methodological Introduction to Key Empirical Studies* 3
Smith, J. M. 221
Smith, W. 220
Snow, D. 152–3
Social Cognition (SC) 3–5, 39, 66, 83, 85, 127, 139, 165, 227–8, 235
  implications 71–2
  misfortune and victim blaming (*see* misfortune)
  research 7
  Social Psychology and 11–13, 105
  traditions and techniques 6
social cognitive biases 36, 203
social conformity. *See* conformity
social connection and attachment compensation 93–5
social contagion 133, 140–2
social embeddedness 179–82

Social Foundations hypothesis 29
Social Identity Theory (SIT) 115–20, 211
  externalizing 120–1
  intergroup bias 118
  internalization and externalization 116
  priming 118–20, 122
  religious and nonreligious 115
  religious prejudice 117, 123
  sacralization 121–3
social influences (R/S beliefs) 5, 103–4, 133, 136, 140
  conformity and 105–10
  culture and environment 112–14
  group influences and 104–5
  social identity (*see* Social Identity Theory (SIT))
Social Intuitionist Model 190, 212
social ostracism 119
Social Psychology 5, 11–13, 39, 105
social reality 104
social transmission 28, 104, 112
social value 166, 190, 202–3
Sousa, P. 136
Spanos, N. P. 21, 139, 143–4, 146, 165
Speed, D. 172
Spilka, B. 42, 44, 46, 49
spiritual darkness 144, 146
spiritual meditation 170–1
spiritual warfare 144, 146
Stavrova, O. 166, 178, 190
Stolle, D. 122
Strandberg, T. 34
strategic processing 20
Sufism 130
sui generis function 6, 14, 127
Sunday Assembly movement 181
sunk cost effect 85
superior effects 172
supernatural belief 24, 30, 46–7, 50, 70, 93–4, 134, 234
supernatural engagement 132
supernatural monitoring 55–6, 187, 193, 208, 223, 236
supernatural punishment (SP) theories 7–8, 55–8, 60–3, 67–8, 71, 223
Swiney, L. 136
system justification bias 7, 54, 211, 232, 235
System/Type One (T1) cognition 8–9, 22–3, 27–8, 31–7, 44, 55, 69–70, 103, 111, 157, 225, 227, 229, 232

System/Type Two (T2) cognition 8–9, 13, 22–3, 25, 27–9, 32–3, 35–7, 69–70, 77, 103, 111, 157, 225, 227, 229, 231–3

Tamarin, G. 121–2, 127
Taves, A. 127, 134
Tehrani, K. 168
teleological and meaning-making tendencies 24, 42–3, 55, 70, 99
tendency, over-detect intentionality/agency 6–7
Terror Management Theory (TMT) 96–7, 99, 119
textual interpretations. *See* scripture
Thauvoye, E. 65, 95
theistic psychology 101, 187, 234–6
themes 3, 6–8, 13, 15–16, 80, 82, 94–5, 105, 151, 218, 222, 237
theory of mind 7, 12, 19, 24, 35, 41, 66–7, 83, 231
Thunstrom, L. 194
Thurow 229
Thurow, J. C. 229
Tinbergen, N. 5
Tix, A. P. 172
Tolstoy, L. 152
Toplak, M. E. 30–1
Tracy, J. L. 99
Transcendental Meditation 170
Tremlin, T. 19, 23, 35, 84
  Mind and Gods 7
Trimble, D. E. 204
truth-tracking 12, 230
Tsang, J. A. 198, 215, 217
Tversky, A. 44, 207
Twelve-Step (TS) treatment approach 152, 159, 173–4
two-factor theory 107
Tyvans studies (southern Siberia) 114

Vainio, O. P. 229
validity tests for spiritual experiences and discernment methods 148–9
  physical reactivity and sense memory 155–6
Van Cappellen, P. 14, 110, 159, 180
Van den Bos, K. 88, 97, 236
Van der Kolk, B. 156
van der Pligt, J. 99

VanDeursen, M. J. 59–60
Van Elk, M. 46–7, 91, 133, 136
Van Eyghen, H. 12, 230–1, 234
van Harreveld, F. 99
Van Tongeren, D. R. 65, 88, 90, 97, 199
Ver Wey, A. L. 201
victim blaming 82–3, 211, 236
    cognitive dissonance 7
    and derogation 57–60
    vicarious punishment and 60–2
violations of beliefs 60, 71, 82
virtual reality paradigms 46, 136
Visser, A. 167, 179, 205
volition attribution process 138–47
Von Hippel, W. 219
Vonk, J. 20, 43, 52
Vonk, R. 205

Wabnegger, A. 165
Wachholtz, A. B. 170–1
Walsh, E. 142
Ward, S. J. 188, 196–7, 200–1, 205, 224–6
warfare and religiosity 92, 113, 122, 144, 146, 218
Warner, R. H. 59–60
Waytz, A. 43, 47

Wegner, D. M. 67–8, 139
    The Illusion of Conscious Will 138
Weisman, K. 154
White Christian Protestant 118
Wilkins, A. C. 166
Williams, T. J. 201
Wilson, T. D. 33, 34, 129, 138, 214
    Strangers to Ourselves 9–10, 31–4, 69, 198, 225
Wlodarczyk, A. 180–1
working model 65–6
worldview-threatening information 29, 60, 73, 75, 79, 89, 99, 119, 175–9, 189, 218, 233
Worthington, E. L., Jr. 173, 198

Xygalatas, D. 84

Yavuz, H. 97
Yilmaz, O. 24–5, 78
Yonker, J. E. 25
Youtz, H. A. 185
Yzerbyt, V. 201

Zhong, C. B. 210, 225
Zuckerman, M. 25–7, 29, 76, 98, 170

www.ingramcontent.com/pod-product-compliance
Lightning Source LLC
Chambersburg PA
CBHW071804300426
44116CB00009B/1202